REVIEW OF BEHAVIOR THERAPY

REVIEW OF BEHAVIOR THERAPY

THEORY AND PRACTICE

VOLUME 11

G. TERENCE WILSON
Rutgers—The State University of New Jersey

CYRIL M. FRANKS
Rutgers—The State University of New Jersey
Carrier Foundation

PHILIP C. KENDALL
Temple University

JOHN P. FOREYT
Baylor College of Medicine

THE GUILFORD PRESS
New York   London

Published by The Guilford Press
A Division of Guilford Publications, Inc.
72 Spring Street, New York, N.Y. 10012

Printed in the United States of America

Library of Congress Catalog Card No. 76-126864
ISBN 0-89862-751-6
ISSN 0091-6595

PREFACE

Volume 11 in this series marks two major changes. First, as foreshadowed in the Preface to Volume 10, we have now switched to a biennial basis. It is our judgment, corroborated by reviewers in the field, that at this stage the behavior therapy literature does not require the intensive appraisal of an annual review. Second, Kelly Brownell, our coauthor for Volumes 8 through 10, has withdrawn from the series to concentrate on other commitments. Although we regret this loss, especially Kelly's expertise in the areas of the addictive disorders and behavioral medicine, we are happy to welcome John P. Foreyt as his replacement.

In the Preface to Volume 9 we noted that as the short history of behavior therapy grows longer, our founding fathers will pass from the scene, unhappily but inevitably. 1985 marked the death of H. Gwynne Jones. Fittingly, Hans Eysenck (1985) offers an eloquent and pithy appreciation of Jones's many contributions to behavior therapy. Eysenck cites Angela Shorr's appraisal in her important work on the history of behavior therapy (Shorr, 1984): "Hans Eysenck and Gwynne Jones were the major forces behind the drive to create modern behaviour therapy at the Maudsley Hospital, Jones in the practical sense, using face-to-face individual teaching for the intensive acceptance of the new prospective, Eysenck in an organizational and science–political sense (Shorr, cited in Eysenck, 1985, p. 173).

Eysenck goes on to state,

> [I]t seems only just that Shorr thus singled out Gwynne Jones as the most important contributor to the development of behaviour therapy at the Maudsley. I always felt that he, more than anyone else, shared my own attitudes and beliefs in this field, and was able to design clinical and experimental studies in a very novel and unique manner which would serve to convince doubters, as well as help patients who had been given up by everyone else. . . . There can be no doubt about the debt which behaviour therapy in this country, and indeed elsewhere also, owes to Gwynne Jones and his pioneering ventures in the 1950s. (p. 173)

We also observe passings of another, fortunately less final, sort. In 1982, Eysenck retired from his position as professor of psychology at the University of London Institute of Psychiatry, The Maudsley Hospital. A year later Jack Rachman left his position as head of the clinical program at the Institute of Psychiatry to become professor and director of clinical training at the University of British Columbia. Eysenck and Rachman—the names and the association are indelibly familiar. Together, in 1960, they launched the world's first journal devoted exclusively to behavior therapy. They published together on many occasions (e.g., *The Causes and Cures of Neurosis*, 1965), and it is difficult to overstate the importance of their collective writings to the field. For more than two decades, they developed and headed a center of behavior therapy that, in terms of influence and distinction, was unsurpassed anywhere. Their respective students over the years number among them some of the most influential behavioral psychologists in the world—in Great Britain, continental Europe, the United States, Canada, India, Australia, and elsewhere.

One of us (CMF), who was there at the start, recalls those exciting early days in which he was privileged to play a formative role. They were indeed exciting times, and those of us who had the opportunity to extend the Maudsley tradition throughout the world think of that unique era in behavior therapy with appreciation and affection that grows as the years roll by (Franks, 1985). The University of London Institute of Psychiatry continues to be a major international center of research and training in behavior therapy, but it will never be the same. An era has come to an end. It is unlikely that we shall see anything quite like it again.

By way of acknowledgments, GTW is grateful, once again, to Barbara Honig of the Rutgers Alcohol Behavior Research Laboratory for her unstinting help in typing his chapters for this volume. Preparation of Chapters 3 and 8 was facilitated by National Institute of Alcohol Abuse and Alcoholism Grant No. AA00259-15. As always, CMF thanks Carol Martin and Sue Wright for their loyal secretarial assistance and transcription services. PCK acknowledges with gratitude the assistance of Elaine Gatsoulas and Jane Burrell for their secretarial assistance. JPF thanks Linda Cate for typing his chapters. Preparation of Chapters 5 and 6 was supported by National Heart, Lung and Blood Institute Grant No. RO1-HL3395. And as always, we are grateful to Elaine Wilson, Violet Franks, and Sue Kendall for their help and support.

G. Terence Wilson
Cyril M. Franks
Philip C. Kendall
John P. Foreyt

CONTENTS

CHAPTER

1

BEHAVIOR THERAPY: AN OVERVIEW

CYRIL M. FRANKS

INTRODUCTION

Some three decades ago, I made the transition from the United Kingdom to the United States, bringing with me certain notions about the role of students in the then fledgling discipline of behavior therapy (Franks, 1985). In 1966, these aspirations culminated in the formation of the Association for Advancement of Behavior Therapy (AABT), modeled on the British Association for Advancement of Science and its American counterpart. Unfortunately, while professional activities have earned the AABT a position as the leading representative of behavior therapy, the founding principles have been given less attention (Franks, in press).

While technology has advanced significantly, the number of concept-oriented books can be counted on the fingers of one hand—and this excludes the thumb. The one volume to deal systematically with such matters is written by a philosopher (Erwin, 1978). To the best of my knowledge, only one recent book of importance has "theory" in its title (Reiss & Bootzin, 1985). Even the scholarly *Advances in Behaviour Research and Therapy* seems to receive manuscripts devoted primarily to methodology and design. The journal *Behaviorism* is interested in philosophical issues, but from a Skinnerian perspective rather than that of behavior therapy at large. Evans and Meyer's (1985) concept-laden text on behavior therapy in education is a rare and successful event in the behavioral literature. Arkowitz and Messer's (1984) comparative evaluation of theory in psychoanalytic therapy and behavior therapy is less successful, in that it largely reiterates the opinions of various individuals on either side or the other.

Throughout the years, I have had occasion to comment upon the competition between traditional behavior therapists and psychopharmacologists. Unfortunately, despite a shared respect for data and similar methodologies, cross-fertilization remains rare, and it is only within recent years that significant communication has occurred. But the pickings remain slim as far as well-designed studies of interactions between drug treatments and behavior therapy are concerned. Hersen's (1986) edited text does little to change this conclusion. Perhaps what is needed is an individually written treatise (and Hersen is eminently capable of accomplishing this) that systematically evaluates the evidence to date, draws the necessary conclusions with respect to clinical applicability, and details research priorities.

Once again, cognition rears its head—ugly or refreshingly vital, depending on one's point of view. Almost a decade ago, Mahoney and Arnkoff (1978) characterized cognitive-behavior therapy as "a relatively diversified amalgam of principles and procedures that have yet to be formalized into a monolithic system or model (p. 69)." In a more recent edited volume, Mahoney and his associates are much more positive. They now see two distinct paths within cognitivism and cognitive-behavior therapy: associationism and constructivism (Reda & Mahoney, 1984). The associationist position is predicated on the assumption that it is contiguity that governs change. Personal meaning can be altered by the substitution of one set of associations for another. By contrast, constructivists view a strictly associationist model of human nature as clinically passive and theoretically impoverished. For the constructivist, cognitive processes are more active and intentional, with an emphasis on so-called "deep structure." Be this as it may, a review of the literature to date suggests that it is Mahoney's 1978 summing-up that still prevails, rather than Eifert's (1984) overoptimistic identification of cognitivism with mainstream behavior therapy (e.g. see Miller & Berman, 1983).

Freeman (1983), an ardent cognitivist, is under no illusion about what he terms the cognitive "myth of simplicity." No one could reasonably accuse Martin and Levey (1985) of being simplistic. In 1983, Levey and Martin distinguished between the contributions of conditioning and cognition to adaptive and maladaptive learning. Two basic modes of data processing govern the learned appreciation of regularities within the external environment. One involves registration of events and their immediately significant consequences; the other summarizes more long-term sequences of events. In their 1985 article, Martin and Levey propose that both forms of learning, though distinguishable, be incorporated into a single, biologically based framework. This framework eliminates conflicts between the cognitive and conditioning models by recognizing the mutually enhancing roles of both. Conditioning theory emphasizes the more phylogenetically primitive mechanisms for evaluation of the external environment. Cognitive theory emphasizes more cognitive summaries of recurring long-term events within the environment. The first step in the formation of a united perspective is the identification of the distinctive features of both processes. Depending on future developments, this model could be highly relevant to behavior therapy.

Wolpe (1984) has entered the cognitive arena to castigate Lazarus once again. It seems that in 1983 Lazarus argued that therapeutic relapses occurred among patients treated with "traditional behavior therapy" rather than his multimodal variation. But Wolpe would have none of this and, correctly, took Lazarus to task for his less than rigorous dismissal of behavior therapy as "a useful psychotherapeutic adjunct" rather than a systematic discipline. By way of response, Lazarus (1985) has attempted to "set the record straight" by drawing attention to the differences between contemporary behavior therapy and the pioneering contributions of Wolpe. While this dispute is rather tiresome and worthy of being laid to rest, it is hard not to sympathize with Lazarus's (1985) summing up:

> Despite our points of departure, however, the theories and methods to which Wolpe and I subscribe, when compared to the views held by psychodynamic practitioners, Gestalt therapists, phenomenologists, person-centered therpists, and so on amount to a just noticeable difference. A dispassionate accounting of technique effectiveness would be greatly facilitated if Wolpe concurred. (p. 1419)

When Wolpe retired, the Behavior Therapy Unit at Temple University Medical Center ceased to exist. Sadly, but probably accurately, Wolpe (1985b) views this as an indication of the prevailing psychiatric appraisal of behavior therapy—a useful adjunct to psychotherapy but not very important. Over the years, observes Wolpe, Temple University's Department of Psychiatry allocated over 20 times as much teaching time to psychodynamic psychotherapy as to behavior therapy! In making this point, Wolpe has taken yet another potshot at the cognitivists, and Beck (1986) has been forced to respond. And so the barrage continues even when I had thought it was beginning to be laid to rest.

In another interchange that has advanced behavior therapy zero paces, Wolpe has engaged a new set of sparring partners. Thompson and Williams (1985) have taken behavior therapists to task for discounting personality variables and treating without first thinking. The thrust of their argument is that methodology must be adapted to people rather than vice versa. Unfortunately, their thesis lack any database, and it is not surprising that Wolpe (1985a) has drawn attention to the empirical core of behavior therapy in his rebuttal.

This otherwise rather tedious interchange has had two mildly interesting spinoffs. Hawkins (1986), staunchly Skinnerian, takes both Wolpe and Thompson and Williams to task for disregarding, or at least de-emphasizing, the development of behavior through systematic manipulation of the environment by way of behavior analysis rather than "mental fictions." For Collins (1986), the major deficiency within behavior therapy is the failure to look at the therapist's behavior; we must define therapy goals empirically and integrate this knowledge base into clinical practice. But how to achieve these goals is something that Collins neglects to specify.

Making the point that behavior therapy is an intellectual movement that values science, technology, and rationality, Woolfolk and Richardson (1984) have succinctly placed behavior therapy in sociohistorical perspective. While applauding its technological achievements, they take sharp issue with behavior therapists on the grounds that they have little to say about the purpose of treatment. Unfortunately, argue Woolfolk and Richardson, behavior therapy can never develop appropriate goals through the utilization of behavior therapy principles alone. Choosing therapeutic objectives is a matter of value judgment that is beyond the domain of behavior therapy.

Hawkins (1985) takes sharp issue with this position. For him, the determination of goals is as much a scientific matter as are questions of technique effectiveness. Defining adaptiveness in terms of the degree to which it contributes to the maximum cost–benefit or punisher–reinforcer ratio for the individual concerned, Hawkins reduces the problem of goal setting to a scientific determination of precisely what will reduce costs and/or increase benefits under what circumstances.

In 1971, Lazarus launched a small and biased sampling of his clinical associates upon the professional world to conclude that behavior therapists take their troubles to nonbehavioral therapists for resolution. While this particular observation is easily dismissed, it is less easy to disregard the 1982 finding of Gochman, Allgood, and Greer that 44% of responding AABT members had experienced some form of nonbehavioral psychotherapy, a result strikingly similar to that of Norcross and Wogan (1983). Unfortunately, as Norcross and Prochaska (1984) note, both of these studies involved small samples of AABT clinicians who did not necessarily ally themselves with any form of behaviorism (AABT is primarily an interest group). But when

Norcross and Prochaska reanalyzed data obtained from a national survey of psychotherapists (Prochaska & Norcross, 1983) and clinical psychologists (Norcross & Prochaska, 1982a, 1982b), similar findings were obtained. Over half of those who identified themselves as behaviorally committed reported having undergone personal nonbehavioral treatment at some time during their lives. It could, of course, have been prior to their becoming behavioral.

In previous volumes, attention has been drawn to the problems involved in the increasing usage of self-help treatment books, manuals, and related aids. As noted, while the potential benefits of self-help books may be great, the risks may be even greater. Do-it-yourself books still have few if any provisions for arriving at a reliable diagnosis or monitoring compliance with instructions, and they have little or no provision for follow-up (Rosen, 1987). In 1976, Rosen noted that behavioral techniques were being marketed as do-it-yourself therapies without benefit of clinical trial, and it was suggested that the only contingency affecting the sale of these programs is monetary. *Caveat emptor*! Now, a decade later, Rosen (1987) arrives at the sad conclusion that his concerns were warranted then and are warranted now. Rather than "giving psychology away," many psychologists are simply finding "new ways to sell it."

The 1978 American Psychological Association (APA) Task Force on Self-Help Therapy recommended certain actions that could be taken by the psychological community to encourage the responsible marketing and development of self-help materials. These recommendations, reports Rosen (1987), have gone largely unnoticed. To bring home his point, Rosen draws attention to the October 1985 issue of *Psychology Today*, a typical issue of a magazine now published under the auspices of the APA. There is a full-page ad that offers "success, mind power, winning, attractiveness, transformation, [and] self-knowledge" to those who purchase the book *Instant Memory*, published by the "Institute of Advanced Thinking." And *Psychology Today* even publishes audiotapes of its own that offer questionable materials for self-help, with such alluring titles as "Discovering Yourself" and "Free Yourself from Guilt."

If Hawkins is correct, and I believe that he is, behavioral principles can be applied to the determination of both individual and societal value judgments. Policy makers rarely utilize behavioral concepts, and, on the few occasions that they do so, these principles tend to be misapplied (Thyer, 1983). On the other hand, there is always the danger, as in the USSR, that behavioral principles can be co-opted in the interests of sociopolitical forces rather than science (Holowinsky, 1985).

Several commentators have drawn attention to the propensity of behavior therapists to favor white, middle-class, "Young, Attractive, Verbal, Intelligent, and Successful" (YAVIS) clients in both research and practice, at the expense of the nonwhite and underprivileged (Smith & Dejoie-Smith, 1984). Behavior therapists have paid little attention to variables related to race or gender. If the stereotyping of women can have adverse affects on mental health (V. Franks & Rothblum, 1983), how much more damaging these issues can be for black women! As Collins and McNair (1986) note, black women, especially if poor, have to cope with stereotypes and prejudices related to race, gender, and class.

Hrop and Rakos (1985) provide a rare example of effective behavioral research in this area. The evidence suggests that empathic assertion in conflict situations is the preferred training goal. But much of this evidence has been generated by white middle-class students, making application with blacks questionable (Lineberger & Calhoun, 1983). No study has assessed the social evaluation of assertion as a function of the race of judge, asserter, or assertee. When Hrop and Rakos had white and black students in various race combinations evaluate videotapes depicting standard and empathic refusal assertions, it became clear that assertiveness training could be enhanced by attention to race variables. More research is indicated.

Feminist behavior therapy is a related area that, in principle amenable to objective study, in practice lends itself to political opportunitism. According to Gerwirtz (1969), the problem is of a quite different order: The behavior therapist's ability to act as an advocate for women clients is muted by a philosophy that considers sex a trivial variable and an imperfect predictor of individual behavior. Perhaps for such reasons, feminist therapists tend to adopt a humanistic rather than a behavioral psychology. But this does not have to be. Hunter and Kelso (1985) make a case, albeit a weak one, for feminist behavior therapy as a modality that combines feminist values and behavioral procedures. Blechman's (1984) case for behavior modification with all women, normal or disordered, black or white, is more powerfully presented. With a few notable exceptions (e.g., Gomberg & Franks, 1979), the behavioral literature tends to ignore issues of gender. Despite certain lacks, such as a neglect of the lesbian female and a failure to consider the treatment of disorders specific to women, Blechman's text is probably the most thorough behavioral study in this area to date.

Finally, in this grab bag of significant new developments and tedious resurrection of shop-worn remainders, attention is drawn to behavioral rehabilitation, an up-and-coming new direction for behavior therapy. The integration of behavior therapy and clinical neuropsychology for the organically impaired—previously presumed to be a notoriously intransient group—assumed significance when Horton (1979a, 1979b, 1981) coined the term "behavioral neuropsychology." In 1978 a special-interest group had been founded at the Chicago meeting of the AABT, and it was out of this meeting that the new title emerged. As yet, the literature on this subarea is sparse. There is a recent review of cognitive and behavioral rehabilitation interventions by Incagnoli and Newman (1985), and *the Behavior Therapist* has commissioned a series of four articles by various members of this group. As yet, only two are in print (Blanton & Gouvier, 1986; Puente & Horton, 1986). In addition, Edelstein and Couture (1984) have edited a volume entitled *Behavioral Assessment and Rehabilitation of the Traumatically Brain-Damaged.* Traditionally, neuropsychologists have concentrated on the contents (both physiological and cognitive) of the so-called "black box," whereas behavioral approaches have not. In this book, the movement is toward a reconciliation of these two perspectives. The major deficit is the misnomer in the title. Readers expecting an emphasis on behavioral techniques will be disappointed; much of the book deals with neuropsychological testing. However, we may hope that, as data accrue, a volume dealing exclusively and directly with behavioral assessment and rehabilitation of the traumatically brain-damaged will emerge. Such a volume will not consist primarily of neuropsychology for behavior therapists. Rather, the main thrust will be the application of a behavior therapy approach to problems in neuropsychology. The two strategies are very different.

PROFESSIONAL AND PARAPROFESSIONAL TRAINING IN BEHAVIOR THERAPY

Training in behavior therapy has two main reference points: the training of behavior therapists and the behavioral training of other professionals and paraprofessionals (Franks, 1984a). Bernstein, the dean of behavioral training, is knowledgeable in both respects. Recently, her focus has been upon the parameters of change agents' competence and the generalization of behavior change skills—complex issues in which what we know is still only a small proportion of what could be known (Bernstein, 1984). Once again, she devotes attention to the teaching of behavior change skills. It would seem that various combinations of instructions, modeling, rehearsal, feedback, and written manuals are more likely to be effective than instruction alone. What is not known are the relative powers of these procedures, either individually or in combination (see also Bernstein, 1982).

As expected, it is the applied behavior analysts who have developed the most meticulous approaches to behavioral training. For example, writing in the pages of *The Behavioral Analyst*, Chase and Wylie (1985) conclude that what is needed is a more detailed analysis of the parameters at stake, and this they proceed to provide. A closely argued rationale is provided for training based upon generalized problem-solving skills. Detailed training programs and evaluation procedures serve as starting points for the future discussions that will doubtless take place.

The AABT is less narrowly focused. Its Continuing Education Committee, established in 1976, has been interested both in assessing educational activities and the development of models for continuing education. In 1983, Clark, Wadden, Brownell, Gordon, and Tarte (1983) surveyed AABT members to determine the roles that other informational sources (journals, conference sessions, newsletters, books, etc.) would play in improving clinical skills. But this is only a beginning. The next level of evaluation will necessitate measurement of the extent to which therapists utilize their training and other experiences. It might also be of interest to determine how the prioritization of educational resources by practicing behavior therapists differs from that of behavior therapists still in formal training (Monti, 1985).

In 1982, a conference on Behavioral Training and Clinical Psychology was held at West Virginia University to discuss strategies for improving graduate education in this field (Foster, Berler, & Collins, 1982). While the participants, most of whom were actively involved in behavioral clinical training, disagreed about virtually everything, unanimity was expressed on two major issues: the lack of pertinent research and the need for empirical training in the study of behavior. As part of this conference, later reported in *the Behavior Therapist*, Russo (1985) discusses training needs in behavioral health psychology. The interactive nature of behavioral health psychology, argues Russo, mandates exposure to nonpsychological content areas such as physiology, pharmacology, and the medical assessment of chronic disease factors, in addition to more traditional behavioral training. Wisely, Russo speaks of "behavioral health psychology" rather than "behavioral medicine." From the perspective of the behavior therapist, "behavioral medicine" is an unfortunate term. Behavioral interventions in health care still tend to be viewed as psychological analogues of physical treatments rather than as expressions of a quite different approach. From this vantage, relaxation and stress management, for example, can be viewed merely as nonpharmacological equivalents of a tranquilizing drug.

Two other contributions to this conference are also of interest. The professional world is primarily nonbehavioral, and behavioral students may need special training for life after graduation. To answer the question of what type of training is needed, Forehand (1985) surveyed graduates of behavioral training programs and nationally distinguished behavior therapists. While both groups acknowledged the importance of preparing behavioral students for the nonbehavioral world, the preferred approach for exposing students to other orientations was through academia rather than experience. While there was substantial support for the acceptance of alien procedures when they could be demonstrated to be effective, conceptual integration at any level was less well received (see also Franks, 1984b).

For McFall (1985), the primary objective of all clinical training programs should be preparing the trainees to function as independent behavioral scientists, rather than teaching specific theories or techniques. While I am well content with this point of view, not all individuals would accept the methodology of behavioral scientists as the ultimate criterion (e.g., Messer, 1985, would not).

In 1984, *the Behavior Therapist* commissioned Bernstein to orchestrate a five-part series on training. In the first article, Kratochwill and Van Someren (1984) have further developed Kratochwill, Bergan, and Mace's (1981) model of competency-based training of school psychologists as behavioral consultants. Then, Ziarnik and Bernstein (1984) take advantage of their experience as consultants to community-based human service agencies to review problems of staff training in such facilities (see also Bernstein & Ziarnik, 1984; Ziarnik & Bernstein, 1982; Ziarnik, Rudred, & Bernstein, 1981).

In the next paper, Bailey and Reiss (1984) offer compelling arguments against the indiscrimnate use of staff training. The usual line of reasoning is this: When the staff members aren't performing properly, send them in for some "in-service training"; that will get them back on track. Unfortunately, the beneficial effects of such training, if any, are ephemeral. What is needed, argue Bailey and Reiss, is a behavioral analysis to determine why the staff members are not performing properly and what can be done about it. Their "behavioral systems management," in which each element of the system addresses a particular problem and each element dovetails with all other elements, offers a nice example of this model put to practice. In their system, theories served up twice a year from someone with little direct experience become things of the past. In-service training, given on site by someone who must demonstrate the procedures, comes in small doses each time a new procedure is to be used or a training program is failing.

Behavioral pediatrics can be criticized on much the same grounds as behavioral medicine. Unwittingly, Friedman and his associates bring this home in their various surveys of something they call "behavioral pediatric residency training" (e.g., Friedman, Phillips, & Parrish, 1983; Zebal & Friedman, 1984). The unwary reader might well conclude that pediatric training programs firmly rooted in behavioral principles are now widely in effect; far from it. Anything vaguely data-based, physiological or sociologically determined is classified as "behavioral" in their lexicon. In sharp contrast, Christopherson, Cataldo, Russo, and Varni's (1984) blueprint for pediatric training is explicitly behaviorally oriented and, so it is claimed, politically acceptable within a medical milieu. To maintain a distinctly behavioral role as an equal partner in an intrinsically medical setting is no mean feat!

The literature is replete with reports of behavioral programs for nonbehavioral professionals and paraprofessionals. To illustrate this point, I discuss two such contexts: the training of nurses and the staff training of those who work with the mentally handicapped.

By far the more sophisticated work in the area of behavioral training for nurses has been carried out by Milne and his associates in the United Kingdom. While senior nurses continually rank behavior therapy as high in their long list of training priorities (Bridge, Dunn, & Speight, 1981), Milne (1985c) was able to locate only 17 inadequate studies anywhere in the world that were of relevance to the training of paraprofessionals (see also Milne, Burdett, & Conway, 1985).

Behavioral ecology takes into account both the complex relationships within the system and the untargeted "side effects" of intervention (Milne, 1985a). When Milne (1985b) evaluated the effects of in-service behavioral training for National Health Service psychiatric nurses from this perspective, the behaviorally trained nurses—surprisingly but explicably—tended to ignore inappropriate behaviors more than did their nonbehaviorally trained colleagues.

The second example stems from the studies by McBrien and her associates of a behavioral in-service training program for those who work with the institutionalized mentally handicapped. Manchester University's Education of the Developmentally Young (EDY) Project maintains two tiers: a behaviorally oriented in-service course for staff members in Educationally Sub-Normal (ESN) schools, and a workshop model for disseminating course content. This project has been the subject of many publications since its inception in 1976 (e.g., Farrell, 1985; Foxen & McBrien, 1981; Milne, 1985a, 1985b, 1985c; Sebba, 1985). A 1985 study by McBrien and Edmonds serves to illustrate recent attempts to evaluate this program. Four teachers at a special school were given EDY training and compared with four control group teachers at pretraining, posttraining, and 40-month follow-up. Following training, the teachers in the experimental group changed their behavior in the expected direction and maintained this change at follow-up. By contrast, the control group teachers showed no consistent behavior change and scored significantly lower than the experimental group on the dependent variable employed.

Finally, attention is drawn to two comparative studies of training programs for nonbehavioral staff members within residental care settings. In the first, 11 residential staffers working in an Australian facility for disruptive or delinquent youths were trained to use a variety of Achievement Place-style behavioral methods and teacher–parent interaction skills to bring about positive behavior change (Spence & Lee, 1985). Three months after termination of this 4-week full-time training program, the staff were observed in the work environment by means of various coding and checklist rating systems. Attempts were made to identify those behaviors that influenced judgments about staff behavior toward the youths under study. Those staff members who asked frequently for information from the youths were generally rated more positively by both colleagues and youths. The judgments of the youths were influenced primarily by the use of praise on the part of the care staff, whereas it was the expression of affection toward the youths that seemed to have most influence on the judgments of the staff by their colleagues. Such findings demonstrate well the utility of direct observation in this context, and it is too bad that program evaluation was not included in the design.

The second study, by Delamater, Conners, and Wells (1984), compared three staff training procedures for those working within a children's psychiatric inpatient setting: in-service training using a 1974 behavior modification skills text; direct feedback of actual staff performance; and role playing, involving instructions, modeling, behavioral rehearsal, feedback, and reinforcement from an experienced behavior therapist. Behavioral data were obtained by direct naturalistic observation of staff members interacting with the children over a 21-year period. As might have been predicted, in-service staff training had little effect on staff behavior. Knowledge and vocabulary improvement do not necessarily produce behavioral change. While direct feedback was sometimes effective in producing behavorial change, the most dramatic improvements occurred as a result of the role-playing sessions.

MENTAL RETARDATION

In Volume 10 I asked, "What's new in mental retardation?" and, from the point of view of behavior therapy, arrived at the answer "Very little." This conclusion is still valid. It may be that the significant advances are going to occur in the areas of biochemistry and brain physiology, with behavior therapy's role relegated to training and rehabilitation. As far as behavior therapy is concerned, it has been customary to think in terms of either a cognitive/learning theory or a developmental/physiological model of mental retardation. Each perspective leads to a different set of research and intervention strategies. For obvious reasons, behavior therapists lean toward the former model.

Whitman, Burgio, and Johnston (1984) critically review cognitive–behavioral interventions with mentally retarded children. But when all is said, if not done, it is still not clear why performance improves during cognitive–behavioral training programs or what this means in real life. Contrived laboratory settings tell us little about socially relevant situations arising out of everyday interactions.

The following three studies are typical of recent self-control projects with the mentally retarded. In the first, Rusch, Morgan, Martin, Riva, and Agran (1985) taught two mentally retarded employees to perform tasks associated with their jobs. What typically happens is that, once the mentally retarded individual has been trained and placed in seemingly appropriate employment, the placement coordinator withdraws from the scene, leaving the employee to sink or swim—and the employee usually sinks (Gifford, Rusch, Martin, & White, 1984). The maintenance of critical employee skills requires continued planning and on-site employee observation. To this end, Rusch *et al.* developed a multiple-baseline design that combined externally generated and monitored strategies with self-generated and self-monitored procedures. This study has obvious practical implications. It is also, to the best of my knowledge, the only sophisticated report to date of vocational self-management training with mentally retarded adults. The use of social validation—the incorporation of coworker performance as an evaluative measure—is another novel feature.

In the second study to be reported here, the self-direction program was directed toward the development and maintenance of physical fitness. Past research has tended to emphasize the inadequate motor performance and limited fitness of mentally retarded individuals. But it would seem that these deficiencies are also related to the limited opportunities for physical education that are available to this population (Coleman & Whitman, 1984). For physical fitness programs to be beneficial, exercise habits acquired within the training program must be maintained outside the training context, and there is reason to believe that mentally retarded clients can be taught how to bring this about by a combination of self-monitoring and self-reward procedures (e.g., Rotatory, Fox, & Switzky, 1980). Previous studies of physical fitness training with mentally retarded persons have relied on external control training procedures. Coleman and Whitman's subjects were also taught how to self-monitor and self-reward independent exercise behavior, both within the training situation and within their natural environments.

It has frequently been suggested that mentally retarded individuals be offered experiences that are as close as possible to those available to their nonhandicapped peers and that they be given opportunities to shape their own lives through the least restrictive procedures available and appropriate to their needs. When compared to other behavior change techniques, Coleman and Whitman's self-directed approach would seem to be both less intrusive than traditional contingency control programs and consistent with the principles of self-enhancement outlined above. In this respect, at least, this study is worthy of note despite follow-up limitations and lack of sampling generality.

The third study was a comparative evaluation of behavioral versus cognitive, self-directed social skills training in intellectually handicapped adults (Jackson, King, & Heller, 1981). It would seem that it was the combination of procedures that produced the maximum verbal and nonverbal changes in these notoriously socially inadequate individuals—a finding that is not at all surprising. But little is known about the long-term maintenance of these skills. Social skills training for mentally retarded people should be age-appropriate, community-referenced, and geared toward integration with nonhandicapped individuals (Wilcox & Bellamy, 1982).

The liberation of the mentally retarded also mandates greater attention to heterosexual interactions. There is a fair amount of pertinent research on such interactions among the general public and college students, but little that is of relevance to the mentally retarded. Not much is known about either the appropriateness of specific heterosexual social behaviors or their social acceptability and it is to this that Cuvo, Gonzalez, and O'Brien (1985) address themselves. It is suggested, perhaps prematurely, that specific findings from their 49-item questionnaire (in which professionals working with mentally retarded persons and college students completed rating scales for hypothetical mentally retarded and nonretarded subjects) could serve as guidelines to behavior therapists involved in heterosexual social skills training with both retarded and nonretarded adults.

A somewhat different skill, of perhaps equal relevance to the socialization of the mental retardate, is that of telephone answering. Matson (1982) defines conversational telephone skills in terms of the ability to give social and appropriate answers to different types of questions imposed by the typical caller. He found that independence training was more effective than modeling in the teaching of telephone-answering skills to the mentally retarded, but that a combination of both was more effective than either treatment alone. Independence training consisted of a treatment package with the following components: instructions, performance feedback, modeling, social reinforcement, shaping procedures, self-evaluation, and self-monitoring. (See Karen, Astin-Smith, & Creasy, 1985, for a very different behavioral approach to this problem—so much so that meaningful comparisons between the two cannot be made.)

Social skills and leisure skills are closely related for all individuals, but especially so for those with limited social and leisure repertoires. Recent research has focused upon social–leisure skills in the higher-functioning mentally retarded. Studies of conversational skills and assertiveness, in particular, have been confined to this group (e.g., Kleitsch, Whitman & Santos, 1983). With the more severely retarded, the emphasis has been upon either simple play development or more global interactions. In either category, programming for generalization and maintenance of responding is rare. In this latter respect, a recent study by Keogh, Faw, Whitman, and Reid (1984), involving an 18-week follow-up, is a notable exception. But even their well-thought-out project achieved limited generalization, and we learn nothing about the relative contributions of the individual components in their complex package.

Although positive consequences now command the most respect in working with the institutionalized mentally retarded, sometimes the carefully monitored application of restrictive and aversive procedures is unavoidable. Understandably, this has become the subject of much legal, ethical, and scientific reaction in recent years. An "aversive" procedure may be defined as any procedure that systematically provides a punishing consequence. A "restrictive" procedure is any intervention that limits or denies the freedom, rights, or habilitation of an individual. The use of psychoactive medications for the purpose of controlling maladaptive behaviors forms a separate and distinct procedure within this latter category. It is only relatively recently that these drugs have been viewed in this manner (Breuning, Davis, & Poling, 1982).

To insure proper use of these procedures, the courts now require the formation of monitoring or evaluation committees to review each program prior to implementation. Sometimes called "human rights" or "behavior management" committees, these groups serve as internal mechanisms to balance possible neglect by withholding proper and necessary treatment against potential misuse or abuse.

Within this context, Egelston, Sluyter, Murie, and Hobbs (1984) have asked what impact these committees have on the use of aversive and restricted programs within residential facilities for the mentally retarded. To answer this question, Egelston *et al.* examined residential records maintained by the behavior management committee of a state facility serving 400 mentally retarded persons from January 1980 to August 1982. Using a systematic sampling procedure, the authors selected 100 records for study after the fact. To compare initial and follow-up programs for each of the 100 subjects in the sample, a simple checklist was devised. The initial program was the first program submitted for approval; the follow-up program was the most recent restrictive program submitted to the same committee during the period studied.

The use of psychoactive medications decreased markedly between initial and follow-up reviews. Professionals tended to rely less on drugs for the modification of behavior and more on other means. Whether this heralds a general change from a medical to a more behavioral model remains to be seen. But the biggest limitations of this study are its retrospective nature and its descriptive rather than analytical focus. It is not possible to point meaningfully to a causal relationship between changes observed and the function of the committee. In addition, the investigation occurred at only one institution. There is a need for further study, and it is encouraging to note in a personal communication (May 28, 1985) from Egelston that this is under way.

INSTITUTIONALIZATON, DEINSTITUTIONALIZATION, AND THE COMMUNITY

In Volume 10, there was occasion to comment in this section about the by then traditional parade of well-designed studies of relevant trivia in an area where so much of significance is happening. This year is no exception. Consider, for example, Benjamin-Bauman, Reiss, and Bailey's "Increasing Appointment Keeping by Reducing the Call-appointment Interval!"

However, one of the more interesting articles pertaining to behavior therapy in institutional settings appears in the new Australian journal *Behavioural Change*. Winkler (1985), long known for his work in behavioral economics and environmental design for mental health settings, reviews some 20 years of token economies in psychiatric institutions. For Winkler, a token economy is more than a token economy; its essence lies not so much in the ostensible token reinforcement as in the larger reward system that defines the environment concerned. This reward system goes well beyond the tangible to include social reinforcements for the staff members in their dealings with patients, with those who enter the institution, and with each other. These patterns of social reinforcement reflect not only the social structure and reinforcement patterns of the institution concerned, but those of the environment in which it is embedded. It follows from this analysis that changes in the larger reward system will affect the token economy itself.

According to Winkler, two main themes characterize the development of token economies within institutional settings. These are problems in the implementation of token economies, on the one hand, and developments in mental health policy on the other. The first theme places the token economy in the context of the social system that is the institution; the second places it within the social system of mental health services as a whole.

Winkler makes the political point that, if the alleged purpose of the token economy is to create an environment resembling that of the community at large, this charge is also accompanied by an implicit request to make the staff's work easier by making residents easier to handle. It was the growing recognition of this potential for abuse that led to the formation of human rights committees and other legal safeguards. These developments coincided with the movement toward deinstitutionalization and the concomitant necessity to demonstrate that institutional token economies facilitate discharge, reduce return rates, and enhance both the process of deinstitutionalization and the well-being of the clients concerned. All too often, residents were leaving the institution for a life of either lonely unemployment or a new kind of institutionalization within the community.

What can be done about all of this? Winkler's proposed remedy is to set up a series of graduated token-related programs leading through a small number of carefully monitored settings to a progressively independent life in the outside world. But for a variety of reasons—scientific, professional, and political—this suggestion has never been implemented. The token economy for long-stay psychiatric patients may have had its day not because it is ineffective, but because it is no longer in accord with contemporary politics. Still, for some individuals, deinstitutionalization will always be an impossibility. For these unfortunate few, the main thrust will still be toward making institutional programs serve the patient rather than vice versa.

No matter how fervent the movement toward deinstitutionalization, behavior modification still seems a promising intervention strategy within the institution. To be maximally effective, such projects need to be ongoing rather than time-limited and subject to continual evaluation. Moyes, Tennent, and Bedford's (1985) package, for example, consists of a basic token economy, individual contingencies, a variety of behavior modification procedures, and a series of comprehensive social and life skills training programs. A total of 78 young men and women with behavior or personality disorders participated in the program for at least 6 months, with 1-year and 2-year outcome evaluations following discharge. The ensuing data were compared with those obtained from a similar group of patients accepted for the program but not admitted. In terms of behavioral outcome measures and levels of independent living, the treatment group did significantly better than the no-treatment controls. However, it should be noted that this study merely shows that behavior modification is better than no treatment at all. Nothing is learned about the efficacy of the package components or how the package as a whole compares with alternative interventions, such as medication, traditional psychotherapy, or milieu therapy.

Social communication is always important. Watson and Singh (1985) come to the conclusion that—at least as far as chronic schizophrenics are concerned—if clinically significant short-term changes can be brought about, the same cannot be said with respect to long-term benefit. Reliable ways of generalizing and maintaining behavior change upon transfer to the community remain to be developed. The relationship between the cognitive dysfunctions of schizophrenics and social skills training is particularly complex. Family, social symptomatic, cognitive, motivational, and learning disturbances all have parts to play in the social skills training of the schizophrenic, and it is probably correct to conclude that any long-term impact is most likely to occur through such a multimodal approach (Liberman, Nuechterlein, & Wallace, 1982).

While nursing homes are assuming increasing prominence as primary care sites for chronic mental patients, the quality of care provided has been studied neither often nor well. The work of Shadish, Silber, and Bootzin (1984) is a rare exception to this generalization. A total of 163 nursing home patients were studied in terms of their needs and the treatments they received. These patients tended to be chronic schizophrenics with an established history of poor social coping but no obvious physical ailments that in themselves would require nursing home placements. The relatively little psychosocial treatment offered tended to decline with time, and most patients were receiving an ongoing average of three to four medications on a gradually increasing basis.

Custodial care has a bad name in the mental health world, and the implication is that we ought to be able to provide something better. But as Shadish *et al.* note, at least for the foreseeable future, society may be unable or unwilling to do better; for many chronic mental patients, custodial care may be the primary need. The best of psychosocial treatment for the chronically mental ill seems to be helpful only while the treatment is in effect. Thus, custodial care may be a necessary part of even a complete-health system for some time to come.

Shadish, Orwin, Silber, and Bootzin (1985) later conducted an intensive comparative evaluation of nursing home residents and other patient and nonpatient groups. Community constraints made it impossible to select truly equivalent groups. Despite this limitation, the results are informative. The nursing home patients reported lower levels of well-being than the general population, but these were not lower than those of other socially disadvantaged groups, such as urban blacks. The nursing home patients all reported levels of well-being similar to those of day hospital patients, participants in innovative community care programs, and psychiatric patients receiving traditional hospital and follow-up care. Neither symptoms nor degree of social integration seemed to be related to self-reports of well-being. Patients in institutions such as nursing homes or mental hospitals do not consistently seem to be either more or less satisfied than patients who are not receiving institutional care—a finding at variance with the "increased quality of life" argument that is one of the most frequently cited justifications for deinstitutionalization. Reappraisal would seem to be in order.

Alternative arrangements for emotionally disturbed individuals now include day hospitals; rehabilitation centers; community clinics; in-home services; and a variety of halfway houses, group homes, and other boarding arrangements. The differing models of community intervention (e.g., psychiatric, rehabilitative, and social support networks) all have different and largely unexplored priorities, goals, and treatment procedures (see Dellario & Anthony, 1981). Stein and Test's (1980) multifactor model, in which patients are taught a variety of coping skills, is a good example of a relatively successful intervention. Comparisons with control groups were encouraging. Stein and Test's subjects evidenced reduced hospitalization, higher income, and improved social relations. Furthermore, relatively little social or financial strain was imposed upon either the community or the families. Unfortunately, at the end of the project all participants had to be referred to traditional community programs, and most of the earlier gains were lost—an outcome all too common in the annals of innovative programs initiated on a research basis.

Fairweather's Community Lodge, originated a quarter of a century ago, was another innovative program for mental patients. Designed to facilitate entry into the larger environment, a four-system process was used to generate increasing responsibilities as patients progressed from one stage to the next. Patients who improved significantly were released much sooner than those in traditional hospital environments. However, these gains deteriorated following discharge, and soon there was no difference in readmission rates between experimental and control groups (Tornatzky & Fergus, 1982). The more recent and less ambitious board-and-care home systems (e.g., see Lamb, 1984), are little more than vehicles for the provision of shelter and social protection. In some ways, board-and-care projects are more indicative of a lack of viable alternatives than anything else (Test, 1981).

When Stein and Test (1980) reviewed 13 comparative studies of alternative community placement facilities, alternative care seemed to produce greater client satisfaction, but there was no fundamental difference in either symptoms or psychosocial functioning. Furthermore, after 1 year the time spent within a particular facility no longer discriminated between the various groups. On the other hand, Kiesler's (1982a) review of 10 well-controlled studies led to more positive conclusions.

All that can be said with certainty about these mixed and conflicting findings is that fundamental questions await investigation. Too many studies use inadequately screened or highly selected populations with a great variety of treatment modalities, settings, program goals, and evaluation criteria. There are also additional methodological limitations, such as lack of controls and observer bias. It may also be, as Burchard and Harrington (1985) suggest, that emphasis needs to be placed upon analyses of the various transition stages rather than straightforward comparisons.

Why is it that so many seemingly ideal alternatives to institutionalization fall so readily into disuse? Once again, it could be because they are inconsistent with existing social structures and ideologies (Shadish, 1984). The Fairweather project, for example, stressed an avoidance of dependence on mental health professionals (see Tornatzky & Fergus, 1982), but it is professionals who control the resources that projects depend upon for continuation. According to Fairweather, it is society that causes many of the problems of mental patients—a view that is in direct conflict with the prevailing belief that individuals are responsible for their own problems. By contrast, nursing homes are in fashion, even though they resemble the type of institution excoriated by those in favor of deinstitutionalization. This may be, in part, because they reflect prevailing American social structures and ideologies. Nursing homes yield profits to the private sector; institutional walls protect middle-class sensibilities; and professionals are relied upon to provide care rather than seen as part of the problem (see also Moss, 1983).

The spectrum of alternatives to institutionalization is but one facet of the struggle within behavioral community psychology as numerous diverse models struggle for primacy. If some form of systems perspective is the current favorite (e.g., Jason & Glenwick, 1984), environmental organization, in which the physical, social, and programmatical variables of the total environment are all seen as closely relevant to the final outcome, is not far behind (Twardosz, 1984). Ecological community psychology, closely related, focuses on the manner in which settings influence behavior. Behavioral ecology and applied behavior analysis, suggests Fantino (1985), complement each other to form an integrated approach to behavior. "Behavioral ecology" is really Jason and Glenwick's term for a synthesis of various streams of research that cut across behavior therapy, environmental psychology, systems theory, ecological and setting theory, and (the newest of them all) the social network—prematurely touted by some enthusiasts as a kind of universal cure-all.

Perhaps the most realistic formulation of social network theory is that of Whittaker and Garbarino (1983): Professional services are strengthened and clients are served better if ways can be found to link both formal and informal helping in an overall frame of human services; this is what social network theory is all about. As with many new movements (one hesitates to use the word "fad"), exaggerated claims based on inadequate data are made in social network research. In general, this "research" utilizes a naturalistic, correlational methodology; construct definitions are vague; and meaningful theory is lacking. The instruments used to assess social support tend to be inadequately standardized, making cross-study comparisons difficult (Schradle & Dougher, 1985).

O'Connor and Lubin's (1984) *Ecological Approaches to Clinical and Community Psychology* will serve to conclude this section on a more positive note. The contributors to this edited volume would probably apply a variety of terms to describe their general orientation. "Ecosystems," "general systems theory," "behavior therapy," "psychosocial," and "interactionist" are all phrases that come to mind. What all of the chapters seem to have in common is a commitment to some form of interactionism based upon hypothesis testing that does not assume a simplistic and linear cause-and-effect model. However, I am still not sure exactly what is meant by either "systems theory" or "ecology," and the diversity of language, definitions, and methodology evidenced in this collection does little to assuage my qualms. Nevertheless, this volume is one of the more encouraging developments in the field of behavioral community psychology to appear in recent years.

INDUSTRY, BUSINESS, AND THE MARKETPLACE

Systems theory in one form or another has been around for decades, but it was not until 1978 with the appearance of Miller's *Living Systems* that it could be meaningfully applied to human behavior. For Miller, all living entities can be classified across seven levels: cell, organ, organism, group, organization, society, and supernational system. Each level incorporates all the lower levels: Organizations are made up of groups, groups are made of organisms, and so forth. The implications of living systems theory for behavior therapy have been discussed in previous volumes in this series. Here the primary concern is with Merker's (1985) extension of living systems theory to the world of business. While intrinsically appealing, Merker's proposal is as yet more of a descriptive outline, a blueprint for future research, than a testable proposal.

Merker uses his framework to clarify the relationship of the organization and its various components to the environment. The word "environment" has different meanings for different people, and all of us develop cognitive maps based on our unique perceptions of events. This cognitive structure contains our knowledge about the organizational environment, imposes meaning upon new information, and assists in adaptation to that environment. As yet, little is known about how different organizational events are perceived and interpreted to generate this cognitive map. Organizationally different reward structures influence individual perceptions of the reward climate in ways that are little understood. In one of the few controlled studies to investigate these notions, Jones (1984) failed to find differences in perception among working nurses subject to different reward climates (tenure-contingent or behavior-contingent), despite the fact that the imposed differences between the two systems were extensive and easily discernible even to an outside observer.

Behavioral economics, a subject much discussed in this series, is receiving a new lease on life with the advent of the Society for the Advancement of Behavioral Economics and the emergence of two major books. Allison's (1983) text is the more basic and therefore the more likely to make psychologists aware of the impact of elementary economic principles upon every situation in which living organisms—be they human beings, rats or even microorganisms—compete for limited resources. Cross's (1983) text is more sophisticated and has a point to make. It is sometimes argued that the economic principle known as "the maximization of utility" provides a viable framework for the analysis of behavioral data. For various reasons, Cross rejects this model. Individuals do not always behave optimally, and the predictability of specific outcomes is limited. Reinforcement theory, according to Cross, can provide a more readily testable model of adaptive economic behavior. At the very least, this book should establish firm links between psychology and economics (Hursh, 1980, 1984).

If certain unifying concepts from economics are in a position to contribute to a more complete science of behavior, the converse is also true. Behavioral accounting, for example, highlights the impact of behavioral principles upon the seemingly mundane world of the accountant. Broadly speaking, the four activities of a business of major concern to accountants are budgeting, decision making, control, and financial reporting. All of these, argues Balachandran (1985), imply more than meets the accountant's eye. Budgeting, for example, can be viewed as a mirror of the total organizational environment rather than as a matter of financial considerations alone. It is, in its own way, a behavioral expression of the bargaining process, a means of expressing managerial style and authority, and a measure of performance evaluation. Far-fetched? Perhaps. As yet, behavioral accounting is still in the descriptive phase; in every sense, there is much accounting to be done.

Consumer behavior research, by contrast, is no longer primarily anecdotal or descriptive. On the contrary, as JAI Press's new series, *Research in Consumer Behavior*, indicates this new field is characterized by an impressive depth of sophistication (Sheth, 1985). General and personal expectations have a large impact on the willingness of consumers to spend large sums of money on the purchase of durable goods, and Pickering's (1981) model of consumer behavior helps make the pertinent parameters more explicit. This model has now been expanded by Winer (1985) to incorporate personal circumstances and general economic expectations within a mathematically based framework capable, in principle, of generating testable predictions. As yet, this is as far as it goes.

Most behavior therapists now view classical conditioning theory as rarely necessary and never sufficient. It is therefore of interest to note the recent incursion of classical conditioning into the domain of advertising behavior (e.g., Hawkins, Best, & Coney, 1983; Schiffman & Kanuk, 1983). Classical conditioning would seem to be one of the few testable frameworks that is capable of accommodating the notion that consumer preferences may develop through some automatic, noncognitive system (Allen & Madden, 1985).

With the exception of Gorn (1982), consumer researchers have generated no substantive information about conditioning mechanisms. Gorn was interested in the manner in which the background features in advertisements influence effectiveness. He showed students slides of either beige or blue pens (the conditioned stimulus, or CS) while they listened to either liked or disliked music (the unconditioned stimulus, or UCS). Subjects were then asked to take a pen. More subjects chose the color of pen associated with liked than that associated with disliked music, thereby suggesting that classical conditioning can change preferences.

Unfortunately, this study suffers from serious methological limitations that contravene basic principles of classical conditioning. Gorn paired his CS and UCS for only one trial. For one-trial learning to occur, the UCS has to be very strong, and Gorn's use of disliked music hardly falls into this category. In addition, Gorn presented his CS and UCS together rather than in the preferred sequence (the CS preceding the UCS). Finally, pseudoconditioning is a well-known hazard; to eliminate this possibility, a variety of readily applicable control procedures are available. Gorn used none of them.

Bierley, McSweeney, and Vannieuwerk (1985) randomly assigned 100 student volunteers to one of four groups in an experimental design that corrected most of the deficits noted above. Colored geometric figures served as the CS, and the theme music from the movie *Star Wars* served as the UCS. Colors and music were chosen because these stimuli had been used by Gorn. The preference ratings for stimuli that predicted pleasant music were significantly greater than those for stimuli that predicted the absence of music. Furthermore, these preferences generalized to new stimuli resembling those actually used. Although this study demonstrates that classical conditioning can alter preferences, what it fails to establish is just how this comes about. There was no control for either demand characteristics or the possibility of some form of cognitive mediation. Nevertheless, if future studies confirm and extend these findings, such data could have implications for the modification of consumer behavior. Advertisers using classical conditioning should present the pleasant stimuli virtually every time their product is seen. And to avoid gratuitous advertising for their rivals, manufacturers should make their products as distinctive as possible (see also McSweeney & Bierley, 1984).

I turn now to a different aspect of the marketplace—employees and their needs. When a prospective employee possesses a wanted skill in abundance, there is little need for vocational counseling. But as all of us know who have occasionally bungled a clinical or academic interview, there is room for guidance under the best of circumstances, and behavior therapists have developed specific helping procedures for just such situations (e.g., Levendosky, 1986; Rohsenow, 1985).

The problem becomes more acute for the individual who has some specific disability. Regardless of skills possessed, handicapped people need some form of training in job-seeking skills. It might be thought that this would take up a significant portion of the rehabilitation counselor's time. Not so. Matkin (1982), for example, found that training in job-seeking skills was offered by fewer than 6% of the private-sector rehabilitation counselors who responded to his survey. Furthermore, despite a growing rehabilitation literature, the effectiveness of those programs that are available remains for the most part unknown.

The work of Mathews and Fawcett (1984, 1985) is a notable exception to this pessimistic summing-up. Their program consists in essence of seven steps: analyzing employment tasks of relevance to the job search; analyzing pertinent behavioral activities for an individual to perform when participating in the various job-related situations; developing and using a behavioral assessment instrument; analyzing the validity of such procedures; developing and pretraining these materials; experimentally validating these materials; and, finally, disseminating the job-finding materials. Role-playing scripts and performance checklists are used to assess employment-related skills. Particular attention is given to generalization of performance to real-life situations (see also Mathews, 1984).

While social skills training is demonstrably effective in helping the unemployed find jobs, less is known about the social skills training needed to maintain this employment. It is for this reason that a case study by Black, Muehlenhard, and Massey (1985) is of interest. The numerous hospitalizations of their 51-year-old chronic alcoholic subject had all been preceded by job-related stresses arising from interpersonal conflicts. The social skills training package provided to the subject included videotaped feedback, videotaped modeling, focused instructions, coaching, and behavioral rehearsal. At a 24-month follow-up, the client had maintained gainful employment, was not hospitalized, had abstained from alcohol, and was functioning relatively effectively on the job. While of clinical interest, case studies of this sort serve primarily as pointers for the future research that we may hope will be forthcoming.

The relationships between job satisfaction and job training have also been insufficiently investigated. In areas where numerous investigations have been carried out, such as nursing, the findings are conflicting. For example, contrary to popular assumption, pay is not a key variable; professional relationships are more important. Nurses (and aides, even more so) need to feel that they are active participants in their work (Thompson, LaBeck, & Zimmerman, 1980).

Thompson *et al.* looked at job-related attitudes of former and current nursing staff members in terms of the four types of facilities within which they were or had been employed: one adult service using behavior therapy; one traditional adult psychiatric service; and one adolescent and one child service, both using interpretative psychotherapy and drugs. Three main factors characterized contented employees: satisfaction with the manner in which psychiatrists and psychologists interacted with the nursing staff; satisfaction with the prevailing theoretical model; and emotional adjustment to the care of psychiatric patients. It should come as no great surprise that, whereas the present nursing employees tended to view professional interactions in a generally favorable light, former employees did not. It would seem that, at least in the settings studies, more care should be taken in evaluating potential employees' attitudes and giving them more exposure to the treatment philosophy and methods used on the service in which they will be working prior to employment rather than after the fact.

Employee absenteeism is another critical issue. In his comprehensive review of antecedents and consequences, Durand (1985) teases out two distinct lines of investigation. Industrial/organizational research tends to be conceptually based and to focus on antecedent conditions. Organizational behavior management typically employs the experimental manipulation of rewards, punishers, and other consequent events. The focus of organizational behavior management is usually upon applied questions, such as how to reduce absenteeism.

Regardless of the model, absenteeism seems to be negatively related to job satisfaction. But this in itself tells us little about either the source of that dissatisfaction or what must be done to bring about change. It is usually assumed that satisfaction with coworkers is negatively related to employee absenteeism. But most studies to date have failed to find any consistent relationship between satisfaction with coworkers and absenteeism. The customary homilies about the need for peer group satisfaction would seem to be premature, to say the least. The assumption that workers involved in decision making are less likely to be absent from work is equally tenuous. When Jackson (1983) attempted to increase the ability of hospital workers to influence job decisions by doubling the number of staff meetings, no significant decrease in absenteeism was observed—a finding that will come as no great surprise to those of us who have been urged to attend yet another meeting!

"Flexitime" is a relatively recent innovation. Narayanan and Nath (1982) offer a good example of research in this area. The experimental group, employees of a large multinational corporation, participated in a flexitime program. A comparison group was required to work the traditional fixed schedule. The flexitime group evidenced a significant decrease of absenteeism, where no such decrease was observed during the same time period for the comparison group.

Efforts to reduce absenteeism focus upon the manipulation of rewards, punishers, and other specific consequences, usually by way of feedback coupled with rewards and punishments for attendance-related behavior. The effects on employee absence of feedback alone have rarely been evaluated (Durand, 1985). Contingent positive consequences continue to be the most frequently employed strategy for reducing employee absences (Durand, 1983; Kopelman & Schneller, 1981; Schneller & Kopelman, 1983). Although these practices are built into the personnel policies of most organizations, formal studies of punishment are rare. Durand was able to locate only three studies involving the analysis of punishment for employer absenteeism. All three suggest that combinations of several punishment procedures reduces absenteeism, but none of the studies has provided an analysis of the package components. In addition, as Durand notes, the uncontrolled correlational designs typically employed prohibit attribution of causal explanation. And even when the findings have been positive, their magnitude has at best been modest. It is premature to arrive at any conclusion about the utility of manipulating antecedent conditions to reduce absenteeism.

It has long been recognized that the interactions between workers and their physical environments are the primary cause of accidents. Unfortunately, management has long tended to ignore safe behavior and, unwittingly, to reward unsafe practices (Peterson, 1982). Incidents involving injury are usually followed up by after-the-fact appraisals of consequences rather than preventative analysis. Learning tends to occur as a by-product of unpredictable, infrequent, and atypical events rather than of formal practice.

Thinking along these lines led Chhokar and Wallin (1984) to make a behavioral analysis of a metal fabrication plant that already had a standard, conventional safety program in operation. Accident reports for the preceding 5 years were analyzed, and a list of key behaviors that most frequently contributed to accidents was developed. The 35 items so identified were abbreviated into a Safety Check List that lent itself to unobtrusive observation and recording. The experimental design consisted of six phases: baseline (15 weeks); training and goal setting (6 weeks); training, goal setting, and feedback once a week (4 weeks); training, goal setting, and feedback once a fortnight (4 weeks); withdrawal phase of training and goal setting only, with no feedback (6 weeks); and the final fortnightly reintroduction of feedback (7 weeks). Training consisted of showing the workers 51 slides about unsafe and safe practices. These slides featured regular employees, thereby enabling ready identification with the work situations. Feedback involved graphic presentations accompanied by explanation and discussion of progress. Additional features of the design included interrater reliability assessment and social validation, but, regrettably, no long-term outcome evaluation.

While the results tend to confirm the applicability of a behavioral approach to accident prevention, at least in this setting, it is of significance that meaningful improvement occurred only when employees were provided with feedback about performance safety rules. But at this stage, as the authors note, the conventional approach has obvious advantages, and behavioral strategies are best considered as complementary rather than supplementary.

Sulzer-Azaroff and Fellner (1984) also think in terms of the manner in which the system itself supports or impedes the promotion of socially meaningful target behaviors. This requires an examination of the network of contingencies of reinforcement within the organization, in order to determine whose cooperation and support are going to be most important for success. Safe and unsafe practices can then be meaningfully related to the selection of socially important, practical, and acceptable performance (Fellner & Sulzer-Azaroff, 1984; Sulzer-Azaroff, 1982).

Following a description of the advantages, development, and implication of appropriate assessment strategies, Sulzer-Azaroff and Fellner (1984) consider in some detail factors relevant to the selection of socially important, practical, and acceptable performances within a particular organization. To illustrate the generality of their strategy, lists of safe and unsafe practices and conditions in several different production plants are documented here and elsewhere (Fellner & Sulzer-Azaroff, 1984).

CRIME AND DELINQUENCY

In Volume 10, I drew attention to the fact that no new behavioral theory of crime or delinquency seemed to have surfaced during the previous year. Nothing that has appeared in the interim changes this summing-up. What does seem to be occurring is a socioeconomic trend that forces a segment of the mentally ill population into the ranks of the criminal system (Lamb & Grant, 1982). If behavior therapists are looking for issues of social significance, the criminalization of mentally disordered behavior should surely receive priority. Individuals who formerly would have been treated in a mental health facility are now being shunted into the criminal justice system. Mentally disordered citizens in the United States now have a significantly greater chance of being arrested than non-mentally-disordered persons for similar offenses (Teplin, 1983, 1984).

Several public policy modifications are suggested by Teplin. First, police officers should receive adequate training in the recognition and management of the mentally ill. Second, the least restrictive alternative should be utilized, and, whenever possible, persons with misdemeanor charges pending should be treated within a mental health facility. Third, programs should be set up to treat patients with complex and multiple problems cutting across a variety of caregiving systems. Fourth, to provide alternatives for police referral of mentally disordered persons, it is necessary to set up care modalities other than hospitalization. Despite the proven efficacy of alternatives (Kiesler, 1982a), current practice is at variance with these recommendations (see also Kiesler, 1982b; Kiesler & Sibulkin, 1984).

Changes in federal policies have been in the direction of reducing both funding levels and federal involvement in mental health programs; as Teplin (1984) notes, these reductions could have serious consequences for the deinstitutionalized. She thinks it likely that maintaining support at the current inadequate levels will increase the probability that mentally ill persons who publicly exhibit their disorders will be processed through the criminal justice system rather than the mental health system.

Correctional systems cope with the increasing influx of mentally disordered offenders by transferring "mental cases" to "more appropriate" settings, such as a secure ward in a state hospital. But this presents major difficulties. Mental health staffs in such facilities are understandably reluctant to treat these individuals, and the hapless patient once again ends up surrounded by prison walls. The "in-house" solution, in which a section of an already hard-pressed correctional facility is designated specifically for the mentally disturbed, presents different but equally formidable problems (Levinson, 1984). No solution is in sight.

For those who work within the correctional system, the problem of prison overcrowding is even more overwhelming. In many instances, crowding is long-term, intense, and inescapable. The numerous investigations of Cox, Paulus, and McCain point convincingly to the causal relationships between crowding in prisons and increased rates of death, suicide, disciplinary infraction, and psychiatric commitment (Cox, Paulus, & McCain, 1984; Paulus, McCain, & Cox, 1985). Suggested and largely unexplored remedies range from circumscribed prison improvements to drastic reappraisal of the entire correctional system and its underlying philosophy.

Dangerousness and its predictability prior to incarceration constitute a frequent topic in this section. Now attention is drawn to the predictability of dangerous behavior *within* the correctional system. Correctional administrators need tools for differentiating potentially dangerous from non-violence-prone inmates. In 1979, Megargee and Bohn developed a promising, simplified Minnesota Multiphasic Personality Inventory (MMPI) typology for use in federal correctional institutions. Unfortunately, subsequent investigations showed it to be ineffective (Louscher, Hosford, & Moss, 1983), and no alternative is in the offing.

In 1958, Clemmer advanced the view that prisons are total institutions that generate a culture of their own, based on the complex dynamics of the prisonization process. In this context, "prisonization" refers to the assimilation of prisoners into the informal normative inmate system, in which both prescriptions and proscriptions are in opposition to the norms of conventional society. A high premium is placed upon physical toughness, group solidarity, disdain for prison personnel, exploitive sex relationships, and mercenary attitudes. This process fosters the criminalistic ideology that reigns within the prison community. Thus, the deprivations resulting from the harsh conditions of confinement are what lead to personal adaptation to the pressures described above.

In 1961, Wheeler introduced a competing model that came to be known as the "importation" model of prisonization. Prior to release, some form of anticipatory socialization takes place in the prison whereby the inmate renounces prison values and attitudes and begin moving towards those that prevail in the outside world. There is empirical support for both points of view, but no conclusive evidence in favor of either (Barak-Glantz, 1983). It may be that prison society is pluralistic rather than monolithic—a matter that awaits further investigation.

It has often been argued that young people are both more amenable to change and of potentially greater social significance in that they have their lives ahead of them. Perhaps for these reasons, social skills training with offenders has concentrated upon young people. In 1979, Spence reviewed 10 pertinent studies and came to the conclusion that most were methodologically defective. Writing in 1983, Henderson and Hollin were not much more encouraging. There is still no unitary concept of "social skills training," and this is reflected in the diversity of methodologies and definitions employed across studies. Few studies build any follow-up into their designs, and those that do are limited mostly to measures of recidivism rather than maintenance (see also Hollin & Henderson, 1984).

In 1977, Emery and Marholin made the important conceptual distinction between first-order and second-order change. The former "rearranges part of the system but does not alter the functioning of that system," whereas the latter "involves modification of the system's functioning, thereby solving the present problem" (p. 861). In other words, if the environment has a significant role to play in delinquent behavior, then attempts to modify such behavior must change the environment in a manner that is meaningful to the individual concerned. The implications, beyond the limits of social skills training as currently formulated, have yet to be translated into practice.

Henderson and Hollin (1983) make a closely related point. It is futile to declare that training programs for young offenders must contain real-life situations without recognition of the fact that, for those who are institutionalized, "real life" has a somewhat artificial tone. For the young offender, it is the penal establishment that defines the parameters of real life. Given that generalization of skills is notoriously difficult to achieve even under the most advantageous of conditions, generalization of skills learned on the "inside" to life on the "outside" seems unlikely. Comprehensive social skills training involves problems associated with both prison life and the demands of life after release (Hollin & Courtney, 1983; Hollin & Henderson, 1981).

There may be another, more covert "payoff" to social skills training with young offenders. It may be, speculate Hollin and colleagues, that a social skills training program in an institution (penal or otherwise) enhances the practitioner's role, leading to acclaim, prestige, and greater cooperation between specialist and staff; life is thereby made more tolerable for both. And at the institutional level, it is conceivable that the presence of a social skills training program could enhance the image of the establishment concerned and thereby lead to both improved recruitment and finances.

Token economies for young offenders continue to be used, but the simpler programs of earlier years are now components of complex packages in which the token economy per se plays a secondary role (see Carpenter, 1984; Carpenter & Carom, 1968). Increasingly, it is suggested that behavioral programs emphasize self-regulation skills and processes of adaptive thinking in addition to traditional operant procedures.

In his review, Kennedy (1984) remains sanguine about cognitive–behavioral interventions with delinquents, despite a lack of outcome evaluation. One long-standing theory of antisocial behavior maintains that certain individuals are able to violate other people's rights with little guilt and even less compunction because of an inability or failure to assume the points of view of the persons whose rights are being violated. Most attempts to train children or adults to take the perspectives of others involve some form of role interchange in analogue conflict or disagreement situations. According to Kennedy, there is now growing evidence of a link between perspective-taking deficits and antisocial behavior. Deficits in impulse control and inability to delay gratification, presumed to be related to deficits in perspective taking, are found to be most pronounced among so-called "psychopathic" delinquents. But as Kennedy points out, even if such individuals were to learn effective problem-solving skills, impulse control, and self-management skills, they still might readily violate the rights of other individuals if they thought that such antisocial behavior would be to their advantage. Whether perspective-taking training is able to deter the delinquent from additional antisocial behavior through a heightened appreciation of his or her potential victim's point of view remains to be seen.

Recent legislation has propelled the mentally retarded adolescent offender into the limelight. The problems that present themselves are not only scientific and professional; they are also political. The aggressive behavior of this group if often too much for community resources to deal with unaided, and a call for institutionalization becomes the typical coping mechanism. However, judicial rulings mandate that these youths be provided with the "least restrictive treatment," a concept that has come to mean, among other things, the right to treatment in small community settings. Unfortunately, while the intent is to divert these highly aggressive young mentally retarded delinquents into such programs, neither technology nor resources has kept up with legal expectations. Denkowski and Denkowski (1985) were unable to locate even one study that described, much less assessed, a program or methodology geared specifically toward residential treatment within appropriate community settings.

In the Denkowskis' own investigation, a basic token economy was implemented within a traditional group home and a token economy was embedded within a more comprehensive behavioral program. The results suggest that a traditional token economy approach is not sufficient by itself. Unfortunately, the groups studied were small; all data were obtained by nonblind recorders; and no follow-up data are reported. All that can be meaningfully concluded is that there is a need for further research in this area as in most others.

BEHAVIOR THERAPY AND THE AGING PROCESS

In 1982, Wisocki and Mosher found that the elderly were featured in less than 9.6% of the behavioral literature. A related survey of other professional journals over the period 1964 to 1980 likewise yielded only 107 articles of relevance. Of these, some three-quarters have dealt with the 5% of the elderly who are institutionalized (Wisocki, 1984).

Hussian is one of the few behavior therapists whose primary interest is in working with the elderly. His recent overviews (1984a, 1984b) make the point that, as currently practiced, behavioral geriatrics consists primarily of strategies geared toward response deficits rather than excesses. Most investigators concentrate on antecedent conditions and/or the provision of differential consequences for different responses. This is accomplished by a removal of barriers, the provision of more varied stimuli, verbal and physical prompts, the provision of positive primary or secondary events contingent upon the occurrence of a desired response, the elimination of negative responses, the enhancement of stimulus saliency, or some combination of these. The rationale seems to be that response deficiencies arise from a failure to emit behavior rather than from any permanent loss. The enhancement of participatory behavior then becomes the primary goal of most clinical and research endeavors (e.g., MacDonald, Davidowitz, Gimbel, & Foley, 1982).

For a variety of reasons, the geriatric population is exposed to a traditional medical approach rather than the very different behavioral model described by Hussian and Davis (1985). Teri and Lewinsohn's (1986) *Geropsychological Assessment and Treatment*, geared toward professionals in training and the more sophisticated practitioners, is another good example of the alternative, behavioral model. Two other related overviews warrant mention: Malatesta's (1985) behavorial formulation of geriatric organic syndromes, and Sufrin's (1984) succinct overview of physical rehabilitation in the brain-damaged elderly from a behavioral perspective. Deliberately avoiding a psychiatric formulation, Malatesta emphasizes instead an operational identification of specific problem areas and their functional relationships.

However it is conceptualized, quality of life assumes particular significance for those in their declining years. While the events themselves are of obvious relevance to quality-of-life determinations, how people respond to the events is of at least equal significance (Reich & Zautra, 1984). Quality-of-life investigations require attention to the events themselves and the needs they provoke, to the responses people make to these events, and to the degree of satisfaction people feel with the outcomes of these responses. Unfortunately, direct research into event–activity–outcome relationships in the elderly is lacking, and Reich and Zautra's discussion of these matters is more of a thoughtfully articulated position paper than a report of accomplishments.

With all its deficits, social network theory has a contribution to make (Berkman, 1983, 1984). The frail elderly, in particular, have few resources to fall back upon; for better or worse, current federal policy is increasingly directed toward the voluntary sector of society for the provision of care services. While many neighborhood-based strategies are available to senior citizens, virtually all of these rely upon a networking confined exclusively to the elderly. The recently completed 3-year demonstration project of Pynoos, Hade-Kaplan, and Fleisher (1984) is unique in that local residents of all ages, young and old, were organized into neighborhood-based helping networks linked to community agencies as needed. Participants were pretested as soon as possible after joining the program, and a posttest was scheduled for not less than 6 months later. Encouraging findings were noted at posttest, with many participants reporting better neighborhood relationships and a stronger sense of community; life satisfaction scores on a standardized questionnaire also increased significantly. But what happened following termination of the project we are not told. Perhaps the primary lesson to be learned is that programs of this sort do not emerge spontaneously. Professionally trained community organizers must be employed; formal and informal support systems must be strengthened simultaneously; consistent definitions must be articulated; and valid measuring devices must be developed. Whether all this can be accomplished on a voluntary basis is quite another matter.

For the impaired elderly in particular, the family and a few close friends assume particular importance. They often constitute the only "network" that is available. As yet, few programs geared specifically toward families are available. Family members and caregivers alike need a technology to alleviate these problems and help them to design better home environments. According to Pinkston and Linsk (1984a), the well-established technology of behavioral parent training (e.g., Dangel & Polster, 1984; O'Dell *et al.*, 1982) could be readily adapted to these ends. Haley (1983), for example, used similar procedures to teach caregivers working with older persons how to reinforce and cue positive behaviors. Pinkston and Linsk have carried this strategy a step further in their Elderly Support Project. Families are trained by supervised social workers to participate in a multistep program consisting of referral, assessment, definition of excesses and deficits, recording of baseline data, the behavioral education of support persons, the development of appropriate intervention strategies, a maintenance program, and finally termination guidelines and follow-up.

Single-case designs made it possible for Pinkston and Linsk (1984a) to analyze such a treatment plan in terms of both baseline and intervention data. Reversal designs were used upon occasion to evaluate those interventions where behavior problems were not life-threatening. A consumer questionnaire, given to both clients and trainers at least 1 month after participation ended, confirmed the program's effectiveness. Activity monitoring and social reinforcement emerged as particularly promising methods for the enhancement of home care. It would seem that, with a little ingenuity, virtually all the time-tested strategies of behavioral parent training can be readily adapted to family intervention with the impaired elderly.

In their later and more detailed exposition, Pinkston and Linsk (1984b) raise a number of key questions that await research. How can behavioral methods be used to provide more systematic support for caregivers? How can other services be incorporated to enhance support and maintenance reinforcers? What training methods are most useful in the transfer of parent training technology to this new setting? How does behavioral family training compare with other approaches? Finally, in terms of the cost–benefit ratio, is group training of caregivers a viable alternative to home visits?

Institutionalization is sometimes an unavoidable response to the decline of advancing years. Once institutionalized, the aged tend to present problems that are relatively specific to this population—enhanced dependency, social withdrawal, a restricted behavioral repertoire, and a certain amount of regression. One positive outcome of the recent increased attention to the psychological disorders of later life has been the design and implementation of innovative assessment and intervention treatment programs for age-related problems. There are many reasons why behavior therapy is well-suited to this population. Behavioral strategies, for example, lend themselves to implementation prior to the occurrence of inappropriate and maladaptive behaviors, thereby exerting their effects even when members of the program staff are not present (Hussian, 1985).

The sensory and central processing deficits shown by many elderly individuals require special compensatory procedures. To facilitate compensation, Hussian (1982) uses supernormal artificial stimuli whose physical characteristics have been simplified and magnified. Response discrimination can then be shaped by the gradual reduction of the supernormal stimuli until naturally occurring stimuli control the ongoing behavior. Exaggerated stimulus objects may be used alone or in conjunction with other techniques, depending on the circumstances. Hussian uses these principles to correct wandering, stereotypic responding, and other frequently encountered inappropriate behaviors.

Moos and Lemke (1985) suggest a more ecological approach to the problems of the elderly institutionalized. The paradigm typically employed within such settings implicitly assumes some form of "closed system" in which older people are exposed only to that particular residential program. But in reality, the residential setting is one of a series of multiple environmental microsystems. Few institutionalized individuals are confined exclusively to one system. To greater or lesser extents, the relatively enduring influences emanating from other microsystems, such as the extended family or pre-existing peer networks, may have stronger effects on the quality of life than the more immediate characteristics of the residential setting alone. Conversely, the residential program could influence these other microsystems, thereby establishing a kind of two-way street. Furthermore, the various microsystems may perform different functions for different individuals, and these functions may interact in a diversity of ways. For example, a residential setting provides a work environment for the residents.

These two facets of the environment are not necessarily independent. Thus, the pressure of required activities may lead the staff to use less time-consuming methods of care, and these, in turn, are likely to reinforce passive/dependent resident behavior. Such behavior, speculate Moos and Lemke, may in its turn lead to the negative stereotyping of older persons and to additional dependency-producing behavior on the part of the staff. This could lead to more rapid functional deterioration among the residents and, eventually, to lower staff morale (Kahana & Kiyak, 1984). Even if irreversible biological processes are present, environmental factors may be associated not only with increased psychological and social dependency, but also with physical dependency (Baltes, Burgess, & Stewart, 1980).

Over the years, Baltes and her group have systematically combined an operant learning model with direct observation to study resident–staff interactions. Among other findings, they report that the staff members tend to ignore rather than reinforce independent behavior and to attend instead to dependency and other undesirable behaviors. To modify the complex interactional patterns surrounding dependent behavior, it is also necessary to think in terms of the ecology of the institution rather than behaviors in isolation (Baltes, Honn, Barton, Orzech, & Lago, 1983).

Few psychologists work with the aged. In 1980—and there is little reason to think the position has changed substantially in the interim—the aged received only 2.7% of the health services provided by psychologists, and 70% of practicing psychologists had never worked with the aged at all (VanderBos, Stapp, & Kilberg, 1980). One possible reason why psychological services for the aged are in short supply is the lack of training facilities (Cohen & Cooley, 1983). In this respect, the Geropsychological Services Program at the University of Oregon is unique. The approach is three-pronged, to use their terminology. Prong 1 establishes mechanisms for reciprocal communication with major community agencies; Prong 2 involves a comprehensive psychosocial assessment; and Prong 3 generates behavioral interventions. Particular attention is given to student training and the acquisition of outcome evaluation data (Lewinsohn, Teri, & Hautzinger, 1984).

While behavioral training for paraprofessionals is well-developed in other areas, the options are few for those who work with the elderly, with most instruction consisting of on-site training. Though a few early descriptions of training programs exist, there is but one recent report of comprehensive behavioral training for paraprofessionals working exclusively with geriatric populations (Patterson *et al.*, 1982). To its credit, this program provides precise descriptions for shaping, modeling, and various reinforcement schedules. But content is only one parameter in the training process. There are many areas of study that should perhaps precede or at least be concurrent with content development (e.g., the most appropriate format, maintenance of skills learned during training, evaluation of the success of paraprofessional training). There is much to keep behavior therapists constructively occupied for decades to come.

CONCLUSIONS

Behavior therapy is now well into its third decade. The first, the 1960s, was a pioneering era of ideology and polemics in which behavior therapists did their best to present a united front against the common psychodynamic "foe." Despite considerable opposition, behavior therapy established itself as a respected method of treatment. As the second decade unfolded, behavior therapists progressively de-emphasized and largely abandoned their missionary zeal. Imperious titles yielded to empirical subtitles, and methods replaced mottos (Franks & Rosenbaum, 1983; London, 1984).

The present decade is characterized by a search for new horizons. Concepts, methodologies, and ways of viewing data beyond those of traditional learning theory but still within the orbit of behavioral science are being tried and tested. As behavior therapy matures, behavior therapists become better able to accept their limitations. *Failures in Behavior Therapy* (Foa & Emmelkamp, 1983), and related texts such as *Failures in Family Therapy* (Coleman, 1985) and *Negative Outcome in Psychotherapy and What to Do about It* (Mays & Franks, 1985), could probably not have appeared even 5 years ago.

Cognitive-behavior therapy, at least to my way of thinking, is now established as a part of mainstream behavior therapy rather than the paradigm shift it was once thought to be. Creativity, once considered beyond the boundaries of behavior therapy, is now yielding to a learning theory formulation (Winston & Baker, 1985). Behavioral models of conflict and cooperation provide other examples of behavior therapy extending itself into new frontiers (e.g., Pulliam, 1982).

In his 1982 presidential address to the British Psychological Society, Blackman has made the telling point that behaviorists interested in meaningful relationships are obliged to engage in more than the trivial examination of an organism in social isolation. Also important is the manner in which we interact with the community through our behavior as psychologists. By this yardstick, it would also seem important to apply some form of behavioral analysis to socioeconomic and political concerns. Meaningful decisions about program design and funding rest upon more than the raw data of outcome evaluations. The contemporary scientist/manager/practitioner needs reliable and valid data about costs and benefits, over and above the methodological effectiveness of variables that he or she can influence directly. Private insurance companies and government agencies are increasingly inclined to base funding decisions on whatever cost-effectiveness and cost-benefit data are available. As Yates (1985) warns, without these data the typically poor legislative impressions of the advantages of our services, not to mention their high estimates of the costs of these services, may be used to justify inadequate or even no funding of our work.

In this context, Fishman (1984) draws attention to what he terms the "adoption gap"—the gap between the scientific and pragmatic potential of behavioral technology on the one hand, and the disappointingly slow rate of its adoption on the other. To make his point, he cites the research of Paul at the University of Illinois. For more than 6 years, Paul worked with institutionalized psychotic patients to develop an effective intervention program. The final project, reported in one of the outstanding volumes in the field, is characterized by exemplary design and outcome evaluation (Paul & Lentz, 1977).

The rigor with which this study was conducted is as extraordinary as are the findings. Some 97% of the intractable, chronic patients in Paul's social learning program were enabled to function on a long-term basis within the community. This program was unequivocally superior to a parallel milieu project, and both were markedly better than the usual psychiatric state hospital regimen. What happened next is summed up by Peterson (1981):

> Talk about effective services? None better. Talk about evaluating programs? None more convincing. So what happened? Were state hospitals in the State of Illinois immediately transformed to take full advantage of Paul's findings? Not exactly. A change of administration in the Governor's office led to a severe budget cut and the programs were discontinued. To quote Liberman's (1980) review, Paul "and his battle-hardened staff stood by helplessly as six years of prodigious accomplishment went down the drain." (p. 310)

The gap between theory and research, on the one hand, and clinical innovation, on the other, is also widening. In the early days, the major thrust was toward the clinical application of principles established in the laboratory (Martin, 1985). The first volume of *Behavior Therapy*, the official journal of the AABT, included numerous references to experimental psychology. Today, some two decades later, the situation is quite different, and references to basic research have practically disappeared from *Behavior Therapy*'s pages (Ross, 1985). To close the gap, will behavior therapy have to modify both its methodology and its stimulus–response learning theory base? If so, how will this come about? What will happen to that unique entity known as behavior therapy? How important all this is in the overall scheme of things, only time will tell (see Franks, 1981, for further discussion of these matters).

More immediate problems include the absence of a meaningful model of man (no sexism intended) and the failure to develop a philosophical framework of relevance to everyday life. Clients grappling with such enigmas as the nature of birth and death rarely turn to behavior therapy for either structure or solution; concerned parents wondering how to discuss interpersonal relationships, sex, and religion with their children are likewise forced to look elsewhere for inspiration. As noted, it is perhaps no coincidence that virtually the only book to deal substantively with conceptual, scientific, and theoretical issues in behavior therapy is written by a philosopher (Erwin, 1978).

Although a small number of psychologists—notably Bandura, Staats, and Eysenck—are attempting to build comprehensive theoretical models, behavior therapy at large is still characterized by circumscribed minitheories. It may be, of course, that a comprehensive theory is not possible at this time. According to Craig and McMahon (1983), advances in behavior therapy must go hand in hand with a sensitivity to alternative paradigms. To a certain extent this is correct, but it could equally plausibly be granted that systematic advances must rest to an even larger extent upon a firm alliance with behavioral theory.

It will be of interest to see how these issues are tackled in the coming years and what new problems emerge. For the present, the fact that behavior therapy is now firmly rooted in inquiry rather than ideology is what really matters. Whatever models and mandates are pursued in the quest for knowledge, it is important that we remain open to change. But it is of perhaps equal importance that this change should take place within some acceptable behavioral framework. When the next history of behavior therapy is being written, this combination could emerge as one of its more enduring assets.

CHAPTER

2

BEHAVIORAL ASSESSMENT AND METHODOLOGY

PHILIP C. KENDALL

Behavioral therapy and behavioral assessment have undergone several modifications over recent years. Behavior therapy, for instance, has expanded its horizons to incorporate contributions from the research laboratories of social, developmental, and cognitive researchers. As part of the expanding boundaries of content, techniques, and target problems, the "performance-based" features of behavioral therapy have become increasingly important in the definitional distinctions among therapies. Behavioral assessment has also experienced some efforts toward redefinition, but it is my view that behavioral assessment has not been as flexible as behavior therapy in responding to the increasing interest in and recognition of the expanding array of influences on human behavior. Behavioral assessment seems to have been somewhat less than optimally successful in accommodating and adjusting to the growth and changes within the field. Although behavioral assessment may have suffered more in the recent past from growing pains, there are now marked signs of adaptation that appear to bode well for the future of the behavioral assessment enterprise.

Both of the journals originally defined as focusing upon behavioral assessment have experienced change. *Behavior Assessment* began its existence as an offshoot of *Behavior Therapy* in some respects, and was published under the auspices of the Association for Advancement of Behavior Therapy (AABT). Presently, the journal has a new home, being published by Pergamon Press. The *Journal of Behavioral Assessment* has enlarged its domain and changed its title accordingly. This Plenum journal is now the *Journal of Psychopathology and Behavioral Assessment*. The prominent location of "psychopathology" in the title suggests that this may be the new main focus of the journal, though it could also be the simple result of a preference for the sound of the title with the order of topics listed as they are.

There is no doubt that a wide range of reactions could be summoned to the changes in the journals associated with behavioral assessment. Some, possibly critics, could suggest that these changes are illustrations of the hard times facing behavioral assessors. Naturalistic observations are too microscopic; role plays lack sufficient external validity; and frequency data are not the sole key to scientific analysis. Others, in a situation not unlike the well-known water–glass metaphor, could see the glass as half full and point to the expanding topics that are now pertinent to the behavioral assessment researcher and practitioner. Independent of a pro or con stance, it seems clear that there may be at least one perspective that helps us to understand the changes without pointing fingers of blame or praise.

Behavioral assessment has made a most significant contribution to the evaluation of the outcomes of treatment. Naturalistic observation of the frequencies of targeted behaviors and the resultant alterations in these frequencies produced by treatment were impressive to both the behavioral and nonbehavioral readership. Behavioral assessment was quite comfortable in its home as a member of an outcome evaluation methodology. Perhaps the phrase "leaving its home too soon" captures some of the changes influencing the behavioral assessment field at present. The sooner behavioral assessment left the nest of outcome evaluation, the greater the extent to which it ran the risk of isolation and impracticality. My own recommendation of a possible title for a journal in this area would be the *Journal of Assessment for Behavior Therapy*. While not wanting to argue about semantics or the felicity of word choices, I do wish to underscore that the message of this journal title more closely associates the assessment field with the treatment field. Moreover, by having the title and aims of the journal focus on the assessments associated with behavior therapy, we might hope that the topics that would be appropriate for consideration would, as behavior therapy enlarged its domain, experience an equal enlargement of content. In some ways the appropriateness of areas of current concern, such as the cognitive and emotional features associated with behavorial changes, would be more apparent. Judging from submissions to *Behavior Assessment* and the *Journal of Psychopathology and Behavioral Assessment*, as well as from some of the accepted papers, there does seem to be a recent trend in this direction, despite the absence of a direct invitation in the journals' titles.

The appearance of the second edition of the *Handbook of Behavioral Assessment* (Ciminero, Calhoun, & Adams, 1986) provides added evidence for the interpretation that the glass is half full. That is, while the field may have experienced certain modifications in the journal outlets associated with behavioral assessment, a major text and several related texts (Barlow, 1981; Hersen & Bellack, 1984; Mash & Terdal, 1981) continue to prosper. And, my sources inform me that the second edition of the influential book edited by Mash and Terdal will be available at about the same time as the present book is published. Indeed, there is evidence that the texts have adapted favorably to the expansion of the defining features of behavioral assessment and therapy.

The addition of three chapters to the second edition of the *Handbook of Behavioral Assessment* reflects its increased coverage. The chapters specific to the assessment of depression, the assessments in behavioral medicine, and neurophysiological assessment, respectively, suggest appropriate attention to the changes taking place in the field. Although it would have been wise to have added a chapter on the assessment of cognitive–behavioral functioning, and perhaps even a chapter on integrating behavioral and other forms of assessment, many of the individual chapters do include consideration of the assessment of cognitive factors and recognition of a need for some degree of integration.

One feature of behavioral assessment that has been a concern to me (see Kendall, 1985a) has been the less than adequate recognition of the need for careful psychometric analysis consistent with that demanded by more traditional approaches to assessment. In the opening chapter of the updated *Handbook of Behavioral Assessment*, Ciminero (1986) takes a position that merits the attention of behavioral assessors: "The clinical utility of the behavioral approach is a function of the same factors (e.g., reliability, validity, reactivity, standardization, and the establishment of norms) with which traditional approaches have been contending for years. Therefore, it appears that behavioral assessors can certainly benefit by attending to the successes and failures of the traditional approach to assessment" (p. 10). Only time will indicate whether this meritorious statement is heeded, and only further time will be able to provide the findings to attest to the true merit of the recommendation. Nevertheless, it is sage to build on the discovery of the wheel, rather than either to discover a crooked wheel or to rediscover yet another simple round one.

In many ways, the approach to assessment that is historically described as truly behavioral is the one that observes and records the rate of behavior in the natural environment. That is, frequency data in the actual context of the behavior in question constitute the target for behavioral assessment. In this light, the chapter by Foster and

Cone (1986) takes on an especially important role within the new *Handbook.* While there may be somewhat fewer therapy outcome studies relying on observed frequency data as the basic ingredients for evaluation, there are numerous studies that do employ observational procedures, and readers of the Foster and Cone chapter will no doubt benefit from its guidebook approach. The chapter not only includes discussion of relevant issues within behavioral assessment, but also provides step-by-step pragmatics for naturalistic observers—everything from selecting and training observers and assessing interrater agreement to procedures for implementing the observational system.

As many who have employed behavioral observations know, assessing interobserver reliability is an important aspect of the methodology, and most journals employ reviewers who seem to be reliable in their recommendation that researchers employ the kappa statistic to reduce the chance occurrence of agreement between observers. To the credit of Foster and Cone, the formula for the calculation of kappa is provided in the second edition of the *Handbook*, as it was in the first. Due no doubt to the number of times I have referred students to that section of my copy of the first edition, the book now opens naturally to page 311 (page 284 in the second edition is due for its own elephant ears).

As most observers of the behavioral assessment literature recognize, there is an increase in the frequency of the use of self-report measures. There are no doubt many reasons for this change in frequency, including the economic and pragmatic advantages of self-report measures over the more time-consuming and costly naturalistic observational strategies; the increased recognition of the need to select or separate subjects according to individual-difference factors in an effort to uncover interactions with types of treatment; and the growing interest in the assessment of nonobservable cognitive factors such as self-statements. Jensen and Haynes (1986) capture many of these facets of the front line of behavioral assessment in their chapter on self-report questionnaires and inventories in the new *Handbook.* Indeed, as the authors state, questionnaires, when properly constructed and evaluated, can provide information with a high degree of reliability, validity, and utility.

BEHAVIORAL ASSESSMENT: A NEW INTEGRATIVE MODEL HOLDING TO ITS ORIGINAL NAME?

What is perhaps most striking about the major works in the assessment literature in general, and the behavioral assessment literature in particular, is the fact that they truly strive for and often accomplish a theoretically reasonable and scientifically sound integration of assessment methods. For instance, the bulk of writers in the field endorse the assessment of the three areas of human functioning: cognitive/verbal, behavioral/motoric, and physiological. The interested reader need only consult the various chapters in the second edition of the *Handbook of Behavioral Assessment* for documentation. Yet, despite this unabashed recognition for the multimethod approach to assessment over the years, there is surprising reluctance to admit or recognize that what has taken place is an integration. The climate for integration across schools of therapy may be more promising than the climate in assessment, but no one would deny that the issues of eclecticism in treatment have been brought before the populace (e.g., Garfield, 1982; Goldfried, 1982b; Kendall, 1982; Wachtel, 1977, 1982b). Perhaps the time is right for a direct examination and statement regarding the costs, risks, benefits, and losses that might derive from an assessment integration. Any respectable effort toward integration must, however, employ scientific criteria in determinations of the methods and/or measures that are to be endorsed, and the proselytizing of even the best of polemicists must not prevent proper precautions. By way of illustration, there has not appeared to be a single instance where the expanding arena of behavioral assessment (the integrative model, in my terms), has opened its arms to unsubstantiated projective testing.

The use of different methods for assessment seems logical and inextricably intertwined within any effort to properly understand the true nature of the disorder being measured. Although assessment of the three areas of human functioning will merit attention in most cases, there are sound arguments for different assessments' being primary for different disorders. This argument is consistent with the following: What sample of data, gathered in what setting, and with what subject and assessor, produces what information? For example, assessing hyperactivity in children would benefit from a strong reliance on observational data and ratings by significant others while little if any confidence should be placed in self-report data. In contrast, childhood depression would be best assessed using self-report and clinical interview methods; behavioral observations as the primary assessment method for childhood depression have yet to be reported. Similar arguments can be made using adult disorders as examples. For disorders such as anxiety and depression (see Bernstein, Borkovec, & Coles, 1986; Carson, 1986), the clients' own statements about their current mood conditions are essential, and this remains true despite the high correlations between these two constructs (see Watson & Clark, 1984). Nevertheless, clinical ratings, such as those obtained from structured interviews, remain essential. Contrast the need for self-report in the negative affective conditions with the limitations of self-report in the area of addictions. Most would place greatest confidence in physiological data such as blood alcohol concentrations, and perhaps observations of consumption in target settings or analogues, while placing only limited confidence in self-reports (and then only when assessing certain types of functioning). Analogue assessments seem to be somewhat important in social skills assessment. Weiss and Margolin (1986), in their introduction to the assessment of marital conflict and accord, offer a position consistent with my argument: "There appears to be movement away from exclusive concern with discrete behaviors (frequencies) and a detente with those advocating the significance of expectancies, meaning, contexts, and other less behavioral notions" (p. 561). (See also discussion in Chapter 4 of this volume; pp. 129–134.)

Behavioral Coding Systems

In addition to the application of behavioral coding systems in the regular fashion, some recent applications can be seen as adaptive and responsive. The following are examples of the diversity of recent applications.

One system, the Marital Interaction Coding System (MICS), continues to be applied in several studies. Arnow, Taylor, Agras, and Telch (1985) used the MICS to evaluate changes produced by an agoraphobia treatment program that included marital communications skills training. Tapes were made of the couples attempting to resolve marital disagreements, and 29 MICS codes were examined. Based on the intervention outcome, it was found that couples who were taught specific skills evidenced improved negotiation. Decreases in negative behavior and increases in positive behavior were seen in the MICS scores on the interaction task.

The MICS and the Structural Analysis of Social Behavior (SASB) systems were applied to father–mother–daughter triads with 16 bulimic–anorexic daughter cases and 24 controls. Humphrey, Apple, and Kirshenbaum (1986) coded SASB observations for content and process of communication, self–other focus, and affiliation–independence, and had mothers make decisions regarding general clusters of patterns. MICS observations, using 18 distinct categories, were reduced to five summary categories (high and low problem-solving effectiveness and positive, neutral, and negative interpersonal transactions). The systems were reported to correctly classify bulimic–

anorexic and normal families 72.57% and 82.5% of the time, respectively.

Humphrey *et al.* (1986) identified the positive–negative dimension as important across both coding systems. For the SASB codes, positive codes included "helping" and "trusting," while negative codes included "ignoring" and "walling off." For the MICS, the "laugh" and "humor" (positive) and "put down" and "complain" (negative) codes contributed to the discrimination of groups: The bulimic–anorexic families were more disturbed (more negative, less positive, more contradictory communication) than the normal control families. The evidence also supports the potentially important role of disturbed family interactions in bulimia and anorexia nervosa. Caution must be exercised in this regard, however, as the data did not address the specificity of the interaction pattern to one disorder: disturbed family interactions may thus be contributory to many disorders, including bulimia and anorexia.

Behavior during a problem-solving task was used by Phelps and Slater (1985) in their study of interactions between single mothers and their sons. Audio-tapes were transmitted and broken into thought units (after Gottman, 1979) and coded into three mutually exclusive categories: "dominance," "submission," and "neutral." These categories come from interpersonal theories of personality and reflect the application of coding schemes to verbal behavior. The coding of verbal behavior—not a major contribution of behavioral assessment, but an associated feature—has received increased attention. Phelps and Slater found that submissive communications from mothers were associated with dominant reactions from sons and that dominant communications from sons were more likely to elicit submissive communications from mothers (in high-problem dyads as compared to low-problem dyads). These findings underscore the need for continued sequential analyses.

A new application of observational systems was reported by Patterson and Forgatch (1985). The behavior of therapists was coded and correlated with client noncompliance, using a mutually exclusive six-category system. The client noncompliance codes were as follows: "interrupt," "negative attitude," "confront," "own agenda," "not working," and a sixth code for all cooperative behavior. The therapist codes were these: "support," "teach," "question," "confront," "reframe," "talk," and "facilitate." In two studies, therapists' efforts to teach and confront produced significant increases in the likelihood that the clients' reaction would be noncompliance. In contrast, the "support" and "facilitate" codes were associated with reduced likelihoods of noncompliance.

Patterson and Forgatch's (1985) results are exciting on one hand and preliminary on the other. The excitement is justified, due to the data base and the empirical evaluation that was conducted. Numerous authors in recent years have written about noncompliance and resistance, but this is one of the first direct observational studies to document therapist behaviors associated with client noncompliance. Referring to this study as "preliminary" is a bit unfair—the pejorative connotation is unearned. It is preliminary only in the sense that much more research is needed. What client behaviors are preceding therapists' teaching or confronting behaviors? What pretreatment characteristics of clients are associated with noncompliant reactions to teaching and confrontation, and what characteristics of clients are associated with more successful teaching and confrontation? In addition, as Patterson and Forgatch have noted, given that experienced therapists produce noncompliant reactions in clients, how does the skilled therapist reduce noncompliance?

In an analysis of the mother–son relationships of juvenile felons, Henggeler, Hanson, Borduin, Watson, and Brunk (1985) used several assessments, including observational measures. The observations were taken during a decision-making task; the categories included "facilitative information exchange," "dominance," and "conflict–hostility." Results indicated that the relationships of mother–son dyads in which the sons were juvenile offenders were less warm, and had less positive and more negative communication, than the relationships of dyads in which the sons were nonoffenders.

Direct behavioral assessment as part of a comprehensive assessment battery is reported by Michelson, Mavissakalian, and Marchione (1985). The battery included numerous self-reports, heart rate measures, therapist ratings, and a behavioral assessment including a motion sensor. The target group was agoraphobics; appropriately, the behavioral assessment consisted of a 1-mile walk beginning at the clinic front door, proceeding to a crowded urban center, and ending at a congested bus stop. Subjects were told to walk as far as they could and to return when they could no longer tolerate experienced anxiety. The walk was divided into 20 segments. Subjects reported subjective distress at each point; heart rate was monitored during the standard walk; and a motion sensor to record physical movements was used.

The results of the treatments used by Michelson *et al.* are of interest in their own right; however, the present focus is on behavioral assessment and what the Michelson *et al.* paper says with regard to trends in behavioral assessment. To me, the Michelson *et al.* paper is evidence that analogues have moved into the real world. That is, behavioral assessments do not mean snake approach–avoidance or role play situations. Rather, as behavorial assessment has argued from the outset, what is desired as evidence of change is change in actual behavior. With significant treatment effects evident in the number of steps completed on the standardized walk, Michelson *et al.* provided behavioral assessment data to document that posttreatment behavior was improved over pretreatment behavior. Importantly, as part of a larger battery, the authors could also document changes in self reported affect.

Jacobson (1985a) has suggested that observational measures are not always directly linked to the targets of therapy and therefore may not be the key as once believed. When the behavior of primary interest is observable, accessible to unbiased raters, and measurable in a reliable fashion, observations are clearly samples of the behavior of interest; however, as Jacobson notes, this is not always the case. Both practical issues, such as those affecting practitioners, and theoretical matters, such as the fact that depression is most accessible to the client and not always seen by observers, contribute to his reservations. When an observational measure is developed to attempt to assess characteristics of the client that are not directly observable, Jacobson points out that the approach no longer has the benefit or merits of being direct observation. It may be an observational modality, but what is being observed is less the target of interest and more an analogue.

Jacobson uses the MICS to illustrate one of his concerns. While the MICS is a solid observational system, the categories that are coded are not always related to the problems that bring couples into therapy. MICS scores do separate distressed from nondistressed couples, but the behaviors, according to Jacobson, are signs of marital distress, not samples of the target problems. To quote Jacobson, "if observational measures do not sample directly target marital problems, they cannot at present be relied upon as primary outcome measures" (p. 302).

Gottman (1985) replying to Jacobson, points out that there is often a bias in self report that is not seen in observational data. Gottman draws examples from literature on child treatment, where behavioral frequencies may show only modest change while parents' judgments suggest grand improvement. Gottman agrees with Jacobson that multimethod assessments should be used and that caution should be exercised when the evidence for effectiveness is inconsistent across measures.

Gottman further examines Jacobson's position that subjects, such as partners in couples therapy, can fake good behavior to please the therapist. Citing Vincent, Friedman, Nugent, and Messerly, (1979) and Lobitz and Johnson (1975), Gottman underscores that subjects "could not fake good [behavior]" when nonverbal behavior was observed. In regard to the separation of behavioral assessment from behavioral therapy, Gottman points to the therapy as the cause: Rather than viewing the assessment as in error, clinicians should adjust the therapy to best meet the needs evidenced in the assessment. (Jacobson uses the word "divorced" to refer to the state of therapies not being based on observations. I prefer the word "separation," as a full divorce is not yet complete. Regarding a settlement, it must be assumed to be no-fault, with both partners, assessment and treatment, contributing to the distressed nature of the relationship.)

Weiss and Frohman (1985) have also responded to Jacobson's article. One point raised by these authors has to do with a topic receiving attention elsewhere, the distinctions between quantity and quality. When the quality of events is a concern, the process of observation is only a part of the assessment and reflects only physicalistic aspects of the events. Self-reports have a place in assessments, but, Weiss and Frohman argue, these assessments are not as direct as Jacobson suggests.

For Weiss and Frohman, what they refer to as "content validity" is the basic issue. Is the content of the observational system or the self-report scale reflective of the content of the marital dysfunction? Even if the behavioral codes do not reflect what the clients describe to be their problems, the clients' construal of their problems may not be an accurate or useful one for planning or evaluating therapy. The changes we seek in therapy, state Weiss and Frohman, are not necessarily those that clients have requested.

In Jacobson's reply (1985b) he restates his point: "[B]ehavior therapy research has been excessively accepting of observational measures, as if they were inherently superior to other assessment modalities." While Jacobson does not wish to abandon behavioral observations, he does seem bent on challenging their lauded position. It is not, he states "that self-report measures are *better* than observational ones, only that *we cannot assume that observational measures are superior to other types of measures simply because they are observational.*" Jacobson seems in agreement with his discussants when he argues for basic multimethod assessment, but may again diverge from them when suggesting that among the multiple assessments are primary and secondary outcome measures and that, in some cases, self-reports can be primary measures of therapy outcome. Jacobson uses marital distress and depression as instances to bolster his position.

When all is done—and I suspect that Jacobson, Gottman, and Weiss and Frohman would to some degree agree—the bottom line is the need for multimethod assessment. Jacobson has challenged the hallowed halls of observational codes, but has not dismissed them entirely. Correspondingly, he has reaffirmed the need for multimethod measurement, but has not opened the door completely to consider the relevance of assessing self statements, dysfunctional thinking, attributions, and other cognitive–behavioral concepts. Judgments of the radical nature of Jacobson's papers vary, depending where on the continuum the observer's own position lies. Certainly, as Jacobson closes his rejoinder, we want to avoid addiction to observational methods, and we need not choose abstinence or abuse. Controlled coding is recommended.

Response-Class Matrix

There have been several discussions of the merits of attempts to standardize behavioral assessments. Without standardization, it has been argued, one can lose comparability of findings across studies. The Response-Class Matrix (Mash, Terdal, & Anderson, 1973) can be viewed as a standardized observational recording procedure (Mash & Barkley, 1986) designed for the behavioral assessment of dyadic interaction in a structured setting. The Response-Class Matrix offers a system that can provide uniformity and standardization of observation measures. Mash and Barkley (1986) review a series of studies using the Response-Class Matrix, highlighting its explicability across various disorders, contexts, and samples, and illustrating its use in treatment outcome.

One reason I have chosen to mention the Response-Class Matrix in this review is that I believe it stands as a reasoned model for advancement in behavioral assessment. Critics of the lack of standardization of behavioral assessment (and its related cost-ineffectiveness) and critics of the noninteractional features of behavioral assessment will find the Response-Class Matrix quite satisfactory. To my surprise, however, the system has been used with child populations almost exclusively and has not been as widely adopted as the system merits. The method can be readily adapted for use in different settings, allows for comparison across time, and represents a reasonable manner in which to approach the complex issue of sequential behaviors.

An example of the application of the Response-Class Matrix is the use of the methodology by Barkley and colleagues to assess hyperactive children's and their mothers' actions and reactions across different doses of Ritalin given to the children. According to Barkley, Karlsson, Pollard, and Murphy (1985), each assessment requires two coders. One coder observes and records the mother's behavior and the child's response, using seven categories of observation for the mother and six for the child. The other coder observes and records the child's behavior and the mother's reaction to it, using the same observational codes. From this data set, Barkley and colleagues report the production of two types of dependent measures: percentage of total interactions and conditional percentages within behavior categories. For instance, "child complies" is calculated by taking the occurrence of a response category of one person relative to an antecedent category (e.g., "mother directs"). Barkley *et al.* (1985), when examining the effects of varying doses of Ritalin on the behaviors of the children and the responses of the mothers, found some data to support a change in compliance. In the high-dose condition (0.7 mg/kg b.i.d.), the medication was effective in improving the children's compliance to the mothers' commands. Correspondingly, mothers then reduced the frequency of their commands and increased their positive general interactions with the children. While compliance is typically viewed as a psychological factor, and correspondingly treated with variations of psychological intervention, there are some data to suggest that medications may alter the behavior of the treated child and have a corresponding result on the controlling actions of the mother, with the result being that the child is less noncompliant. It is through this application of the Response-Class Matrix that one can accomplish an analysis of differential compliance rates across types of parental action, and, more generally, can determine sequential and interactional patterns (see also Barkley, Karlsson, Strzelecki; & Murphy, 1984).

ASSESSING DEPRESSION: SELECT MATTERS OF MEASUREMENT WITH CHILDREN, ADOLESCENTS, AND ADULTS

The assessment of depression has become an important assessment focus. Perhaps more than in any other individual area during the period reviewed, there seems to be activity on numerous fronts, all concentrating on the measurement of depression in children and across the life span: self-report scales, peer nominations, task performance measures, ratings by significant others (e.g., parents and teachers), behavioral observations, and clinical structured interviews. The assessment of depression is the topic of an entire book edited by Sartorius and Ban (1986). These editors have gathered an international collection of contributions, each of which focuses on the measurement of psychological depression. Chapters include coverage of assessments for French, German, Spanish, Polish, Indian, Scandinavian, Japanese, and African populations. Other chapters note specific assessment procedures and devices, but there remains an international flair throughout the volume. In the following discussion, assessment research and procedures are reviewed and recommendations provided.

Self-Report Instruments

The Children's Depression Inventory (CDI) described by Kovacs (1979, 1981), a downward extension of the Beck Depression Inventory (BDI; Beck, Ward, Mendelson, Mock, & Erbaugh, 1961) consists of 27 forced-choice items with three choices each (e.g., for question 2, "Nothing will ever work out for me," "I am not sure if things will work out for me," or "Things will work out for me O.K."). To assure that the scale taps current mood, the instructions ask the child to pick the sentence that best describes him or her for the last 2 weeks. Question 9 has to do with thinking about killing oneself, and more than an occasional researcher/clinician has eliminated this item from the scale, following the assumption that there might be iatrogenic effects. Internal consistencies for the scale average approximately .80; test–retest reliabilities range from .70 to .82; and there are correlations in the .50 range between CDI scores and clinician ratings. Helsel and Matson (1984) conducted three studies using the CDI, including a factor analysis, age analyses, and relationships with a measure of social behavior.

Saylor, Finch, Spirito, and Bennett (1984) reported that the CDI discriminated depressed from normal children, but did not reliably differentiate children diagnosed as depressed according to the *Diagnostic and Statistical Manual of Mental Disorders*, third edition (DSM-III) from nondepressed disturbed children. This finding raises the question of the lack of specificity of the scale scores to depression alone, and suggests that, in part, the CDI also taps some generalized psychopathology. Saylor *et al.* (1984) also reported that the CDI scores were related to self-reported self-concept. In a second set of studies, Saylor, Finch, Baskin, Furey, and Kelly (1984) reported that self-reported depression, using a multitrait–multimethod approach, was related to other self-report measures (e.g., anger), but not related to measures of depression gained from other sources. In this study, the method variance (variance accounted for by the type of assessment method used—self-report) accounted for twice that produced by the trait effect (depression).

When one is considering the self-report assessment of depression, it is essential to consider the specificity of the measurement. That is, does the self-report scale select depressives, or does it select persons with general maladjustment or a composite of psychopathologies? A key concept associated with depression is anxiety. Are they separable? Do self-reports overlap excessively? Watson and Clark (1984) have introduced the important concept of "negative affectivity" and stressed that anxiety and depression are both negative affective conditions.

Research by Finch and colleagues (e.g., Wolfe *et al.*, in press) has examined the negative affectivity issue in children. Using three different assessment methods (self-report, teacher ratings, and structured clinical interview) and measuring both anxiety and depression allowed these researchers to test the separateness of the two constructs. Their results indicated that the anxiety and depression measures, independent of the type of assessment method, were significantly correlated and seemed to lack discriminant validity. The findings were interpreted as support for the notion of the larger conceptual construct, negative affectivity (Watson & Clark, 1984) (see also pp. 58–59).

It is worth noting at this juncture that the often used scale for assessing anxiety in adults, the State–Trait Anxiety Inventory (Spielberger, Gorsuch, & Lushene, 1973), has been revised. Items on the earlier version that were seen as tapping a depressive pattern were replaced. It would be useful to pursue a similar strategy with the children's version. For example, one item on the scale asks for a frequency assessment tied to the item "I feel like crying," Not that the item content offers the best explanation of the degree of overlap between anxiety and depression, but a true test of the separability of the constructs of anxiety and depression, based upon self-reports, may require more differential self-report instruments. Nevertheless, the broad-band construct of negative affectivity seems to capture the pattern of results reported across studies.

Reynolds, Anderson, and Bartell (1985) report on the development of the Child Depression Scale (CDS). The CDS has 30 items, a reported internal consistency of .90, and a correlation of .70 with the CDI (in a population of third- to sixth-grade children). As customary, though unfortunate, the CDS and the CDI were also found to correlate substantially with self-reported anxiety (.67 and .58, respectively). While both scales seem to have similar difficulties with the assessment of depression specifically, and not anxiety and other psychopathologies, each has reasonably sound psychometric properties.

Self-ratings of depression by children admitted to a psychiatric facility have been investigated by Asarnow and Carlson (1985). The Depression Self-Rating Scale (DSRS; Birleson, 1981) asks children to self-rate experiences over the preceding 2-week period. The DSRS contains 18 items that refer to the affective, cognitive, and behavioral symptoms of depression; a 3-point scale is employed (present always, sometimes, or never). The modified DSRS used by Asarnow and Carlson included additional depressive items, such as hopelessness items. A total of 82 consecutive admissions to a child psychiatry facility participated. The children were 8–13 years of age, had IQ's over 70, and were not seriously confused. DSM-III diagnoses (reached according to the Schedule for Affective Disorders and Schizophrenia for School-Age Children [Kiddie-SADS, or K-SADS]) identified depressed and nondepressed cases. The depressed and nondepressed groups could be reliably differentiated using the DSRS (both the 18-item form and a modified form); with very few false positives, the DSRS reached 66–77% correct classifications. DSRS scores were correlated with CDI scores (self-report), but were not meaningfully related to ward ratings of depression.

A Cognitive Bias Questionnaire for Children (CBQC) was developed and investigated by Haley, Fine, Marriage, Moretti, and Freeman (1985). DSM-III criteria for depression were applied to 39 recent admissions to a child psychiatry clinic. Of these, 11 met DSM-III criteria for Major Depression and 6 for Dysthymic Disorder ($n = 17$), while other diagnoses included Conduct Disorder ($n = 9$), Adjustment Disorder ($n = 6$), Anxiety Disorder ($n = 4$), and Attention Deficit Disorder ($n = 1$). The remaining 2 children did not receive a DSM-III (Axis I) diagnosis. The children completed the CDI (Kovacs, 1981), the Children's Depression Scale (Lang & Tisher, 1978), and the CBQC. The CBQC consists of brief vignettes describing a school, home, or social situation with four response options. The options reflect depressed–distorted, depressed–nondistressed, nondepressed–nondistressed, and nondepressed–distorted thinking styles. Controls for age effects, and nonsignificant effects for socioeconomic status, IQ, and sex, were reported along with the main findings. The depressed–distorted category of response was related to severity of depression and reliably distinguished between the children with and without an identified affective disorder. Given the hypothesis that certain psychopathologies may be more related to cognitive distortions (e.g., depression), while others (e.g., impulsivity, antisocial behavior) are more the result of cognitive deficiencies (Kendall, 1985b), the CBQC and its assessment strategy may be helpful in future studies of several psychopathologies where there is an effort to identify the extent to which distortions (or deficiencies) are implicated in the disorders.

The Hopelessness Scale (Beck, Weissman, Lester, & Trexler, 1974) has been shown to have some predictive validity regarding suicide. For example, Beck (personal communication, 1986) mentioned that 10 of 11 clients with initial suicidal ideation who scored 10 or more on the Hopelessness Scale committed suicide within a ten-year follow-up period. This information is potent and mandates that clients who may be at risk for suicide be assessed for hopelessness.

Kazdin, Rodgers, and Colbus (1986) have described the evaluation of a Hopelessness Scale for Children aged 6–13. Internal consistency and 6-week test–retest reliabilities were good. Hopelessness correlated positively with depression and negatively with self-esteem and social behavior. The 17-item scale (e.g., "I want to grow up because I think things will be better") merits further investigation to determine the predictive criterion-related validity (e.g., suicidal behavior). Although one can readily generate enthusiasm for this line of inquiry, especially given the relationships found with the adult Hopelessness Scale, there is the major reservation having to do with the fact that children may not yet have developed the futuristic perspective necessary to understand a long-term concept such as hopelessness. True, the scale may function adequately even in instances where the respondent does not have a full grasp of the concept, but it is important to determine whether there exists a cutoff age or level of cognitive functioning that might moderate the validity of the scale. Developmentalists suggest that children approximately 10 years of age or older can begin to master a view of the future, but that younger children may have particular difficulty with the concept. Further investigation employing developmental (e.g., age) factors and cognitive ability measures might further elucidate the efficacy of the Hopelessness Scale for Children.

Notes on Adolescents

Reynolds has reported on the development of a specific scale for assessment with adolescent cases. The Reynolds Adolescent Depression Scale (RADS; Reynolds, 1986) is a 30-item self-report measure normed on over 8,000 13- to 18-year-olds. Internal consistencies over .90 and a 6-week test–retest reliability of .84 have been reported; these, coupled with concurrent validities with other self-report measures (.71 to .89) and high correlations with Hamilton Rating Scale for Depression (Hamilton, 1960) scores (.84), suggest that the RADS has positive psychometric qualities. As far as structured clinical interviews are concerned, the SADS can be used for adolescents, as can the Hamilton ratings. Reynolds (1986) has reported acceptable psychometric qualities for these interviews and ratings with adolescent cases, and has noted that the administration can be as brief as 20 minutes (range 20–30 minutes).

Carey, Kelley, Buss, and Scott (1986) report on the development of an Adolescent Activities Checklist (AAC) for use with depressed adolescent cases. The scale contains 50 pleasant and 50 unpleasant activities and is designed to allow for assessment of the frequency and pleasantness of activities. There was a .36 correlation between depression scores (BDI) and the frequency of unpleasant activities, but a nonsignificant relationship with pleasant activities.

There are reasons to be pleased with the development of scales specific to adolescent samples. First, these youngsters are often put off by language that may be more appropriate for younger children. Second, adolescents are developmentally more capable of understanding concepts such as a negative view of the future. Third, adolescents are a "marginal" group (Kendall & Williams, 1986)—not children and not adults—and they may therefore respond differently to adult questionnaires. Finally, the increased incidence of suicidal behavior among adolescents (Pfeffer, 1986) in itself warrants more detailed assessments specific for this group. A problem remaining with the RADS, as with self-report measures of depression, is the degree to which the scale specifically taps depression and not related negative affective conditions such as anxiety or anger, or social patterns such as withdrawal.

In one study of the later effects of depression in adolescents, Garber, Kriss, Koch, and Lindholm (1987) examined the outcome of depressed adolescents using a longitudinal design. The range of ages was 10–17 years, with 10 males and 10 females in the overall sample. Controls, matched for sex and age, were nondepressed psychiatric patients. Adolescents with an affective disorder received significantly higher ratings for sleep problems, loss of interest, low self-esteem, psychomotor agitation, suicidal ideation and behavior, and social withdrawal. The nondepressed controls received significantly higher severity ratings for conduct problems. As the authors note, these results document that adolescents seem to show the same depressive symptons as are associated with the major affective disorders in adults. One of the most striking findings was that 7 of the 11 depressed subjects had had at least one other episode of major depression since their original hospitalization. Only 1 of the nondepressed control subjects had an episode meeting the criteria for major depression. Although the authors note the limits of their follow-up duration (an average of 8 years), I was impressed by that interval of time. Indeed, since adolescent depression is so infrequently targeted, it is pleasing to see researchers paying attention to the later effects of affective problems in earlier years. Indeed, as these results suggest, there is a continuity of symptoms in depressive disorders of adolescents and adults; it sends a clear message that direct attention to the treatment of the symptomatology is needed earlier than in the adult years.

Beck Depression Inventory

An enormous quantity of research using the BDI has appeared in the recent past. Because of its widespread usage and the need for certain consistencies, a set of recommendations for use of the BDI has been prepared (Kendall, Hollon, Beck, Hammen, & Ingram, 1987). The recommendations concern the stability of depression and the need for multiple assessment periods; specificity and the need for multiple assessment measures; and selection set points and the need for terminological accuracy. The following material on the BDI is adapted from the Kendall *et al.* (1987) paper, and each of the authors is thanked for his or her unique contributions.[1]

STABILITY OF DEPRESSION AND THE NEED FOR MULTIPLE ASSESSMENT PERIODS

Despite relatively high rates of test–retest reliability, recent studies have shown that over 50% of those who initially score above cutoff criteria for depression change classification when retesting is conducted within hours (Hatzenbuehler, Parpal, & Matthews, 1983), days (Zimmerman, 1986), or 1–4 weeks (Deardorff & Funabiki, 1985; Hammen, 1980). Many change from some classification of depressed to nondepressed, while others change from more to less depressed. The overall stability coefficients appear to be contributed largely by relatively nondepressed scorers. One implication of the issue of instability, raised by Sacco (1981), is that the experimenter bears the burden of proof in demonstrating that the status of participants at selection and experimental testing is the same.

We (Kendall *et al.* 1987) have concurred with Sacco's (1981) recommendation that the presence of depressive affect must be verified prior to any experiment, and have also noted that subjects should be assessed during at least two time periods (once at initial selection and once immediately preceding the experiment) to insure that the depressive affect appears relatively "stable" over some period of time. Research based solely on a single-administration BDI classification

1. The author wishes to thank Steve Hollon for his comments on earlier drafts of this section.

cannot be generalized to imply stable, dispositional attributes of the person.

SPECIFICITY AND THE NEED FOR MULTIPLE ASSESSMENT MEASURES

The specificity issue, as related to the BDI, is largely an issue of construct validity (Cronbach & Meehl, 1955). A "construct" is a concept that is "constructed," based on scientific information, to explain and organize aspects of existing knowledge. A psychological instrument is said to have "construct validity" only when a number of studies are integrated and judged to support the underlying theoretical construct. To what extent does the BDI demonstrate construct validity specific to depression? The issue of psychopathological specificity concerns both (1) high-end specificity (the degree to which high scores on the BDI are associated solely with increased levels of depression and not other disorders) and (2) low-end specificity (the extent to which the BDI assesses a continuum ranging from no depression to severe depression, with low scores indicating the absence of psychopathology).

High-End Specificity. The specificity of the BDI for the assessment of "depression" as a homogeneous psychopathological entity is a concern. Recent data are consistent in suggesting that the instrument is relatively sensitive but not entirely specific. Several investigators have shown that in both community samples (e.g., Oliver & Simmons, 1984) and samples of college students (Deardorff & Funabiki, 1985; Hammen, 1980), significant proportions of high scorers do not have diagnosable disorders, and of those who do have disorders, many are not current primary affective disorders. Elevated depression scores appear to reflect a variety of dispositional qualities, various psychiatric entities, responses to stressful life events or other transitory happenings, and the like. Research has found high correlations between BDI scores and other self-reported symptoms (e.g., Gotlib, 1984). As noted earlier, Watson and Clark (1984) argue for a construct of "negative affectivity" as a term for the general tendency to experience and report discomfort, and to display negative views of the self and situations; the term encompasses what has been termed "trait anxiety," "low ego strength," "neuroticism," and the like.

Evidence attests to the fact that depressive and anxious affect are correlated in many cases. For example, we (Hollon & Kendall, 1980) reported a correlation of .79 between depression and generalized anxiety in a sample of college students. Tanaka-Matsumi and Kameoka (1986) reported correlations based on college students' responses to several measures of anxiety, depression, and social desirability that indicated strong relationships between measures of depression (e.g., .54 to .60) and between measures of anxiety (e.g., .79). However, anxiety and depression measures also correlated highly (e.g., .71, .73). All scores on the affective self-report scales were associated with social desirability (e.g., −.67, −.75). The data were also analyzed separately for a group of "moderately depressed" subjects, and the correlational patterns held. This association has important interpretive implications: Results obtained from a "depressed" sample may be a reflection of depressive affect, other negative affect, or some interaction between the different affective states. Indeed, recent research (Ingram, Kendall, Smith, Donnell, & Ronan, in press) found that depressed college students evidenced one pattern of automatic thoughts, while test-anxious subjects evidenced a different pattern. However, subjects who were *both* depressed and test-anxious evidenced still another pattern. It would be potentially misleading to report that a certain pattern of psychopathological features is characteristic of depression when it may be characteristic of other disorders as well.

The specificity sword cuts both ways. While depression researchers must be aware of the potential confounding effects due to the presence of other types of negative affect, so must researchers who study anxiety or other affective states. Researchers who have relied on psychometric subject selection of a specific psychopathological state have typically not acknowledged this potential affective overlap and its implications. Future work would benefit greatly from the inclusion of assessments of other affective states besides depression, and analyses of the results, to determine what effects are specific to depression relative to other mood conditions. The burden of proof must fall on the investigator to demonstrate the generalizability of the sample to particular clinical groups, or to show that the results may be applied specifically to depression rather than to nonspecific distress conditions or other nosological categories.

Low-End Specificity. Studies often use control groups composed of nondepressed individuals for comparison with their depressed groups. While this is an appropriate strategy, the selection of such groups on the basis of low BDI scores can at times be problematic. Using an extremely low-scoring group as a "normal" control may lead to inferential errors, since this cell would probably be composed of "Pollyannas," professional daredevils, incipient hypomanics, and the kind of people who want to talk to you when you sit next to them on an airplane.

Hammen (1983) has noted that individuals selected for very low levels of depressive affect (e.g., a score of 0 on the BDI) may be characterized by other forms of psychopathology (e.g., psychopathy, hypomania) rather than, or in addition to, the absence of depression. Use of such subjects as a "normal" comparison group is thus inappropriate. We (Kendall *et al.*, 1987) have recommended that researchers select control groups for being statistically "average" in level of depression, or that three groups be selected: one high in depressive affect, one at the mean for depressive affect, and one low in depressive affect.

Use of the BDI in conjunction with other measures—the hallmark of the classic multimethod approach to assessment—promises to provide the most convincing diagnostic statements. It is recommended that multimethod measurements be undertaken in conjunction with the need for multiple assessment periods. Use of a multiple-gate approach is discussed in a later section, and the reader is encouraged to read that section with the BDI in mind.

SET POINTS AND THE NEED FOR TERMINOLOGICAL ACCURACY

Variations in the set points (cutting scores for initially selecting depressed cases and those used to reflect clinical improvement) used in research with the BDI create the potentially troublesome situation where different studies cannot be readily composed and/or integrated. It may be desirable to establish a minimum set point in order to have greater comparability between studies; as a practical matter, however, it is difficult to suggest universal set points, since the problems of instability and heterogeneity occur when scores of both 10 and 16 are used to identify relatively depressed samples (e.g., Deardorff & Funabiki, 1985; Hammen, 1980). The adoption of a higher cutting score would surely reduce false positives at the expense of false negatives (e.g., Oliver & Simmons, 1984), but would not insure stability or eliminate heterogeneity. Most researchers probably care more about reducing false positives and may find that adoption of higher set points increases the likelihood of finding significant predicted effects. Nevertheless, interpretation of such outcomes and their range of generalizability must be cautious.

While we are not inclined to offer a rigid recommended set point for different degrees of depression or for clinically meaningful change, we (Kendall *et al.*, 1987) have suggested that one consider the following stance. Large-sample psychometrics for the BDI evidence a skewed distribution, with a mean often in the area of 4–6. The range of scores from 0 to 9 may be viewed as normal, but it must be noted that selecting subjects whose scores are at the extremely low end may produce a comparison group with other real abnormalities rather than properly labeled normals. Mild levels of depression are associated with BDI scores of 10–20, with scores of 10–17 suggesting dysphoria and, scores greater than 17 more closely associated with depressive states. Scores of 20–30 reflect moderate depression, and scores greater than 30 reflect severe depression. Studies that have selected outpatients on the basis of meeting Research Diagnostic Criteria or DSM-III criteria for Primary Unipolar Depression typically report mean BDI scores around 30 (e.g., Murphy, Simons, Wetzel, & Lustman, 1984). Consistent with these parameters, clients with BDI scores of 0–9 after clinical intevention may be reasonably viewed as remitted (e.g., Rush, Beck, Kovacs, & Hollon, 1977).

Related to set points along the continuum of BDI scores is the issue of the continuity hypothesis. Are changes in measured level of depression matched by similar changes in some potentially covariant construct of interest? Or, stated differently, as one moves up the units of the BDI (e.g., specific scores or set point cutoffs), is there necessarily corresponding movement along another dimension of interest? For example, we know that psychomotor retardation is found in at least some severe depressives. Would we necessarily expect a mild level of psychomotor retardation in the presence of a mild level of "depression"? Continuity becomes particularly critical when we use analogue studies to test causal models; if modest levels of syndrome depression are relatively detectable (easily measured), and modest levels of some purported causal factors are less sensitively directed, then we could erroneously reject the hypotheses of covariation.

To the extent that depression is a continuous phenomenon, then a study that contrasts a group very low in measured depression with one only moderately low in depression might indeed yield valid inferences about the phenomenon. This would be equivalent to contrasting retardates and dull normals on performance in vocational school and finding that greater intelligence facilitates learning. While one might not be comfortable calling either group "intelligent," most would be fairly comfortable talking about the role of intelligence based on such a design. This situation holds true, of course, when depression is viewed as a single straightforward continuum.

Base rates will influence the acquired mean scores on the BDI. Samples of college students will produce dramatically lower mean scores than samples of outpatient cases. Patients who score at the high end of the BDI and who come from settings where persons with other disorders congregate (e.g., outpatient settings, all-night diners, self-help groups) would not be properly selected for depression using simply set points on the BDI. The odds for having elevated scores on the BDI for reasons stemming from causal processes different from those working in depression would be too great. When certain set points are implemented with college students (e.g., scores in the 10–15 range), it seems wise to refer to these subjects as "dysphoric," unless detailed assessments using other measurement methods are employed (e.g., structural clinical interviews). Only when there is consistent agreement in the assessment of depression across measurement methods (e.g., BDI scores beyond a set point, passing criteria on a structured clinical interview) would one be safe in assuming some degree of symptom covariation and secure in using the label "depressed." Thus, unless it can be demonstrated through the use of clinical interviews that BDI-evaluated samples meet diagnostic criteria for some category of depression, it might be desirable to avoid the term "depression" altogether in favor of a term like "dysphoric" that implies nonspecific negative affectivity.

Behavioral Observations

Though lagging behind, in terms of the quantity of research effort, some studies have begun to examine the observed frequencies of specific behaviors and their relationship to depressive symptomatology. At least one study with children and one with adults have tried to tackle the challenge of an observational coding system for depression.

In one study, childhood depression was assessed by self-report and interview measures administered separately to the children and their mothers. This report (Kazdin, Esvelt-Dawson, Sherick, & Colbus, 1985) included direct observations of the children obtained during free-time periods on several days. Activity, solitary behavior, and affect-related expressions (i.e., smiling) were assessed. The results indicated that depressed children engaged in significantly less social activity and exhibited fewer affect-related expressions than did the nondepressed peers. Overt behavior measures were consistently related to parent-completed but not to child-completed measures of depression. That is, when the mothers rated the children as depressed, there was a meaningful relationship between the severity of those depression ratings and the frequency of the depressive behaviors described above. The major findings, according to the authors, were that depressed children engaged in significantly less social activities and exhibited fewer affect-related expressions than did the nondepressed peers.

A coding system designed for the naturalistic observation within interactions within families has been described by Biglan *et al.* (1985). The Living in Family Environments Coding system (see also Arthur, Hops, & Biglan, 1982, and the Family Interaction Coding System, Reid, 1978) includes behaviors from prior coding systems but added codes pertinent to depression and to affect in general. There are a total of 31 content and 7 affect categories. Samples of the depressive codes include "ignore," "complaint," and "self-derogation."

The addition of depressive codes adds meaningfully to the breadth of content that can be measured with the observational system. Equally, if not more advancing, is the fact that many features of the behaviors are assessed. To quote from Biglan *et al.* (1985), "The coder keyed in a five digit number indicating the person behaving, the content of their behavior, the aspect associated with the behavior, and the target of the behavior. Changes in content of affect were recorded independently" (p. 436).

It is far too soon to draw conclusions about the efficacy of coding systems for assessing depression. Clearly, more work is needed to determine the proper codes for each of the age groups and the validity and cost-effectiveness of this method of measuring depression. The final result may be that observations of depression will take somewhat of a back seat to self-report, since the source of the disorder (the person) is involved in the experience of the condition.

Interview Methods

Similar to the CDI as a downward extension of the BDI, the Children's Depression Rating Scale (CDRS; Poznanski, Cook, & Carroll, 1979) is a downward extension of the Hamilton (1960) Scale used with adults that requires approximately 30–40 minutes to administer. The CDRS is appropriate for 6- to 12-year-olds and includes 15 items rated along a severity continuum by a trained clinician. Poznanaki *et al.* noted that a high correlation was found between the global ratings of two psychiatrists of the severity of depression and the scores on the CDRS. Specific items on the CDRS that correlated highly with overall ratings included social withdrawal, capacity for fun, irritability, hypoactivity, and depressed mood. The efforts of these researchers were focused on the use of trained observers to rate the actual behaviors of the target children in an interview situation. As they concluded in their discussion, "Depression in children is characterized not only by unresponsive and unhappy faces but also by other characteristic behaviors. These include anhedonia, social withdrawal, decreased schoolwork, poor appetite, sleep difficulty, excessive fatigue, retardation of language and/or hypoactivity and lowered self-esteem and/or guilt" (p. 447). The authors went on to note that "It is important to underscore that depression in children can be assessed by these directly observable behaviors, and that it is usually not 'masked' by other presentations, such as enuresis, pain, or school refusal" (p. 447).

The Poznanski *et al.* report should no doubt bring pleasure to the hearts (pleasure centers?) of behavorial assessors, as it is clear that the CDRS seems to have observable behavioral sequelae. What is less pleasurable, and noteworthy, is that the interview method of observation and rating seems to be receiving greater use then the observational assessment of depression! If this were 10 years ago, when "the" disorder was hyperactivity, we would be witnessing the concurrent development of observational systems for the measurement of behaviors that differentiate behavior problem cases from normal cases. Today, in contrast, the energies seem directed toward the development, examination, and evaluation of self-report and other instruments, and their correlates.

The K-SADS (Puig-Antich, 1986; Puig-Antich & Chambers, 1978) has been devised to allow the user to proceed along a branched series of questions that will eventually lead to diagnostic decisions according to DSM-III criteria. The complete interview takes approximately 90 minutes to complete. It should be kept in mind that although the title (K-SADS) refers to schizophrenia and affective disorders, the interview includes questions designed to aid in the diagnosis of other disorders (e.g., conduct disorders, emotional disorders). Parent(s) and child are interviewed (separately), and the interviewer provides ratings based on the data provided. These summary ratings are subjective, though based on the interview, and interviewers are advised to use clinical judgment. Whereas one applauds the increased structure offered to interviewers, one must simultaneously experience some discomfort with the confidence placed in "judgments"; this is often the source of unscientific inquiry.

One positive feature of the K-SADS (Puig-Antich, 1986), related to its assessment of emotional difficulties, is the expressed concern for the child's use of the proper language. That is, a child subject may be saying that he or she is depressed, but may be using the term inaccurately due to a parent's similar incorrect use. The K-SADS has a section where the child interviewee and the interviewer work to come to an agreement about the words to be used. Depressed mood, irritability/anger, elation/euphoria, and anxiety are differentiated. Later, when interviewing for an assessment of depressed mood, the interviewer is instructed not to include in his or her ratings reports of feelings of anxiety or irritability. In this manner, the unwanted influences of confusion among feeling "bad," "sad," and "upset" are given direct attention.

The structured interview methodology has been widely accepted, and both the CDRS and the K-SADS are worthwhile procedures. Recently, both have undergone revisions. There is a CDRS-R and an updated K-SADS as well. Researchers and clinicians interested in these interview schedules and in information regarding the latest versions of them are encouraged to contact the authors directly.

All of the interview methods for assessing depression require pretraining and practice before implementation with actual research or clinical subjects. One is not certain of the preferred method for the acquisition of such training. For instance, if two or three colleagues work together and "teach" each other, it is possible that they could achieve a high degree of reliability, but they could well be idiosyncratically divergent from the also-reliable ratings made by another set of observers trained elsewhere and/or by others. Is a uniform training program required? Could training cases be taped and new interviewers required to achieve reliability with the experts on the taped cases? With the intent of structured interviews to increase diagnostic reliability, the issue of training and the training criteria should not be taken lightly.

Parents and Peers as Raters

Ratings by parents and peers are typically employed with child and adolescent, but not adult, cases. Perhaps the most often used child behavior rating scale at present is the Child Behavior Checklist (CBCL) developed and described by Achenbach and Edelbrock (1983). Among the 118 items on the scale, 17 are identified as Depression items. Raters endorse either 0, 1, or 2 to indicate the severity/frequency of the item. The Depression scale is one of five that contribute to the "Internalizing" behavior problems factor. Curiously, a Depression factor did not emerge from the data set for 12- to 16-year-old boys.

Some data on the CBCL Depression scale suggests that it can separate DSM-III-diagnosed depressed and nondepressed children; yet, as noted in a paper by Reynolds (1986), mother and father reports on the CBCL did not correlate with child reports on the CDI (see also Kazdin *et al.* 1983).

Within the Personality Inventory for Children (PIC; Wirt, Lacher, Klinedienst, & Seat, 1977), a 600-item Minnesota Multiphasic Personality Inventory (MMPI)-like parent rating form, there is a 46-item Depression scale. This parent rating scale has been used to separate depressed and nondepressed cases within a normal school system, but has not received widespread use in the literature.

The use of peers in psychological assessment among child and adolescent researchers has grown dramatically within the last few years (e.g., Schneider, Rubin, & Ledingham, 1985). Perhaps as a combined result of the influence of Hartup's (1970, 1983) work on peer relations in developmental psychology and the increased use of peers to identify children at risk for psychopathology, peers have become an important source of data. Indeed, there is an increased use of peers among child interventionists as well, suggesting that one way to increase treatment generalization is to place the treatment directly in the context where one hopes to attain generalization—that is, bring the peer group into the program (cf. Howard & Kendall, 1987).

Peer nominations, as typically used in sociometric assessment, have a place in assessing depression. Lefkowitz and Tesiny (1980) described the psychometric qualities of a Peer Nomination Inventory of Depression, (PNID) constructed with fourth- and fifth-graders (averaging approximately 10 years of age). The PNID consists of 19 peer nomination items (e.g., "Who often plays alone?"), 13 of which assess depression, 4 of which tap happiness, and 2 of which are popularity items. The reliabilities for the PNID are quite satisfactory, and there were meaningful relationships with self-ratings and teachers' ratings. Children who were nominated as depressed "were also viewed as depressed by their teachers and tended to rate themselves as depressed" (p. 48). The authors' confidence in their results was buttressed by a cross-validation and evidence of discriminant validity.

Multiple Methods, Multiple Assessments, and a Message from Epidemiology

Having now considered measures available for use in the assessment of depression, one must wrestle with the question of how best to proceed when implementing an assessment battery in order to identify depressed cases for inclusion in a specific research project. The following suggestions reflect both a critical view of the measures themselves and a consideration of the sequence of events that would be most profitable in related research. The proposed sequence of screening procedures has merits identified by epidemiological researchers, and, quite pleasingly, has a sense of pragmatics and recognition of the attendant difficulties in large-scale screenings.

The first matter requiring consideration is the selection of a self-report measure. While self-report may be of limited value in assessments of hyperactivity in children or the addictions in adults, it is essential when one is examining internalizing disorders such as depression. Several scales are worthy of consideration. For adults, the BDI seems to be the dominant self-report index. Perhaps the child scale most often used is the CDI, with the more than occasional removal of the item having to do with suicide.

The second matter for consideration is the use of other types of assessments such as the clinical interview. Recommended are structured interviews that allow for conclusions consistent with DSM-III categories. Again, there are several methods available for different-age clients.

A third matter concerns the method of screening. A multiple-gate procedure is recommended (see Cronbach & Glaser, 1965; Loeber, Dishion, & Patterson, 1984; Wiggins, 1973). In such an approach, large numbers of persons are administered the self-report scale(s), and these data are used to select potentially depressed cases. A somewhat less stringent criterion might be employed at this first point, since there will be a repeated assessment using the same self-report scale(s). That is, in order to insure that the cases to be investigated have a relatively consistent pattern of experiencing depression, two administrations of the self-report measure(s) are recommended (see also Lewinsohn & Teri, 1982; Sacco, 1981). The second administration of the self-report scale(s) comes when the clinical interview is implemented and is undertaken only for those persons who scored in the depressed category at the first administration. Thus, for a person to qualify for inclusion in the final group of depressives, he or she must first score beyond a criterion cutoff score on a self-report scale; must again score above a criterion score (perhaps a more restrictive score) on a second administration; and finally, must also be categorized as depressed on the basis of the structured clinical interview. This multiple-gate methodology has the stamp of approval of epidemiologists. Other assessments could also be conducted, as appropriate, at the second testing.

Interestingly, in a paper I received after completing the first draft of this section, Reynolds (1986) reports having employed "multiple-stage" (multiple-gate) procedures with over 8,000 children and adolescents (beginning with third-graders). His rationale for the multiple-gate methodology parallels the points raised above (e.g., potential for overendorsement of depressive items on a single initial assessment) and adds the fact that parent and teacher referrals of children for depression are relatively rare. It is not that depression does not exist, but that teachers and parents who do refer children for mental health services most often refer for undercontrolled, externalizing problems (e.g., acting out, hyperactivity, and impulsivity). Reynolds (1986) states, "The screening model proposed . . . utilizes successive administrations of self-report measures and further refinement of identification via an individual interview as a third stage" (p. 120).

Data reported by Asarnow and Carlson (1985) are consistent with the need for multiple-gate assessments. They found a high degree of covariation among self-report measures (the DSRS and the CDI), but no relationship between the self-ratings and ratings of ward behavior. As the authors themselves note, optional clinical and research procedures for assessing depression may involve the combined use of measures completed by different sources.

Use of a two-stage process for screening psychopathology in general epidemiological investigations is further buttressed by Shrout, Dohrenwend, and Levav (1986). As these authors note, both economy and validity of classification are increased when a first stage using a screening questionnaire is followed by a second stage with detailed diagnostic assessment conducted by a clinician.

ASSESSING SELF-CONTROL

Two scales for assessing self-control have continued to receive research attention: the Rosenbaum (1980) Self-Control Schedule (SCS) for adults and the Kendall and Wilcox (1979) Self-Control Rating Scale (SCRS) for children. The SCS and task-specific self-efficacy estimates were used in predicting cold-pressor task performance (Barrios, 1985). While the SCS was not predictive, task-specific self-efficacy estimates did predict cold-pressor tolerance. Barrios noted that self-control may not be a unitary construct with cross-situational consistency. The more situational assessments (task-specific self-efficacy ratings) do not invoke cross-situational consistency and have proven more predictive.

The SCS has been successful as a predictor of response to therapy for depression. Simons, Lustman, Wetzel, and Murphy (1985) found that level of self-control (learned resourcefulness) interacted with different types of treatment. Clients entering cognitive therapy with high SCS scores did better than patients with low SCS scores. Clients receiving nortriptyline improved more when their initial SCS scores were low. It should be noted that cognitive therapy and pharmacotherapy were equally effective in treating depressed cases. These findings parallel some data reported with children (see Kendall, 1984a) where medications were more effective for children with external attributional styles and a cognitive–behavioral treatment was superior for children with an internal attributional style. The larger picture seems to suggest that there is a match between type of treatment and individual differences that would optimize outcome.

The SCRS is favorably reviewed by Barkley in his National Institute of Mental Health (NIMH)-sponsored evaluation of child behavior rating scales and checklists (Barkley, 1987). Barkley notes that the SCRS "is a quite useful scale where measures of self-control utilizing parent or teacher reports are of interest. The scale has satisfactory test–retest reliability, construct and discriminant validity, as well as sensitivity to treatment effects. Concurrent validity studies suggest a strong relationship with other scales having conduct problem factor dimensions." It should also be noted, however, that Barkley identifies a need of the SCRS: more normative data with a sample that has representatives for the general population. Norms for various ages, and for parental report using the SCRS, are also needed.

Translations of the SCRS make it appropriate with Spanish-speaking persons. For example, Montero (1985) has developed a Spanish version of the SCRS, *Escalar de Evaluacion del Auto Control para Ninos*. This translation was undertaken in Lima, Peru. A second Spanish translation, done in Spain (*Escala de Classificacion de Auto Control*), is also available (Miranda, 1985). Research evaluation of the Spanish version of the scale is needed, as are normative data and evidence of construct consistency across the languages. An adapted version of the scale for use with attention deficit disordered preschoolers is also available (Pisterman, 1985).

COGNITIVE–BEHAVIORAL ASSESSMENTS

Approaches to cognitive assessment may differ on a number of variables: the manner of assessment, differential sensitivity, reactivity, and so on. To what degree can we expect different methods of assessment to produce comparable data? Addressing this question using think-aloud and thought-listing methods, Blackwell, Galassi, Galassi, and Watson (1985) presented two sets of math problems to highly math-anxious subjects; during one set the subjects were instructed to think aloud, and during the other they completed thought listing. Eleven cognitive content categories were used: review of information, strategic plans, strategic calculations, conclusions and solutions, attention control, positive self-evaluation, positive problem-solving evaluation, irrelevancies, negative self-evaluation, negative problem-solving evaluations, and neutral statements. Subjects were found to be significantly more anxious and took longer when listing thoughts than when thinking aloud. Thinking aloud produced twice as many thoughts as thought listing, and more thoughts in the categories of review of information, strategic calculations, conclusions, and attention control. However, there were more positive problem-solving evaluations and more positive self-evaluations produced during thought listing; obviously, the two methods did not produce comparable data. Blackwell *et al.* noted that the methods vary and that, after correction for the overall number of thoughts produced, thought listing may be superior for accessing evaluative and other non-problem-solving cognitions. However, thought listing has its reactive effects. It takes longer and can increase anxiety and/or reduce the number of thoughts reported. These data support a speculation I have noted elsewhere (Kendall & Hollon, 1981): Thought listing, as opposed to an ongoing cognitive assessment such as thinking aloud, may encourage more "editing" and fewer reported responses. Also, when one has to recall thoughts from memory, there can be some processing errors that may be less likely with an ongoing assessment.

The differences documented by Blackwell *et al.* are important. Not only do they provide support for an earlier notion that all cognitive assessment methods are not equal, but they also provide data to allow more accurate understanding of other studies. That is, if assessment methods can influence the data gathered and the findings reported, then we need to know in advance whether any assessment methods are especially likely to produce particular types of data. We want to be able to identify those aspects of assessment methods that may account for any reported differences in otherwise well-controlled comparisons.

Think-aloud assessments were used by Houston, Fox, and Forbes (1984) in their study of children's anxiety and performance under stress. A math task was used in both a high-stress and a low-stress condition. Subjects were assessed for levels of trait and state anxiety. Tape-recorded verbalizations were scored according to seven categories: analytic attitude, derogation of other, justification of positive attitude, performance denigration, performance reassurance, preoccupation, and situation-irrelevant thought. From an analysis of interrelationships, Houston *et al.* reported that subjects who thought more reassuring things about the upcoming task had fewer derogatory thoughts and more thoughts justifying their positive outlook. Highly trait-anxious subjects evidenced more preoccupation and (for females) more justification of positive attitude, and their performance was affected by the levels of stress.

Derived from Beck's cognitive theory, the Dysfunctional Attitude Scale (DAS) is a 100-item scale designed to assess depressogenic schemata. Oliver and Baumgart (1985) reported test–retest reliability of .73 over 6 weeks. The DAS and BDI were correlated .41. Item-to-total correlations for the DAS were "modest." It was not stated whether there were item-to-total-remainder correlations. A lack of factorial congruence between the two short forms of the DAS suggests that the short forms should not be used interchangeably.

The DAS, administered shortly after remission, was found by Rush, Weissenburger, and Eaves (1986) to relate positively to later depressive symptoms. That is, dysfunctional attitudes were a predictor of subsequent depression. A depressive attributional style and the presence of automatic thoughts (assessed by the Automatic Thoughts Questionnaire [ATQ]) were also related to subsequent depression, though less strongly.

Wise and Barnes (1986) hypothesized that dysfunctional attitudes could serve to moderate the effects of negative life events on the onset of depression. In a sample of several college students, there was a significant interaction: Low DAS scorers were relatively unaffected by negative life events, whereas the high DAS scorers were more depressed when they had been exposed to high levels of negative events. Here, the DAS evidenced predictive validity by separating those individuals who were predisposed to depression from those who were less so.

Using a set of assessments of cognition associated with depression, Dobson and Shaw (1986) reported that the measures were specific to depression, possessed strong internal reliabilities, and correlated among themselves and with severity of depression. Three groups of hospitalized patients were used (depressed psychiatric, nondepressed psychiatric, and nonpsychiatric) to test specificity, and repeated testing was used to examine change. The assessment battery, said to tap different levels of depressive thinking, was generally supported by Dobson and Shaw's data. The scales are listed here for consideration for use in future research: (1) the ATQ, a measure of depressotypic automatic thoughts; (2) the DAS, a measure of depressogenic assumptions; (3) the Interpretation Inventory, a measure of dysfunctional interpretations of situations; (4) the Cognitive Response Test, an open-ended test of a subject's thoughts in 30 potential situations; and (5) the Differential Anxiety and Depression Inventory.

Anxious persons engage in more negative self-talk than nonanxious persons. Bruch, Kaflowitz, and Kuethe (1986) went beyond this somewhat routine finding and examined the role of beliefs and the subjective meaning of thoughts in the relationship of self-talk and academic test performance. Using college students as subjects and academic competence classification criteria, Bruch *et al.* found that negative thoughts were not related to beliefs about competence, but that beliefs about competence were related to subjective meanings assigned to thought-listed cognition. The only measure predictive of actual performance was subjective meaning. Subjective meaning was assessed by having subjects respond to questions for each of the thoughts they provided on a thought-listing form. Also, judges coded transcripts of thoughts as facilitative, nonfacilitative, or neutral. Differences in competence were associated with differences in subjects' interpretations of their thoughts: Regardless of the proportion of negative thoughts listed, the highly competent persons were less likely to see their thoughts as being detrimental to performance. In this study, then, even when the persons' self-talk could be blindly considered negative, it was not viewed as negative by the persons themselves. Correspondingly, a client's reported self-talk that appears to be negative to a therapist may actually be quite different functionally, given the meaning associated with it by the person.

The Social Interaction Self-Statement Test (SISST) was psychometrically evaluated by Zweig and Brown (1985). They reported test–retest correlations ranging from .72 to .89 and alpha coefficients of .88 to .95. Validity data included significant correlations with social anxiety, fear of negative evaluations, and irrational beliefs. There was also a nonsignificant correlation with social desirability. The authors are positive in their views on the SISST, but do note the need for additional evaluation of the SISST in terms of its sensitivity to treatment effects.

Harris (1985) considers the target for cognitive assessment, the assessment techniques used, and the related issues (e.g., temporal relationships, structural differences). Going further, Harris (1985) addresses some of the challenging conceptual issues facing cognitive–behavioral assessment—for instance, the need to pay greater attention to the reciprocal influences of organism and environment; of cognition, affect, and behavior; and of the various features of cognition (e.g., processes, structures). The developmental factors across the life span and situational specificity are examined, as are needed research topics. On the clinical side, Harris (1985) looks to the need for strategies that move us from the nomothetic to an ideographic approach. The clinician needs cutoff scores (for individual subjects) that assist him or her in the determination of the treatment of choice.

In this, the fourth volume in this series in which I have contributed on the topic of cognitive–behavioral assessment, I continue to note with pleasure the presence of positive moments; each volume has had its "ups." However, there is presently a need for a directive challenge. It is true that progress has been evident; it is also true that some of the critical tests have yet to be performed. I speak here of the need to pursue studies of the incremental validity of cognitive–behavioral assessments. Assessments of irrational beliefs have been available for some time, though we readily recognize their psychometric limitations. The question in regard to incremental validity, is this: What do assessments of beliefs tell us that other assessments do not? The other assessments that may be most challenging are existing measures of what have been referred to as personality dimensions, such as neuroticism, anxiety, and the like. One of the reasons why personality scales will be a challenge for the incremental validity of cognitive–behavioral assessments is the similarity of the assessment method employed (i.e., self-report). Documentation of incremental validity relative to assessments gathered via other methods may be less challenging but no less important. What can be predicted from assessments of self-talk that cannot be predicted as well from behavioral observations?

A related issue has to do with the timing of the assessment of self-statements. If these are assessed at the same time as personality dimensions, and especially if they are assessed using the same method (self-report), then documenting their incremental validity will be particularly challenging. If, however, self-statements are assessed in the *situation* of interest, and perhaps assessed using an inventory or think-aloud method, then the data gathered have greater potential to pass the test of incremental validity.

SURVEYS OF PSYCHOLOGICAL TEST USAGE

Members of various groups have been surveyed to determine their views of psychological tests. Members of the Society for Personality Assessment reported that projective tests were the major instruments utilized (Piotrowski, Sherry, & Keller, 1985). Respondents from American Psychological Association-approved clinical training programs saw projective testing as declining and not supported by research; more objective approaches were viewed favorably in terms of academic preparation, future emphasis, and research credibility (Piotrowski & Keller, 1984a). But our interests lie more within AABT, and it is to the Piotrowski and Keller (1984b) survey of AABT members that I now turn.

Fully 60% of AABT members saw the use of projective measures decreasing in the future, while 50% saw the use of objective assessment increasing. Not surprisingly, 76% saw the use of behavioral assessment increasing. Regarding which tests professionals should have competence with, 34% said the Rorschach (projective), 70% the MMPI (objective), and 20% observation (behavioral). Most thought that behavioral assessment based on research was warranted 75% of the time, and that objective assessment (40%) and projective tests (11%) were less so.

What is not surprising is that AABT members were endorsing behavioral assessment methods. What may be surprising to some is that the degree of endorsement was not greater and that the endorsement given other approaches (e.g., 70% for the MMPI) was as high as it was. These surveys seem to document that AABT members' views of assessment are integrative, even if not specifically identified as such.

EXPECTANCIES AND ALCOHOL

Expectational analyses, such as self-efficacy expectations and client expectations of therapy outcome, have welcome company with the addition of expectational views of the effects of alcohol. Expectations can mediate levels of consumption of alcohol, as well as level of sexual arousal and eating patterns following alcohol consumption. The role of expectancies as a factor in the development of alcohol problems among adolescents was studied by Christiansen and Goldman (1983) (see also Kendall, 1985a). Taking an important and related step, Brown, Goldman, and Christiansen (1985) examined expectational contributions in adult alcoholics. Three groups of subjects were compared: college students, medical patients, and participants in an alcohol treatment program (total $n = 580$).

The Alcohol Expectancy Questionnaire (AEQ) and data sheets to assess demographics and drinking patterns were completed by subjects. The AEQ consists of six factors regarding the expected effects of alcohol: (1) Positive Global Changes, (2) Sexual Enhancement, (3) Social and Physical Pleasure, (4) Social Assertion, (5) Relaxation and Tension Reduction, and (6) Arousal with Feelings of Power. Across the comparison groups, an increased set of expected effects from alcohol was associated with increased levels of alcohol consumption. These findings extend earlier work to include patterns of excessive and abusive drinking and add support to the mediational role of expectations in alcohol consumption. Alcoholics and excessive-drinking subjects scored higher on the Positive Global Changes, Social Assertion, and Social and Physical Pleasure factors of the AEQ than did nonproblem drinkers. It seems reasonable to conclude that persons with inordinate expectations regarding the effects of alcohol will be those most susceptible to its abuse and its negative effects. The belief that alcohol is a panacea appears to produce, paradoxically, the painful side of its effects.

Brown (1985) reported two studies that examined the alcohol expectancies of college students as a function of their pattern of drinking and compared expectancies to demographic variables for their ability to predict problematic and nonproblematic drinking patterns. A total of 321 college students, who ranged from nondrinkers (6%) to heavy drinkers (13%), reported their alcohol expectancies, customary drinking patterns, and demographic data. The first college sample was divided into three groups, ranging in severity of drinking. Brown's data indicated that demographics and expectancies were useful predicors of alcohol consumption among college students. The single best predictor of each drinking pattern was a specific expectancy of alcohol effects, rather than any background characteristic. As a composite, demographics were slightly better at predicting drinking patterns.

The second set of subjects provided data for cross-validation. As in the first study, expectancies associated with the effects of alcohol helped identify patterns of alcohol consumption. Also, background data contributed to the prediction. Among college students, the Relaxation and Reduction factor of the AEQ was the single best predictor of a problematic drinking style.

There are problems and promises associated with the study of expectations related to alcohol. A primary concern that can be remedied via use of more naturalistic behavioral assessment (and/or laboratory analogue measurements) is the reliance on self-reported data. Hard data on drinking practices would contribute meaningfully to a more compelling argument for the mediational role of expectancies. On the promising side, the data provide potent suggestions for prevention. Given that expectancies occur before behavioral events, and that expectational styles develop after repeated behavioral events (Kendall & Braswell, 1982), it seems quite reasonable to recommend that attention be paid to the initial experiences adolescents have with alcohol and to preliminary education regarding alcohol's actual effects. With an expectational set of accuracy and preparedness, those who have been trained may be maximally likely to practice nonproblematic alcohol ingestion. Monitoring expectational effects across multiple experiences, thus guiding the development of an expectational style in regard to alcohol, would maximize preventive efforts.

It should be noted that, in addition to these expectational factors implicated in alcohol consumption, Collins, Parks, and Marlatt (1985) have reported two studies with data to support the influence of modeling on alcohol consumption. In the first study, when a model behaved sociably, the drinking behavior of the model was evident in the drinking behavior of the observer. Unsociable models, however, did not have this effect. In Study 2, the modeled rate of alcohol consumption had a significant impact on subjects' drinking behavior. Heavy-drinking models produced greater alcohol ingestion in subjects than light-drinking confederate models. Collins *et al.* provide a detailed and enlightening analysis of the role of conflictual/aversive situations in increased alcohol consumption, and interested readers are referred to their paper. At present, however, it is interesting to note the modeling effects and to speculate about the role of cognitive processes in modeling effects. What were observers saying to themselves? What expectations did they hold for the effects of alcohol?

ASSESSING THE QUALITY OF THERAPY: THE CASE OF DEPRESSION

The Cognitive Therapy Scale (CTS; Young & Beck, 1980) was developed to evaluate the degree of competence evidenced by a cognitive therapist. The idea of the CTS is consistent with the call for greater calibration and examination of the quality of the therapy provided (see Kendall & Hollon, 1983) and its relation to the differential effectiveness of treatment strategies and techniques.

The CTS is an 11-item observer rating scale, with two subscales: General Skills and Specific Cognitive Therapy Skills. The General Skills subscale consists of items concerning establishment of an agenda, obtaining of feedback, therapist understanding, interpersonal effectiveness, collaboration, and efficient use of time (pacing). The Specific Cognitive Therapy Skills subscale includes items to assess empiricism, focus on key cognitions and behaviors, quality of homework, and use of cognitive and behavioral techniques. Items are rated on a 7-point Likert Scale.

Interrater reliability estimates range from .54 to .96 (see Vallis, Shaw, & Dobson, 1986), though Vallis *et al.* note methodological shortcomings in the early work and proceed to provide additional data. All raters (seven) used by Vallis *et al.* were cognitive therapy experts. Interrater reliability, based on 10 randomly selected topics from a pool of 94, was estimated to be .59. Internal consistency, based on 90 of some 700 tapes, was high as determined by item-to-total correlations. It should be noted that the appropriate correlation is an item-to-total-remainder coefficient, where the total is not inclusive of the item itself. These remainder totals are not capitalizing on the inclusion of the specific item in the total. It was not clear, but the report seems to have used item-to-total correlations.

Factor analyses revealed one major factor (64.8% of the variance accounted for) with all but three items loading highly; it included items from both the General Skills and the Specific Cognitive Therapy Skills subscales. A second factor, accounting for 8.9% of the variance, concerned items having to do with the therapist trying to structure therapy. These factors do not correspond to the two CTS subscales. This finding is not surprising to me, as the original subscales were "armchaired" and do not seem to be accurately separating specific from general skills. For instance, "collaboration" is listed as an item in General Skills, yet appears to be a skill more specifically tied to cognitive–behavorial therapies.

Based on 53 tapes and raters' decisions as to whether or not the tapes depicted acceptable or unacceptable cognitive therapy, analyses of discriminant validity were performed. All items significantly differentiated the acceptable from the unacceptable tapes, with significant additions to a discriminant-function analysis contributed by application of cognitive and behavioral techniques, feedback, empiricism, interpersonal effectiveness, and collaboration. The resulting discriminant function predicted classification with 84.9% accuracy (about 35% better than a 50% base rate).

The CTS, based on Vallis *et al.* (1986) and other work (e.g., DeRubeis, Hollon, Evans, & Bemis, 1982), seems to be a useful scale for assessing the quality of cognitive therapy provided by various therapists. Although estimates of internal consistency may be less than optimal (needed item-to-total-remainder correlations, limited factorial consistency), the scale will be a worthwhile addition to efforts to try to determine the degree to which variations in the *quality* of therapy (Kendall & Hollon, 1983) are associated with indices of gainful outcome.

SEPARATING OVERACTIVITY/INATTENTION AND AGGRESSION

The ability to separate, and the meaningfulness of separations of, inattention/overactivity and aggression in children continue to be targets for assessment research. Using 48 clinic-referred boys and three classroom setting conditions (large group, small group, independent seat), Milich and Fitzgerald (1985) reported that teachers' ratings did discriminate the behavior patterns. The ratings were obtained on the Conners Teacher Rating Scale, and scores for Inattention/Overactivity, and Aggression, were used in the analyses. The Inattention/Overactivity ratings were related to behaviors such as failing to attend and failing to comply, whereas the Aggression ratings were associated with talking out in class, talking back to the teacher, and being aggressive with peers. As Milich and Fitzgerald (1985) noted, these findings are in contrast to those of Lahey, Green, and Forehand (1980) and may be due to sample differences: Lahey *et al.* used nonreferred girls, while the Milich and Fitzgerald study used referred boys. It is possible that nonreferred girls display an overall reduced rate of externalizing behavior problems.

What is the nature of the deficit in childhood hyperactivity? Assuming that there are behavioral problems, and that these frequencies can be observed and coded (e.g., Abikoff, Gittelman-Klein, & Klein, 1977; Abikoff, Gittelman, & Klein, 1980), there remain questions concerning the information-processing, attention-focusing, and social-cognitive features of the hyperactive behavior pattern. In an elaborate and interesting follow-up study of a large sample of New Zealand children, McGee, Williams, and Silva (1985) conducted canonical correlations of a diversity of ratings and abilities. Cognitive and motor abilities best predicted parent and teacher ratings of inattention. The inattention factor identified by McGee and colleagues was a behavioral dimension relating to planning, organization, and execution of tasks and activities, and resembled "impulsivity." The Hyperactivity factor consisted of restlessness and overactivity, and the Antisocial Behavior factor also emerged as separate.

Milich, Loney, and Roberts (1986) followed children who were originally observed as part of a diagnostic evaluation, and observed them again 2 years later. Observations during a free-play period and a restricted academic period were recorded and compared to earlier data. In all, 6 of 8 free-play variables and 4 of 10 academic situation codes (wrist actometer readings and grid crossings were significant in both situations) demonstrated significant stability. Although actometer readings are not actual observational frequencies, grid crossings, though not a microbehavior, are behavioral frequencies and did show 2-year stability. Thus, these results can be seen as initial support for the use of playroom observations as a procedure for assessing activity and attention. However, an index of stability, such as test-retest reliability, is positive to the degree that a meaningful intervention does not take place during the test-retest interval. According to this reasoning, the Milich *et al.* (1986) data may be subject to potential confusion by the extent of and effectiveness of any intervening interventions.

Whereas the recent data seem to converge on the opinion that overactivity/inattention and aggression can be reliably separated, there remains a body of literature that has not found such a distinction to be easy. What remains to be determined, if advocates of the distinction are correct, is whether or not there are treatments or treatment strategies that are differentially effective for the separated groups. It is this test of the potency of an assessment distinction that appears most needed at present.

METHODOLOGY

Clinical Significance

As readers of this continuing series are aware, the concern with clinical significance, normative comparisons, and normative data and outcome has been ongoing. As stated elsewhere (Kendall & Norton-Ford, 1982), "clinical significance refers to the meaningfulness of the magnitude of change, the remediation of the presenting problem to the point that is no longer troublesome" (p. 449).

Recently, the matter of clinical significance has received increased attention, with Jacobson, Follette, and Revenstorf (1984) proposing a reliable change (RC) index. When referring to clinical significance, these authors have adhered to a definition regarding return to a nondistressed group: "[A] change in therapy is clinically significant when the client moves from the dysfunctional to the functional range during the course of therapy on whatever variable is being used to measure the clinical problem" (p 430). They have further described the RC as equivalent to a pre–post difference score divided by the standard error of measurement, and have noted that an RC index larger than ± 1.96 would be unlikely to occur ($p < .05$) in the absence of real change. The authors viewed their initial article as one that would stimulate discussion, and, as hoped, there have been several replies.

Wampold and Jenson (1986) have pointed to several concerns with the RC index, one of which has to do with the nature of the distributions of scores obtained from functional and dysfunctional groups. They have argued that when the two groups come from a single distribution, measures of clinical significance as proposed would *not* be appropriate. This issue concerns me, and as I have learned from reading Jacobson *et al.*'s reply, concerns them as well. It strikes both them and me that comparisons of two groups drawn from a larger population is what statistical (inferential) testing is all about. The two groups may produce different-shaped distributions of scores (different even from the shape of the combined distribution), but the notion that they are two samples from a population and that the testing concerns whether or not these two samples are statistically different is a reasonable thing to pursue. Wampold and Jenson (1986) have also noted that using a more dysfunctional sample (and its related parameters) makes it easier to move from the dysfunctional to the functional range. If one begins with very distributed scores, the posttest score required for "clinical significance" will be lower than it would be if the initial scores were less deviant.

Christensen and Mendoza (1986) have identified what they called a "basic problem with the RC index as specified by Jacobson *et al.*" (p 305). As Christensen and Mendoza continue, they point to the needed remedy:

> The standard error of measurement is an index of the dispersion of an obtained score about a true score. However, the RC index makes use of two obtained scores. For the RC to be an accurate measure of whether or not a change is greater than that which would be expected by chance one must be interested in whether or not an obtained score exceeds a *true score* by an amount which exceeds the measurement error. (pp. 305–306, italics in original)

The proposed modification of the RC index is the significant change (SC) index, where the difference between the pretest and posttest scores, as in RC, is divided by the standard error of difference between two test scores (S_{diff}) (as opposed to the standard error of measurement as the divisor, as in the RC index).

Jacobson, Follette, and Revenstorf (1986), in their reply, seem to be pleased by both the increased attention given the issue and the apparent improvement made to the change index. They acknowledge that use of the standard error of the difference scores is entirely appropriate, and state that "we will use their corrected formula rather than our original one" (p. 309).

It is my own opinion that the proposed indices of clinically significant change are valuable additions to the therapy outcome literature. True, there are issues to be resolved, and some have begun to be addressed by the authors of the replies and commentaries. What remains, for the larger outcome research community, is the effort to make applications of additional statistical analyses that may make the claim of success more difficult. Those looking for data simply to say that "what we do works" may shy away. Those seeking to advance the scientific study of psychological therapies will, it is hoped, continue to apply critical tests to the evaluation of the entire therapy enterprise.

Placebo

One of my pleasurable duties is the casual reading of excerpts from the many new books that appear in our discipline each year. I engage in this pleasurable behavior at conventions, in libraries, and when visiting friends' offices. Somewhere, though I cannot recall where, I read a statement from a biofeedback researcher that ran something like the following: Biofeedback does not have a specific mechanism of change, but rather seems to work because people are believers. To what extent are psychotherapeutic effects the result of active psychological mechanisms of change, and to what extent is there a generic effect of personal beliefs and expectations?

The use of "placebo" controls has a meaningful history within behavioral and clinical research in general. For instance, as Huesmann (1982) noted,

> In manipulation studies where one is testing alcohol or drug effects it is critical to control subject expectations. The best manipulations appear to be those that vary actual substance does and expected substance dose orthogonally. The control group receives a placebo that is indistinguishable from the "real thing." (p. 228)

Within the therapy outcome literature, placebo (or attention placebo) controls have been used to rule out threats to internal validity. Participants in attention placebo controls receive contact with and attention from a therapist, as well as a therapy rationale. The rationale that is provided is intended to mobilize an expectancy of positive gains (Kendall & Norton-Ford, 1982). Such attention placebo controls allow researchers to identify the changes produced by specific therapeutic interventions, over and above any effects that may be attributed to nonspecific factors (e.g., contact, attention). Methodologically, the need for proper controls cannot be sidestepped. Nevertheless, there have been several papers appearing in the recent literature in which the concept of placebo has been "worked over."

In an early paper concerning placebos, O'Leary and Borkovec (1978) identified several problems with their use. For instance, when long-term therapy is being evaluated, it is questionable from an ethical point of view to offer some clients a placebo. On methodological grounds, O'Leary and Borkovec pointed to the difficulty of creating the same degree of positive expectancy in subjects receiving a placebo condition.

But how do we best view placebo effects—as purely expectational or attributional (see Ross & Olson, 1981)? As Karoly (1982) has noted, the fact that placebos produce health benefits is rarely questioned. He continues, however, "that placebos produce health benefits to the individual is no longer taken as evidence that the patient's disorder was purely functional. Rather, placebo effects support the notion of the *brain as a self-correcting, multimethod–multiorgan health care system*

(Schwartz, 1979)" (Karoly, 1982, p. 426, italics in original). Could placebo effects merely be the start of a naturally occurring biological health process? Do placebos have differential effects on different types of disorders (e.g., effects with unipolar depressives, but no effects with bipolar depressives)? Ross and Buckalew (1983) note that a particularly impressive number of behaviors have been found to be amenable to influence by placebos. These data appear to have been a secondary focus, with few studies being directly interested in the investigation and maximization of the potency of placebo. When research is directed toward increasing the placebo effect, we may indeed produce potent procedures. In a sense, the suggestion is that we go beyond accepting placebo effects and begin investigating placebo effects—that we do not avoid placebo control groups, but that we include measures to help determine what takes place that can account for placebo-produced change. For what disorders are placebos more or less influential?

Methods of Subject Solicitation

Do the methods we use to acquire cases for inclusion in our outcome research alter the sample characteristics (influence representativeness) or moderate the treatment effects? In view of the multitude of recruitment procedures described in the literature, it may be sensible to wonder about the potential effects of these solicitation procedures. As noted in an earlier volume (see Kendall, 1984a), Hersen, Bellack, and Himmelhock (1981) compared solicited and unsolicited depressive female subjects and reported an absence of significant differences in terms of self-report, observer, and behavioral measures for depression, assertiveness, and social adjustment. Also noted was the fact that data on male subjects, and perhaps level of social support (implicated in treatment outcome), should also be investigated.

Breckenridge, Zeiss, Breckenridge, Gallagher, and Thompson (1985) compared elderly subjects solicited for depression by traditional, semitraditional, and nontraditional methods. The traditional group included referrals coming from typical channels with no direct appeal to clients. The clients in the semitraditional group were recruited through channels that are often used to inform community members of available services (e.g., church flyer, talk in community). The nontraditional group included clients recruited through direct media-related appeals to potential clients (e.g., newspaper story, radio talk show). The clients were compared across referral sources on demographic data, treatment history, pretreatment status, treatment completion, and treatment outcome. The results were nonsignificant differences; when added to the extant literature on the comparability of subjects from different sources, they indicate that subject source may not be a confounding factor.

In a review of 14 studies that compared solicited and nonsolicited patient groups, it was concluded that the groups were generally similar (Krupnick, Shea, & Elkin, 1986). That is, it seems possible to generate comparable samples via different methods as long as adequate screening procedures are employed.

While there does appear to be some consistency in the evidence that different methods of solicitation do not produce different cases with different nomological networks, the data sets are typically made up of depressive individuals. It is entirely possible, and consistent with my own experience, that persons with different disorders may not produce similar results. For instance, in an effort to recruit "impulsive" adults via an ad in a newspaper, *no* phone-in responses were generated. One postcard was sent, containing the message that "Mary" (someone other than the respondent) was impulsive and providing Mary's phone number. It seems reasonable to expect depressed persons who are motivated to alleviate their situation to call for help, and it may also be reasonable to assume that recruitment ads will be effective methods for gaining subjects. However, other disorders, such as impulsivity, do not produce personal distress to the disordered individual or self-perceived need to seek service. Impulsive persons create conflict in the surrounding environment and social context, and others may thus be much more likely to refer impulsives. Methods of subject recruitment may be differentially successful for clients with different disorders.

CHAPTER

3

FEAR REDUCTION METHODS AND THE TREATMENT OF ANXIETY DISORDERS

G. TERENCE WILSON

The assessment and treatment of the anxiety disorders continue to constitute one of the most active and significant areas of research and practice in behavior therapy. As in past years, the evaluation of the effects of behavioral treatment has been a prominent feature. Prominent, too, has been the comparison of behavioral treatment with pharmacological methods—a subject that was a major focus of discussion in the corresponding chapter in Volume 10 of this series. Some new trends have also emerged.

One of the newer directions has been the greater emphasis on the treatment of panic disorders, generalized anxiety disorders, and social phobia than in the past. Another noticeable direction may be seen in analyses of these disorders in the behavior therapy literature. Attention has been focused not only on the treatment of these and other anxiety disorders, but also on their diagnosis and conceptualization. Some of the most recent and exciting research in the field of panic and phobic disorders is summarized in a scholarly volume edited by Hand and Wittchen (1986). This volume brings together the findings from several prominent research groups in England and Europe whose work is at the cutting edge of the field.

Innovative cognitive–behavioral treatment strategies have appeared. For example, 1985 saw the publication of Beck and Emery's extension of Beck's cognitive therapy, hitherto honed to the treatment of depression, to the anxiety disorders. The mechanisms of effective therapeutic methods have remained an important focus of theoretical analysis, together with papers on the etiology of phobic disorders.

PANIC DISORDER

The Nature of Panic

In the *Diagnostic and Statistical Manual of Mental Disorders*, third edition (DSM-III), panic is described as "the sudden onset of intense apprehension, fear or terror often associated with feelings of impending doom" (American Psychiatric Association, 1980, p. 230). One of the arguments for singling out Panic Disorder (PD) as a separate diagnostic entity in DSM-III was the view that it responds differently to treatment than do other forms of anxiety disorder, such as Generalized Anxiety Disorder (GAD) (Spitzer & Williams, 1980). Thus PD is thought to be uniquely responsive to treatment with tricyclics and monoamine oxidase inhibitors whereas GAD may be more appropriately treated with benzodiazepines (Sheehan, 1982; Zitrin, 1983). Implicit in this view is that PD has a different biological basis from that of other anxiety disorders. Nevertheless, this conceptualization is not without its difficulties.

PD AND DIFFERENTIAL RESPONSE TO DRUG TREATMENT

Evidence does exist showing that imipramine is effective in reducing panic attacks, although most of the studies can be faulted on methodological grounds. Yet it is not entirely clear that this is a differential response. Imipramine may also be effective in reducing generalized anxiety (Kahn *et al.*, 1981; Kahn *et al.*, 1986), and one study even suggests that diazepam may be useful in the treatment of panic attacks (Noyes *et al.*, 1984). A careful review of the drug literature indicates that the claim for specificity of drug treatment of panic attacks has little unequivocal support (Margraf, Ehlers, & Roth, 1986). And then there are data (discussed below) indicating that at least in some patients, cognitive–behavioral methods may be effective in treating panic attacks.

Rapee (1985c) carried out a direct test of the hypothesized differential drug responsiveness of PD and GAD. Patients carefully screened to meet the DSM-III criteria for each of these disorders were treated with either imipramine or diazepam in a 2 × 2 factorial study. The results revealed a trend ($p < .10$) for PD patients to respond more favorably to imipramine, while patients with GAD responded more favorably to diazepam. Among the PD patients, imipramine produced a mean reduction of 81% in the frequency of panic attacks, whereas diazepam produced a reduction of only 13%. As Rapee notes, however, the mean dose of imipramine in this study (79 mg/day) may not have been high enough to produce the results reported by Kahn *et al.* (1981).

PD VERSUS GAD

In addition to providing tentative support for the hypothesis of differential drug responsiveness between these two groups of anxiety patients, Rapee has reported other diagnostic differences. Rapee's PD patients had a more rapid and abrupt onset of symptoms than their GAD counterparts. The symptoms of the PD patients were more somatic (with hyperventilation especially prominent) and were interpreted as evidence of physical illness, whereas GAD patients tended to attribute their symptoms to anxiety and stress (Rapee, 1985b). Another study by Rapee (1986) found that PD patients presented with more distress and reported a greater number of physical symptoms in response to a brief period of voluntary hyperventilation than did patients with GAD. These findings are consistent with Barlow *et al.*'s (1984) data showing that the anxiety of patients with PD has a stronger somatic component than that of patients with GAD. Finally, studies have shown that the cognitions of patients with these respective disorders are different, as discussed below.

DO PANICS OCCUR IN OTHER ANXIETY DISORDERS?

Although PD is a separate diagnostic entity, panic attacks do occur in other anxiety disorders. Barlow *et al.* (1985) assessed the incidence of panic across the different anxiety disorders using the DSM-III classification. A high percentage of individuals within each diagnostic category reported having had a panic attack. Individuals with PD and Agoraphobia reported a higher frequency of panic attacks than did those with Simple and Social Phobias, but there were few differences among these categories in terms of the severity of the panic attacks as measured by the 12 DSM-III symptoms of panic. Unexpected panic attacks were associated with a greater number of the 12 symptoms than were expected (predicted) attacks. However, the severity of symptoms was comparable for both expected and unexpected panic attacks. In particular, the symptoms of dizziness and loss of control appeared to discriminate expected from unexpected panic attacks.

Rachman and Levitt (1985) found that panics or near-panics occurred in their claustrophobic subjects in the course of a controlled experimental analysis of anxiety in response to anticipated and actual time in a small, dark room. The details of the rich data set this experimental investigation yielded are beyond the scope of the present summary review. Suffice it to point out, however, that 75% of the subjects (n = 17) experienced a panic attack on at least one occasion and 65% did so on at least two occasions. Panics were defined by subjective reports, and, in most cases, by subjects' checking at least three items from the DSM-III panic checklist. Significantly, the occurrence of a panic attack was followed by an increase in predicted fear for the following trial. Yet actual reported fear on this subsequent trial did not show an increase from the preceding trial. Thus panics produced expectations of increased fear, but these expectations were not confirmed. Commenting on this result, Rachman and Levitt observe that it is consistent with theories assuming a causal connection between panics and avoidance behavior (i.e., agoraphobia): "It could be therefore, that a main effect of panic is precisely to increase anticipatory anxiety. The effects of panic on later fear may be minor. To recall a phrase used by Chambless and Goldstein (1982), panic engenders a 'fear of fear' " (p. 597). In this regard also, Thyer and Himle (1985) have reported evidence indicating that agoraphobia develops as a secondary response to the occurrence of panic attacks.

Roughly two-thirds of the panics were correctly predicted by subjects, but there was a high rate of overprediction. Consistent with cognitive explanations of fear maintenance and reduction, disconfirmations of expected panics resulted in significant decreases in fear. Consistent with Barlow *et al.*'s (1985) data summarized above, Rachman and Levitt also found a significant difference between expected and unexpected panics. Unexpected panics produced significantly greater increases in predicted fear on the next trial than did expected panics. Beyond the specifics of the findings of this study, it might be noted that Rachman and Levitt have come up with a promising methodology for carrying out experimental analyses of panic attacks in the laboratory.

Cognitive–Behavioral Treatment of PD

Behavior therapy for PD is still in its early stages. Exposure treatment may produce significant reductions in agoraphobic patients with panic attacks, as noted in the discussion of agoraphobia below. Nevertheless, there is clearly a need for alternative treatment strategies, particularly in those cases where particular situations cannot be avoided. Taylor *et al.* (1986) have shown that distinctions can be reliably drawn among situational and spontaneous panics. The latter call for treatment methods other than conventional exposure.

ANXIETY MANAGEMENT AND COGNITIVE RESTRUCTURING

Barlow *et al.* (1984) treated five patients with PD and five with GAD with a procedure that combined electromyographic (EMG) biofeedback, relaxation training, and cognitive restructuring. The latter was largely based on Beck and Emery's (1985) cognitive therapy for anxiety disorders. Compared to a waiting-list control group, treated patients improved significantly on a broad range of outcome measures, including clinicians' ratings, psychophysiological measures, and patients' daily self-monitoring of background anxiety and panic attacks. The waiting-list control patients did not improve. Although the PD patients showed greater somatic reactions on self-report and physiological measures prior to therapy, both groups of patients responded equally well to the treatment. This lack of differential response to treatment is not consistent with the view that PD is a biologically unique disorder.

Studies of the treatment of PD have often been limited by inadequate measurement of panic attacks per se. Barlow *et al.* (1984) closely monitored the occurrence of panic attacks. They summarize their results as follows:

> At posttreatment 2 patients reported essentially no panic. One of these patients continued to report occasional episodes of intense anxiety which he no longer labeled as panic. The additional patients reported that panics that did occur were less frequent, less severe, and shorter. Two of these three patients also reported identifying consistent cues or 'triggers' that set off the remaining panics and a greatly increased sense of control or mastery over the attacks. (pp. 443–444)

Improvement was maintained at follow-ups ranging from 3 to 6 months. These data replicate and extend previous findings by this group (Waddell, Barlow, & O'Brien, 1984). The well-documented efficacy of this cognitive–behavioral treatment in reducing panic attacks calls into question the view that, as a specific biological disorder, PD can be treated effectively only through the use of tricyclic drugs.

RESPIRATORY CONTROL TRAINING AND COGNITIVE RESTRUCTURING

The similarity between the symptoms of panic attacks and the effects of hyperventilation have been noted by several investigators over the years. These observations have led to the view that hyperventilation may play an important, possibly even causal role in panic attacks (e.g., Lum, 1976). As noted above, Rapee (1985b, 1986) confirmed that hyperventilation is prominent among the self-reported symptoms of patients with PD, and showed that such patients responded differently to a brief period of voluntary hyperventilation than did patients with GAD. Nevertheless, Rapee found that hyperventilation-produced distress did not mimic naturally occurring panic attacks. A study by Gorman *et al.* (1984) found similar results. Rapee attributed this to the absence in his subjects of the dysfunctional, catastrophic cognitions that are typically associated with panic attacks. In the presumed safety of the laboratory, and given an explanation of the anticipated effects of hyperventilation, his subjects did not interpret their physical symptoms in a manner that would evoke intense anxiety or panic.

Consistent with the foregoing explanation, a subsequent experiment showed that patients with PD who engaged in hyperventilation without any explanation of its likely effects reported greater panic—and reactions more similar to naturally occurring panics—than those who were given an explanation. Accordingly, Rapee has hypothesized:

> [P]anic attacks involve a physiological discharge of a set of somatic sensations (possibly due to hyperventilation) for which the sufferer has no explanation. The individual thus engages in a set of catastrophic thoughts, misattributing the source of the symptoms to serious physical or mental disease. This results in an affective component of panic and the overall experience is labelled a panic attack. (1985b, p. 156)

Following up on this hypothesis, Rapee (1985a) has reported a case study illustrating how a respiratory control technique designed to slow breathing and obviate hyperventilation, combined with a cognitive reinterpretation of the symptoms of panic, proved highly effective.

A similar conceptualization and treatment strategy has been developed by Clark and his colleagues at Oxford University (Clark, 1986; Clark, Salkovskis, & Chalkley, 1985). Panic attacks are viewed as the catastrophic misinterpretation of different bodily sensations. The diverse pharmacological and physiological reactions that have been shown to trigger panic attacks (e.g., lactate infusion, hyperventilation, and normal sensations such as increased heart rate) are assumed not to have a direct panic-inducing effect. They provoke panic only if misinterpreted.

This cognitive model accommodates panic attacks that are preceded by heightened anxiety as well as those that come "out of the blue." The model fits well with the broad scope of empirical evidence that bears on panic attacks. For instance, both Hibbert (1984) and Ley

(1985) found that panic patients reported that they first noticed an unpleasant bodily sensation followed by negative cognitions. A particularly important line of evidence is the research on lactate-induced panic. Here Clark shows that patients perceive the many physiological sensations lactate induces before the onset of panic. If these sensations are misinterpreted, then the resultant panic is explained. Clark also notes that in some studies, panic patients are given different instructions from nonpatient controls, a serious confound:

> For example, in their pre-infusion instructions, Appleby *et al.* (1981) told patients that they "might experience a panic attack" (p. 413) but told controls that they "might experience an attack with symptoms analogous to those of 'public speaking' " (p. 143). As the controls presumably had never experienced a panic attack but probably had been slightly nervous during public speaking these instructions are likely to lead controls to expect a less-frightening experience than patients. Such differences in expectation can have marked effects on the affect produced by biochemical interventions. (1986, p. 465)

Finally, initial evidence from psychological treatments provides tentative agreement with Clark's model.

On the basis of this model, Clark *et al.* devised and tested a respiratory control method that appears to be a promising means of substantially reducing panic attacks. They divided patients with panic attacks into "situationals" and "nonsituationals." The latter, whose anxiety and panic were unrelated to any situation, seem similar to PD patients. It must be noted that they selected patients in whom "there was some evidence to suggest that hyperventilation may play a role in the panic attacks" (Salkovskis & Clark, 1984, p. 3). Treatment consisted of (1) brief, voluntary hyperventilation, which was intended to induce a mild panic attack; (2) explanation of the effects of overbreathing and reattribution of the cause of a patient's attacks to hyperventilation; and (3) training in slow breathing incompatible with hyperventilation.

The results have been most promising. In their first study, a brief period of 2 weeks of this intervention produced significant reductions in panic attacks. A pre–post behavioral test (for the "situational" patients) confirmed that the patients rated themselves as less anxious after treatment. Most importantly, patients were asked not to engage in any self-exposure activities during the 2 weeks of treatment, thereby eliminating a confound that has complicated the interpretation of other drug studies. Therapeutic improvement was maintained at a 2-year follow-up. A second study replicated these results and added a measure of carbon dioxide pressure (PCO_2). Consistent with the authors' model of panic attacks, their patients had a significantly lower resting level of PCO_2 than normal controls. However, after only 1 week of treatment, the level of PCO_2 increased to the point where it was comparable to that of the normal controls. This second study also showed that this respiratory control treatment, even in the absence of scheduled or unscheduled exposure, produced reductions in avoidance behavior in the situational patients.

In commenting upon their treatment effects, Salkovskis and Clark (1984) speculate upon the possible therapeutic mechanisms. They suggest that the cognitive reframing is a critical element. Nevertheless, the self-control or mastery experience provided by the controlled breathing technique, or the repeated exposure to the physiological symptoms of panic during the breathing exercises, could be factors.

In other studies, Salkovskis and Clark and their colleagues have shown that patients do hyperventilate acutely during actual panic attacks. In a creative case study, Salkovskis, Warwick, Clark, and Wessels (1986) monitored changes in PCO_2 and blood pH in a man who experienced panic attacks while undergoing renal dialysis. Consistently, PCO_2 dropped and pH rose during panic attacks. Encouragingly, treatment with their combination of respiratory control and cognitive restructuring rapidly abolished these panic attacks. The results reported by Salkovskis and Clark (1984) and Rapee (1985a) require replication with larger samples of patients and with superior controls. Nevertheless, they encourage the use of cognitive–behavioral strategies in the treatment of PD, a disorder that is commonly said to be responsive only to tricyclic drugs.

All the support for the cognitive model reviewed above is of an indirect nature. Margraf *et al.* (1986) have recently reported an experimental test of a key tenet of the model by directly manipulating patients' perceptions of somatic changes using false heart rate feedback. The heart rate feedback paradigm consists of true binary auditory feedback followed by false feedback of an abrupt heart rate increase (equal to a heart rate increase of 50 bpm over 30 sec). Both panic patients and controls accepted the false heart rate as accurate and showed increased self-reported anxiety. However, only the patients showed increased actual physiological arousal in response to the false feedback. Margraf *et al.* conclude that these data indicate that "perceived cardiovascular arousal may act as an internal cue that, together with other factors, triggers or exacerbates panic attacks. Only panic patients showed the pattern necessary for positive feedback in that they responded to perceived physiological arousal with further increases in arousal" (1986, pp. 36–37).

Cognitive–behavioral research following up these exciting leads is underway both in Europe and North America, and we can anticipate that these new experimental analyses will pave the way to a better understanding of panic disorders.

AGORAPHOBIA

The assessment and treatment of agoraphobia continue to constitute an area of major research activity.

Assessment

Chambless and her colleagues have developed three new questionnaires that promise to improve the assessment of agoraphobia. Two of these measures are designed to assess the often elusive concept of "fear of fear" (Chambless, Caputo, Bright, & Gallagher, 1984). The first is the Agoraphobic Cognitions Questionnaire, which measures thoughts about the negative consequences of experiencing anxiety; the second is the Body Sensations Questionnaire, which assesses sensations associated with autonomic arousal. Chambless *et al.* (1984) report data indicating that these measures are reliable and valid instruments. At present, as Chambless *et al.* point out, they are optimally suited to evaluating the process and outcome of treatment of agoraphobia. A third questionnaire—the Mobility Inventory for Agoraphobia—assesses avoidance behavior and the frequency of panic attacks in agoraphobics (Chambless, Caputo, Jasin, Gracely, & Williams, 1985). Again, commendably, Chambless *et al.* (1985) report data showing that the Mobility Inventory is reliable and valid. It should facilitate both studies and treatment of agoraphobia.

The Fear Questionnaire (Marks & Mathews, 1979) is a widely used measure of treatment outcome in research on agoraphobia. Mavissakalian (1986) provides further support for its validity, and suggests that a cutoff score of 30 may be used as a sensitive diagnostic criterion.

Finally, Himadi, Boice, and Barlow (1985) review the evidence on triple-response assessment with agoraphobia. They provide a useful summary of the complex conceptual and measurement issues that this type of assessment has raised and has yet to resolve. Grouping patients as either synchronous or desynchronous responders has not been shown to have prognostic value. However, patients who at pretreatment show higher heart rate reactivity do seem to respond more successfully. This relationship remains to be explained, although the data fit Lang's (1979) bioinformational theory.

Agoraphobia and Marital Adjustment

The matter of whether marital adjustment is a cause, concomitant, or consequence of agoraphobia has been discussed in previous volumes in this series. A familiar, albeit empirically unsupported, theme in the clinical literature is that agoraphobia is a product of an interpersonal (marital) problem. Assortative mating and marital dysfunction have both been proposed to explain this alleged connection between marriage and agoraphobia. Recent evidence from controlled studies discredits these interpersonal viewpoints still further.

Arrindell and Emmelkamp (1985a) compared female agoraphobics and their spouses on measures of marital adjustment to three control groups: (1) nonphobic female psychiatric patients and their husbands; (2) maritally distressed couples; and (3) maritally nondistressed (happily married) couples. Consistent with the findings of the only other controlled study of agoraphobics' marriages (Buglass, Clarke, Henderson, Kreitman, & Presley, 1977), Arrindell and Emmelkamp found that neither the agoraphobics nor their spouses rated their marriages as more maladjusted or characterized by dependence. Rather, "agoraphobics and their spouses were found to be more comparable to happily-married couples than to maritally-distressed controls. By contrast, nonphobic psychiatric patients and their partners were generally found to rate their marriages as being just as distressing and unpleasant as maritally-distressed control spouses did" (1985a, p. 1).

In another investigation, Arrindell and Emmelkamp (1985b) tested the notion that the psychological characteristics of agoraphobics' spouses are connected to the development or maintenance of agoraphobic symptoms. They compared the male partners of female agoraphobics with those of nonphobic psychiatric patients and normal control subjects on a variety of personality measures. Arrindell and Emmelkamp have summarized the data as follows: "[T]he present findings indicate that the partners of female agoraphobics cannot be characterized as more defensive than those of non-phobic psychiatric or normal controls. Further, no evidence was found to support the view that partners of female agoraphobics are more neurotic, more socially anxious, more obsessive, or more seclusive than partners of controls" (1985b, p. 412).

A third study failed to show any difference between female agoraphobics and normal controls in their degree of marital satisfaction as measured by the Locke–Wallace questionnaire (Fisher & Wilson, 1985). The only counter to these data is that agoraphobics may not recognize ("deny") their lack of marital satisfaction. The problems with this sort of interpretation are obvious, however.

Using a different approach to assessing agoraphobics' response to marital distress, we (Fisher & Wilson, 1985) recorded agoraphobics' heart rates and subjective reactions to a videotaped sequence of marital conflict (a husband and wife arguing). Compared to their responses to a neutral scene, agoraphobics' heart rates and self-reports of fear in reaction to the marital conflict videotape were lower. In contrast, the normal controls' heart rates and self-reports of fear and anger increased significantly over the neutral scene in response to the marital conflict scene. This pattern of results

> is consistent with the notion that agoraphobics do not react with fear, anger or panic in response to marital conflict. An analysis of these data, however, provides little direct support for theories in which the etiology of agoraphobia is predicated on marital conflict, displaced anger and mislabeling of external stimuli. First, no subject reported any increased likelihood of an anxiety or panic attack following exposure to this scene—or to comparable experiences in their own marriages. Second, the agoraphobics did not mislabel their anger as fear, since their fear ratings also decreased. (Fisher & Wilson, 1985, p. 104)

The Nature of Agoraphobia

Aside from the interrelationship between marital factors and agoraphobia, other common assumptions about the development and maintenance of agoraphobia have been the focus of research. One such assumption is that separation anxiety is critical to the etiology of agoraphobia. Nevertheless, Thyer, Nesse, Cameron, and Curtis (1985) found that agoraphobics did not report any greater degree of childhood separation anxiety than did a comparison sample of simple phobics.

Examining the fear of fear hypothesis about agoraphobics, we (Fisher & Wilson, 1985) studied patients' attention to internal cues and their processing of this information. Compared to a group of normal controls, the agoraphobics did not differ in their attention to internal cues. The agoraphobics did, however, mislabel cues to a greater extent and reported significantly different attributions than did controls. The agoraphobics attributed the causes of negative outcomes to themselves and rated this internal cause as more consistently present, as influencing more life situations, and as more important than did controls.

Chambless (1985) surveyed the characteristic psychopathology of a large group of outpatient agoraphobics (n = 378). On the basis of her findings, Chambless cautions that samples of married agoraphobic women are not necessarily representative of the general population. Similarly, she argues that the exclusion of very depressed agoraphobics from studies will introduce bias. Chambless also reaffirms that in agoraphobics, depression is secondary—perhaps a "result of the demoralization associated with a low sense of self-efficacy in relation to phobias, anxiety and panic" (p. 310).

Treatment

BEHAVIORAL TREATMENT VERSUS PHARMACOTHERAPY

The evidence on the separate and interactive effects of behavioral treatment and the use of tricyclic antidepressants or monoamine oxidase inhibitors was reviewed in Volume 10 of this series (Wilson, 1985b). At best, the evidence on the specific therapeutic value of these drugs is mixed. Telch, Agras, Taylor, Roth, and Gallen (1985), in one of the best-controlled studies to date, showed that imipramine alone did not reduce panic attacks or avoidance. However, combining imipramine with *in vivo* exposure produced significantly greater reductions in panic attacks than exposure treatment alone.

Noting that one factor that complicates comparisons among the different, conflicting studies is the use of different doses of the same drug, Mavissakalian and Perel (1985) examined the dose–response relationship in the treatment of agoraphobia with imipramine. Unfortunately, the findings are unlikely to clarify the debate over the putative effects of imipramine. The study did show that some therapeutic effects of imipramine are dose-dependent. The optimal dose appeared to be 150 mg/day or greater; at these levels, imipramine was significantly more effective in reducing anxiety and depression than a placebo condition. The authors conclude that the "dose-response relationships obtained in this study are compelling evidence in favor of a specific pharmacological effect of imipramine in agoraphobia" (p. 1035). Yet this conclusion would seem to be undermined by what is an even more important finding—namely, that there was no difference in effects on panic between the patients receiving high and low doses. Moreover, the low-dose group did not differ significantly from the placebo group. Mavissakalian and Perel comment, "These findings are unexpected because the control of panic attacks is generally considered central to imipramine's action in agoraphobia" (p. 1035).

Mavissakalian and Perel's findings are unexpected only if studies such as Telch *et al.*'s (1985) are disregarded. The failure to find a specific antipanic effect is damaging to the theory that PD and agoraphobia with panic are distinct biological disorders. This view rests heavily on the putative unique response of panic attacks to drugs such as imipramine, as mentioned earlier in this chapter.

Despite the overall finding that imipramine alone does not appear to be effective in treating agoraphobia and should be combined with exposure treatment, the often exclusive use of pharmacotherapy continues to be extremely popular among psychiatrists. A particularly unfortunate instance of this uncritical advocacy of drugs was featured on television in the United States in the ABC News program *20/20*

(Sheehan, 1985). Behavioral treatment, at least as represented by the TERRAP program (Hardy, 1969, cited in Bandura, 1972), was dismissed as largely ineffective, while drugs were extolled. Sheehan, a participant in this program, declared, "There's no reason now why the vast majority of these patients, that is, upwards of 90% of the victims of this disease, really can't make a satisfactory, sometimes complete recovery of their condition." Responding to this exaggerated assertion, *20/20* host Barbara Walters commented, "Isn't it amazing . . . that all these years everyone thought it was emotional, and it turns out to be biological, physical, and curable." One can only hope that the impact of this particular television program will be short-lived.

Michelson and Mavissakalian (1985) have reported the psychophysiological outcome measures of the same behavioral and pharmacological treatments that formed the basis of the Mavissakalian and Perel (1985) dose-response analysis. A main effect was that the patients treated with flooding showed decreases in arousal (heart rate) across the course of therapy. Patients receiving imipramine showed a mixed profile, with increases on some indices of psychophysiological arousal and decreases on others. Combining imipramine with flooding resulted in increased arousal (heart rate) at the 1-month posttreatment assessment. Michelson and Mavissakalian comment that this result "suggests that physiological habituation processes might have been delayed or inhibited" (p. 235). Assuming that this speculation is correct, the finding is at odds with the conditioning interpretation of exposure treatment as one of passive habituation or extinction (Borkovec, 1982; Emmelkamp, 1982). It constitutes one more finding indicating that arousal level is unrelated to treatment outcome. An alternative explanation in terms of self-efficacy theory is discussed below.

SPOUSE-ASSISTED EXPOSURE TREATMENT

The interrelation between marital adjustment and cause and cure of agoraphobia is addressed above. The related matter of involving agoraphobics' spouses in exposure treatment has been discussed in previous volumes, and has again been the focus of research in recent publications.

Cobb, Mathew, Childs-Clarke, and Blowers (1985) compared *in vivo* exposure with and without the involvement of spouses as cotherapists in the treatment of agoraphobics. Their results were straightforward: Including the spouse as cotherapist did nothing to influence treatment outcome. Contrary to previous studies (e.g., Bland & Hallam, 1981), Cobb *et al.* found that initial poor marital adjustment (assessed by questionnaire) did not predict less therapeutic improvement. And, finally, marital adjustment tended to improve as patients' agoraphobia was eliminated. In contrasting their results with prevailing clinical stereotypes about "the agoraphobic's spouse," Cobb *et al.* echo a previous interpretation made by Mathews, Gelder, and Johnston (1981). They suggest that the odd case in which improvement in the agoraphobic behavior is associated with marital deterioration is an exception but is "memorable." Another way of saying this, as I have indicated before (Wilson, 1984b), is that this clinical stereotype owes more to therapists' peculiar judgmental heuristics (e.g., the availability heuristic) than to the actual occurrence of the phenomenon. Arrindell and Emmelkamp (1985b) quote Hafner (1982) to the same effect: "[A] self-perpetuating myth has arisen, with clinicians seeing in their own patients only what has been reported by other clinicians. The more powerful the myth, the wider the clinical consensus, which in turn strengthens the myth" (1985b, p. 413).[1]

A second well-controlled study by Arnow, Taylor, Agras, and Telch (1985) evaluated the effect of adding a communication skills training component to exposure treatment. Clients were initially treated for 4 weeks with *in vivo* exposure. They were then assigned to two groups matched for degree of improvement they had shown to that point. One group received the communication skills training, and the other received a couples relaxation training program. Clients receiving the former fared significantly better than the latter on the Fear Questionnaire, on unaccompanied excursions out of the home, and on a standardized behavioral test. Arnow *et al.* were able to show that their communication training did significantly improve communication skills, as evidenced by the Marital Interaction Coding System MICS),

In trying to explain the incremental advantage of the communication skills program, Arnow *et al.* 1985) make the following observations:

> In accounting for the success of communication skills training when compared with relaxation training, it is important to reiterate that couples were encouraged to use communication skills to discuss, identify, and change interactional patterns that may have been impeding the agoraphobic's progress in overcoming the symptoms. For example, one

1. I have previously (Wilson, 1982a) challenged the notion, popular among some clinicians, that a consensus of opinion among therapists provides *ipso facto* evidence of the "truth" of the phenomenon on which there is agreement. This consensus on a "marital myth" about agoraphobia may be another example of the limitations even of consensus.

> subject persuaded her husband to stop mentioning his fears for her safety when she went out alone. Others reached new agreements with their partners regarding more overt demonstrations of interest in their progress. In other cases, partners were asked to be less accommodating to subjects' fears; in these instances, subjects' complaints that their partners "anticipate[d]" their anxiety and were overly helpful were translated into specific behavioral change requests. (p. 464).

It may be recalled that a previous study by Chambless, Foa, Groves, and Goldstein (1982) failed to show the benefit of adding a communication training component to flooding in the treatment of agoraphobics (see Wilson, 1984b). This discrepancy is not addressed by Arnow *et al.*, and the reason remains unclear.

Hand, Angenendt, Fischer, and Wilke (1986) have reported the long-term results of the treatment of 75 agoraphobics in Hamburg, West Germany. Although not a formal, controlled outcome study, this clinical series provides a good deal of useful clinical information. Three closely related treatments were used: individual exposure; group exposure, as developed by Hand, Lamontagne, and Marks (1974); and home-based treatment using German translations of the manuals of Mathews, Teasdale, Munby, Johnston, and Shaw (1977). Hand *et al.* (1986) provide a detailed breakdown of the patients, treatments, evaluation procedures and criteria, and outcome. Suffice it to note here that, overall, 70% of patients showed clinically significant and lasting improvement. Therapeutic progress was broad-ranging, extending from the target phobic anxiety and avoidance to depression and general life activities. This is, of course, consistent with previous behavioral research and once again contradicts tiresome allegations of symptom substitution. Among the severely agoraphobic, monosymptomatic patients fared better than their multisymptomatic counterparts. The reasons for this difference are unknown; nor is it clear how to spot the multisymptomatic patients who do not respond to exposure prior to treatment. There was no apparent difference among the three forms of exposure, although group therapist-guided exposure seemed superior to home-based treatment in the severe, monosymptomatic patients.

Finally, two prognostic variables are of note. First, the occurrence of panic attacks during treatment emerged as a good predictor of a favorable therapeutic response. This finding is consistent with the conceptual basis of exposure treatment used by Hand and his colleagues at the Hamburg Behavior Therapy Unit, as discussed below. It also suggests that patients can be reassured that the occurrence of panic attacks during *in vivo* exposure is not countertherapeutic. Second, failure to find a decrease in depression by posttreatment predicted nonresponse to treatment at the 6-month follow-up. Hand *et al.* observe that patients who have not shown an improvement in depression are at risk for relapse after 6 months.

VARIATIONS OF EXPOSURE TREATMENT

Previous research has indicated that home-based self-exposure treatment can be effective in the treatment of agoraphobia (Mathews, Teasdale, Munby, Johnston, & Shaw, 1977). Ghosh, Marks, and Carr (1984) compared three variations of self-administered exposure in the treatment of phobic (predominantly agoraphobic) patients: therapist-instructed, manual-instructed, or computer-instructed exposure. Patients in all three groups improved significantly to a similar extent on various phobic measures at the end of the treatment and maintained their treatment gains at a 6-month follow-up. Mean clinicians' time spent with each patient was 40 minutes, 4.2 hours, and 3.2 hours in the respective groups. These findings encourage the use of self-administered exposure treatment as a cost-effective strategy, where appropriate. Ghosh *et al.* prudently point out, however, that their manual-instructed and computer-instructed procedures were implemented in a context in which patients had to complete weekly assessments and did retain contact with a therapist. There is no telling how well an agoraphobic would fare when simply buying the manual in a shop and setting out to follow instructions. Indeed, as we have discussed in Volume 5 of this series, the existing evidence suggests that the results would be far less successful (Rosen, 1976).

In previous volumes of this series, I have pointed out how exposure treatment is not a standard form of therapy and how different theoretical frameworks can lead to procedural differences in actual clinical practice (Wilson, 1984b). These comments are underscored by observations from Hand *et al.* (1986) in the course of their description of the results of their follow-up study of the treatment of agoraphobics. Hand *et al.* emphasize the importance of both panic (or peak anxiety) management and the management of depression and emotional distress during exposure therapy. Few accounts are as explicit, and their comments are worth stressing.

Hand *et al.* routinely withdraw patients from medication prior to exposure treatment, with the goal that "patients are to experience exposure under difficult environmental and emotional conditions, in order to rebuild lasting self-confidence" (p. 106). Hand *et al.* note the similarity of this view to Bandura's (1977) self-efficacy theory. This parallel is evident also in their guidelines for when to push patients to approach a new phobic situation: "The criterion for moving is the patient's experience-induced new cognitive response: 'I can cope' " (p.106).

Intermittent escape is allowed during exposure, and the rationale is distinctly more akin to social learning theory than traditional conditioning notions:

> It appears important not to threaten a patient's autonomy by contracts in which he subscribes himself to "being held" in the phobic situation if he cannot manage to do so by himself. Some treatment centers seem to apply much more direct external control, and patients not infrequently seem to expect, and to be afraid of, such a therapist attitude. Though this attitude may seem plausible from learning theory concepts, it appears rather dangerous from an interactional point of view. Therefore, when intermittent avoidance occurs, we try to reassess motivation for change (in phobic as well as in daily life activities) with the patient—and this usually leads to the patient's decision to enter the situation again at his own will. (p. 107)

Finally, patients who experience depression or other emotional distress prior to an exposure session are helped to relabel that feeling as an opportunity to cope with one of the major triggers of avoidance. To quote Hand and his colleagues once more

> We never raise the expectation that treatment will completely eliminate episodes of anxiety or depression. Instead, we want to provide the real-life experience that the consequences of "giving in" to those feelings on a motor-behavior level probably create to a large extent the "illness" of chronic agoraphobia. If disconnected from phobic anticipatory cognition (with low self-esteem), the occurrence of further anxiety attacks and depressive episodes will, for the majority of patients, be rare and usually manageable events. (p. 107)

It is now widely assumed that *in vivo* exposure is superior to imaginal exposure in treating phobic disorders. Nevertheless, James (1985) has recently questioned the evidence on which this assumption is based. He argues that the evidence does not support such a clear-cut conclusion, and recommends that therapists combine *in vivo* with imaginal exposure.

SOCIAL PHOBIA

Social phobia, like PD and GAD, has received relatively little attention in the behavior therapy literature compared to simple phobia and agoraphobia. However, the past couple of years have marked an increase in research on social phobia.

Amies, Gelder, and Shaw (1983) conducted a comparative clinical study of social phobics and agoraphobics that yielded useful information about this disorder. Amies *et al.* found that social phobics had an earlier age of onset than agoraphobics, typically between 10 and 19 years of age. A greater proportion of social phobics were men. Their most prominent somatic symptoms were blushing and muscle twitching—symptoms that, as Amies *et al.* point out, can be seen by other people. Simple phobias were less often associated with social phobia than was agoraphobia. Phobic disorders were present in the families of 20% of both social phobics and agoraphobics. Depression was also common among social phobics—a finding corroborated by Liebowitz, Gorman, Fyer, and Klein (1985) in their recent review of social phobia from their more biological perspective.

Gelder's group at Oxford University also reported the results of a rare controlled, comparative outcome study of the treatment of social phobics. Butler, Cullington, Munby, Amies, and Gelder (1984) compared two behavioral methods to a waiting-list control group in the treatment of social phobics. One method was *in vivo* exposure plus anxiety management (EX/AM) training. AM, based on Suinn and Richardson's (1971) technique, consisted of training in progressive relaxation, distraction, and "rational self-talk" (a form of cognitive restructuring in which clients identified negative or self-defeating thoughts and then rehearsed more constructive alternative thoughts). The other method, EX alone, focused exclusively on encouraging clients to participate in situations they had been avoiding; no instructions about coping with anxiety were given. Instead of AM training, clients in the EX-only group received a comparable amount of a placebo procedure called "associative psychotherapy." Treatment was composed of seven weekly sessions and two booster sessions at 2 and 6 weeks during follow-up.

Both treatment groups improved significantly more than the waiting-list control group, which showed no improvement on most measures. Treatment effects were maintained, or increased, at a 6-month follow-up. At posttreatment, the EX/AM group had lower scores than the EX group on two cognitive measures of social anxiety. Six months later the EX/AM group had lower scores on four additional measures, including patients' self-ratings of phobic severity. Only the EX/AM group showed generalized treatment effects to fear in situations other than social ones. This finding is consistent with the view that AM training provides clients with skills that can be used in different situations. No patient in the EX/AM group requested further treatment within a year, whereas 40% of the EX group did so. All patients showed satisfactory compliance with therapeutic instructions, with no difference between the two treatment groups. Patients also expressed comparably high ratings of the credibility and suitability of both treatments.

In another comparative outcome study, Emmelkamp, Mersch, Vissia, and van der Helm (1985) examined the effects of exposure, rational–emotive therapy, and self-instructional training. All three treatments resulted in significant reductions in anxiety at posttreatment, after a mere six therapy sessions. Exposure was superior to the other methods only on pulse rate, while the cognitive treatments alone were associated with improvement on a measure of irrational cognitions. The absence of a suitable control group makes it difficult to rule out placebo effects and therefore complicates interpretation of the results.

Both the Butler *et al.* (1984) and Emmelkamp *et al.* (1985) studies—and our own work (Biran, Augusto, & Wilson, 1981) previously—found exposure to be effective in the treatment of social phobia. Nevertheless, all three studies reported incomplete improvement of one sort or another. On the basis of experience in the comparative outcome study at Oxford, Butler (1985) has spelled out a number of difficulties in the implementation of exposure treatment with social phobics. She lists four major problems in using exposure treatment:

> 1. [*In vivo* tasks] could not always be clearly specified in advance, repeated or graduate[d] because social situations are variable and unpredictable. 2. Many social situations have an intrinsic time limit and cannot be prolonged. Entering a room, saying good morning or buying a drink are example of such situations. 3. Social phobics often appear to avoid relatively few situations; they may continue to go to work or to other places where they will meet people, and may be forced to do some things that provoke anxiety. However, this continued exposure is not apparently beneficial, as the problem frequently persists despite it. 4. Thoughts and attitudes seem to play a central role in the maintenance of social phobias. (p. 651)

Exposure alone does not directly address these thoughts and therefore leaves part of the problem unaddressed. In pointing out these difficulties, Butler not only raises important clinical concerns for the practice of exposure treatment; she also calls attention to the mechanisms responsible for the success of exposure. By way of illustration, consider her point about persisting anxiety despite continued exposure.

Butler offers some helpful practical advice for the practitioner confronted with the failure of continued exposure to reduce social phobia. Her major tactic is to increase the extent to which patients are "engaged" in their activity. This concept of engagement (DeSilva & Rachman, 1981) presumably insures that patients do not cognitively avoid the feared situation. Borkovec's (1982) notion of "functional exposure" captures roughly the same point. Butler recommends that patients be encouraged to practice specific elements of social interaction, such as engaging in eye contact or active listening. A breakdown of the components of social skills is used to guide these activities. Related to this point is Butler's recommendation that patients take an active role in seeking out suitable social interactions. And finally, she instructs patients deliberately to provoke anxiety (e.g., "a man who sweated distressingly when in company was able to increase his practice by moving away from the open window, wearing an extra sweater or accepting hot food and drink" (1985, p. 654).

It remains to be seen how these suggestions might improve the efficacy of exposure with social phobics. Theoretically, the concerns Butler raises and the recommendations she makes underscore the importance of advancing our understanding of the mechanisms underlying exposure treatment. It can be argued that the need to facilitate "engagement" or "functional exposure" indicates that what is vital is more than mere attention to relevant anxiety-eliciting cues. Rather, it then becomes important how the information gleaned from these cues is processed, encoded, and stored in memory. In short, active (and complex) cognitive processing is at work, and it is the modification of the nature and product of this processing that is probably the goal of exposure or of any treatment (Goldfried & Robbins, 1983; Wilson, in press-a).

THEORETICAL CONSIDERATIONS IN FEAR REDUCTION

Animal Models of Fear and Fear Reduction Methods

In its early stages, behavior therapy was, of course, closely connected to research from the animal conditioning laboratory. The development of fear reduction methods and the theories used to explain their effects relied heavily on animal research. In recent years, however, the influence of animal conditioning research on behavior therapy has waned significantly. The reasons are several. Behavior therapy has become far more cognitive in nature, emphasizing concepts that owe more to current human experimental psychology (e.g., information processing, attribution theory, and social cognition) than to basic conditioning research (Bandura, 1986; Wilson, in press-b).

Nonetheless, it would be unfortunate if more recent developments in animal conditioning research were to be overlooked as we search for improved theories of behavior change. Eelen (1982), in a theoretical paper discussed in Volume 9 of this series, suggested how modern analyses of classical conditioning in terms of correlational or contingency relations may dovetail with the principles of attribution theory. He argued for another look at the cognitive commonalities between learning in animals and people. The past several years have seen other findings from the animal conditioning laboratory that warrant attention.

Mineka (in press) has provided a comprehensive and thoughtful analysis of the usefulness and limitations of animal models in understanding and treating the anxiety disorders. Her analysis documents how conditioning formulations have changed and grown more sophisticated. In many ways, these conditioning formulations more closely resemble cognitive social learning theory (Bandura, 1986), which is derived primarily from research with people. Two sets of important findings from Mineka's own research on the acquisition of fear reactions illustrate this view.

In the first example, Mineka reports recent findings showing that a "sense of mastery" can significantly reduce fear in infant primates. Monkeys reared in an environment in which they could control important events, such as the delivery of their food and water, were compared with yoked controls who received the same consequences but on a noncontingent basis. Subsequent tests of these monkeys' fear reactions (at ages 7–9 months) to standardized laboratory stressors showed that the mastery group displayed significantly less fear than their yoked controls. Mineka (in press) comments that "a generalized expectancy of control or a sense of mastery can indeed have profound effects on an animal's reaction to fear or anxiety provoking situations. This is obviously a way in which personality variables stemming from a person's experience with control or mastery over his/her environment may influence or interact with the development and maintenance of phobic fears." The relevance of these findings and Mineka's concept of "sense of mastery" to self-efficacy theory (Bandura, 1977) and related theories that underscore the importance of control and predictability in coping with stress (Miller, 1979) hardly needs emphasizing.

Mineka and her colleagues have also conclusively demonstrated the influential role of observational learning in the acquisition of snake fear in primates (Mineka, Davidson, Cook, & Keir, 1984). In a series of well-controlled experiments that corrected for methodological flaws in previous research, Mineka *et al.* (1984) showed that adolescent monkeys developed an intense and lasting fear of snakes as a result of observing their wild-reared parents act fearfully in the presence of real or toy snakes for a brief period of time. Several aspects of these experiments are worthy of note.

First, the rapidity with which such an intense fear was acquired must be emphasized. Second, Mineka and her colleagues demonstrated that this observational learning affected both the behavioral and autonomic components of fear. Third, the learned fear was not specific to one context, but was generalized to environments other than the original learning context. Fourth, the fear was lasting; follow-up assessments 3 months following the initial learning showed no diminution of intensity of fear. And fifth, fear did not develop either when the observer failed to pay close attention to the parents' behavior or when the parent displayed relatively low levels of distress in the presence of the snake.

Finally, these results may offer useful suggestions for preventing the development of phobic fears. Specifically, Mineka *et al.* (1984) found a high correlation between the parental models' and the observing offspring's level of fear. This led them to suggest the following:

> [P]arents who have strong fears or phobias should avoid confronting their phobic object as much as possible in the presence of their children. Although one might expect that such avoidance, especially if it were obvious, might suffice to instill a fear in the children, [our results] suggest that the level of disturbance exhibited by the parental model is more important than behavioral avoidance per se. This suggestion stems from the observation that, although all of the models showed virtually complete and equivalent behavioral avoidance, it was their level of disturbance that correlated so highly with the level of fear conditioned in their offspring. Thus, to the extent that parents can prevent themselves from exhibiting their fear in a dramatic way, they may be able to help prevent the observational conditioning of fear in their children or, at a minimum, to reduce the extent of such conditioning. (pp. 370–371)

Self-Efficacy Theory

SELF-EFFICACY AND THE MECHANISMS OF FEAR REDUCTION

Self-efficacy theory (Bandura, 1977) continues to generate wide-ranging research, much of it directly relevant to the analysis and modification of phobic reactions. This research and its implications for understanding behavior are detailed in Bandura's (1986) recent book, *Social Foundations of Thought and Action: A Social Cognitive Theory*. This comprehensive volume provides a rich source of information and ideas for the behavior therapist. Suffice it here to summarize, selectively, some of the recent research on self-efficacy theory that relates to the treatment of anxiety and anxiety disorders.

The effect of changes in self-efficacy on physiological indices of fear arousal (e.g., heart rate and blood pressure) has been demonstrated (Bandura, Reese, & Adams, 1982). A subsequent study has gone further in exploring the mechanisms through which self-efficacy might influence fear by analyzing the correlation between self-efficacy and the neuroendocrine responses involved in fear arousal (Bandura, Taylor, Williams, Mefford, & Barchas, 1985). Simple phobics were presented with the task of coping with their feared object in their high, medium, and low ranges of self-efficacy for the task in question. High perceived self-efficacy was accompanied by low levels of plasma epinephrine and norepinephrine during interaction with a phobic object, whereas moderate perceived self-inefficacy gave rise to substantial increases in levels of plasma catecholamines. Levels of both catecholamines dropped sharply when phobics refused to attempt tasks at which they judged themselves to be inefficacious. Release of dopac rose significantly even when subjects contemplated a task with which they believed they could not cope. Of particular clinical importance is the finding that after perceived self-efficacy was strengthened to the maximal level by participant modeling, all of the tasks were performed without any differential catecholamine responses. These data not only provide additional support for the causal action of self-efficacy on fear reactions, but also address the processes that mediate elimination of phobic fear. Bandura *et al.* (1985) comment that their pattern of results is "in accord with a mechanism involving controllability rather than simple extinction or adaptation over time" (p. 413).

In Volumes 8 and 9 of this series, I addressed the emerging question of the interaction between cognition and affect (Wilson, 1982b, 1984b). It seems well established that affect, or mood, can critically influence cognitive processing. For example, there is Bower's (1981) research on the effects of mood on memory, demonstrating a mood congruity effect (meaning that people attend to and learn more about events that match their emotional state). He proposes that emotion serves as a memory unit that can enter into associations with coincident events. People tend to recall more experiences that are affectively congruent with their feeling state during recall. In view of affect's strong influence on cognitive processing, it becomes important to ask how affect or mood might influence judgments of self-efficacy.

A recent study by Kavanagh and Bower (1985) investigated the effect of hypnotically induced mood on subjects' self-efficacy regarding social, academic, and athletic capabilities. The findings were striking: Mood inductions had a significant effect on efficacy judgments. Of particular note is that this effect was widespread; mood altered self-efficacy beyond the particular domain of functioning in which the mood was experienced. Johnson and Tversky (1983) have similarly reported the broad, generalized effects of a highly specific affect induction on cognitive processing. This finding explains the common clinical observation that patients (e.g., agoraphobics) who experience depression, for whatever reason, find it more difficult to continue their attempts at coping and may suffer temporary setbacks. Since moods can alter self-efficacy, which, in turn, can determine individuals' capacities to cope with stressful or threatening situations, direct means of modifying mood are called for, as Rachman (1981) and Kihlstrom and Nasby (1981) have previously pointed out.

SELF-EFFICACY THEORY AND EXPOSURE TREATMENT

Self-efficacy theory not only provides a plausible explanation of the mechanisms of fear reduction methods; it also suggests ways in which exposure treatment might be most effectively used. In Volume 9 of this series, I made this point and sketched out ways in which the clinical practice of exposure methods could be usefully informed by cognitive social learning theory in general and self-efficacy theory in particular (Wilson, 1984b). The past few years have seen the publication of studies providing empirical support for this contention.

Williams, Dooseman, and Kleifield (1984) compared the conditioning view of exposure treatment, which emphasizes the extinction of conditioned anxiety responses to phobic stimuli, to the social learning model, which emphasizes the development of coping and personal mastery. The subjects were severe acrophobics or driving phobics. Degree of overall exposure was equated between the two treatment conditions. The critical procedural difference between the two conditions was the extent to which the therapist provided subjects with driving and height phobias with "mastery induction aids." The latter included active guidance by the therapist during exposure tasks, setting proximal goals to overcome lack of progress, and varied performance. Both treatments were more effective than a no-treatment control condition, and guided mastery was significantly superior to exposure modeling on measures of behavior, self-efficacy, and self-report of fear. Self-efficacy measures predicted therapeutic change significantly better than measures of anxiety, duration of exposure, or level of performance during treatment.

The foregoing finding was replicated in a second study by Williams, Turner, and Peer (1985). Simple phobics (acrophobics) were randomly assigned to one of three groups: a guided-mastery treatment, based on social learning/self-efficacy theory, as described briefly above; a "performance desensitization" treatment, based on conditioning theory, which placed primary emphasis on stimulus exposure and corresponding extinction of classically conditioned anxiety; and a no-treatment control group. Although the performance desensitization group actually received longer exposure to the phobic stimuli, guided mastery was significantly more effective in reducing phobic behavior and self-reported fear. As in the former study (Williams *et al.*, 1984), self-efficacy measures predicted outcome more accurately than measures of anxiety arousal.

A frequent objection to self-efficacy theory has been that outcome expectations alone might predict behavior without any need to invoke the construct of self-efficacy (e.g., Kazdin, 1978). The evidence thus far, however, has indicated otherwise (Bandura, 1986). Williams and his colleagues have conducted the most detailed empirical analysis of the relative predictive accuracy of the two sets of expectations. Their results are summarized in a report by Williams and Watson (1986) as follows:

> [T]his conclusion [that outcome expectations are superior] was not supported in Williams and Telch's (1984) analysis of 15 sets of data from five experiments in which perceived self-efficacy, anticipated anxiety, and phobic behavior were measured in 140 severely debilitated phobics before and after treatment. These studies replicated [Kirsch, Tennen, Wickless, Saccone, and Cody's] (1983) findings of high correlations between self-efficacy and anticipated anxiety, and between anticipated anxiety and behavior. However, partial correlation analyses revealed that in 13 of the 15 data sets perceived self-efficacy remained significantly predictive of phobic behavior with anticipated anxiety partialled out, whereas in only 3 of the sets did anticipated anxiety significantly predict behavior with self-efficacy partialled out. (p. 137)

A basic behavioral assumption in the treatment of phobic and obsessive–compulsive disorders has been that "The golden rule is to try never to leave a [phobic] situation until the fear is going *down*" (Mathews, Gelder, & Johnston, 1981, p. 182). This "golden rule" has been an article of faith among behavior therapists and is based squarely on Mowrer's (1960) two-factor theory of avoidance learning. According to this theory, if the classically conditioned anxiety that motivates the avoidance (phobic) behavior is undiminished as a result of exposure to the feared stimulus, any escape or avoidance behavior will simply be maintained because of secondary reinforcement via anxiety reduction. For this reason, it is typically recommended that exposure be prolonged. The case has been made that if exposure is too brief, it not only may be inefficient, but may exacerbate the phobia (see Wilson & O'Leary, 1980).[2]

DeSilva and Rachman (1984) carried out a direct test of this widely shared assumption that patients who escape from phobic situations while experiencing high levels of fear will fare more poorly than those who wait for the fear to diminish. Agoraphobics receiving *in vivo* exposure treatment were randomly assigned to one of three treatment groups. In one condition, patients were instructed to leave their fear situations only when their anxiety had dropped to at least half of peak anxiety experienced; in a second condition, patients were instructed to withdraw from feared situations when their anxiety reached 75% of maximum; the third condition was a waiting-list control. Each treatment group received eight weekly treatment sessions. The results showed that both treatment conditions resulted in significant reductions in phobic fear and avoidance behavior, whereas the waiting-list control group showed no improvement. As DeSilva and Rachman note, "The study provides preliminary data that escaping and/or avoiding while still fearful does not necessarily lead to increased fear and to increased avoidance. On the contrary, an exposure strategy incorporating systematic escaping proved to be as effective as the widely-used therapeutic strategy of ensuring exposure to fear situations until anxiety drops by a significant amount" (p. 91).

These results call for an explanation. They run counter to the firm prediction of two-factor conditioning theory and the conventional conditioning view of exposure treatment (Borkovec, 1982; Emmelkamp, 1982). Unlike a conditioning explanation, self-efficacy theory is not embarrassed by these findings. DeSilva and Rachman unfortunately did not assess changes in patients' self-efficacy, but it is not far-fetched to speculate that both exposure treatments produced comparable changes in self-efficacy, which, in turn, resulted in similar therapeutic outcomes. Just as amount of exposure to the phobic stimulus cannot explain the usual finding of considerable variability in how much patients benefit from exposure treatments (Bandura, 1986), so it might be that escape or avoidance behavior per se is less important than the ramifications of such behavior for self-efficacy. It is possible

2. Marshall (1985) has shown that brief exposures to phobic stimuli in acrophobics do not enhance phobic sensitivity. Rather, even brief exposure without extinction of fear arousal may produce some reduction in behavioral avoidance.

for patients to experience increases in strength of self-efficacy despite elevated levels of anxiety arousal. As Bandura (1986) observes, cognitive social learning theory "posits an interactive but asymmetric relation between perceived self-efficacy and fear arousal, with coping efficacy exercising the much greater sway" (p. 444). Another explanation of this finding is put forward by Rachman (1984) in his safety-signal perspective. Subsequent research should address these alternative views, and DeSilva and Rachman have indicated a useful methodology for examining a theoretically and practically important assumption of clinical practice in behavior therapy.

Marshall (1985) studied the effects of different durations of exposure and the addition of coping self-statements to exposure in the treatment of acrophobics. He found that longer exposures were more effective than shorter exposures. Marshall points out that prolonged exposure to the point where subjects did not experience anxiety did not change behavior via automatic habituation of fear, but by prompting a cognitive reappraisal of the situation. This formulation is consistent with self-efficacy theory. Another finding was that adding coping self-statements to exposure facilitated treatment outcome. Marshall states,

> [This result] strongly supports the idea that treatment initiates processes of reappraisal which interact with opportunities to test these reappraisals behaviorally, and that these processes are crucial to deriving maximal benefits from flooding therapy. This is not to say that some degree of passive extinction or habituation is unnecessary to effect flooding. Rather, these processes appear to be preliminary and set the stage for the behavioral/cognitive interactions which result in a reappraisal by the subjects of both the power of the stimulus to control them and their own capacity to deal with the situation. (1985, p. 132)

Marshall goes on to assert that "optimal treatment effects will ensue when exposure to the feared stimuli are continued after the subject reaches a state of relative quiescence, so that training in coping skills can occur in the phobic situation while the subject is in a state (i.e., low arousal) where learning capacity is maximal" (1985, p. 132). This assertion is questionable. Anxiety arousal during exposure has not been shown to predict treatment outcome on phobic disorders (e.g., Bandura, 1986), as noted above in connection with the Michelson and Mavissakalian (1985) results. The results of the Williams *et al.* (1984) and Williams *et al.* (1985) studies, summarized above, show this. Optimal treatment effects are more likely to ensue when treatment (be it *in vivo* exposure or other fear reduction methods) raises subjects' self-efficacy to the point where they are confident they can cope with threatening situations.

Beck's Cognitive Theory

Given the very influential impact and therapeutic success of Beck's cognitive theory and therapy of depression (Beck, Rush, Shaw, & Emery, 1979), his recent volume with Emery on the nature and treatment of anxiety disorders (Beck & Emery, 1985) warrants serious attention from behavior therapists. The book provides some insightful analyses and rich clinical material for understanding the anxiety disorders. Clinicians will find the treatment manual especially helpful. In particular, Beck's cognitive therapy seems, on the face of it, to be well suited to the treatment of problems such as GAD, the cognitive nature of which has often been recognized. Beck and Emery differentiate their theory of generalized anxiety from Beck's previous analysis of depression in terms of the "anxious patient's more positive self-image, more optimistic outlook for the future, and more pleasant recollection of past experiences. Attention is paid to the tendency of the anxious patient to criticize himself for specific deficiencies and performance (behavioral self-blame), in contrast to the depressive who is more likely to attribute his problems to a global, structuralized deficiency (characterological self-blame)" (Beck & Emery, 1986, p. xvii).

Beck and Emery's cognitive view of panic is also timely. Essentially, it involves the patient's misinterpretation of internal physiological sensations. There is considerable similarity between Beck and Emery's position and the conceptualizations of panic developed by Clark and Salkovskis and by Rapee, as discussed earlier in this chapter. The initial success achieved by these latter investigators in England and Australia provides initial support for Beck and Emery's position. All in all, one must concur with Rachman's (1986) judgment that "there is not much to choose between the instructions recommended for anxiety disorders and those previously set out for the treatment of depression. Certainly, there are some differences, but the similarities between the two treatment manuals easily outweigh them" (p. 96). One of the more interesting differences, however, is the greater emphasis on imagery and its modification in this more recent volume on the treatment of anxiety disorders. The remaining comments here draw selectively on features of Beck and Emery's theory rather than their actual therapy, and to issues discussed in this series over the past few years.

For Beck and Emery, the "core psychological problem in anxiety disorders" is "vulnerability," which refers to

> an individual's tendency to devalue his problem-solving ability as well as to exaggerate the degree of threat in a problematic situation. The dys-

> functional behaviors are seen as basic functions or strategies used for self-protection. These self-protective patterns are likely to become mobilized in areas where the individual feels specifically vulnerable. These vulnerable areas involve public and private sectors and consist specifically of threats to a person's social bonding or sense of individuality, freedom, and identity. (1986, p. xvii).

In view of this cardinal theoretical tenet, it is disappointing not to find a discussion of how this concept relates to Bandura's self-efficacy theory. The overlap would seem to be considerable. For example, Bandura (1978), in the course of distinguishing between efficacy and outcome expectations, has stated that "*perceived vulnerability* to potential hazards generates thoughts of injurious consequences, high arousal, and avoidance" (p. 241, italics added). Among the obvious questions that come to mind are the following: Does Beck and Emery's theory accommodate the now substantial body of empirical support enjoyed by self-efficacy theory? Do the two theories make differential predictions? How can these predictions be tested, both in the laboratory and in the clinical setting? In a similar vein, Rachman (1986) has remarked on the absence of attempts to link this cognitive theory to existing conceptual models such as self-efficacy theory, the three-response system, and others.

I would also have liked to have seen more discussion of the difference and interaction between cognition and anxiety, particularly in view of the debate on this important topic that has been spurred by Zajonc's (1980) provocative paper (see Wilson, 1982b, 1984b). This becomes a vital issue for Beck and Emery, since they introduce the questionable assumption of a fundamental distinction between fear and anxiety. The former, they contend, is an emotional process; the latter is a cognitive one. This distinction is unlikely to be successful, and it requires a far more detailed conceptual justification. It is here that the absence of consideration of Lang's (1969) three-response analysis of fear, and of more integrative theories such as Bandura's (1986) social learning framework, is most acutely felt.

Butler and Mathews's (1983) research on cognitive processes in anxiety disorders was noted in Volume 10 (see Wilson, 1985b). They argued for the existence of "danger schemata," cognitive structures involved in evaluating personal threat. A subsequent study in this line of investigation has yielded data consistent with Beck and Emery's view of generalized anxiety (Mathews & MacLeod, 1985). Groups of generally anxious patients and nonanxious controls were administered the Stroop color-naming task, in which some words referred to physical or social threat and others were unrelated to any threat. The results showed that the anxious patients were significantly slower in responding to the threat words than were their nonanxious counterparts. The slower responding was presumably a function of the interference in naming the correct color caused by simultaneous activation of competing cognitive activity. Mathews and MacLeod (1985) interpret these results as evidence of the activity of the distinctive danger schemata in patients with generalized anxiety.

Williams and Watson (1985) reported an empirical test of another prediction from Beck's (1976) cognitive theory. Specifically, they tested Beck's assumption that negative outcome expectations maintain phobic fear and avoidance:

"[P]atients . . . are afraid not of a particular object or situation in itself, but of the consequences of their being in the situation or in contact with the object. A person with a phobia of heights indicates that he is afraid of falling; a person with a phobia of social situations states that he is afraid he will be humiliated or rejected" (1985, p. 167). Acrophobics rated their perceived danger of ascending to different heights, and these ratings were compared with comparable self-efficacy ratings. Whereas self-efficacy expectations accurately predicted behavioral performance at both pretreatment and posttreatment, ratings of perceived danger were only weakly related to behavior. Williams *et al.* (1985) replicated these findings in a study referred to above.

As I have suggested elsewhere (Wilson, 1984b, in press-a), there is a natural affinity between cognitive social learning theory and Beck's clinical concepts, particularly those regarding the processing of information. It is in the latter domain—the distorted processing of information—that Beck's concepts are most likely to enrich social learning theory. At the present time, however, cognitive social learning theory stands unmatched in scope, development, and empirical support as a cognitive–behavioral account of anxiety and its modification.

CHAPTER

4

COGNITIVE PROCESSES AND PROCEDURES IN BEHAVIOR THERAPY

PHILIP C. KENDALL

Having written about the cognitive processes and procedures in behavior therapy for Volumes 8, 9, and 10 of this series, I have come to note and take stock of certain landmark-like events in the years that have passed us by. For example, the Association for Advancement of Behavior Therapy (AABT) has passed somewhat of a milestone in the form of its 20th National Convention in 1986. What may be more surprising to some is that *Cognitive Therapy and Research* has now passed its 10th volume, representing over 10 years of publication. These time markers make it clear that the cognitive influences within behavioral therapy have now played a significant role for fully half the period of AABT's existence.

The international behavior therapy scene has witnessed equal movement in the tilt toward cognitive–behavioral approaches. To use the 1985 Congress of the European Association for Behavior Therapy (EABT) in Munich as a metric, the evidence included cognitive–behavioral workshops, symposia, lectures, and posters. Traditional behavioral themes were also represented, though the presence of a cognitive emphasis was buttressed by the fact that the theme of the entire Congress was "15 years of progress." The international interest was not unbridled; participants and presenters were not simply seduced by a different drumbeat. Rather, the need for further research and empirical support was clearly stated in most cases. In the Congress's opening address, for instance, nonempirical efforts were severely chastised, and new "marriages" were advocated only when each partner had empirical data and references. It was my reaction that this opening address referred more to a "wedding" with physiological than with cognitive colleagues.

Being chosen as a level of an independent variable in studies of schools of psychotherapy can also verify one's standing in the community of therapies. The cognitive–behavioral orientation was one of four "schools" used by Kopta, Newman, McGovern, and Sandrock (1986). These authors were interested in how various therapists of different therapeutic orientations would conceptualize treatment plans and how much these plans would cost. The therapists/subjects were cast into one of four categories: psychodynamic, cognitive–behavioral, family systems, and eclectic.

Despite the apparent longevity of the cognitive–behavioral enterprise, there remain several topics that are debated and discussed. What is cognitive–behavioral therapy? To what degree do the cognitive and behavioral approaches overlap, and to what degree have they been integrated? What is the proper place for integrative eclecticism? As a self-identified cognitive–behavioral therapist, I find some of these issues to be dated; they were hot at the outset, but have cooled substantially over time. Nevertheless, as mandated by the continued discussions in the literature, there appears to be more grist for the mill, and updates and clarifications are in order.

At least a decade has passed since the "revolutionary" period within the behavioral camp—perhaps best viewed as an "evolutionary" period. It would be far from the facts to attempt to argue that changes have not taken place. Thought and action are now often associated with each other, with affect increasingly joining the group. An earlier review of thought and action in psychotherapy (Kendall & Bemis, 1983) provided a description of related studies and their outcomes. More recently, Bandura (in press-a) provides several interesting accounts of the interrelatedness of thought and action; for instance, "The apparent divergence between cognitive theory and action-oriented treatments can be reconciled by distinguishing between process and means." Cognitive processes are the ingredients of changes produced by an individual's experience of mastery.

Behaviorists (often described with the adjective "radical" attached) prefer to dismiss the influence of cognition and invoke explanations involving rule-governed behavior (e.g., Zettle & Hayes, 1982) or the notion that thought is also behavior and therefore subject to the same laws that apply to observable action. Bandura (in press-a) argues, "The field of psychological change is not well served by false dichotomies that there exist pure cognitive and pure behavioral treatments. One would be hard pressed to find a 'behavioral' method that does not rely, at least in part, on cognitive conveyance, or a 'cognitive' method that is devoid of any performance elements." Along these lines, let us consider the early celluloid treatment of Ellis's rational–emotive therapy in the film *Three Approaches to Psychotherapy* (also affectionately referred to as the "Gloria" film). There were several descriptive adjectives ascribed to Ellis by several classes of viewers of this film; it consistently emerged that he was viewed as extremely verbal and that he talked at the client an inordinate amount. It is interesting to note, however, that one of the directives most often stated to Gloria, and therefore one of the major contributors to the content of Ellis's verbal behavior, was that Gloria needed to try some of the ideas she had and see what would happen. "Try" meant to take action and evaluate the consequences. In his postsession reflections, Ellis commented that he had instructed Gloria to try certain strategies because of the importance of practice. Indeed, I can readily recall his repetitious statement that she needed to practice, practice, practice. This behavioral feature in the strategy of the pre-eminent spokesperson for rational–emotive therapy is readily apparent. Similarly, cognitive therapy for depression is cognitive–behavioral. Self-monitoring, the related actions necessary to gather the data required by cognitive therapists, the scheduling of pleasant events, and mastery experiences—all these combine to underscore the interplay of cognitive and behavioral strategies.

From the behavioral side, one must recognize that there are mediating factors that may help us to understand what might be viewed as a purely behavioral procedure. How does extinction work? Can we not benefit greatly from both the knowledge that a discontinuance of contingent reward produces a reduction in the probability of a response, and the knowledge that there may be a process change in the expectations of the individual? Altered expectations may underlie the changes observed in extinction-like methods. What is the current status of the differential effectiveness of performance-based procedures versus cognitive ones in achieving desired gains? Bandura's (in press-a) statement that behavioral methods are preferable in the production of cognitive changes, which seems destined to become a classic (see below, p. 123), requires added empirical scrutiny.

Other issues continuing to confront the future of behavior therapy are the trend toward eclecticism and the associated sidelining of the more technological aspects of behavioral interventions. Articles by Thompson and Williams (1985) and Wolpe (1985a) in *the Behavior Therapist*, and associated replies from various readers, highlight the continued interest in and concern about the defining features of "behavior therapy." To some minds, it is the influence of the cognitive–

behavioral therapists that is responsible for the initial undermining of more pristine behavioral enterprises, and it is in this context that I wish to address the trend toward eclecticism.

It is my belief that eclecticism can be a good thing, but only when the ingredients within the eclectic approach are each the recipient of careful evaluation and empirical scrutiny. The methods and manners of evaluation that have been employed in the behavioral and cognitive–behavioral literatures should be required of the other intervention strategies before the supposed benefits and/or advantages of such strategies are integrated within empirically established approaches. Accordingly, I see the cognitive–behavioral integration as quite acceptable, desirable, and to be encouraged. Clearly, many of the varieties of cognitive therapy have been subjected to the rigors of scientific testing. As Beck (1986) argued in his reply to Wolpe (1985a), there are quite a number of studies, conducted by various researchers across several continents, that endorse the merits of a cognitive–behavioral approach to the relief of depressive symptomatology.

If we can assume that the newly integrated cognitive slants on behavioral therapy have rushed, pledged, and completed the other rites of passage into the behavioral fraternity, then what other features of proposed integrationism have been similarly successful? Neurolinguistic programming (NLP), according to mass media reports and local conversations, has enormous potential—and even claims to cure anxiety in a single 1-hour session (see Krugman *et al.*, 1985)! However, Krugman *et al.*'s evidence does not support the fact that NLP does anything but reduce anxiety to the extent that occurs simply by waiting for an hour to pass. That is, speech-anxious subjects evidenced reductions in their anxiety, but the degree of change was similar for NLP, a waiting-list control, and a 1-hour self-control desensitization treatment. The effects of the NLP treatment were apparently no greater than those of the passage of time; thus, as Krugman *et al.* accurately note, the rapid changes ascribed to NLP may be merely the changes that occur from the passage of time. Also, self-control desensitization has been found to be more effective than a waiting-list control when the treatment is longer than a single session, and the limited effects for this treatment in Krugman *et al.*'s study may have been due to the brevity of the experiment. However, in regard to the NLP claim of rapid treatment, the *findings*, not the claims, are important.

To return to a consideration of candidates for integration, it must be concluded that there is as yet no systematic evidence that NLP merits consideration for inclusion in a systematic behavioral eclecticism. Indeed, I have chosen two extremes—cognitive–behavioral approaches and NLP—to highlight my point that growth and advancement require that new information be gathered and incorporated when appropriate. My positive endorsement for integrative efforts rests on the approach taken by the cognitive members of AABT. It is my hope that the future includes more careful and detailed evaluations of treatments with a focus on emotional processing, interpersonal relationships (including therapist–client relationship factors), and the crises facing the human organism as they vary developmentally across the life span. Perhaps we can avoid the hyphenated hybrid, "cognitive–behavioral–affective–social–developmental therapy," but we need not be avoidant of the underlying multifaceted approach to treatment.

COGNITIVE DISTORTIONS AND NEGATIVE THINKING: CAN THEY BE FUNCTIONAL?

One feature of the behavioral therapy of maladaptive functioning that has particular appeal is its recognition that the process of learning is neither good nor bad; the behaviors that are learned may or may not be adaptive, but the learning process is itself not culpable. Much of the theorizing within the cognitive arena seems to have leaned heavily on the negative aspect, with distorted processing of information viewed as causal in the development of psychological pathology. Distortions have been routinely cast as unwanted, pathological, erroneous, and detrimental ways of experiencing, viewing, and making sense of the world.

What the behavioral model suggests, and what the cognitive side of the model needs to pay more attention to, is the potential explanatory power that can be afforded to positive, adaptive distortions. What I am suggesting here is that distortions, the negative connotations of the word aside, may have both functional and dysfunctional roles in psychological adjustment.

The dysfunctional qualities of distortions have been described early and extensively (e.g., Beck, 1967; Ellis, 1962). The functional value of certain distortions, however, has received modest attention at best from those with clinical interests. One might think of the "sadder but wiser" study of Alloy and Abramson (1979) and call attention to the notion of the "rosy glow" that nondepressed persons are said to maintain, often by distorting what in reality might be more negative than is perceived.

The functional distortions that are in need of further investigation, from the standpoint of increasing our understanding of psychological adjustment, are the "normal" information-processing distortions that affect all of our thinking. Tversky and Kahneman's work (1973, 1974) deserves greater attention. Consider, for example, the confirmatory bias that is said to permeate much of our information processing. We tend to seek data to confirm our original, initial hunches, and fail to gather the data that would support rival hypotheses or disconfirm our initial notions. When told a series of numbers (e.g,, 4, 6, 8), and instructed to try to determine the rule that governs the set of numbers by offering other sets of numbers that will then be judged as correct or incorrect, persons typically try several series of three-digit numbers something like the following: "10, 12, 14? 20, 22, 24? 2, 4, 6?" In each instance the judgment is "Yes, the sequence of numbers fits the rule," and in many cases the subject then assumes to have determined the rule "Even numbers increasing by two." As Mahoney (1986) discovered in some of his early research on the cognitive processing styles of scientists, many researchers who should have known better were also subject to confirmatory bias. The scientists, to a significantly greater degree than Protestant ministers, concluded that they had determined the rule after many fewer trials and without proper attention paid to the disconfirmation of alternative hypotheses. As scientists and clinicians, we, too, are subject to the information-processing biases that affect humankind.

Turk and Speers (1983) have provided a clinical case illustration of confirmatory bias (see also Turk & Salovey, 1985a). The client, a so-called "Mr. Smith," experienced mistrust and paranoia in regard to persons who wear glasses. Those wearing eyeglasses were evil and conspiratory, and he often brought pictures of criminals and other unscrupulous persons to the therapist to demonstrate how true his belief was. The patient obviously failed to attend to the numerous cases of people who wear glasses but who have not committed crimes, or of people who do *not* wear glasses but *have* committed crimes!

Consider the following scenario: A client comes to the office of a practicing cognitive–behavioral therapist, provides a reasonable description of his or her life's course and current state of difficulty. The clinician suspects that depression is the proper nosological category and proceeds to conduct proper evaluations to determine the nature of the client's problems. If the confirmatory bias holds, the clinician will give tests to assess level of depression, will look for indications of the features of depression that covary with depressive symptoms, and may even begin to ask the patient to talk about what makes him or her so depressed. Clearly, a detailed functional analysis of the problem behavior and a detailed and systematic assessment of all features of potential pathology, to eliminate some difficulties while tuning in on others, would be the procedure of choice. But what actually happens in most offices? To what degree are we practicing within a confirmatory bias that influences our ability to be most efficacious?

The availability heuristic (Tversky & Kahneman, 1973, 1974) again exemplifies a feature of routine information processing that suggests a distortion. When one tries to make sense of an enormous amount of information, or even a small amount of discrepant new information, an efficient approach to processing is to use short cuts or heuristics. Heuristics affect what information is retrieved from a person's memory and how it is brought to bear on the current question. The availability heuristic is said to operate when a person estimates the frequency or probability of an event or an outcome by the ease with which the instances are brought to mind. When working in clinical settings, we are especially prone to misrepresent base rates of particular behavior patterns, as the more maladaptive patterns are brought to our attention and these disorders are more available to us than to others. Correspondingly, if we have success in treating a single case with a specific form of intervention, we are particularly prone to see that intervention as the best approach for other similar candidates. Indeed, we may even go so far as to make a case for a particular client's needing a form of therapy that we have found to work or that we are particularly skilled at implementing. What is available to us influences how we proceed cognitively.

To return to the original concern that has launched this brief digression, if there are naturally occurring and perhaps therefore functional distortions (and there seem to be many), how must we operate as diagnosticians? As therapists who recommend "proper" thinking for our clients? Do we want clients to correct their unwanted distortions to the degree that they overcome confirmatory bias and/or the availability heuristic, or do we want clients simply to return to a level of processing at which most people function effectively, even if it means that they will be employing certain distortions (though perhaps functional distortions) in their thinking?

Some irrationality seems to have spurred success in certain persons. Business executives, sports figures, and academicians may be dedicated to certain achievements with irrational passion; for example, "I must create a better computer," as an absolute self-directive, can have beneficial effects. Individuals with exceptional or special skills have worked to perfect these skills beyond average or temperate goals. Irrationality may be a part of passion.

Research addressing these and related questions would provide much needed and markedly exciting data that would allow cognitive–behavioral therapists to begin to better understand what it takes cognitively to attain and maintain satisfactory adjustment. We already have a strong hunch that inflexible thinking, illogical and irrational thinking, and an absence of thinking are correctly associated with various forms of psychopathology. What is lacking, and what would be of great importance to the advancement of the field, is a more in-depth and detailed depiction of the types of cognitive functioning that are adaptive and maladaptive, together with a reasonably descriptive template for nonpathological cognitive functioning. Admittedly, and quite interestingly, those persons not suffering from psychological disorders may indeed be exercising functional distortions.

Popular depictions of psychological therapies are not noted for their accuracy or insight. Behavior therapy has certainly experienced its share of misrepresentation and misinterpretation. A popular misconception of cognitive therapy is its definition as teaching positive thinking. Other terms and phrases (e.g., "positive power," "self-affirmations") are also used when inaccurately popularizing aspects of cognitive–behavioral therapy. As noted in earlier volumes of this series (Kendall, 1984a, 1985a), there are data suggesting that there is power not in positive thinking, but in nonnegative thinking. Does this mean that the desired outcome of treatment is an absence of negative thinking? Is some degree of negative thinking functionally adaptive? Theory and research on the balance of positive and negative thinking appear promising.

Schwartz and Garamoni (1986) have described various states of mind and detailed hypothetical relationships between positive and negative thinking and psychopathology (such as depression). The internal dialogue associated with depression is hypothesized to contain a 50–50 split of positive and negative thinking, with increased levels of depresssion associated with increased negative thinking. The ratio of positive and negative thinking for an adjusted person is hypothesized to be 2:1. This optimal balance of positive to negative thinking parallels the "golden section" (a preferred ratio where a:b as b:[a + b]) and is calculated to be .618:.382.

Following the notion of the "power of nonnegative thinking" and guided by the "golden section," we (Kendall & Hays, 1986) conducted a series of studies to evaluate the predictive accuracy of various ratios of positive to negative thinking in the differentiation of adjusted and maladjusted persons. Using dual criteria for depression (i.e., BDI and Minnesota Multiphasic Personality Inventory [MMPI] *D* scores) and hypomania (i.e., General Behavior Inventory [GBI] and MMPI *Ma* scores), separate groups of depressed, hypomanic, and nondisturbed cases were determined. Subjects also completed inventories designed to measure the frequency (and meaning) of positive, negative, and neutral self-statements. These data were converted to ratio scores for each of the groups.

The initial findings indicated that subjects classified as depressed evidenced a .45:.55 positive-to-negative ratio and that nondisturbed subjects showed the predicted 2:1 ratio. The actual numbers so closely resembled the hypothesized ratios that a cross-validation was undertaken. Again, on the basis of similar measures and procedures, the ratios were again as predicted. The data regarding hypomania were not as consistent, but the evidence was reliable in documenting that our adjusted profile of self-talk includes approximately one-third negative material.

It appears that some degree of negative thinking is functional and that when positive thinking outweighs negative thinking 2:1 there is reasonable adjustment. Not thinking negatively some of the time would be dysfunctional, and perhaps reflective of an absence of a reality base to cognitive processing. A storehouse of positive self-talk to counter the reasonable and realistic negative self-talk appears to be a part of adjustment demands.

Recent reports of research include some data bearing on this general issue. Using a checklist to assess the behavioral and cognitive approaches used by participants in a stop-smoking contest, Glasgow, Klesges, Mizes, and Pechacek (1985) documented that subjects reported using a variety of cognitive strategies but relatively few behavioral ones to attempt to quit. Use of self-statements such as "I don't need a cigarette" was reported by 81% of participants, and self-reminders of the commitment to quit were reported by 80%. Behavioral techniques, such as self-reward, self-punishment, and self-monitoring, were used infrequently (by fewer than 20%). Those who were successful abstainers used self-statements and self-reward more often than the less successful participants in the contest. It should also be noted that demographic factors and data on smoking patterns (e.g., sex, quantity/duration of smoking) were not found to be meaningfully related to success among smokers trying to quit without professional help. Stress was related to less successful efforts to quit.

In a study of the social-cognitive processing of boys with peer adjustment problems, Asarnow and Callan (1985) reported several interesting findings. For instance, boys with negative peer status generated fewer alternative solutions, proposed fewer assertive and mature solutions, showed less adaptive planning, and evaluated physically aggressive responses more positively and positive responses more negatively than boys with positive peer status. Of particular interest in the present context is the authors' report that the boys with negative and positive peer status did not differ in their endorsement of positive self-statements. According to the authors, the findings concerning negative self-statements were difficult to interpret. Clearly, more research in this area is needed, but the lack of differential predictions associated with the frequency of positive self-talk is not consistent with the power of positive thinking and more closely parallels notions of the power of nonnegative thinking (Kendall, 1984a).

The concern with the balance of positive and negative thinking has created an interest in the sequence of training experiences having to do with positive and negative thinking. For example, G. Thorpe (personal communication, July 1986) has reported that when treating phobic clients, he finds it more effective first to reduce the negative thinking and then to build the positive thinking, as compared to other sequencing of the training.

Clearly, more research is needed for a better understanding of the true nature of adaptive cognitive functioning. The apparent presence of functional distortions and the apparent benefit of a balanced degree of negative thinking document that simple pieces of advice such as "Think positive" or narrow directions such as "Don't think distorted" are not only inaccurate platitudes but also potentially disturbing suggestions.

COGNITIVE–BEHAVIORAL PROCEDURES WITH ADULTS AND ADOLESCENTS

One of the classic statements in clinical psychology and behavior therapy has been attributed to either of two people (Kiesler, 1966, or Paul, 1967b) and has to do with the several "whats": What treatment provided by what therapist produces what effects when measured in what ways? This near-platitude has had a deserved and desired effect on the field. We no longer assume that therapists, clients, types of changes, or outcome measures are all the same. The field has progressed markedly as a result of this classic statement of purpose.

Although perhaps it is too soon for a confident declaration of the "key" comment of the recent past, it seems likely that time will support me in suggesting the following: Bandura's (in press-a) proposal that cognitive process and behavioral procedures are both important but express their potency in different ways may be the prime candidate for the status of classic statement. Stated in Bandura's own words, "Cognitive factors mediate psychological changes, but the cognitive factors can be developed and altered most readily by enactive mastery." Reference is made to both the development and alteration of cognitive processes and the employment of behavioral enactive methods to treat the cognitive processes most effectively. But one must note that the cognitive side is not unidimensional. *Developing* or building cognitive factors is more appropriate for those disorders where *deficiencies* are prominent, while the *altering* of cognitive factors is more appropriate for conditions where the disorder results in part from *distorted* cognitive functioning (see also Kendall, 1985b). In each instance, consistent with a cognitive–behavioral and social learning analysis, behavioral performance-based strategies along with a focus on cognitive processing are preferable.

This review of cognitive–behavioral procedures with adults and adolescents cannot, due to the bulk of published work, attempt to be exhaustive and encyclopedic. There are several recent books and chapters on cognitive–behavioral procedures that may be examined by readers with specific interests (e.g., Beck & Emery, 1986; Dobson, 1987; Hollon & Beck, 1986; Jacobson, 1987; Kendall & Braswell, 1985; Meichenbaum, 1985). The present review builds on earlier volumes in this series and touches on select topics of current interest in the areas of depression, stress inoculation, problem solving, anger, and bulimia. Particular targets with children, such as hyperactivity, anger, and learning difficulties, are discussed in a later section.

Depression

In an earlier volume of the *Annual Review* (Kendall, 1984b, pp. 146–148), I discussed some of the research on the application of cognitive–behavioral strategies to the treatment of geriatric depression. At present, this issue and the prevention of relapse in depression are considered.

Briefly, Steuer *et al.* (1984) reported on a comparison of two forms of group therapy for depressed elderly patients. A psychodynamic group therapy was compared to a cognitive–behavioral group therapy. The authors reported that patients in both groups showed statistically and clinically significant improvements, and that these gains were evident in observer ratings of anxiety and depression and on self-report measures of depression. The only statistically significant difference in the outcomes of the two groups was a better result on the BDI for the subjects receiving the cognitive–behavioral treatment.

The cognitive–behavioral treatment was reviewed by personnel at the Center for Cognitive Therapy, and observers were able to distinguish the two types of therapy. Groups met twice a week for 10 weeks and once a week for the following 26 weeks, resulting in a total of 46 sessions over a 9-month period. There was no control group, and the authors presented their reasoning for the lack of a control condition. Basically, ethical and pragmatic considerations were predominant; for instance, it would be ethically indefensible to withhold treatment for a 9-month period. The main question was one of differentially superior outcomes and not one of "Does therapy work?," and this also buttressed the argument for not including a control group.

In a reply to the Steuer *et al.* (1984) report, Riskind, Beck, and Steer (1985) pointed out that the earlier concern with the magnitude of observed differences (Steuer *et al.* stated that only 25% of treated patients met BDI criteria for mild depression or complete remission) must be reconsidered in light of the fact that the earlier research used a short form of the BDI, and cutoffs (or set-point scores for different levels of depression) are different for the long and short forms. Using regression to determine equivalent short-form values from long-form scores, and applying these scores to the Steuer *et al.* data, Riskind *et al.* found that close to 50% (not 25%) of the cognitive therapy patients and only 30% of the psychodynamically treated patients met the criteria for improvement (mild depression or in remission).

Other criteria for this magnitude of change, such as Klerman, DiMascio, Weissman, Prusoff, and Paykel's (1974) notion of 50% decrease in initial depression, and Smith, Glass, and Miller's (1980) residual-gain method, also support the greater effectiveness of cognitive therapy over psychoanalytic therapy for the treatment of depression.

Mintz, Mintz, and Jarvik (1985) have replied to Riskind *et al.* and acknowledged the BDI results, but have again raised the issue of why the BDI is potentially sensitive to cognitive therapy. These authors, like Steuer *et al.*, seem to be concerned that cognitive–behavioral therapy for depression is not more effective, but more direct in teaching answers to the BDI. Admittedly, the BDI is often a scale that is used in outcome research and that has been found to be sensitive to treatment efforts, but there is a long list of outcomes that have employed measures in addition to the BDI, and the improvements are often seen across measures.

A digression on short forms seems to be in order here. The interchange noted above is but one illustration of a larger issue: Short forms are notoriously troublesome. It is possible for correlations between long and short forms to be significant, and for *t* tests between the mean short form and long form to be nonsignificant, and yet the short form can still be incredibly inaccurate in classification. To use IQ as an example, long and short forms can correlate in the .80–.90

range, with no mean differences in IQ, and yet the accuracy of classification can be so dramatically reduced as to preclude the use of the short form (see Kendall & Little, 1977).

A classic statement in psychology—indeed, so classic that it is perhaps the leading candidate for a psychological law—is the notion that the best predictor of future behavior is past behavior. Job candidates with a list of high-quality publications are the best candidates for research/academic positions because this statement is true. Graduate students who fall asleep in class, are years late with required work, and constantly generate lame excuses for their incompletes are the best candidates for the list of people most likely not to complete the PhD. There is some consistency in behavior.

Some recent work by Gonzales, Lewinsohn, and Clarke (1985) has provided data relevant to the "law" that past behavior is the best predictor of future behavior. I will provide some of the details of the research before reaching the main point. Gonzales *et al.* tracked down 125 of the 167 outpatients who had completed a cognitive–behavioral treatment (note that this treatment was not an instance of the application of a Beck, Rush, Shaw, and Emery [1979] program). The investigators assessed recovery and relapse, and examined a host of variables to determine the best predictors of relapse. The cases were divided into three groups: major depression, intermittent depression, and major depression with underlying intermittent depression (double depressives). The recovery rates after a 1-year period were 70%, 43%, and 27%, respectively; the relapse rates were 31%, 33%, and 14%, respectively. Predictors of the relapse included the following six variables: the number of previous episodes of depression, history of depression in first-degree relatives, health problems, dissatisfaction with major roles in life, initial level of depression, and age at entry (with younger age more closely related to relapse). The main predictor of relapse was the number of previous episodes of depression. In other words, the best predictor of future behavior was past behavior.

A surprising finding was reported by Baker and Wilson (1985). These authors followed a cognitive–behavioral therapy for depression with either cognitive–behavioral booster sessions, nonspecific booster sessions, or no booster sessions for a period of 3 months. Depression, assessed throughout the booster period, was not favorably affected by the boosters. Posttreatment effects were maintained during the booster period, but there was no evidence of prevention of relapse. It could be that the relatively brief initial treatment (seven $1\frac{1}{2}$-hour group treatments) reduced the potency of the initial program and thereby reduced relapse prevention, but it remains that the boosters did not boost. Using other analyses, Baker and Wilson (1985) reported that clients who were "good" responders for the initial treatment remained improved through the booster period, with "poor" treatment responders continuing to do poorly during boosters. The authors then concluded that "subjects who improve during treatment remain improved." To return to the earlier concern about the length of the initial treatment, it is possible that stronger effects could have been produced with a more extended, though typical, length of treatment. Consistency, however, was again evident, as the most succssful treatment cases initially were also the least likely to have a relapse.

Stress Inoculation

Stress inoculation training has been described as involving three components (e.g., see Meichenbaum, 1985; Meichenbaum & Turk, 1976). The first of these is educational in nature and presents an overview of the psychological dimensions being focused on in treatment (such as anxiety and/or stress). The second component teaches the client coping skills relevant to the target situation, while the third component consists of exposing the client to practice using the recently acquired coping skills. The theoretical underpinnings and especially the procedural strategies of stress inoculation training are detailed, along with clincial anecdotes, in Meichenbaum's (1985) practitioner guidebook. As researchers and practitioners continue to employ the stress inoculation approach to help clients manage stress and overcome anxiety, component analyses and long-term follow-ups are needed.

In a dental phobia context, Moses and Hollandsworth (1985) examined the relative potency of education alone; coping skills and application training; and coping skills and application training plus education. A waiting-list control was used for comparison purposes. Significantly more subjects from the three treatment conditions scheduled posttreatment dental appointments than subjects from the waiting list. However, significantly more subjects from the two treatments that involved training in the application of coping skills actually went through the scheduled dental appointments, as compared with those from education training alone. These findings suggest, as the authors have noted, that education may motivate individuals but that more is needed in terms of getting them to follow through with the complete dental process. The subjects in the study were indeed dental-avoidant (having avoided a dental situation for a year or longer as a result of excessive fear), and the clinical meaningfulness of this study is evident. While the study does support the position that stress inoculation procedures do enhance dental-phobic patients' follow-through on dental work, the researchers also assessed clients using ischemic muscle pain and a cold-pressor task, and it was found that there were no significant differences in terms of pain tolerance.

Stress inoculation and aerobic conditioning were used to reduce anxiety in 61 stressed community residents. At a 15-month follow-up (Long, 1985), it was found that both treatments reduced anxiety and increased self-efficacy. Stress inoculation was seen as superior, in that it increased positive and decreased negative self-statements (assessed via thought listing). More work in this area seems warranted, as a question of current concern for stress inoculation, as well as for other cognitive–behavioral interventions, in the explication of the process of change and the mechanisms of change; cognitive assessment (such as assessment of self-statements) is essential to address these matters.

Problem Solving

The application of problem-solving training has expanded to include samples and types of disorders that heretofore have not been targeted. The generic applicability of problem-solving training is fairly evident from its basic tenets: Psychological maladjustent results, in part, from an inability to solve life's problems, and adjustment is enhanced by development of improved problem-solving skills (see also D'Zurilla, 1986; D'Zurilla & Nezu, 1982). Examples of this expanding application include such diverse groups as chronic psychiatric patients, conflicted marital couples, depressives, shy adolescents, alcoholics, and counseling students.

Applying problem-solving training to the difficult cases in a chronic aftercare situation produced some promising results in one study. Hansen, St. Lawrence, and Christoff (1985) treated seven chronic psychiatric patients who were in a partial hospitalization program and evaluated the problem-solving training via a multiple-baseline design. The standard problem-solving training seems to have been administered, with a focus on problem identification, goal definition, solution evaluation, evaluation of alternatives, and selection of the best solution. Treatment was provided in a group, and sessions were conducted twice weekly. When one component of the problem solving was acquired, training progressed to the next component; in each case the therapist provided instructions, modeled use of the skill, requested that each subject demonstrate use of the skill, and provided involved and corrective feedback and praise.

The overall effectiveness of the intervention suggests that group interpersonal problem solving with chronic aftercare patients has some potential. The training effects generalized from training situations to unfamiliar problem situations. There was also evidence of maintenance of gains at 1- and 4-month follow-ups. Importantly, the authors proceeded to conduct a normative comparison: They contrasted the degree of improvement in the subjects with the level of functioning among community members, and in so doing documented that the patients' problem-solving skill at posttreatment was equivalent to the competency level of individuals who were functional in the community at that time. These normative comparisons add to the documentation of the importance of the outcome. However, one must recognize that while these data do document improved problem solving, they do not provide evidence to address the degree to which the patients' improvement in problem-solving skills translated to improved levels of behavior adjustment in a generalized fashion outside of treatment.

A problem-solving intervention and an experimental intervention in relation to the resolution of marital conflict were the topics of a study by Johnson and Greenberg (1985). These authors chose a sample of 45 couples who were evidencing marital discord and seeking therapy, and then randomly assigned them to a waiting-list control condition or to one of the two treatment conditions: (1) a cognitive–behavioral intervention teaching problem-solving skills, and (2) an experiential intervention focusing on the emotional experiences underlying interpersonal interaction. The treatment was provided in eight sessions by experienced therapists, and the treatments were monitored and found to be as described in the written procedures. The assessments included the Test of Emotional Styles; the Couples Therapy Alliance Scale (Pinsof & Catherall, 1983); the Dyadic Adjustment Scale (Spanier, 1976); a target complaints assessment; goal attainment scaling; and the personal Assessment of Intimacy in Relationships (Schaefer & Olson, 1981).

The problem-solving treatment used in this study taught subjects to be skilled at negotiations and to avoid unnecessary negative communications; they were also taught some behavior management skills and ways in which to enhance positive exchanges (see manual by Jacobson & Margolin, 1979). These clients were exposed to consideration of the rules for effective communication, problem definition, problem solution, and making contractual agreements, and in each case they observed a model and had an opportunity to rehearse. In contrast, the emotional-focus treatment was concerned more with the experiential and emotional aspects of the dyadic experience. In this treatment, the clients were viewed primarily as emotional processors, dealing with their current emotional state, their understanding of their current emotional state, and their understanding of their current environment; problems were viewed as ways of maintaining reciprocal negative interpersonal relationships. The therapist therefore identified negative interaction cycles and worked with each couple to help them understand the feelings associated with each of these negative cycles and each spouse's role in that cycle. As various problems were described by the couple, the therapist used various techniques to heighten emotional responses, to reframe the problems, and then to help the couple consolidate their new experiences in relationship to each other.

The outcomes of this study indicated that both treatments significantly improved the quality of the relationship for the couples involved. This is consistent with the existing literature supporting the effectiveness of the problem-solving approach with couples, but the results also indicate that there were improvements in the emotionally focused group. While it is true that these two treatments each had unique features, there were aspects of similarity across the two. Although there was an emphasis on the rational aspects of problem solving in the problem-solving approach, emotions nevertheless entered into the interactions and their evaluations. Similarly, in the emotionally focused treatment, there were some considerations of the negative interaction patterns in the cycles of negative emotional responding; this is a facet of the problem-solving approach. Thus, the results suggest, as in good clinical practice, that both rational and emotional approaches would probably be desirable. Although the findings were consistent across measures, it is important to note that there was an absence of measures beyond self-report. Though self-report is important in a marital interaction situation, it would also be helpful to know whether there were actual changes in the interaction patterns in addition to the assessments conducted via self-report; this could have been determined via naturalistic behavioral observations, for example. (See also discussion in Chapter 2 of this volume, pp. 44–45.)

An application of social problem-solving therapy to unipolar depression has been reported by Nezu (1986). Individuals diagnosed as unipolar depresives according to the Research Diagnostic Criteria were assigned problem-solving therapy, problem-focused therapy, or a waiting-list control. The problem-solving therapy was based on the training described by D'Zurilla and Nezu (1982) and focused on problem orientation, problem definition, generation of alternatives, decision making, and solution implementation and verification. Homework assignments were also a part of this 8-week program with $1\frac{1}{2}$- to 2-hour sessions per week. The problem-focused therapy was based on the same rationale in the problem-solving therapy but did not include the systematic problem-solving approach. Subjects discussed their problems during the sessions, thus constituting a reasonable comparison group, along with the waiting-list controls.

Evaluative assessment included the BDI, the MMPI *D* scale, and the Problem-Solving Inventory. The problem-solving approach to therapy was successful in reducing depressive symptomatology, as evidenced by substantial reductions in scores on the BDI and the MMPI *D* that were maintained after 6 months. Clients receiving the problem-solving therapy also reported increases in their self-appraised problem-solving effectiveness (and showed an increase in internal locus of control). Nezu (1986) also reported the clinical significance of the changes produced by the problem-solving therapy. According to Jacobson, Follette, and Revenstorf's (1984) reliable change index, 10 of 11 cases treated with the social problem-solving therapy evidenced meaningful BDI changes (e.g., pretreated means in the mid-20s to posttreatment means of approximately 10). Equally positive changes were evident on the MMPI *D*. The two other groups (the problem-focused and waiting-list groups) did not experience comparable gains.

Shy adolescents, while in a period of particular importance for later adjustment, have not received a great deal of research attention until recently (e.g., Kendall & Williams, 1986). However, Christoff *et al.* (1985) have produced some evidence that problem-solving training is an effective means of increasing the social skills of shy young adolescents. Several measures were used in the study to evaluate the outcome. For example, Christoff *et al.* employed the Means–End Problem Solving measures described by Shure and Spivack (1972) and assessments of conversation skills. In these conversation assessments, the subjects were paired and asked to engage in a 5-minute conversation, which was taped. In the analysis of these tapes, the researchers studied the frequency of occurrence of several conversational problem-solving skills. Self-report measures were employed, including a conversation diary, a self-esteem measure, and a social interaction assessment. To measure changes in behavior in a real situation, observations were conducted in the school cafeteria during the students' normal lunch period. This observation took place four times prior to the onset of training and following each phase of training. Lastly, the students, their parents, and their teachers rated the subjects on six different dimensions in an effort to assess the social validation of the outcome.

The intervention procedures included a problem-solving focus and a social skills focus. Within the problem-solving component of the program were the more or less standard approaches following the work of Spivack and Shure (1974). The factors involved recognizing a problem situation, defining the problem completely, generating multiple solutions, evaluating the positive and negative consequences of each potential solution, determining the most reasonable solution, and developing a plan for implementing that solution. Among the social skills foci were listening skills, talking about oneself, ways of beginning a conversation, and making requests of others. Using a multiple-baseline approach to the evaluation of the outcome, Christoff *et al.* (1985) reported that group training in social skills and problem-solving abilities provided positive improvement. There were improved social interactions, for example, as seen in the increase in the frequency of daily interactions among the formerly shy adolescents, positive reports of social interaction, and more positive patterns of self-evaluation. Although preliminary in several respects, the Christoff *et al.* study does suggest that problem-solving approaches have potential, if not conclusively demonstrated efficacy, and that their application to a wide variety of problems—now including shy adolescents—seems to be reasonable.

An evaluation of a sequential application of the components of problem-solving training with alcoholic cases was reported by Kelley, Scott, Prue, and Rychtarik (1985). Using a multiple-baseline design, five subjects, and training in three phases (problem definition, solution generation, and predicting consequences), Kelley *et al.* reported increases in the participants' skills level. However, the training did not improve the overall quality of the subjects' solutions to difficult and relevant problems. This finding is important for at least two reasons: (1) It suggests that merely treating or assessing the quantity of problem solutions is not equivalent to a concern with the quality of solution; and (2) the trend in assessment is to go beyond the frequency count of quantity analysis and toward an increased emphasis for ratings of quality. In related research, we (Fischler & Kendall, 1986) found that quality of generated alternatives, but not quantity, was associated with various indices of child adjustment. It should be noted that the method of assessing quality of problem solutions may be particularly important in producing meaningful research data. When subjects are asked to select a high-quality answer from a multiple-choice list, the task is one of "quality recognition." However, when no choices are provided and subjects are asked to produce high-quality solutions, they must themselves think of them! One can be misled into thinking that response quality has improved when a multiple-choice assessment procedure is employed, whereas a truer test of improved quality of problem solutions would be an open-ended assessment method.

Cormier, Otani, and Cormier (1986) examined the effects of components of a problem-solving program on counseling students. The treatment group consisted of the following modules: (1) general orientation, (2) problem definition, (3) generation of alternatives, and (4) description of behaviors used to solve problems. Using different combinations of the self-paced learning modules, students proceeded through the treatment program (perhaps best described as an educational course). Cormier *et al.* found that training was significantly effective in enhancing subjects' ability to select the best alternative, with all treatment groups performing better than an attention placebo control group.

Experts generated lists of alternative solutions, and there were then rated for effectiveness; "effectiveness" was defined as the maximizing of positive consequences and minimizing of negative consequences—long-term as well as short-term, and social as well as personal (after Nezu & D'Zurilla, 1979). The solutions were arranged according to rated level of effectiveness in advance of the subjects' being asked to select the best one. As noted earlier, use of "selecting" the best solution as a dependent measure has a potential weakness: Recognition of a high-quality solution is not identical to being able to generate a high-quality solution.

Some studies have begun to address the psychopathologies associated with low problem-solving skills. Using the Problem-Solving Inventory (see Heppner & Petersen, 1982), Nezu (1985) compared self-perceived effective and ineffective problem solvers on measures of depression, anxiety, and personal problems. Those who perceived themselves as ineffective problem solvers reported more depression and anxiety, had more problems, and reported more distress associated with these problems. In a separate study, Nezu, Kalmar, Ronan, and Clavijo (1986) found that problem-solving scores were significant predictors of depression even after attributional styles were taken into account. While these data do imply that self-perceived effective problem solvers are less emotionally distressed, the reliance on self-report measures alone can contribute to realistic fears of method variance.

Research in the area of social/interpersonal problem solving has grown, and applications have broadened to include diverse samples. Future work would benefit from less reliance on multiple baselines, a greater focus on the quality of problem solutions, continued efforts toward normative comparisons, and a universal concern for the contribution of overall intelligence. This last point emerges from studies with children, where careful assessment of intelligence and its inclusion in predictions of adjustment have suggested that problem-solving skills count for meaningfully less variance when general intellectual ability is included in the analysis (Fischler & Kendall, in press; Kendall, 1986).

Anger

Relaxation and cognitive treatments for anger were compared to a no-treatment control condition in a study reported by Hazaleus and Deffenbacher (1986). The "angry" clients[1] scored in the upper 25% on the State–Trait Anger Scale (STAS; Spielberger, Jacobs, Russell, & Crane, 1983) and reported personal problems with anger. The effectiveness of a relaxation program and cognitive modification program was assessed using self-reports of anger on the STAS and the Anger Inventory (Novaco, 1975), reports of situation-specific anger, an anger log (average daily ratings), and pulse rates following visualization of an anger-producing scene. Coping, anxiety, and depression were also assessed.

The relaxation-based program used anger-arousing situations (instead of anxiety-producing ones), but followed the anxiety management program of Suinn (1977). Trained skills included progressive relaxation, coping without tension, relaxation imagery, and deep-breathing-cued relaxation. After training these skills, subjects were taught to apply them to imaginary anger-arousing situations, as well as anger-producing situations that they actually experienced outside of the sessions.

The cognitive program consisted of stress inoculation and rational restructuring. Initially, treatment focused on identifying cognitions associated with anger and with more adaptive coping. Later, specific anger-producing situations were created, and clients practiced anger control. Over time, clients were encouraged to apply cognitive coping to increasingly angering situations.

Both the relaxation and the cognitive programs produced significant anger reduction on self-reports and daily logs. Indeed, with few exceptions, treatment produced desired changes across the dependent measures. There were only minor initial differences in the effects of the two programs (slightly in favor of the cognitive program), and a 4-week follow-up indicated the compatibility of the gains produced by the two different programs. Another advantage for the cognitive training group was seen in the reduction of anxiety scores over those produced via relaxation—a somewhat surprising finding,

1. Though the treated subjects were not clinical cases, the authors documented (p. 223) that they did have meaningful problems associated with anger control.

given that relaxation is typically viewed as a more direct treatment of certain anxieties. Nevertheless, the bottom line is that the programs were effective and that, in clinical practice, some combination of these procedures may prove maximally efficacious. Future research could address this issue.

Adolescents with disruptive behavior problems were given an anger control training program in 10 biweekly 50-minute sessions (Feindler, Marriott, & Iwata, 1984). Modest support for the program was provided, with some reduction in the frequency of daily fines resulting from disruptive behavior. Changes in other measures were nonsignificant. The authors reported that on the Self-Control Rating Scale (SCRS), the change in the treatment group was "significant . . . indicating an increase in self-control subjects [*sic*]" (p. 308). Unfortunately, when the means on the SCRS are checked (see Feindler *et al.*, 1984, Table 3), the increased scores actually reflect an increase in treated children's *deficits* in self-control. In essence, then, the data suggest an effect opposite to the predicted and intended one.

Bulimia

A cognitive–behavioral conceptualization guided the treatment approach used in an evaluation of the length of intervention with bulimic patients (Ordman & Kirschenbaum, 1985). Full treatment lasted an average of 15.3 weeks and consisted of 1- to 2-hour sessions; brief intervention consisted of three interactions for purposes of screening and assessment. Bulimia was viewed as a type of obsessive–compulsive dysfunction, including preoccupation with food, irrational concern about body weight and fat, and the ritualistic nature of binge–purge behavior. Accordingly, the intervention involved cognitive restructuring, exposure with response prevention, behavioral contracting, and process-oriented psychotherapy. Therapists helped clients identify unrealistic and self-defeating cognitions and assumptions regarding eating; assisted clients through exposure sessions with response prevention; and required self-monitoring of bingeing–vomiting and level of discomfort after every eating episode. There was also a special effort to establish rapport with and be supportive of the clients, and a willingness to discuss conflictual relationships and other associated difficulties.

The authors reported that there seemed to be merit in viewing bulimia as an obsessive–compulsive disorder, since the interventions so designed were found to be quite successful. For instance, the clients receiving the full cognitive–behavioral intervention evidenced a reduced frequency of binging–vomiting, as well as decreases in depression and improvements in general psychological adjustment. In actual eating situations, treated cases showed a reduction in urges to vomit and levels of discomfort.

A cognitive–behavioral group treatment for bulimia was compared to a nondirective group treatment (Kirkley, Schneider, Agras, & Bachman, 1985). In the cognitive–behavioral program, but not the nondirective treatment, groups were instructed to eat regularly (three daily meals), decrease vomiting, increase food variety, decrease eating rate, eat only when sitting at table and using utensils, modify any vomiting rituals, eat "forbidden" foods in nonbinge settings, and use relaxation tapes. Self-monitored food records, several self-report scales, and ratings of treatment credibility were analyzed. The reported findings suggested that the cognitive–behavioral approach, focusing on specific behavior changes, resulted in superior improvements to those achieved with the nondirective approach. Both treatments produced significant improvements on the self-report measures (e.g., depression, anxiety), but only the cognitive–behavioral treatment resulted in significant greater reductions in binge eating and vomiting. While the study is hampered by self-report data as the criterion, as in much bulimia research at present, the cognitive–behavioral group also produced fewer dropouts—a favorable outcome that is a bit surprising, given that both groups enjoyed high (and similar) ratings of credibility.

COGNITIVE–BEHAVIORAL PROCEDURES WITH CHILDREN

Some striking, if not surprising, consistency has emerged in the analyses of the cognitive–behavioral literature on procedures with children. Comments offering conclusions, cautions, and future directions were remarkably similar across the first three papers of the 1985 special issue of the *Journal of Abnormal Child Psychology*. For instance, each of these papers (i.e., Craighead, Meyers, & Wilcoxon-Craighead, 1985; Kendall, 1985b; Reeve & Brown, 1985) suggested that there is evidence to document that cognitive–behavioral treatments have produced desirable gains (see also Hollon & Beck, 1986). Craighead *et al.* stated, "Clinical interventions derived from the cognitive–behavioral model have been demonstrated to be effective with children" (1985, p. 334). Reeve and Brown observed, "Metacognitive training, in the form of teaching general problem solving principles, has been particularly successful in facilitating the intellectual performance of children with learning problems" (1985, p. 343). Finally, I commented that "the outcomes of cognitive–behavioral interventions have potential" (1985b, p. 358). In addition to this level of agreement on the effectiveness of the programs, there were equally consistent suggestions for how to reach the as-yet-unachieved full potential of the cognitive–behavioral integration and its resultant interventions.

The role of "involvement" was a consistent concern in these papers. For instance, I (Kendall, 1985b) pointed out that data on the frequency of occurrence of in-therapy events that were classified as "involvement" produced strong relationships with independent data on the successful outcome of the treatment (Braswell, Kendall, Braith, Carey, & Vye, 1985). As noted by Reeve and Brown (1985), Brown and Palinscar (in press) have found that reciprocal training is superior to direct instruction. In their work, poor learners in junior high school were given small-group training. In the reciprocal teaching experience, students and teachers took turns "being the teacher." Reeve and Brown (1985) reported that the intervention resulted in dramatic improvement in laboratory and classroom tests of comprehension, as well as on standardized tests in a follow-up study. Use of a "taking turns" procedure no doubt increases a child's involvement in the educational activity, and it would be of interest to learn whether involvement mediates the beneficial gains. It should be noted that a directed-discovery approach to teaching children self-instructions was found superior to a direct approach in work by Meyers and colleagues (see Meyers & Cohen, 1984).

Hyperactivity/Attention Deficit Disorder

Seeking to determine whether cognitive training is a useful adjunct to the treatment of hyperactive children with stimulant medication, Abikoff and Gittelman (1985) evaluated the outcome of a 16-week cognitive training program. According to the authors, the cognitive training program employed self-instructional procedures and cognitive modeling strategies to teach reflective problem solving. The first half of the treatment took place twice weekly, with 1-hour sessions employing psychoeducational tasks. To foster the verbal control of behavior, sessions used "say it before you do it" exercises and reminder cards. The second half of the program sought to instill social problem-solving skills. Children were exposed to hypothetical problems and asked to identify interpersonal problems, to generate solutions, and to evaluate the likely consequences. Children also had to suggest means of implementing the alternatives and ways to follow through with the chosen solution.

Despite the 16-week treatment and the inclusion of social problem-solving curricula, the reported outcomes were decidedly nonsupportive. That is, there were no significant treatment effects on academic, behavioral, or cognitive measures. Given the design of the study, in which medicated hyperactive children received either cognitive training, attention control, or no training, and with the inclusion of a subsequent division of the cognitive training group into two subgroups receiving continued medication or placebo, it was possible to address several questions. For instance, did the cognitive training facilitate withdrawal of stimulant treatment? Did the cognitive training enhance the maintenance effects of academic performance following medication? The authors reported that there were no beneficial effects from the cognitive training.

These findings are surprising, but they become understandable after a detailed evaluation. Possible explanations for the lack of additive effects of cognitive training in this study include (1) differences in the subsamples studied (subject characteristics), (2) variations in the treatment provided (therapy characteristics), (3) differences in the features of the therapists who conducted the intervention, and (4) the possibility that cognitive training as described does in fact not help the treatment of hyperactive children.

Characteristics of the sample may help us understand the reported findings. In the area of social problem solving, major differences have been found across studies with different samples of subjects. Socioeconomic status, for instance, has been found to influence the ability of measures of interpersonal problem solving to predict adjustment (Gesten *et al.*, 1982; Kendall & Fischler, 1984; McKim, Weissberg, Cowen, Gerten, & Rupkin, 1982; Spivack & Shure, 1974). Middle-class subjects generally evidence variability in social problem-solving responses, but the quantity of solutions offered does not always predict adjustment as well as the quality of the responses (e.g., Fischler & Kendall, 1987). In general inappropriate responses are usually associated with maladjustment. Some responses were rated as aggressive among Fischler and Kendall's middle-class cases, but this finding is in contrast to those for the lower-socioeconomic-status sample of inner-city children, who typically show more aggressive responses to interpersonal problems. Given that some of the positive findings for the efficacy of cognitive–behavioral training have employed middle-class samples only, moderator effects due to social class may require further attention.

Variations in the treatment provided may also help us understand the variations in outcomes observed by different reseachers. Judging from the written report provided by Abikoff and Gittelman (1985), the intervention included many of the training materials that have been used by researchers who have reported positive findings. The length of the treatment was consistent with that reported by others, and the use of some individual sessions and some group sessions should not necessarily be considered a feature that would reduce program effectiveness. However, there were some features of the treatment that were less than optimal. First and foremost was the lack of inclusion of systematic behavioral contingencies within the training. Cognitive training and cognitive–behavioral training are two different treatments. To my mind, "going cognitive" is not a step in the right direction unless one maintains the demonstrated effective qualities of behavioral interventions (Kendall & Hollon, 1979). The cognitive features of the intervention are best learned when in the context of a behavioral program. Although Abikoff and Gittelman reported that children were given 25 points that could be traded for toys and games, the rewards were "noncontingent . . . ostensibly dispensed for working hard and trying your best" (p. 954). The failure to tie successful use of the cognitive strategies with the earning (not dispensing) of rewards may prove to be a serious obstacle to drawing any conclusions from the study.

The treatment may have been less than optimal for other reasons. For instance, at the heart of the cognitive–behavioral effort is the desire to increase generalization of gains. One does not accomplish such gains by keeping one's fingers crossed, but rather strives for generalization via its inclusion in the training program. Abikoff and Gittelman's anecdote about the lack of generalization seen in an interaction between children and a cab driver illustrates what could have been done. That is, rather than seeing the situation as a lack of generalization, they could have viewed the situation as a context for treatment and included role-play training sessions that indeed focused on the proper strategies for handling the problematic social interaction. In this manner, generalization could have been directly trained (see Kendall & Reber, 1987).

Variations in the therapists may also have been related to variations in the efficacy of the treatment. This is not to suggest that the therapists were of poor quality, but that variations in the degree of high-quality training that was provided may have interfered with maximal gains. In one study of the process of therapeutic change and outcome from cognitive–behavioral therapy with impulsive children, Braswell *et al.* (1985) reported that "involvement" was a strong predictor of treatment success. Unfortunately, it is not possible to evaluate the involvement process in the Abikoff and Gittelman study, based on their report. Nevertheless, it may have been the case that there was a low degree of "involvement" on the part of the children in the study, and that this moderating factor undermined the eventual outcomes.

Yet another possibility is, of course, that the cognitive training as described does not offer the needed intervention for hyperactive children. This issue deserves attention. To the extent that the training was solely cognitive, then it may indeed suggest that cognitive training is lacking in potency. To the degree that the training did not reflect cognitive–behavioral procedures, then the report is not an indictment of cognitive–behavioral procedures. Since there has been some discussion of the relative efficacy of the various components of cognitive–behavioral training, with special mention of the importance of the behavioral procedures, it is possible that differences in the defining features of the treatment are responsible for treatment outcome. One must, however, entertain the possibility that cognitive training simply is not what is needed. This type of conclusion could have been reached in the present case if something else had been found to be an effective adjunct treatment. One must be cautious, however, since the absence of significant findings means that the null hypothesis was confirmed; such a confirmation, as we all know, cannot be given the weight of a confirmation of the experimental hypothesis. By the way, this is not to say that only supportive findings can be published. Rather, if one intervention is not as good an another, then the significant differences will provide such evidence and the lesser intervention must be considered less efficacious. It is when differences are nonsignificant and could be due to chance that caution must be exercised.

On the flip side of the "Medications work; what can be added?" stance is the position that medications produce unwanted psychological side effects. Research on the treatment of hyperactivity has resulted in some interesting analyses of the detrimental effects of the use of stimulant medication. For example, Rosen, O'Leary, and Conway (1985) reported on a case analysis of procedures used to overcome the detrimental attributions associated with stimulant medication. Tom, a 9-year-old boy who performed well in class when on medications but was rated as very hyperactive when off drugs, was given an opportunity to demonstrate improvement in a behavioral training program in the classroom. As part of the assessment and modification of the attributional processes associated with the medications, the researchers provided Tom with a placebo tablet during a time when he was not taking medications and when his behavior was somewhat troublesome. Recording some of his attributions while taking the placebo was informative. For example, the authors noted that Tom would say, "You see, the pill helps me," or "I need it to do my work." Rosen *et al.* proceeded to withdraw the child from placebo while simultaneously attempting to modify his attributions, in order to avoid the detrimental effects of stopping the taking of the pill. Training involved getting the child to have such self-statements as "I finished and I did it on my own," and having the teacher instruct and encourage the child to be responsible for his own actions.

The authors noted that the results of this case suggest that the child's behavior was in part being controlled by factors other than the medication's psychological components. The authors noted that placebo and a typically ineffective dose of the medication were associated with good classroom performance, which deteriorated when the pills were not administered—even though the pills should not themselves have been effective. Their hypothesis, confirmed by their data, was that the attributions were causally related to the classroom behavior. Indeed, the positive effects of the attributional training were found to persist through the beginning of the next school year. The authors have stated that there may be some reasons for qualifying their findings, but the degree to which attributions play a significant role in controlling behavior cannot be discounted. It is important that attributional training, in which children are taught to make internal explanations of their own efforts and the benefits of their efforts in controlling their behavior, be a part of treatment regimens.

In earlier volumes of this series, I have noted the distinction between concrete (task-specific) and conceptual (general) self-instructions. In a project with two children (aged 9 and 10) who had attention deficit disorder with hyperactivity, Guevremont, Tishelman, and Hull (1985) reported successful application of a self-instructional program that focused on each child's specific behavioral problems and used both concrete and conceptual training. The program involved several features: seven or eight 50-minute sessions with each child and mother; self-instructions; response-cost programs; and home practice (30 minutes a day, 4 days a week). The program produced improvements in daily classwork and in mothers' and teachers' ratings of improved self-control. This paper not only presents evidence that endorses such an intervention with 9- or 10-year-olds; it also highlights two advances—systematic use of the mother, and tailoring the self-instructions to individual problems. While this second feature is sought in other programs (e.g., Kendall & Braswell, 1985), Guevremont *et al.* have provided a special operationalization of how to involve parents that deserves continued application and evaluation.

Anger

Lochman and colleagues have conducted a series of studies designed to evaluate an anger control program for children. In a 2 × 2 factorial design, Lochman, Burch, Curry, and Lampron (1984) examined the efficacy of an anger control intervention for aggressive boys. Anger coping, goal setting, anger coping plus goal setting, and no treatment were compared. The anger-coping groups met weekly for 12 sessions that focused on social problem solving. Goal setting involved 8 weeks in which weekly goals were monitored by classroom teachers, who provided contingent rewards for goal attainment. The authors reported that the children in the anger-coping intervention groups displayed significant reductions in disruptive and aggressive off-task behaviors at follow-up, but that there were nonsignificant changes in passive off-task behaviors. Goal setting was seen as having augmented treatment effects in the classroom; this result, as in other work, documents the benefits of both combining cognitive and behavioral procedures and using these treatment components in the applied setting. However, there were limitations to the breadth of effects reported; for example, there were no meaningful changes in peers' perceptions of the treated boys.

In a separate paper, Lochman, Lampron, Burch, and Curry (1985) reported that greater reductions in rates of disruptive and aggressive off-task classroom behavior were predicted by higher initial rates of these behaviors, and that greater reductions in parents' ratings of aggression were predicted by initially low problem-solving skills. Boys in a no-treatment group who improved over time were initially the best problem solvers and had higher levels of self-esteem. Putting a regression or change explanation aside, Lochman *et al.* (1985) concluded that client characteristics do seem to be related to improvements following cognitive–behavioral treatment, and that the treatments seem to be most effective for those children with the greatest deficits—those most in need of the program.

It has also been reported (Lochman, 1985) that a longer (18-session) cognitive–behavioral program for aggressive boys produced greater improvement in on-task classroom behavior and reductions in passive off-task behaviors than a shorter (12-session) program. One must keep in mind, as Lochman noted, that the study was quasi-experimental and involved separate, though comparable, aspects of the different treatment programs.

Lochman and Curry (1986) compared two cognitive–behavioral interventions for aggressive children. In one, an anger-coping intervention, children received 18 sessions in which an operant reward system was operative and in which they worked toward inhibiting impulsive behavior, learning social problem-solving skills, making plans, and making a videotape of their problem solving. In the second intervention, the anger-coping program was preceded by the first six sessions of a self-instructional program described elsewhere (Kendall, Padawer, Zupan, & Braswell, 1985). The anger-coping interventions produced significantly greater reductions in disruptive and aggressive off-task behavior, with the addition of self-instructions tending to produce greater reductions in passive off-task classroom behavior. Both treatments produced reduction in parents' ratings of aggression and in the children's self-reported self-esteem.

The use of multiple measures is a strength of the Lochman and Curry (1986) report, and the findings that both treatments led to gains in parent ratings, self-reports, and some observed behaviors lend support to the efficacy of the treatments. However, the absence of a no-treatment control restricts one's ability to draw more definitive conclusions regarding the agents responsible for observed gains. The limited additive effect of the self-instructional component does not surprise me. That is, for an aggressive sample, the self-instructional part of a cognitive–behavioral program is only the beginning of treatment. Later sessions focus on problem solving, role plays, and basically the ingredients in what Lochman and colleagues refer to as "anger coping." The potent program contains contingencies, a problem-solving focus, concern with self-talk, and role playing for practice. The additive efficacy of the self-instructional feature may be selective, seen primarily in those cases where aggressive responding is impulsive.

A "cognitive control therapy" program has been described by Santostefano and colleagues (e.g., Santostefano, 1984; Santostefano & Rieder, 1984). The program focuses on restructuring the cognitive–affective balance; this balance has to do with the coordination of information from feelings and from thoughts and fantasies. According to Santostefano, deviant children have a control orientation that is not balanced. The treatment concerns a series of graded tasks designed to restructure the cognitive controls that are said to be deficient. The tasks, quite rationally, go from simple to complex, from neutral to emotional, from physically active to cognitively active, and toward increasing delay in responding. Perspective-taking tasks are employed, as are nonverbal reactions for handling resistance. The interested reader is referred to Santostefano's (1986) practitioner guidebook.

This program has many interesting features and several resemblances to cognitive–behavioral programs. Santostefano's integration, however, is more cognitive–psychoanalytic than cognitive–behavioral; accordingly, there are areas where increased methodological rigor would be beneficial. For instance, there is a need for the use of control groups in treatment evaluation and greater concern with the specificity of the treatment for distinct types of childhood disorders. Nevertheless, there are meritorious ideas and intervention strategies in Santostefano's writing, and more prescriptive efforts (e.g., detailing how treatments need to be modified for different types of child disorders) will no doubt contribute to maximal therapeutic gains.

The road to behavioral change via cognitive programs is not limited to the more or less standard fare. To illustrate, consider Arbuthnot and Gordon's (1986) use of a training program in moral reasoning. Juveniles at risk for delinquency received a cognitive based moral-reasoning development program that involved 16 to 20 sessions lasting 45 minutes each. The teenage clients and their nondisturbed control comparisons were assigned to the treatment or the control condition (no treatment) by means of a randomized block procedure blocking on initial social adjustment scores.

The treatment program involved group discussions, with group size varying from five to eight pupils. Initial sessions were for building rapport, demonstrating warmth, and being humorous and directive. The bulk of the treatment concerned guided discussions of moral dilemmas. Group leaders tried to work toward gradually higher levels of moral reasoning. Role plays were used, with group participants having an opportunity to participate in different roles and to discuss related moral obligations. Leaders asked probing questions to examine role obligations and conflicts of loyalty and the law. Role reversals were employed to facilitate perspective taking.

Both cognitive and behavioral improvements were evident from the training program's effects on several dependent measures. The clients' maturity of social–moral reasoning was improved, and various indices, such as court/police contacts, teacher ratings, and behavior problem referrals, evidenced desired gains. The authors were also quick to note that moral-reasoning change scores were associated with all of the change scores on outcome measures, and to suggest that behavior change "can be effected through development of the underlying structural bases of decisions" (p. 213). The absence of an attention control group, as the authors themselves stated, leaves open the possibility that the adolescents improved because of the attention given them (as compared to the controls) instead of or in addition to the actual training in moral reasoning. Nevertheless, the positive changes produced with a group of youths typically viewed as nonresponsive to treatment suggest that this cognitively based approach merits additional research attention.

Educational Applications

The application of cognitive–behavioral procedures to education has made substantial gains in recent times. There have been increased applications, innovative modifications, and some improved research evaluations. Haywood, Brooks, and Burns (in press), for instance, describe a cognitive curriculum for young children that is designed to address specific thinking processes and teach children how to think effectively. This curriculum is for 3- to 6-year-olds and strives to enhance basic cognitive skills, to remediate deficiencies, to improve motivation, and generally to enhance learning readiness. Haywood *et al.* are preparing children to think and to benefit maximally from education. Feuerstein's instrumental enrichment for activating intellectual potential in learning-disabled children is another illustration of how cognitive influences are active within educational environments (cf. Messerer, Hunt, Meyers, & Lerner, 1984), though research evaluation of it is surely needed.

The effects of a cognitive–behavioral program (e.g., self-instructions, tokens, modeling) on the academic performance of emotionally disturbed children have been reported Swanson (1985). The program integrated both general strategies and task-specific components to teach the children to pay attention. A multiple-baseline design was used in two separate studies. In terms of percentage of correct responses, the program favorably improved academic performance. Treatment maintenance occurred across settings and responses.

Self-instruction, relaxation, and a no-treatment condition with learning-disabled children were compared by Zieffle and Romney (1985), using cognitive tasks requiring deliberation and concentration. Only the two treatment groups showed significant overall improvement on dependent measures such as the Porteus Mazes, the Matching Familiar Figures Test, and the Coding and Digit Span subtests of the Wechsler Intelligence Scale for Children. However, cautious conclusions are required, given the potential of general "nonspecific" treatment effects to explain the findings.

Cognitive self-control procedures were applied to 12-year-old learning-disabled children in an effort to improve academic performance (Brown & Alford, 1984). Children were assigned randomly to training or control groups, and those receiving training received two 1-hour sessions per week over 2 months for a total of 16 sessions. On several dependent measures that could reflect gains, treated children indeed showed improvements. For instance, there were significant gains in the Reading subtest of the Wide Range Achievement Test. Caution must again be exercised, however, as there was no control for the role of nonspecific, attentional factors as a rival hypothesis to that of the effectiveness of the treatment. In general, evaluations of cognitive–behavioral strategies in education would benefit from added control groups that allow for clear conclusions.

Concern about the age of children treated with self-instructions remains an issue. The point has been made several times over the years (e.g., Kendall, 1977; Braswell & Kendall, 1987), and additional related data have appeared. Billings and Wasik (1985) in an effort to replicate the results of Bornstein and Quevillon (1976), taught self-instruction to boys 4 years of age. Given the lack of supportive data, Billings and Wasik correctly concluded that something other than the treatment alone may have been responsible for the Bornstein and Quevillon outcomes. Therapist quality and teacher attention are two candidates for the active features of the successful program. As I see it, however, age of the subjects is a more compelling concern. In general, 4-year-olds may simply be developmentally unprepared for training involving self-guiding internal mediation. Some 4-year-olds may be more developed than others, and an individual-difference factor, such as the cognitive levels of the target children, may help to explain differential treatment outcomes.

ATTRIBUTIONS

Among the major influences on the cognitive–behavioral approach to research and therapy have been the analyses of individuals' characteristic explanations for the causes of their behavior or attributions. These studies have had both an initial and a continuing impact. Research on attributional processes has already been welcomed into the clincial arena, and there is presently added evidence of a wider series of investigations. Data attest to attributional differences among groups of disturbed and nondisturbed pesons, to attributional biases associated with specific psychopathologies, and to moderator effects of attributional styles on the effects of some forms of therapeutic intervention.

Working with distressed and nondistressed couples, Jacobson, McDonald, Follette, and Berley (1985) examined partners' attributions for positive and negative behavior. Subjects were involved in a role play where they acted either positive or negative, and each partner was asked to explain the other partner's behavior on a questionnaire of internal and external causal attributions. Jacobson *et al.* documented that members of distressed couples were particularly likely to make internal attributions for their partners' negative behavior. In contrast, members of nondistressed couples were particularly likely to make internal attributions for their partners' positive behaviors. Such attributional patterns may contribute to maintenance of dissatisfaction among distressed couples and require attention in programs designed to improve marital/couples relationships (see also Fincham, 1985).

Attributional analyses have been applied to assertion. Alden (1984) found that assertive subjects attributed positive outcomes more internally than negative outcomes, and that nonassertive subjects responded similarly to positive and negative feedback. Nonassertive subjects attributed both outcomes to more stable factors than did the assertive subjects. The differences were greater in the positive-feedback condition, where self-attributions for positive outcomes were seen in the assertive subjects.

Following success and failure in several situations (social, athletic, academic), children high in self-esteem were more likely than children low in self-esteem to attribute their success to "ability" and their failures to "lack of effort" or "bad luck" (Fielstein *et al.*, 1985). The low-self-esteem children attributed their success more to "good luck" and their failures more to "lack of ability" than did the high-self-esteem children. The most pronounced differences were seen in the social domain, the least in the academic domain. Thus, as the authors noted, the low-self-esteem children (more than the high-self-esteem children) attributed their success to unstable factors (e.g., luck) and their failures to more stable factors (e.g., lack of ability). In contrast, success was attributed to ability and failure to unstable factors by the high-self-esteem children. Given the relationship between self-esteem and depression, it should not be surprising to note the consistency between the present attributional differences and those reported between depressed and nondepressed children.

How can one best characterize healthy attributions for negative events? It has been suggested that external, unstable, and specific attributions for negative events would be adaptive, and O'Hara, French, Zekowski, Neunaber, and Schroeder (1985) reported data to support this notion. Subjects made attributions for hypothetical events under instructional sets that were either neutral or adaptive (i.e., subjects were told to "think about causes that would make you feel good about yourself"). Subjects' ratings and coders' ratings of the attributions were relatively consistent; thus, adaptive attributions for negative events do seem to be external, unstable, and specific. Also, subjects responded to the "adaptive" instructions as predicted. These data suggest that there is general knowledge of how to attribute unsuccessful behavior in order to reduce maladaptation, but that it may not always be employed. To what extent can already distressed/disordered persons be responsive to "adaptive" instructions? It would be interesting to learn whether disordered persons lack the knowledge of adaptive attributional patterns or fail to use adaptive attributions.

It is likely that the majority of readers either have heard Don Meichenbaum speak about cognitive-behavior modification or have read the opening of his book on stress inoculation (Meichenbaum, 1985). It is also likely, therefore, that readers have heard or read his delightful story about his watching the children at home when a series of unwanted events led to increasing confusion and annoyance. To summarize briefly, Don describes his plans to watch a special program on television and his efforts to complete some child care chores (e.g., bathing a son) to insure being able to view the program from its beginning. As one thing and then another served to interrupt his plans, he reports feeling a sense of being overwhelmed, and it is at this point in the story that he asks, "Why isn't there more child abuse?"

Don is not an abusive parent (quite the contrary is true), but his story does illustrate that even a relatively even-tempered adult can be pushed to such thoughts (but not actions). What factors are involved in such a dilemma? Some initial answers seem to be emerging (see Azar & Twentyman, 1986). For instance, Bauer and Twentyman (1985) studied the reactions and responses of abusing, neglectful, and comparison mothers to a number of aversive stimuli. Both child-related and non-child-related stressful circumstances were employed. Abusing mothers were found to be more annoyed across both the social and nonsocial stressors. Abusing mothers consistently attributed more malevolent intentionality to their children. The authors have also suggested that abusive parents evidence a pattern of hyperresponsivity to stress: All mothers were relatively less annoyed when the situation involved a hurt child, but less obvious contexts, such as a misbehavior in the presence of others, produced added annoyance for the abusive mothers. A striking and important finding was that abusing mothers were most likely to view the child as acting intentionally to annoy them.

There is a parallel between these data from abusing parents and the data from aggressive children (see Dodge, 1985). Evidence presented by Dodge also suggests that aggressive behaviors displayed by children are in part associated with misperceptions of others in terms of their intent to harm. Accidents are viewed as provocations. With such similarities in mind, it seems reasonable to suggest that an essential treatment ingredient for these groups would be some version of a cognitive–behavioral program in which the therapist makes an effort to change the clients' perceptions of intentionality. Role-play exercises, in which clients play each of several roles to gain perspective-taking skills, and a direct focus on the attributional process may well combine to be especially helpful in reducing the unwanted effects of misperception of intentionality.

RESISTANCE

Wachtel (1982a) has presented an edited volume on resistance. As in other volumes, such as *Failures in Behavior Therapy* (Foa & Emmelkamp, 1983), the contributors to the *Resistance* volume draw readers' attention to the simple fact that therapy, as all practicing clinicians know, does not always proceed smoothly and without glitches. Although the concept seems to have originated within the psychoanalytic schools, therapists of various theoretical persuasions are nevertheless having to confront the problem of resistance, whether it is called "resistance," "noncompliance," or any other term (see also Chapter 8 of this volume).

Ellis (1985) has written a book on overcoming resistance from the rational—emotive standpoint. He provides a lengthy section on the potential sources of resistance, and he recognizes that part of the client's resistance may be due to the therapist. Despite the diversity of his described sources of resistance, there is still the common theme that it is all a spinoff from irrational thinking. For instance, in the section on environmental factors in resistance, several sources are noted (see also Golden, 1983); again, however, the individual's personal interpretation of the environment in irrational terms is seen as primary: "I must not change myself too drastically, even when I want to do so, in case others do not approve of me with my new thoughts, feelings and behaviors" (Ellis, 1985, p. 29).

Consistent with Ellis's earlier works, he recommends that the treatment for resistance be the disputation of the irrational beliefs associated with resistance: "RET's primary cognitive technique of combating resistance, therefore, consists of showing clients that they do not 'just' resist and that they do not merely resist *because* they find it difficult to change, but that they *choose* to subscribe to a philosophy of LFT [low frustration tolerance] and/or self-deprecation which, in turn, largely 'causes' their resistance" (p. 35; italics in original).

Ellis's position on resistance reflects his consideration of various efforts at behavioral change. He speaks of trying to sell the challenge and adventure of self-change, as well as of the benefits of proselytizing others. He describes the use of humorous songs to combat irrationality, and suggests that when the songs are well learned they are internalized and hence can come to govern behavior. Emotive, behavioral, and cognitive strategies are described by Ellis, as is the potential for the therapist to be contributing to the client's resistance. In the end, as throughout, the underlying difficulty leading to resistance is the philosophical adherence on the part of the client to an irrational belief about self-change.

Although Ellis remains a radical adherent of the need for disputational strategies in therapy, he does have a behavioral side (though this is less obvious). Indeed, he often has clients do things to experience their effects. In the now-classic film depicting three approaches to the treatment of Gloria, Ellis spoke repeatedly of the merits of practice, as noted earlier. In fact, students who have watched the film have often described Ellis as being behavioral and pragmatic because of this use of homework assignments and his recommendations for practice (as well as describing him as a bit too verbal and confrontive). This behavioral side is not clearly visible in Ellis's new book, though he does see merits in performance-based strategies as they get a person to act differently. He writes of reinforcements for clients who follow the therapist's assignments, and of stiff penalties for not doing the tasks—for instance, burning $20.00 for failure to comply with an assignment.

One cannot read one of Ellis's works without recognizing the strength of his adherence to his system. The present work on resistance is no exception, as the entire treatise fosters a further reliance on the principles of rational–emotive therapy as the solution to maladaptive behavioral problems through modification of irrational beliefs. To be fair, Ellis covers a wide range of topics and pays proper respect to the cognitive, behavioral, and emotive features of the helping process. Nevertheless, the variety of strategies discussed (and used to create headings in the various chapters of the book) do not truly reflect a multiplicity of perspectives. Rather Ellis's integration involves an acceptance of such behavioral procedures as role plays and reinforcement, but seemingly only when the role play or reinforcement experience is used to dispute an irrational view of the world or irrational self-demand.

PERSONAL CONSTRUCTS

Many who enjoy tracking the history of psychology take pleasure, when scanning a new publication, in being able to refer to an older citation that made a similar point years earlier. Such efforts do not always result in a reference to Freud, James, Pavlov, or the like, nor can one reliably cite ancient Greek philosophers. Historical accuracy is not served by vacuous reference to the ancients.

When we refer to the early theoreticians within the cognitive and cognitive–behavioral frameworks, we are typically speaking about Beck and Ellis. To be sure, there were and are others, but this pair has received the widest attention. It may be more accurate, I propose, to create a cognitive–behavioral triumvirate by adding George Kelly to the list. Indeed, Kelly's classic works on personal construct theory have had an impact on key writers in the field (see Mischel, 1980), have influenced current cognitive–behavioral psychotherapies, and contain rich insights awaiting further methodological amplification and evaluation (see Kelly, 1955). A number of recent writers have begun to address personal constructs (e.g., Bannister & Fransella, 1986; Beail, 1985; Button, 1985), and some have done so with a specific focus on the cognitive–behavioral therapies (e.g., Neimeyer, 1985).

Neimeyer (1985) has noted that the integration of Kelly's work into cognitive–behavioral therapy is incomplete. He points out that of the writers who mention Kelly, most mention the repertory grid technique and fixed-role therapy, but he notes further that there is a massive literature, with an international basis, that appears to go relatively unnoticed. Kelly's work is significant, and advances in related research are significant as well. Do Kelly's work and the related research fit within cognitive–behavioral therapy? What has been written on this point in recent years is quite interesting.

Bannister and Fransella (1986), in the third edition of their *Inquiring Man: The Psychology of Personal Constructs*, provide remarks that are at one point troublesome and at others quite reasonable. Perhaps the most troublesome stance taken by Bannister and Fransella concerns their view of the relationship of Kelly's perspective to cognitive–behavioral therapy. To aovid unwanted inaccuracy, I quote from the authors:

> Personal construct therapy is often classed as a cognitive therapy. But it is not. It differs from the approaches of Beck (1976), Ellis and rational emotive therapy (Ellis & Grieger, 1977), or Meichenbaum (1977) by being based on an integrated, total psychological theory about the whole person and by giving primacy to neither cognitions nor emotions nor behaviours—there cannot be one without the others. In personal construct theory there is no dualism, no dividing up of the person into "bits." (1986, p. 115)

These writers are, of course, entitled to their views. However, their perspective becomes troublesome when the details of the supposed differences are illuminated. For instance, Bannister and Fransella (1986) argue that a personal construct approach is one that does not try to change a client's constructs, but focuses on helping the client to test his or her own constructs. The resemblance of this focus to the strategy of collaborative empiricism, person-as-scientist, and hypothesis testing put forth by the bulk of contemporary cognitive–behavioral therapists leads one to question how personal construct therapy would be unique. Similarly, Bannister and Fransella state that the client and therapist are partners in the therapeutic enterprise. Again, this closely resembles the collaborative empiricism described by Beck and colleagues (e.g., Hollon & Beck, 1978). Both the theory of personal constructs and the intervention style associated with the theory play an important role, albeit sometimes behind the scenes, in cognitive–behavioral therapy. However, the differences suggested by Bannister and Fransella are not differentially true for a personal construct approach and false for a cognitive–behavioral one. Apparently, the systems are more similar than some of the personal construct writers seem to see it.

Neimeyer (1985) has written of a gentle irony in his chapter on personal constructs in *Advances in Cognitive–Behavioral Research and Therapy*, Volume 4 (1985). The irony he refers to is Kelly's wish not to be viewed as a cognitive theorist. Neimeyer (1985) goes on to add that "despite Kelly's reservations, substantial commonalities have developed between his thinking and that of other cognitive–clincial theorists" (p. 321). One area where there seems to be agreement among cognitive theorists and therapists is the adoption of Kelly's "person-as-scientist" model. Neimeyer notes this, but goes on to add that while the scientific enterprise did much to bring differing views together, it also, through distinct interpretative emphases, distinguished the positions as well. Kelly, less interested in modifying irrationality or illogical thinking, was more interested in understanding the client's personal idiosyncratic construct network.

One area where the various models seems to differ, according to Neimeyer (1985), is in the view of cognition and emotion. Ellis, and to a degree Beck, see faulty cognition as the causal core in emotional disturbance. Kelly considered his views as neither cognitive nor emotional, and he further preferred that the two concepts be viewed as one. While I do not want to put words into others' mouths, my experience suggests that the majority of cognitive–behavioral theorists and therapists view cognition and emotion (and behavior) as causally interrelated (see Beck *et al.*, 1979; Kendall & Bemis, 1983; Mahoney, 1977), but do not take a stance that any one of the three is uniformly primary.

A few words about the therapist's behavior are also in order. What are the behaviors that the personal construct therapist views as potent? It is my opinion that one of the similarities among the various cognitive–behavioral therapists is their active stance. This is true, too, of Kelly's therapy; he wrote of active strategies that would either tighten or loosen the client's constructions, or both. By way of contrast, Ellis's approach is more disputational, and Beck's is more focused on the modification of the distorted thinking. To quote Neimeyer (1985), "while Ellis may be seen as more attacking and disputational, and Beck as more directive and experimental, Kelly may be seen as more invitational and exploratory" (p. 328).

Earlier efforts to distinguish among the various cognitive–behavioral strategies have produced only moderate success (see Kendall & Kriss, 1983). That is, there have seemed to be more similarities than differences among the major cognitive–behavioral theorists. The present examination of personal construct materials suggests again (though not in great detail) that Kelly has many commonalities with others in the generic cognitive–behavioral school. True, there are fine-tuned distinctions, but the personal construct approach more closely resembles other cognitive–behavioral approaches than it does any of the other forms of psychological therapy. Thus, contemporary cognitive–behavioral therapy may share more with a Kellyian framework than is typically recognized. Indeed, several writers of the current stance of personal construct theory who seem to be seeking to make distinctions may actually be recognizing similarities. It may be hoped that others, as I have, will return to copies of the original Kelly and see what he had to say.

CHAPTER

5

BEHAVIORAL MEDICINE

JOHN P. FOREYT

INTRODUCTION

If the ever-increasing number and size of the latest books in behavioral medicine are indications of interest and activity, we are a healthy, rapidly growing field. Matarazzo and colleagues' latest tome, *Behavioral Health*, for example, has 95 chapters and runs 1,292 pages (Matarazzo, Weiss, Herd, Miller, & Weiss, 1984). Division 38 (Health Psychology) of the American Psychological Association (APA), and the Society of Behavioral Medicine (SBM), both have increased in membership. Division 38's journal, *Health Psychology*; SBM's two journals, *Behavioral Medicine Abstracts* and *Annals of Behavioral Medicine*; and the *Journal of Behavioral Medicine* update professionals on the latest research in the area. The federal government continues to show considerable interest in behavioral medicine. The National Heart, Lung and Blood Institute (NHLBI) of the National Institutes of Health (NIH) supports the Behavioral Medicine Branch under the direction of Dr. Steven M. Weiss. The National Cancer Institute (NCI) has a Health Promotion Sciences Branch, and the National Institute of Child Health and Human Development has a section on behavioral medicine. The Behavioral Medicine Study Section, a group that reviews grant applications from several NIH Institutes, is busier than ever. The field appears firmly established.

As in previous reviews, this chapter covers several topics of importance to behavioral medicine. The first one concerns the relationships of psychosocial variables to health and disease. The results of a recent study indicated the lack of such relationships for predicting survival or time of recurrence of cancer, and an accompanying editorial suggested that beliefs about relationships between psychosocial variables and disease state are based largely on "folklore." The issue is clearly a complex one, due in part to the difficulty in the assessment of these variables. The second topic reviews the findings and recommendations from a workshop on epidemiological methods for measuring psychosocial factors in cardiovascular diseases (CVD). The workshop illustrates the contributions that the field of psychosocial epidemiology is making in this area.

The third topic indicates the American Heart Association's (AHA's) increasing interest in the field. The AHA, a private organization, recently sponsored a conference on behavioral medicine and CVD, focusing on biobehavioral approaches to the development, treatment, and prevention of hypertension, coronary heart disease (CHD), and sudden cardiac death. Results and recommendations from this conference are summarized.

Fourth is the area of cardiovascular risk reduction. In Volume 10 of the *Annual Review*, Brownell (1985a) discussed the work being done with children. This year, cardiovascular risk reduction in adults is covered. An update on the multiple risk factor reduction programs and the progress they have made is provided.

Finally, the topic of behavioral medicine and minority groups is reviewed. Although blacks and Hispanic Americans make up the two largest minorities in the United States and suffer disproportionately from many diseases and disorders, there are relatively few intervention studies with these groups in progress. There is much more that can be done to help alleviate the health problems that currently afflict minorities in this country.

PSYCHOSOCIAL STATUS AND PHYSICAL HEALTH

A recent study by Cassileth, Lusk, Miller, Brown, and Miller (1985) in the *New England Journal of Medicine* investigated the role of social and psychological factors as predictors of longevity in cancer patients. In their study, 204 patients with unresectable cancers and 155 patients with melanoma or breast cancer were followed to determine their length of survival or time of relapse, respectively. All patients were given a self-report questionnaire assessing seven variables found to predict longevity or survival in previous studies: social ties and marital history, job satisfaction, use of psychotropic drugs, general life evaluation/satisfaction, subjective view of adult health, degree of hopelessness/helplessness, and perception of the amount of adjustment required to cope with the diagnosis.

A total of 154 of the 204 advanced cancer patients (75%) died during the 3½ years of the study. Their median survival was 7 months.

Of the 155 patients treated for melanoma or breast cancer, 41 (26%) had recurrences of the disease.

None of the analyses indicated any relationship between the psychosocial factors studied and either survival or the time to recurrence of the disease. The researchers concluded that the psychosocial factors studied were not useful clinical predictors of either the length of survival in newly diagnosed patients with advanced metastatic disease or the time of recurrence of disease in patients with high-risk primary melanoma or breast cancer. Cassileth *et al.* stated, "Our study of patients with advanced, high-risk malignant diseases suggests that the inherent biology of the disease alone determines the prognosis, overriding the potentially mitigating influence of psychosocial factors" (1985, p. 1555).

An accompanying editorial by Marcia Angell (1985), the *Journal's* deputy editor, entitled "Disease as a Reflection of the Psyche," questioned the whole belief in possible mind–body links to illnesses. She wrote, "The evidence for mental state as a cause and cure of today's scourges is not much better than it was for the afflictions of earlier centuries. . . . In short, the literature contains very few scientifically sound studies of the relation, if there is one, between mental state and disease" (Angell, 1985, p. 1571). She further stated, "It is time to acknowledge that our belief in disease as a direct reflection of mental state is largely folklore." (p. 1572).

Reaction to the Angell editorial by behavioral researchers was predictably swift. A letter to the *Journal's* editor by the past president, president, and president-elect of SBM, Redford B. Williams, Jr., Herbert Benson, and Michael J. Follick (1985), respectively, expressed concern about the editorial, commenting that although the Cassileth *et al.* study failed to predict outcome once cancer was established, results of the study did not rule out involvement of psychosocial factors in the initiation of disease. They also stated that Angell ignored the "voluminous *positive* evidence that psychosocial factors do predict adverse health outcome" (Williams *et al.*, 1985, p. 1357) in healthy persons and patients with CHD.

At the August 1985 meeting of the Council of Representatives of APA, a resolution from Division 38 was introduced concerning Angell's editorial. Both the Division and the Council viewed the editorial as "inaccurate," in light of a substantial body of laboratory and clinical research findings in behavioral medicine and health psychology. At the meeting, the Council voted to send a letter to the *Journal* from APA's president calling attention to the "editorial's inaccuracy"; it also voted that representatives from Division 38 work with APA's public information officer to prepare an appropriate press release stating APA's position (Abeles, 1986).

In reading both the Cassileth *et al.* paper and Angell's editorial, it is important to separate the conclusions of the two. Over half of the patients in the Cassileth *et al.* study suffered from advanced metastatic disease. In a sample of patients like this, the role of behavior as a possible modifier of the disease state is highly unlikely, and the authors' conclusion that "the inherent biology of the disease alone determines the prognosis" is reasonable. Few behavioral researchers would argue that psychosocial factors play a major role in determining length of survival in patients near death. The study did not investigate the role of psychosocial factors in the acquisition, progress, or outcome of disease in patients with other diseases or with more favorable diagnoses of cancer. Furthermore, the questionnaire used in the Cassileth *et al.* study was put together by the authors from a number of instruments developed and tested on other populations, rendering its reliability and validity on this sample suspect.

Angell's editorial has raised the broader question concerning the potential relationship between psychosocial factors and disease. There is a substantial body of literature investigating this relationship. Fox (1976, 1978, 1981, 1983), Levy (1983), and Cox and Mackay (1982), for example, reviewed both positive and negative findings in this area as related to cancer incidence. Vaillant (1979) reported a significant relationship between previous mental health and subsequent physical status in a 40-year prospective investigation of college men. Psychosocial factors predict poor health outcomes in healthy individuals (Barefoot, Dahlstrom, & Williams, 1983; Shekelle, Gale, Ostfeld, & Paul, 1983). There is a significant relation between individual temperament and health and disease (Betz & Thomas, 1979). Palmore (1969) concluded that the best predictors of longevity are work satisfaction and happiness.

There is also a strong negative effect of bereavement and grief on physical health and general well-being (Klerman & Izen, 1977). Divorced, single, and widowed individuals have higher mortality rates than married individuals (Kraus & Lilienfeld, 1959; Ortmeyer, 1974).

Social support is another important variable for predicting morbidity and mortality. Ruberman, Weinblatt, Goldberg, and Chaudhary (1984) found that socially isolated male patients with high degrees of life stress were over four times more at risk of death than patients with low levels of both isolation and stress. High levels of social isolation and stress were most prevalent among least educated men and least prevalent among those educated. Individuals who lacked social community ties were found to have a risk of dying two to three times greater than patients with more extensive social contacts (Berkman & Syme, 1979). Syme (1984) and Berkman (1984) have published excellent reviews of the relationship between disrupted social ties and the onset of disease. The literature on social support and physical health, however, is more modest (Wallston, Alagna, DeVellis & DeVellis, 1983).

Published evidence clearly suggests a relationship of psychosocial factors to both health and certain diseases. This relationship appears to be oftentimes subtle, complex, varied among diseases, and difficult to assess. Because of the *New England Journal of Medicine's* strong influence on both the medical community and the lay public, the publication of an editoral ignoring a large body of published literature investigating relationships between psychosocial factors and health–disease was unfortunate and unfounded.

ASSESSMENT OF PSYCHOSOCIAL VARIABLES

Related to the complex question of the role of psychosocial variables in disease states, a workshop (Ostfeld & Eaker, 1985) sponsored by NHLBI in conjunction with the University of Texas Medical Branch, Galveston, examined epidemiological methods for assessing potential psychosocial factors in CVD. It was interesting to note that in the foreword to the volume of the workshop proceedings, Claude Lenfant, director of the NHLBI, wrote, "It is no longer questioned, as it was in the early 1960's, whether psychologic and social factors are implicated in the etiology of cardiovascular diseases" (Lenfant, 1985, p. vii). He pointed out that life style makes the largest contribution (54%) among four determinants (the others are biology, environment, and health care services) to deaths from CHD. The six areas reviewed at the workshop were socioeconomic factors; social support and social networks; life change events and chronic life situations; Type A behavior, anger, and hostility; personality characteristics; and acute physiological reactivity (Ostfeld & Eaker, 1985). The results of the workshop are of particular interest to behavioral researchers in the psychosocial area.

Socioeconomic Factors

With respect to the empirical evidence linking socioeconomic factors with health, Morgenstern (1985) concluded:

- Socioeconomic status (SES) has remained inversely related to total mortality since before 1900.
- The effect of SES on CHD has changed from positive to inverse

over the past several decades, but this change appears to be confined primarily to men.

- The current inverse association between SES and CHD cannot be explained in terms of known risk factors for the disease.

Greater emphasis should be given to identifying specific associations between SES and risk of CVD in future research (Shekelle, 1985). It was recommended that the minimum information to be collected on SES in epidemiological studies of CVD include the following:

- Years of education completed
- Employment status
- Occupation
- Total household income
- Gender
- Race and ethnicity
- Marital status

Social Support

Berkman (1985) reviewed the role of social support and social networks and their relationship to CVD. Among the conclusions of the working group on this topic (Ostfeld, 1985) were these:

- The scientific literature relating CVD and social networks and social support is small and contradictory. Standardized instruments for assessing social support are greatly needed.
- Social support is not a unitary construct. Components include quantity, quality, type, and source of support.
- A definition of "social support" based on observable, verifiable personal behavior as well as on individual perceptions is needed, along with the development of models that identify both the network structures permitting social support behaviors and the responses of the recipient of support to such behaviors.
- The mechanisms through which social support can have beneficial effects on health include playing a facilitating role in getting good health care; acting directly to expedite care (money, transport); enhancing group norms of behavior that promote health; influencing the neuroendocrine and immune systems that promote resistance to disease; and promoting a sense of well-being, which, by operating through behavior and the neuroendocrine system, induces good health.

Life Change Events

Wells (1985) presented a comprehensive review of the literature relating life change events and chronic life situations to CVD. His review indicated the general lack of standardized assessment methodology and objective measures, along with the paucity of prospective studies in this field. Among the recommendations of the working group in this area (Kasl, 1985) were an endorsement of the strategy of studying major consequential events (e.g., bereavement, job changes, marital status changes, residential changes, and disasters) "one at a time." The work setting was seen as a potential area of fruitful research; particularly relevant subareas for research within this setting were quantitative overload, high levels of responsibility, and high job insecurity.

Recommendations for future study included the following:

- Comparison of the differential outcomes of adaptation versus chronic reactivity.
- The implementation of longitudinal studies at crucial stages of adaptation.
- The examination of self-report and recall biases that influence measures.

Type A Behavior

Matthews (1985) reviewed existing measures of Type A behavior, anger, and hostility, and their ability to predict CVD. Her paper highlighted the problems common to all measures in this area. The working group (Jenkins, 1985) summarized the reasons for the growing negative evidence of the role of Type A behavior in CHD. Research priorities include analytic studies of anger–hostility–aggression measures that have been found to be predictive of CHD. Further studies of the dimensions that are being measured and the underlying physiological mechanisms are needed. An especially helpful paper for the behavioral researcher studying Type A, anger, and hostility is Matthews, Jamison, and Cottington's (1985) review of measures of these constructs.

Personality Characteristics

Siegel (1985) summarized research findings suggesting that personality characteristics, anxiety, and neuroticism are related cross-sectionally to CVD. Among the recommendations of the working group on this topic (Eaker, 1985) were these:

- Because of the positive prospective relationship between certain personality variables and angina pectoris, it would be worthwhile to determine whether personality is related to actual disease processes or only to the propensity to report symptoms, and whether certain components of the personality variables are more highly related to angina pectoris.
- There is little support for future studies of the main effects of personality characteristics. However, personality variables combined with other host and environmental characteristics (e.g., anxiety or depression with self-esteem) should be studied in association with CVD.
- Previously unexplored aspects of personality, including coping style, sense of self, sense of belonging, sense of control, and vital exhaustion, should be studied in terms of CVD endpoints.
- Multiple and repeated measures of the same personality characteristic should be included in studies.
- CVD endpoints (angina pectoris, fatal and nonfatal myocardial infarction, arrhythmias, blood pressure, and cardiac death) should be considered separately rather than as a group.

Acute Physiological Reactivity

Krantz and Manuck (1985) reported studies linking physiological reactivity to pathogenesis of disease. Although a number of studies indicate an association between acute physiological reactivity and CVD, there is little convincing evidence that this association has any cause-and-effect relation. As Herd (1985) pointed out, it is unlikely that periodic elevations of heart rate and blood pressure have any lasting effect on cardiovascular function or arterial disease. However, acute physiological reactivity as an indicator of CVD risk appears to be a helpful concept. The working group (Glass, 1985) had several recommendations:

- The inclusion of several of the more common and easily administered reactivity-eliciting tasks in ongoing epidemiological studies.
- The development of standard definitions of reactivity.
- The implementation of a rigorous epidemiological study that would include refined measures of reactivity, including measures of plasma or urinary levels of catecholamines and cortisol.

Summary

This workshop illustrated the complexity involved in the assessment of psychological factors and CVD, current progress being made, limitations, and research needs for the future. Psychosocial epidemiology continues to make excellent contributions in the area of assessing psychosocial variables and their relationship to disease. The next few years should yield significant findings for behavioral medicine.

CONFERENCE ON BEHAVIORAL MEDICINE AND CVD

The AHA, stimulated by a growing number of requests for its interpretation of developments in the field of behavioral medicine and CVD from both medical professionals and the lay public, sponsored a conference on the topic in February 1985, on Sea Island, Georgia (American Heart Association, in press). The NHLBI, which had previously sponsored a Review Panel to evaluate the evidence linking behavior to CHD (Review Panel on Coronary-Prone Behavior and Coronary Heart Disease, 1981), joined the AHA as a cosponsor. The conference focused on biobehavioral approaches to the development, treatment, and prevention of hypertension, CHD, and sudden cardiac death. Participants evaluated evidence in three areas: association between behavioral–environmental factors and the disease state under consideration; basic mechanisms responsible for this relationship; and clinical investigations of primary and secondary prevention strategies.

Presentations at the conference addressed three main topics: the connections beteen the central nervous system and the cardiovascular system; the impact of the environment on the brain and cardiovascular system; and the effects of personality and personality traits on the cardiovascular system and on CVD. Studies on the first of these topics, the neurological and neurochemical relationships of the brain and the cardiovascular system, have made significant progress. Clarkson (cf. Kaplan *et al.*, 1983), for example, presented the effect of stressors and their ability to influence the development of atherosclerotic lesions in normocholesterolemic primates. Discussing the second topic, Syme (cf. Syme, 1984) illustrated the impact the worksite has on the cardiovascular system in a discussion of studies of hypertension among bus drivers.

Not surprisingly, the third topic—the effects of personality and personality traits on the cardiovascular system and on CVD—proved to be by far the most controversial one at the conference. In contrast to earlier work, a number of major studies have now indicated the lack of a significant relationship between Type A behavior and various cardiovascular endpoints. It has become increasingly uncertain whether the Type A behavioral pattern predisposes an individual to ischemic heart disease or whether some particular aspect of personality, such as anger or hostility, might be the key element (cf. Chesney & Rosenman, 1985). At the conference, it was pointed out that there is a pressing need for a standardized methodology for assessing the Type A behavioral pattern. Written instruments to define the Type A individual were criticized, and the "structured interview" was emphasized as necessary for diagnosis. However, until reliable, reproducible criteria become available for assessing behavioral patterns, the usefulness of the Type A concept is questionable.

Presentations at the conference emphasized that efforts to modify cardiovascular risk factors must continue. While substantial progress has been made in the use of certain drugs to reduce risk of cardiac death, nonpharmacological approaches have also been shown to be effective. Treatment of mild hypertension with nonpharmacological approaches (cf. Cottier, Shapiro, & Julius, 1984) was used as an example where biobehavioral approaches may have therapeutic effects without producing electrolyte abnormalities or other complications sometimes seen with pharmacological management.

SES as a risk factor for CVD was highlighted at the conference. A number of studies have suggested that SES has a very strong inverse relationship to death rates (e.g. Ruberman *et al.*, 1984). Behavioral interventions designed by and for educated middle-class individuals usually do not reach lower-SES groups or are ineffective when they are utilized. Development of effective strategies for lower-SES groups was seen as a priority.

It was pointed out that the ability to take advantage of further opportunities for research and treatment in this area will require increasing interdisciplinary collaboration among individuals from a wide diversity of disciplines. New and better animal models, with constant attention to the necessity that interventions be validated in humans once they are found to be reasonably safe, are required. Finally, the need for training individuals in a wide variety of disciplines and backgrounds for careers in research was emphasized.

The conference (American Heart Association, in press) illustrated the AHA's strong interest in and commitment to the role of behavioral medicine and CVD.

CARDIOVASCULAR RISK REDUCTION FOR ADULTS

In 1983, nearly 50% of all deaths in the United States, 989,400 individuals, were due to CVD (American Heart Association, 1985). One-fifth of all people who died from CVD were under 65 years of age. The cost of CVD in 1986, including physician and nursing services, hospital and nursing home services, medications and lost productivity resulting from disability, was estimated at $78.6 billion.

Table 5-1 illustrates the estimated deaths due to CVD by major type of disorder. Heart attack is the leading killer, accounting for 547,100 deaths, making it the leading cause of death in the United States today. A total of 4,740,000 people alive today have a history of heart attacks, angina pectoris, or both. In 1986, about 1,500,000 Americans had a heart attack, and about 550,000 of them died from it. About 5% of all heart attacks occur in individuals younger than 40 years of age and 45% in individuals younger than 65 years old.

Stroke killed 156,400 individuals in 1983, and another 1,930,000 victims suffer limitations from stroke. It is the third largest cause of death (after heart attack and cancer). About 500,000 individuals will suffer a stroke this year.

Hypertensive disease accounts for about 31,900 deaths. High blood pressure afflicts approximately 54,990,000 adults and 2,720,000 children aged 6–17 years. The threshold criterion for high blood pressure is now 140/90 mm Hg.

Rheumatic heart disease killed about 6,700 Americans in 1983. It afflicts approximately 1,980,000 adults and 100,000 children.

Other CVDs include congenital or inborn heart defects. There are about 35 recognizable types of defects.

Atherosclerosis: Major Modifiable Risk Factors

Atherosclerosis is a degenerative disease that narrows the arteries of the heart, brain, and other parts of the body. Over the years, the

TABLE 5-1. Estimated 1983 Deaths Due to Cardiovascular Diseases

CVD type	Number of estimated deaths	%
Heart attack	547,100	55.3
Stroke	156,400	15.8
Hypertensive disease	31,900	3.2
Rheumatic fever and rheumatic heart disease	6,700	0.7
Other CVD	247,300	25.0

Note. Adapted from *1986 Heart Facts* by the American Heart Association, 1985, Dallas, TX: Author. Copyright 1985 by the American Heart Association. Adapted by permission.

inner walls of the arteries become lined with deposits of fat, cholesterol, fiber, calcium, and cellular waste products. As the arteries narrow, blood flow is reduced and clots may form, shutting off the flow of blood to the heart, brain, or other internal organs, and eventually resulting in a heart attack or stroke.

Epidemiological studies have identified factors associated with increased incidence of atherosclerotic disease. Major modifiable risk factors are hypercholesterolemia, hypertension, and cigarette smoking. Diabetes mellitus also appears to be an important risk factor. Other modifiable risk factors include obesity, lack of physical activity, Type A behavorial pattern, and hypertriglyceridemia. Nonmodifiable risk factors include age, sex, and family history of CVD.

HYPERCHOLESTEROLEMIA: LIPIDS AND LIPOPROTEINS

Plasma lipids include cholesterol, cholesterol esters, triglycerides, and phospholipids. These lipids are transported in association with protein compounds (apolipoproteins) in macromolecular complexes called lipoproteins (Gotto, Jones, & Scott, 1986). The five major lipoprotein families are chylomicrons, very-low-density lipoproteins (VLDL), low-density lipoproteins (LDL), intermediate-density lipoproteins (IDL), and high-density lipoproteins (HDL).

The apolipoproteins (or apoproteins) are listed alphabetically (apoA through apoE). In the next few years, we will see increased research on the relationship of the apolipoproteins to coronary artery disease (CAD). For example, apoB has already been shown to be correlated directly to increased incidence of CAD (Avogaro, Bon, Cazzolato, & Rorai, 1980).

Severe hypercholesterolemia is based on the 90th percentile of the general population; moderate hypercholesterolemia is defined as the 75th–90th percentile. Table 5-2 illustrates the new values for selecting adults at moderate and high risk requiring treatment (Con-

TABLE 5-2. Hypercholesterolemia Values for Selecting Men and Women at Moderate and High Risk Requiring Treatment

Age (years)	Moderate risk (mg/dl)	High risk (mg/dl)
20–29	>200	>220
30–39	>220	>240
≥40	>240	>260

Note. Adapted from "Lowering Blood Cholesterol to Prevent Heart Disease" by the Consensus Conference, 1985, *Journal of the American Medical Association*, *253*, 2080–2086. Copyright 1985 by the American Medical Association. Adapted by permission.

sensus Conference, 1985). Individuals who fall in either the moderate- or the high-risk category should be treated. The values illustrated in Table 5-2 are considerably less than values traditionally used in the past in the United States. Data suggest that levels above 200 mg/dl in 20- to 29-year-old individuals are associated with increased moderate risk of developing premature heart disease.

Concentrations of LDL are also closely associated with prevalence of CHD. An LDL value greater than 170 mg/dl is considered significantly elevated (Gotto *et al.*, 1986). On the other hand, HDL may facilitate cholesterol transport from the peripheral tissues to the liver; there is an inverse relationship between concentrations of HDL and the occurrence of CHD. Aerobic exercise increases HDL levels. Adult male marathon runners have an averge HDL of 65 mg/dl; male joggers, 58 mg/dl; and inactive males, 43 mg/dl (Hartung, Foreyt, Mitchell, Vlasek, & Gotto, 1980). Adult female runners have an average HDL of 74 mg/dl, and inactive females have an HDL of 60 mg/dl (Hartung, Reeves, Foreyt, Patsch, & Gotto, 1986).

In individuals with elevated cholesterol levels, the goal is to encourage reduction through low-fat, low-cholesterol diets to approximately 180 mg/dl for adults less than 30 years old and to approximately 200 mg/dl for individuals aged 30 or older. Drugs may also be prescribed if diet does not normalize lipids. Figure 5-1 illustrates the percentage of persons 35–74 years of age with high-risk serum cholesterol levels, according to age, sex, and race in the United States. Prevalence of elevated serum cholesterol is fairly similar for both white and black individuals 35–74 years of age. However, for both white and black individuals, a substantially larger proportion of females in the 55–74 age range have elevated cholesterol levels than younger females. For males, the proportions are similar. Prevalence of elevated cholesterol is higher for females than males above age 55 years, but there is little difference in prevalence rates below age 55.

HYPERTENSION

Blood pressure is the force of the blood against the walls of the arteries and veins created by the heart as it pumps blood. The cause of high blood pressure is unknown in 90% of all cases. The percentage of persons aged 35–74 years with elevated blood pressure has declined substantially for blacks, especially black females, through the 1970s. Over this time, prevalence of elevated blood pressure has remained stable for white males and declined slightly for white females. These declines in prevalence of high blood pressure during the 1970s have been attributed largely to increased awareness of the condition, better

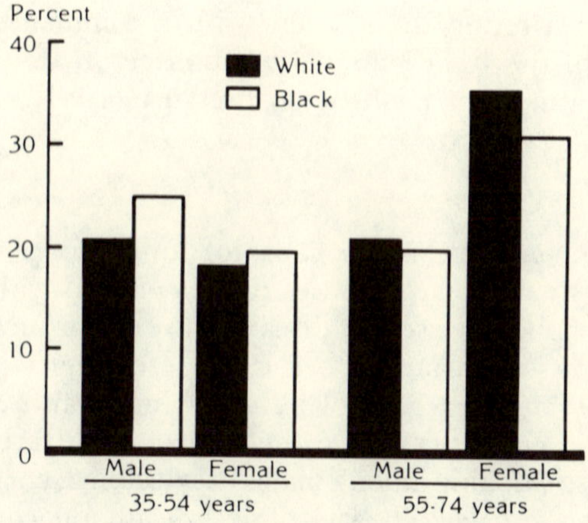

FIG. 5-1.
Percentage of persons 35–74 years of age with high-risk serum cholesterol levels, according to age, sex, and race, United States, 1976–1980. High-risk serum cholesterol levels are defined by age-specific cutoff points of the cholesterol distribution as follows: 20–29 years, greater than 220 mg/dl; 30–39 years, greater than 240 mg/dl; 40 years and over, greater than 260 mg/dl. Risk levels defined by NIH Consensus Development Conference statement on lowering blood cholesterol, Dec. 10, 1984. (From *Health United States, 1985* [DHHS Publication No. PHS 86-1232], 1985, Washington, DC: U.S. Government Printing Office).

treatment, and better control of elevated blood pressure—the result of increased public hypertension education and intervention programs. However, even though the prevalence of hypertension has declined at a greater rate for blacks than whites, the proportion of blacks with hypertension is still considerably larger than that of whites. During the period 1976–1980, the age-adjusted percentage of individuals between the ages of 35 and 74 with elevated blood pressure was 35% for black males, 26% for white males, 33% for black females, and 21% for white females.

Figure 5-2 illustrates the age-adjusted percentage of persons 35–74 years of age with elevated blood pressure, according to sex and race, in the United States between 1971 and 1974 and between 1976 and 1980. Elevated blood pressure was defined as systolic pressure of at least 160 mm Hg or diastolic pressure of at least 95 mm Hg or both, based on a single measurement. Prevalence figures for high blood pressure were much higher in 1986, since the threshold for hypertension was recently lowered to 140/90 mm Hg. This change in the definition was made because data have shown that individuals with blood pressure readings of 140/90 mm Hg and above are at increased risk of disease or premature death from high blood pressure. The new criterion is consistent with recommendations of the recent report of the Joint National Committee on Detection, Evaluation, and Treatment of High Blood Pressure (1984).

CIGARETTE SMOKING

Cigarette smoking is the major cause of lung cancer and is also a major risk factor for heart disease. It is associated with CHD, arteriosclerotic peripheral vascular disease, chronic bronchitis, emphysema, and cancers of the larynx, oral cavity, esophagus, pancreas, and bladder. In 1965, about 52% of all adult males and 33% of adult females smoked cigarettes. Since then, this sex differential has decreased, because smoking among males has declined at a much greater rate than among females. The lack of decline among women has been attributed to increases in smoking among young adult females. In 1986, about 30% of adults smoked—33% of males and 28% of females (see Chapter 6 for additional comments about cigarette smoking).

Reducing Cardiovascular Risk Factors

A number of large multiple risk factor reduction programs have been implemented since the 1970s. Among the best-known of these projects

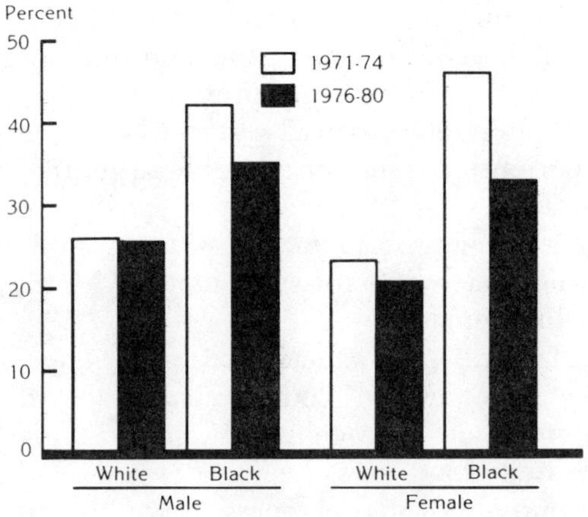

FIG. 5-2.
Age-adjusted percentage of persons 35–74 years of age with elevated blood pressure, according to sex and race, United States, 1971–1974 and 1976–1980. Elevated blood pressure is defined as systolic pressure of at least 160 mm Hg or diastolic pressure of at least 95 mm Hg or both, based on a single measurement. (From *Health United States, 1985* [DHHS Publication No. PHS 86-1232], 1985, Washington, DC: U.S. Government Printing Office.)

are the Oslo Heart Study (Hjermann, 1980; Leren *et al.*, 1975); the Multiple Risk Factor Intervention Trial (MRFIT; Multiple Risk Factor Intervention Trial Research Group, 1982); the Belgian Heart Disease Prevention Project (De Backer, Kornitzer, Thilly, & Depoorter, 1977); the U.K. Heart Disease Prevention Project (Rose, Tunstall-Pedoe, & Heller, 1983); the Rome Project of Coronary Heart Disease Prevention (Research Group of the Rome Project of Coronary Heart Disease Prevention, 1986); the Community Syndrome of Hypertension, Atherosclerosis and Diabetes (CHAD) Program in Jerusalem (Gofin, Gofin, Abramson, & Ban, 1986); the Stanford Heart Disease Prevention Program (SHDPP; Maccoby, Farquhar, Wood, & Alexander, 1977); the Stanford Five-City Project (SFCP; Farquhar *et al.*, 1984); the Pawtucket Heart Health Project (Lasater *et al.*, 1984); the Minnesota Heart Health Program (Blackburn *et al.*, 1984); the North Karelia Project (Puska *et al.*, 1985); and the Lipid Research Clinics' Primary Prevention Trial (Lipid Research Clinics Program, 1984a, 1984b).

OSLO HEART STUDY

The Oslo Heart Study (Hjermann, Velve Byre, Holme, & Leren, 1981) was a randomized trial of primary intervention in normotensive, high-risk, middle-aged men. The primary targets of intervention were reduction of saturated fat and cholesterol and cessation of smoking. Results indicated that serum cholesterol values were 13% lower in the intervention group than in the control group and that average use of tobacco decreased 45% more in the intervention group. At the end of the 5-year study, incidence of myocardial infarction and sudden death was 47% lower in the intervention group than in the control group. The authors reported that 60% of the benefits were derived from reduction of serum cholesterol and 25% from reduction of smoking (Hjermann *et al.*, 1981).

MULTIPLE RISK FACTOR INTERVENTION TRIAL

The MRFIT was a randomized, collaborative trial to test the hypothesis that a 6-year program for lowering serum cholesterol level, diastolic blood pressure, and cigarette smoking would reduce mortality from CHD among men at risk. Reduction in risk factor levels occurred in both the experimental special-intervention group and the usual-care group intended as a comparison. A nonsignificant 7.1% reduction in coronary mortality occurred in the experimental group, without any difference in overall mortality. Both the experimental and the usual-care groups did extremely well in regard to overall mortality, experiencing only approximately 60% of that expected from the risk factor makeup of the subjects. The low mortality rate made it difficult to compare the two conditions. However, higher mortality rates were seen in subjects who continued to smoke than in those who quit smoking regardless of condition. Serum cholesterol lowering was similar in both conditions. Blood pressure control was somewhat better in the experimental group than in the usual-care condition (Multiple Risk Factor Intervention Trial Research Group, 1982, 1985, 1986).

BELGIAN HEART DISEASE PREVENTION PROJECT

The Belgian Heart Disease Prevention Project (Kornitzer, De Backer, Dramaix, & Thilly, 1980) was part of the larger World Health Organization (WHO) European Collaborative Group (1974, 1980). The project was directed toward five risk factors: serum cholesterol, hypertension, cigarette smoking, obesity, and sedentary life style. Subjects were recruited from 30 factories throughout Belgium. The factories were paired by industry and then randomly assigned to treatment or control groups, with 15 factories in each condition. Overall results indicated that total mortality was 17.5% lower in the intervention group, coronary mortality was reduced by 20.8% (nonsignificant), and total CHD incidence (including nonfatal CHD) was reduced by 24.5% (significant) (Kornitzer *et al.*, 1983).

U.K. HEART DISEASE PREVENTION PROJECT

Results of the U.K. Heart Disease Prevention Project, also part of the WHO European Collaborative Group, showed little change in risk factors following intervention efforts. Data showed no clear effect of treatment on CHD endpoints or on all causes of mortality. Intervention subjects, however, showed a 36% reduction in angina (Rose *et al.*, 1983).

ROME PROJECT OF CORONARY HEART DISEASE PREVENTION

The Rome Project of Coronary Heart Disease Prevention, part of the WHO European Collaborative Group in the Multifactorial Prevention of CHD, was a primary preventive trial carried out on 6,027 middle-aged working men (3,131 in the treatment group and 2,896 in the control group). The goals of the project were to reduce serum cholesterol, high blood pressure, smoking, obesity, and sedentary life style. Intervention lasted 6 years and consisted of individual sessions for about one-third of higher-risk subjects and mass education for the rest of the treatment group. Net changes for the treatment group after 6 years were −0.71% for body weight, +0.77% for cigarette consumption, −3.00% for systolic blood pressure, −5.39% for serum cholesterol, and −18.00% for the estimated multivariate coronary risk. After 8 years, mortality from all causes was lower by 9.8% in the treatment group, and mortality from CHD was lower by 23.7%. Incidence of fatal plus nonfatal CHD events after the first 6 years was reduced by 30.9% in the treatment as compared to the control group (Research Group of the Rome Project of Coronary Heart Disease Prevention, 1986).

THE CHAD PROGRAM IN JERUSALEM

The CHAD Program is a community health project for control of hypertension, obesity, elevated cholesterol, and smoking. It has operated in a neighborhood of western Jerusalem since 1971. The program was set up within a family practice and is directed toward all adults living in four adjacent housing projects. Initial results were promising (Abramson *et al.*, 1981). A follow-up of 441 people exposed to the program for 10 years showed that mean blood pressures and prevalence of hypertension continued to decrease. Prevalence of cigarette smoking among individuals 30 years or older also showed a continuing decline. Results did not show favorable changes in cholesterol or weight (Gofin *et al.*, 1986).

STANFORD HEART DISEASE PREVENTION PROGRAM

The SHDPP was a 3-year intervention study begun in 1972 in three northern California towns. One community, Tracy, served as a control and received no direct intervention; a second community, Gilroy, received a 2-year multimedia intervention; and a third community, Watsonville, received the same multimedia intervention supplemented by an intensive instruction program for high-risk individuals (Farquhar *et al.*, 1977; Maccoby *et al.*, 1977). To assess the effectiveness of the interventions, surveys were conducted at baseline and yearly follow-ups from random samples of adults in all three communities. Behavioral interviews measured knowledge about heart disease and specific individual behaviors related to cardiovascular risk, including dietary and smoking habits. Physical examinations included measures of plasma lipids, blood pressure, body weight, and electrocardiograms. All data were combined to yield an estimate of risk of developing CHD over the following 12 years.

Results showed that the communities receiving intervention made significantly greater improvements than the control community on all measures except relative weight. At the end of the 2 years of intervention, there was a net difference of 23–28% in estimated total coronary risk between the combined treatment samples and the controls. The high-risk participants who received intensive instruction showed the greatest beneficial effects, primarily due to reduction in smoking. Half of the high-risk smokers exposed to intensive intervention had stopped smoking after 3 years. Although diet and blood pressure also improved in the treated high-risk samples compared to the control sample, there was no differences between treatment methods. Relative weight and physical activity did not change significantly in treatment groups. Overall, the SHDPP demonstrated that a mass media intervention program can substantially reduce risk factors for CHD, particularly when the mass media efforts are complemented by face-to-face education.

STANFORD FIVE-CITY PROJECT

The ongoing SFCP differs from the SHDPP in extending the outcome measures to include CVD morbidity and mortality. The project includes two treatment and three control cities. Independent surveys of population samples are used to measure community impact on knowledge, behavior, and risk factors. In addition, repeated surveys of longitudinal cohorts allow use of correlational, network, and path analysis (Farquhar, 1978). An epidemiological surveillance system is monitoring all CVD events occurring in the five cities over the 8 years of the study.

The community education program is aimed at producing a 10% reduction in overall risk status after 2 years of intervention. The Stanford group estimates that a reduction greater than 20% in overall risk will be achieved if there is a 9% change in the proportion of smokers, a 2% net change in relative weight, a 7% change in systolic blood pressure, and a 4% change in blood cholesterol (Farquhar *et al.*, 1984). The education program will continue for a total of 6 years in order to detect changes in morbidity and mortality. Preliminary results are encouraging. Farquhar and Wood (1985) reported that changes in smoking, blood pressure, and cholesterol levels have resulted in a reduction of approximately 15% in cardiovascular risk in the treatment versus the reference cities. After 28 months of intervention in one cohort of adults, the multiple CVD risk logistic for total mortality and for CHD events was 10.4% ($p < .001$) and 11.1% ($p < .01$) less, respectively, in the treatment versus the reference cities (Farquhar *et al.*, 1986).

PAWTUCKET HEART HEALTH PROJECT

The Pawtucket Heart Health Project is also assessing the effectiveness of a community-based program for modifying cardiovascular risk factors. Specifically targeted are smoking, high cholesterol diets, blood pressure, obesity, physical inactivity, and stress. The primary deliverers of this project, however, are not professionals, but volunteers recruited from within the Pawtucket community. Led by these volunteers, intervention for each risk factor includes social skills training along with stimulus control and individual self-management methods. Overall outcome is based on cross-sectional random sample surveys of 1,400 adult subjects in the intervention city and a comparison community. Assessment occurs at baseline and at 2-year intervals. Along with changes in risk factors, actual morbidity and mortality are also being assessed, based on review of clinical records. Community participation in heart health activities increased over the first 26 months of the study (Elder *et al.*, 1986). The study is currently in progress, and outcome results should be available in the late 1980s (Lasater *et al.*, 1984).

MINNESOTA HEART HEALTH PROGRAM

The Minnesota Heart Health Program is a 9-year project in CVD prevention. The overall goals of the project are to measure change in disease risk and behavioral characteristics of communities and to relate these changes to the effects of the intervention. Surveillance is carried out in yearly population-based surveys, along with periodic cohort studies. Three intervention communities and three comparison communities of progressively larger size comprise the populations under study.

Risk factors being measured are blood pressure, plasma lipids and lipoproteins, cigarette smoking, and physical activity. Intervention is occurring through mass communications, direct education and special adult classes, professional education, youth education, and community-based activities. Baseline and annual surveys of risk characteristics along with morbidity and mortality surveillance, are currently being carried out. Preliminary data suggest that the program has generated community awareness of its health messages and community exposure to health promotion activities (Mittelmark *et al.*, 1986). Results of the project also should be available during the next several years (Blackburn *et al.*, 1984).

NORTH KARELIA PROJECT

The North Karelia Project began in 1972 in Finland's easternmost county. Because Finland's CHD mortality rates were the highest in the world at the time the study began, the project attempted to carry out a planned, comprehensive intervention in the entire community of North Karelia for control of CVD. The original project extended for 5 years, but later it was lengthened, and in 1982 a 10-year survey was carried out.

Risk reduction programs were aimed at control of smoking, serum cholesterol, and blood pressure. The intervention model included improved preventive services, education, persuasion, training in self-management, environmental control, social support, environmental change, and community organization.

Results have been encouraging. When the study began in 1972, 52% of adult males smoked. This rate was reduced to 44% in 1977 and to 38% in 1982. Smoking rates of women were small—1.1% in 1972, 1.1% in 1977, and 1.7% in 1982. Mean serum cholesterol concentrations showed a significant lowering of 4% between 1972 and 1977 and 3% between 1972 and 1982 in men. Nonsignificant lowerings of 1% were seen between 1972 and 1977 and between 1972 and 1982 for women. Mean blood pressure was reduced significantly; a 3% decrease was seen for both periods in men and a 5% decrease in both periods for women. During 1974–1979, reduction in male CHD mortality was 22% in North Karelia, compared with a 12% reduction in the reference community and 11% in all Finland excluding North Karelia. A significant decrease in CHD mortality among women in North Karelia compared with the rest of Finland was also significant (Puska *et al.*, 1985).

Overall reductions in risk factor levels seen in North Karelia during the 10 years were substantial for men: 36% in smoking, 11% in mean serum cholesterol concentration, and 5% in mean diastolic blood pressure. Results of the North Karelia Project suggest that well-run community-based programs can have an important positive impact on life styles and risk factor levels in the population. With sustained intervention, maintenance of change also appears favorable. The long-term effects appear to be an increase in health and well-being and a decrease in the rates of CVD among the entire population.

LIPID RESEARCH CLINICS' PRIMARY PREVENTION TRIAL

The Lipid Research Clinics' Primary Prevention Trial was a 7-year study investigating whether the risk of myocardial infarction and CHD mortality could be reduced in adult men with elevated cholesterol. It was not a multiple risk factor reduction study like the others reviewed here; however, its size, scope, and findings suggest that it should also be included in the present discussion. Results have provided the most conclusive evidence to date of the potential for primary prevention of CHD through reduction of elevated serum cholesterol values. At-risk males received either a drug (cholestyramine resin) or a placebo, plus a low-fat diet. Diet produced a 5% reduction in total serum cholesterol in both the treatment and the placebo groups. Combination of diet and cholestyramine produced an 8.5% greater reduction in total cholesterol and a 12.6% greater reduction in LDL cholesterol in the treatment group than in the placebo group. Participants achieving the improvements in their lipids had a 24% reduction in CHD mortality and a 19% reduction in coronary attacks compared to the placebo-treated participants. The results add evidence incriminating both total and LDL cholesterol in the development of CHD. Although the study was not designed to test the efficacy of a low-fat, low-cholesterol diet, the results—when taken together with additional extensive evidence linking diet, plasma lipids, and CHD—clearly support the conclusion that reduction in lipids through diet is beneficial.

The researchers suggest that if Americans were to reduce their plasma cholesterol by 25%, there would be a 50% reduction in incidence of CHD (Lipid Research Clinics Program, 1984a, 1984b). Although results were produced by a combination of diet and drug, presumably reduction of cholesterol by dietary means alone should have a similar effect.

Implications for Behavioral Medicine

Persons at risk for CVD are easily identified. New instruments for providing cholesterol values within minutes are now available (Boehringer Mannheim, 1986). Cholesterol screenings can easily be completed in community settings, just as blood pressure screenings are now routinely done. Effective prevention efforts require aggressive promotion of the cardiovascular risk profile concept, using optimal plasma cholesterol (Consensus Conference, 1985) and blood pressure (Joint National Committee on Detection, Evaluation, and Treatment of High Blood Pressure, 1984) values, rather than "normal" or "average" values. Although the results of many of the multiple risk factor intervention trials are not yet in, and the results of those completed have not shown conclusively that recommended life style interventions do in fact lower incidence of CHD, there is abundant evidence to suggest that modifications in life style *should* reduce CHD morbidity and mortality. Furthermore, what is being advocated in the trials is certainly not dangerous to health. CHD is such a massive public health problem that definitive proof of the efficacy of the potential benefits of life style modifications is not necessary before recommending them. The potential consequences of inaction while awaiting definitive evidence may be too great. It is especially important to protect children from developing an atherogenic way of life.

The general public has made some favorable changes in diet, cigarette smoking, and exercise patterns. Multiple risk factor reduction studies have suggested the potential for further beneficial changes. Although these studies are very expensive to run, their potential benefits are enormous. Prevention and control of CHD in the United States continue to be major challenges. The decline in cardiovascular mortality and predisposing risk factors are reasons to be optimistic about the value of multiple risk factor control in communities. These trials are making major contributions to knowledge for risk factor modification. The continuing declines in deaths due to CHD and CVD appear to be at least partially due to widespread changes in life style and improvements in health behaviors. These trials should provide additional information about the behavioral strategies that may be required to hasten the decline in CHD mortality currently observed.

BEHAVIORAL MEDICINE AND MINORITY GROUPS

At the turn of the century, the life expectancy for the white U.S. population at birth was 47.3 years; for blacks it was 33 years. In 1983, the life expectancy was 75.2 years for whites and 69.6 years for blacks. In 1981, whites suffered 10.5 infant deaths per 1,000 live births, compared to 20 for blacks (U.S. Department of Health and Human Services [DHHS], 1985).

This section of the chapter examines the health status of blacks and Hispanics in the United States and the potential role of behavioral medicine in helping to alleviate the serious health discrepancies that presently exist.

Characteristics of Blacks

Blacks are the largest minority group in the United States, accounting for 11.5% of the population (U.S. DHHS, 1985). According to the 1980 census, blacks numbered 26.5 million. Almost 59% live in central cities, and about 53% live in the southern United States. Median age is 24.9 years, with a current life expectancy of 65 years for men and 74 years for women. The average black family has 3.7 members. Approximately 79% of blacks have completed high school, and 13% have graduated from college. Median income of black families in 1981 was $13,270, and one out of every three lived below the poverty level. The unemployment rate in 1982 was 18.9%.

Characteristics of Hispanic Americans

Hispanic Americans are the second largest minority group in the United States, numbering 14.6 million in 1980 (U.S. DHHS, 1985). Of this total, 9 million are Mexican Americans, 2 million are Puerto Ricans, and 1 million are Cubans. The Hispanic population is growing 6.5 times faster than the general population (Guernica & Kasperuk, 1982). They currently total 6.4% of the population. By 1990, they may comprise 20% of all U.S. residents (Guernica & Kasperuk, 1982). About 60% of all Hispanics live in Arizona, California, Colorado, New Mexico, and Texas. California and Texas account for half of the total. Median age is 23 years. Number of children per family is 2.3. Only 58% of Hispanics have completed high school, and only 10% have graduated from college. Median income in 1981 was $16,228. About 30% of all Hispanics were living under the poverty level in 1982, and about 13.8% were unemployed.

Mortality and Morbidity of Blacks and Hispanic Americans

Figure 5-3 shows the average annual excess deaths for blacks between 1979 and 1981. The index "excess deaths" expresses the difference between the number of deaths actually observed in blacks and the number of deaths that would have occurred had they experienced the same death rates as whites. Most of the excess deaths are attributable to six causes: (1) homicide and accidents, (2) infant mortality, (3) CHD and stroke, (4) cirrhosis, (5) cancer, and (6) diabetes. Among blacks under the age of 45 years, homicide and accidents, infant mortality, CHD and stroke and cirrhosis account for the greatest number of excess deaths. CHD, stroke, and cancer show large increases when deaths up to age 70 are plotted. These same six causes for excess deaths also apply to Hispanic Americans, although the percentages are not available at this time.

HOMICIDE AND ACCIDENTS

Homicide and accidents account for about 35% of excess deaths in blacks under 45 years of age. Data are not yet available for Hispanic Americans; however, rates are probably similar to those of blacks.

- Although blacks represent only 11.5% of the population, they accounted for 43% of homicide victims in 1983 (Federal Bureau of Investigation, 1984).
- The lifetime chance of becoming a homicide victim for black

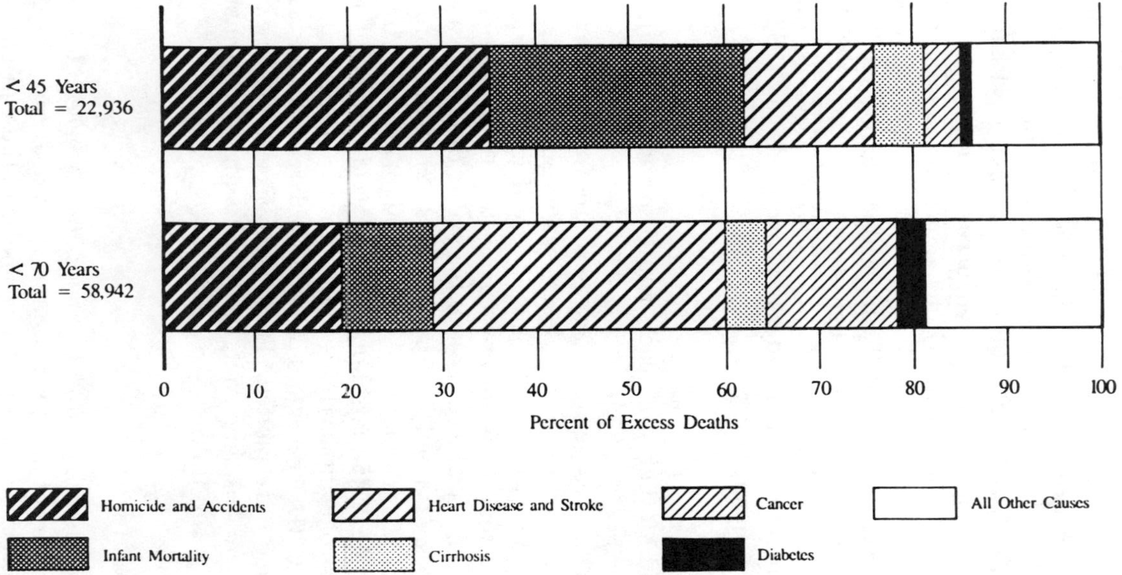

FIG. 5-3.

Average annual excess deaths for blacks, 1979–1981. The base of "zero" is equal to the mortality rate for whites. "Excess deaths" indicate those observed in excess of the white rate. (From *Report of the Secretary's Task Force on Black and Minority Health: Vol. 1. Executive Summary* by the U.S. Department of Health and Human Services, 1985, Washington, DC: U.S. Government Printing Office.)

males is 1 in 21; for white males it is 1 in 131 (U.S. Department of Justice, 1985).

- The lifetime chance of becoming a homicide victim for black females is 1 in 104; for white females it is 1 in 369 (U.S. Department of Justice, 1985).
- Homicide is the leading cause of death for black males between the ages of 15 and 44 years (National Center for Health Statistics, 1984). The homicide rate for black males is 69.2 per 100,000, compared with 10.3 for white males (National Center for Health Statistics, 1984).
- The homicide rate among black females is 12.9 per 100,000, compared to 3.1 for white females (National Center for Health Statistics, 1984).
- For black males between the ages of 15 and 24 years, the homicide rate in 1981 was 78.2 deaths per 100,000, compared with 14.4 for white males of the same ages (National Center for Health Statistics, 1984).
- For black males between the ages of 25 and 34 years, the homicide rate was 136.9 per 100,000 in 1981, compared with 17.6 for white males of the same ages (National Center for Health Statistics, 1984).
- For Hispanics, the homicide rate was 21.6 per 100,000, compared to 7.7 in whites, in a five-state Southwestern region between 1976 and 1980 (Smith, Mercy, & Rosenberg, 1984).

Homicide has been linked to psychological, environmental, life style, and physiological factors. Among the primary life style variables associated with homicides are alcohol and drug usage. About half of all homicides are related to the use of alcohol (John, 1978). In New York City, for example, over 20% of homicides are drug-related (New York City Police Department, 1982). The most prominent physiological risk factors for being involved in a homicide are being young and male.

INFANT MORTALITY

Infant mortality, the rate at which babies die before their first birthday, was 10.9 per 1,000 births in the United States in 1983. Black rates were about twice those of whites—20.0 versus 10.5 per 1,000 births. Infant mortality rates include both neonatal (within the first 28 days of life) and postneonatal (from 28 days to 1 year) rates. About 7% of babies are born with low birth weight; however, they account for about two-thirds of the deaths in the first month of life and about

60% of all infant deaths (McCormick, 1985). Among black babies, 12.4% are of low birth weight, compared to 5.7% for Mexicans, 5.8% for Cubans, 9.1% for Puerto Ricans, and 5.6% for whites (U.S. DHHS, 1985).

CHD AND STROKE

CHD is the leading cause of death among blacks in this country (Gillum, 1982). The average annual age-adjusted death rates for CHD between 1979 and 1981 per 100,000 population were 319.4 for black men, 274.4 for white men, 194.4 for black women, and 131.9 for white women. For persons under the age of 45 years, the age-adjusted death rates per 100,000 population were 34.9 for black men, 15.3 for white men, 17.2 for black women, and 5.1 for white women (U.S. DHHS, 1985).

Mean blood pressures are greater and there is more hypertension among blacks than among whites. Prevalence of hypertension in blacks is 1.4 times that of whites (Rowland & Roberts, 1982). Mean systolic blood pressure decreased from 138 to 130 mm Hg in black men between 1960 and 1980, and from 138 to 126 mm Hg in black women. Between 1960 and 1980 there was also a nonsignificant decline of definite hypertension among blacks, from 33.6% to 28.6%. In 1975, blacks were more likely to be aware of their elevated blood pressure than whites, and black hypertensives were as likely as whites to be treated with antihypertensive medications and to have their blood pressure under control. Between 1960 and 1980, there was an increase in awareness, treatment, and control of hypertension among blacks.

End-stage renal disease is caused by hypertension and occurs more commonly in blacks than whites (Rostand, Kirk, Rutsky, & Pate, 1982). Blacks treated with dialysis have lower death rates than whites undergoing the same procedure (Krakauer, Grauman, McMullan, & Creede, 1983).

Death rates from stroke are much higher in blacks than whites (Kuller, 1986; Stolley *et al.*, 1977). The highest rates of stroke have been detected in black men in the Southeast United States, an area commonly referred to as the "stroke belt." Although deaths from stroke have declined in blacks at a greater rate than in whites, their incidence of stroke is still higher.

Data on CHD and stroke mortality in Hispanic Americans are very limited at this time, although forthcoming data from the nationwide Hispanic Health and Nutrition Examination Study (HHANES) will provide current health status and behavioral data on Mexican Americans, Cubans, and Puerto Ricans. Regional mortality rates in

Los Angeles suggest that CHD is a major cause of death for Hispanics, but is lower than in whites (Frerichs, Chapman, Nourjah, & Maes,1984). Age-adjusted prevalence rates of hypertension are similar for Mexican American and white men (10% and 9.8%, respectively) and slightly lower for Mexican American women than white women (7.8% and 9.7%, respectively) in Texas (Franco *et al.*, 1985).

CIRRHOSIS

Alcohol abuse is a major health risk in minority populations. Deaths from cirrhosis of the liver are an indicator of excessive alcohol use. Although blacks' drinking patterns appear similar to those of whites when social class is controlled for (National Institute on Alcohol Abuse and Alcoholism, 1980), blacks may be at a disproportionately high risk for some alcohol-related health problems. Consumption of alcohol appears to be a primary etiological agent in the development of esophageal cancer, and the incidence rate for this cancer among middle-aged black males between 1979 and 1981 was 10 times that of whites (U.S. DHHS, 1985).

Average annual age-adjusted death rates for cirrhosis and chronic liver diseases for 1979–1981 per 100,000 population were 29.4 for black men, 15.4 for white men, 13.5 for black women and 6.0 for white women. Although Hispanic data are not yet available, Hispanic males aged 18–29 years drink more heavily than either white or black youths of the same age (34%, 17%, and 29%, respectively) (Caetano, 1985).

CANCER

The average annual age-adjusted death rates for cancer between 1979 and 1981 per 100,000 population were 227.9 for black men, 159.2 for white men, 127.3 for black women, and 106.9 for white women (U.S. DHHS, 1985). The major risk factors of tobacco, combined effects of alcohol and tobacco, nutrition and dietary factors, and occupation account for about 69% of incidence and 72% of cancer mortality (Doll & Peto, 1981). Tobacco is the greatest risk factor for cancer in blacks, with tobacco-related cancers accounting for about 45% of new cancer cases in black males and 25% in black females, and about 37% of cancer deaths in black males and 20% in black females (U.S. DHHS, 1985).

Although the overall age-adjusted cancer incidence rates for Hispanics are lower than for whites or blacks, the rates for some cancers, such as stomach cancer, are higher than for whites. The incidence of stomach cancer, which is twice as high in Hispanics as whites, has been associated with diets high in spiced, pickled, and smoked foods. Surveys of tobacco use among Hispanics in California, Texas, and New Mexico indicate that Hispanic males smoke at least as frequently as white males, while Hispanic females smoke at a considerably lower rate than white females (Marcus & Crane, 1985).

DIABETES

The two major types of diabetes are insulin-dependent diabetes mellitus (IDDM), which usually develops in childhood and accounts for 5–10% of all cases, and non-insulin-dependent diabetes mellitus (NIDDM), often developing in adulthood, which accounts for 90–95% of all cases. The prevalence of diabetes in blacks is about 33% higher than in whites (Bonham & Brock, 1985). The rate of diabetes is 50% greater in black females than white females, possibly due to the striking prevalence of obesity among black females (see Chapter 6 for more information on rates of obesity in black females).

The prevalence rate of diabetes among Hispanics is over three times that of whites (Stern *et al.*, 1981; U.S. Bureau of the Census, 1981). Prevalence of NIDDM is significantly greater in Mexican Americans than whites, even when obesity is controlled for (Stern, Gaskill, Hazuda, Gardner, & Haffner, 1983). It is related to SES, falling in both Mexican American men and women with rising SES (Stern, Rosenthal, Haffner, Hazuda, & Franco, 1984). More specific data on the prevalence rates of diabetes among Hispanic groups will be available with the publication of the HHANES.

Implications for Behavioral Medicine

HOMICIDE

Several opportunities for behavioral scientists exist in the areas of primary and secondary prevention of homicides (U.S. DHHS, 1985). Among them are the following:

- Developing community self-help programs that include the use of culturally relevant messages, featuring appropriate role models suitable for specific target populations, in media campaigns for educating the community about the unacceptability of violence and high homicide rates.

- Working with organizations such as the National Parent–Teachers Association to reinforce parents for choosing programs on television that demonstrate appropriate prosocial behaviors; also, working for the reduction of violence on television.
- Increasing greater awareness of homicide as a public health problem, and incorporating information on it into the curricula of graduate schools and continuing professional education courses.
- Developing programs to assist in the acquisition of parenting skills and effective forms of discipline that avoid excessive punishment, in order to reduce the amount of family violence.
- Adding school-based programs for homicide prevention in the elementary schools, aimed at teaching children how to manage hostility and aggression through nonviolent means.
- Incorporating programs to reduce chemical dependence into strategies aimed at the prevention of homicide.

INFANT MORTALITY

Although there are no simple solutions to the problem of infant mortality, behavioral researchers can play an important role in several areas (U.S. DHHS, 1985):

- Offering behavorial programs to help pregnant women stop smoking. Additional research is needed to identify other health-related behaviors in which women engage during pregnancy that may be related to pregnancy outcome.
- Developing comprehensive health education programs that address avoidable health risks during pregnancy.
- Researching behaviors associated with unplanned pregnancies, including the perceived risks and benefits of methods of fertility regulation, particularly for teenage women.
- Investigating strategies for the reduction of injuries in infants, such as the role of seat belts in child safety.

CHD AND STROKE

Behavioral medicine has much to offer in the prevention and treatment of CVD and cerebrovascular disease with minority groups. Behavioral interventions aimed at promoting dietary patterns to lower blood lipids, reduce tobacco use, increase exercise, lower blood pressure, and reduce obesity are needed. Although there is voluminous literature on risk reduction interventions in the areas of CVD and cerebrovascular disease with white populations, little exists to date on such interventions with minorities. Among the specific needs are these:

- Developing specific behavioral interventions for reduction of elevated plasma cholesterol levels, blood pressure, tobacco use, and obesity in black and Hispanic populations.
- Developing primary prevention programs in these areas targeted to minority groups.
- Investigating strategies to increase compliance with therapeutic regimens among minority groups.
- Designing programs for treatment of diabetes, particularly among Hispanics.

CIRRHOSIS

Among the many research needs in this area are the following (U.S. DHHS, 1985):

- Promoting the initiation and continuation of efforts to help both children and adolescents in minority groups develop coping skills to delay or prevent the use of alcohol.
- Developing peer group instruction programs in schools, designed to strengthen resistance to the use of alcohol ("Just Say No") among minority groups.

CANCER

Behavioral researchers have a major role to play in the development of programs aimed at reduction of risk factors associated with the development of cancers. Among the recommendations are these:

- Developing smoking prevention and cessation programs targeted specifically to minority groups.
- Developing low-fat, high-fiber, culturally adapted dietary programs.

DIABETES

Behavioral researchers can contribute significantly to the prevention of diabetes and its complications through the initiation of prevention programs for the reduction of obesity in minority groups. It has been estimated that control of obesity might prevent almost 300,000 cases of diabetes per year (U.S. DHHS, 1985). Among the many opportunities in this area are the following:

- Developing culturally relevant obesity treatment programs for minority groups.
- Developing culturally relevant behavioral strategies for promoting compliance with dietary recommendations among these groups.
- Developing programs to foster control and management of diabetes with minority groups.

Example of an Intervention Program with Hispanics

Few studies exist that have attempted health behavior change intervention with minority groups. One exemplary program that has attempted to reduce cardiovascular risk is the San Diego Family Health Project (FHP; Nader *et al.*, 1985). The aim of the FHP is to help families initiate and maintain healthy dietary and physical activity behaviors. The three specific goals of the intervention are to reduce sodium intake to 3 grams per day; to reduce saturated fat intake to 10% of total calories; and to increase exercise to at least 20 minutes per day, three times a week. At the beginning of the project, 12 San Diego elementary schools were randomly assigned to treatment or control conditions. Both Hispanic and white families with a fifth- or sixth-grade child were recruited; a total of 203 families (627 participants) joined the study. Families met in groups for 12 weeks of intensive behaviorally oriented intervention, followed by 9 months of maintenance sessions. Each session included family physical activity, learning sections for adults and children, family behavior management instruction, and a healthy snack. The investigators plan to assess changes in both Hispanic and white subjects. Although outcome data are not yet available, the FHP should contribute to our understanding regarding the Hispanic families' role in promoting health behaviors; the maintenance of behavior change; and specific behavioral methods needed for reinforcing change among Hispanic groups. The FHP is an excellent example of innovative approaches for initiating and maintaining healthy behaviors in minority populations. It is hoped that many other projects aimed at these groups will be carried out over the next few years.

Summary

Behavioral scientists can play a significant role in influencing the overall health status of minority groups in this country. Unfortunately, many of the prevention and treatment programs developed for white populations may not be relevant for minorities because of differences in social characteristics, including demographic profiles, dietary practices and nutritional status, environmental and occupational exposures, and stress and coping patterns. To date, relatively little attention has been paid to the development of such programs with these groups. We may hope, however, that this sad fact will soon be changing. The 1986 Forum on Cardiovascular Disease Risk Factors in Minority Populations, sponsored by the NHLBI Ad Hoc Committee on Cardiovascular/Pulmonary Disease Risk Factors in Minority Populations, and the National Medical Association, focused on the specific needs of these groups. The next few years should show an increase in awareness and sensitivity to the issues of minority health, as well as the development of behaviorally oriented, culturally relevant programs to help end the health disparity that these groups currently experience.

CHAPTER

6

THE ADDICTIVE DISORDERS

JOHN P. FOREYT

This chapter on the addictive disorders continues the tradition maintained by its predecessors. Issues of general interest, trends, and specific contributions that behavior therapists are making in the areas of obesity, tobacco use, and alcoholism are covered. Because the areas have grown so rapidly, overviews of relevant topics are summarized and the reader is referred to other published works for more detailed review.

OBESITY

This section on obesity reviews five topics. First, new studies on genetics and weight cycling provide a broader perspective on the development of obesity and the difficulties involved in losing weight. A recent study on rats that were allowed access to a high-fat diet until obese, then restricted and refed for two cycles of loss and regain, may have implications for human chronic dieters and help explain why many obese people cannot lose weight even on highly restrictive diets. Second, I report on the results of a workshop on methods for characterizing human obesity. This work may lead to standardized methods for data collection in this field, which would be extremely useful for behavioral researchers. Third, I review several large studies that report new data on the prevalence of obesity, its definition, and its association with excess mortality. Fourth, I report on the results of two consensus development conferences sponsored by the National Institutes of Health (NIH), one on cholesterol and the other on obesity. These conferences indicate the strong interest the federal government has in these topics. And, finally, I update what is happening in the behavioral treatment of obesity. The review illustrates the contributions that behavior therapy continues to make in helping patients both lose and maintain body weight. It also points out the limitations of our approaches and the challenges that remain. Overall, it has been an exciting year in the obesity area.

Bad News for Dieters

Two recent articles by Stunkard and colleagues (Stunkard, Foch, & Hrubec, 1986a; Stunkard *et al.*, 1986b) have re-examined the old question about the role of genetic factors and the family environment in the development of obesity, with some important findings. In the first-published of these studies (Stunkard *et al.*, 1986b), a sample of 540 adult Danish adoptees was divided into four weight classes: thin, median weight, overweight, and obese. The weight classes of the adoptees were then compared to the body mass index values of their biological parents and to that of their adoptive parents. Results showed a clear relation between the body mass index values of the biological parents and the weight classes of the adoptees; however, there was no relation between the body mass index values of the adoptive parents and the weight classes of the adoptees. These findings suggest that genetic influences are major determinants of body fatness and that childhood family environment alone has little or no effect. In the second study (Stunkard *et al.*, 1986a), height, weight, and body mass index were measured in 1,974 monozygotic and 2,097 dizygotic male twin pairs. The authors found that the concordance rates for different degrees of overweight were twice as high for the monozygotic twins as for the dizygotic twins. A high degree of heritability for height, weight, and body mass index, both at age 20 (.80, .78, and .77, respectively) and at a 25-year follow-up (.80, .81, and .84, respectively), was found. Stunkard and colleagues' conclusion in both reports is that human body weight, including fatness, is under strong genetic control.

The results of these studies are clear and unequivocal; they suggest strong and undeniable genetic influences on body weight. Family environment alone seems to have little influence. What are the implications of this research for behavior therapists? Are behavioral interventions doomed to failure with individuals genetically programmed to be obese? Stunkard and colleagues' data illustrate the enormous difficulty we face in trying to treat individuals with strong genetic tendencies toward obesity. Their results also may help explain the relatively modest results that behavior therapists, relying primarily on self-monitoring and stimulus control strategies, have achieved with obese patients and may indicate why they have not been more successful. Much more aggressive programs, such as the ones reviewed later in this chapter (see "Trends in the Behavioral Treatment of Obesity," below), seem necessary if behavior therapists are ever going to play an important role in the treatment of patients with moderate or gross obesity.

Van Itallie (1986) points out that although genetic factors may explain much of the individual variation in fatness within a society, environmental influences can help account for the differences in fatness that occur among societies and social groups whose characteristic diets, activity levels, and attitudes about physical appearance differ. As described later in this chapter (see "New Data on Prevalence of Obesity," below), major epidemiological studies show that the prevalence of obesity in human populations is related to a number of factors, in addition to genetics, including social conditions and economic circumstances (e.g., the prevalence of obesity is much higher among women below the poverty line than above it).

Stunkard and colleagues' studies also have implications for the prevention of obesity. They (Stunkard *et al.*, 1986b) argue that current efforts at preventing obesity are generally directed toward all obese children and their parents. If their data suggesting that family environment alone has little to do with the development of obesity are correct, then prevention efforts now directed toward children at low genetic risk of becoming obese could be refocused toward those at high risk (i.e., the children of obese parents). Only 14% of children of two parents of normal weight become obese, compared with 80% of children of two obese parents (Mayer, 1965).

If these two studies are not discouraging enough for dieters, a third one, investigating the metabolic effects of weight cycling (i.e., repeated attempts at weight loss followed by regain), has reported more bad news. Brownell, Greenwood, Stellar, and Shrager (1986) assigned adult male Sprague–Dawley rats to three groups: (1) chow controls (*ad libitum* access to chow throughout the study); (2) obese controls (*ad libitum* access to a high-fat diet); and (3) obese cycling (*ad libitum* access to a high-fat diet until obese, then restricted, and then refed for two cycles of loss and regain). Results showed that the rats in Group 3 (the obese-cycling animals) had significant increases in food efficiency in the second restriction and refeeding periods compared to the first such periods. Weight loss occurred at half the rate and was regained at three times the rate in the second cycle. Equivalent weight losses required 21 days in the first cycle and 46 days in the second. Equivalent regain of weight took 46 days in the first cycle compared to only 14 days in the second. The obese-cycling animals had a significantly higher percentage of body fat and a lower percentage of body water. They also had a significantly increased number of fat cells. Results of the study demonstrated the strong metabolic effects of cycles of restriction and refeeding in obese animals. At the end of the study, Group 3 animals were maintaining the same body weight as the control group (Group 1), while consuming significantly less food. The authors speculated from their animal results that obese humans who lose and regain weight repeatedly may also have a dieting-induced metabolic deficiency that inhibits weight loss and promotes regain. These data may help explain the difficulty that many patients who have dieted for long periods of time have in losing weight, even on calorie-controlled diets. Further studies such as this one will help increase our understanding of the complexities involved when patients lose and regain body weight. They also illustrate the breadth of research in which behavior therapists are involved.

Characterizing Human Obesity

The condition we refer to as "obesity" is in fact a heterogeneous group of disorders, and new work in better defining these disorders is a welcome addition to the field. For many adults, the obese state may be the result of inactivity; for others, it may result from overeating. Hormonal changes may be a cause or a consequence of obesity. Obesity may be due to specific enzymatic or endocrine effects. Because of its heterogeneous nature, many classification systems over the years have been devised to attempt to bring some clarity to the ambiguity. Von Noorden originally proposed the dichotomous classification of "exogenous" versus "endogeneous" obesity in the early 1900s. It is still widely used, despite the fact that almost all obese patients are classified as "exogeneous" (Sims, 1979). Other classification systems have been based upon the age of onset, presumed etiology, adipose cellularity (i.e., hypercellular vs. hypertrophic), or metabolic origins ("regulatory" vs. "metabolic" obesity) (Callaway & Greenwood, 1984).

The proceedings of a workshop on methods for characterizing human obesity, funded by NIH and held at Vassar College, have now been published. In attendance at the workshop were researchers in nutrition, genetics, physical anthropology, experimental and behavioral psychology, exercise physiology, endocrinology, and other areas of clinical medicine (Callaway & Greenwood, 1984).

At the workshop, Harrison (1984) described four types of classification systems that have been used by obesity researchers.

1. Etiologic classifications, as commonly used today, consist of a few rare types of genetic, endocrine, and central nervous system causes, and place the rest of obese individuals into a category labeled "exogeneous," "idiopathic," or "unknown origin." Harrison believes that etiological classifications will eventually evolve to a point at which "unknown origin" will account for only a small number of obese cases.

2. Prognostic classifications predict the probability of successful weight loss or weight maintenance. Behavioral studies, for example, have suggested that a high number of unsuccessful attempts at weight loss may be a negative prognostic factor. Other possibilities may include childhood onset of obesity, increased adipose cell number, and high percentage of body fat.

3. Therapeutic classifications attempt to identify what types of obesity are most responsive to specific therapeutic interventions. Therapists with certain personality traits may work better with some patients than others; specific behavioral strategies (e.g., cognitive–behavioral interventions) may be more effective with some types of individuals than others; and so forth.

4. Functional classifications are aimed at describing the consequences of obesity with respect to their significance to the patient's physical or mental well-being. For example, changes in blood pressure for an obese, hypertensive patient may be of more importance than measuring therapeutic outcome by weight loss.

A manual about standardized data collection and methodology for characterizing human obesities may soon be published, and could prove extremely useful for behavior therapists as a guide for helping standardize data collection. It will provide recommendations for what baseline data should be routinely assessed and what descriptive measures collected in obese subjects who are part of clinical studies; it should also help provide the standardization needed when evaluating and interpreting published data.

New Data on the Prevalence of Obesity

The National Health and Nutrition Examination Surveys of the National Center for Health Statistics, covering the years 1971–1974 (NHANES-I) and 1976-1980 (NHANES-II), assessed height, weight, and skinfold thicknesses in large samples of the U.S. population (Abraham, Carroll, Najjar, & Fulwood, 1983; McDowell, Engel, Massey, & Maurer, 1981; Miller, 1973). Overweight in NHANES-II was defined by a body mass index (i.e., weight in kilograms divided by height in meters squared) equal to or greater than the 85th percentile of men and women in their 50s. Men were defined as "overweight" with a body mass index equal to or greater than 27.8 and "severely overweight" when the index equaled or exceeded 31.1; for women, the indices were 27.3 and 32.3, respectively. These cutoffs points correspond closely to our commonly used definitions of mild obesity (20–40% over ideal body weight) and moderate obesity (40–100% over desired body weight).

According to NHANES-II, 26% of U.S. adults (about 34 million individuals) aged 20–75 years were overweight between 1976 and 1980. Over 12 million were severely overweight. These results compare unfavorably with the earlier NHANES-I data, which suggested that 20.8 million adult Americans were obese, including 8.4 million who were severely obese.

Figure 6-1 illustrates the percentage of males and females who are overweight by race and age; it also shows the percentage of males and females who are overweight by poverty status and age (Van Itallie, 1985). According to Figure 6-1A, the prevalence of overweight rises in both white and black males until age 54, at which time it declines. Overweight is more common among black men than white men between the ages of 35 and 54.

The data on white and black females in Figure 6-1B are especially interesting. Unlike the situation with males, the prevalence of overweight in white females continues to increase with age from 20 to 74. But the prevalence of overweight in black females is much higher at all ages, and, in the 45–54 age range, over 60% of black females are overweight. This percentage remains relatively constant through age 74. This incredible prevalence of overweight cries out for the development of culturally relevant behavioral intervention programs for this underserved group (see Chapter 5).

Figure 6-1C, which illustrates the same data with respect to poverty, shows that with men there is a slightly higher prevalence of overweight at all ages among those above the poverty line. This is in striking contrast to Figure 6-1D, which clearly indicates that women below the poverty line have a much higher prevalence of overweight at all age categories, except ages 20–24. The figure suggests an obvious question: Are race and socioeconomic status confounded? According to Van Itallie (1985), multivariate analysis indicates that race and poverty status are *independent* predictors of overweight for women; race is an independent predictor of overweight status after adjustment for sex, age, and poverty status. The association of poverty status and overweight is thus independent of race and different for men and women.

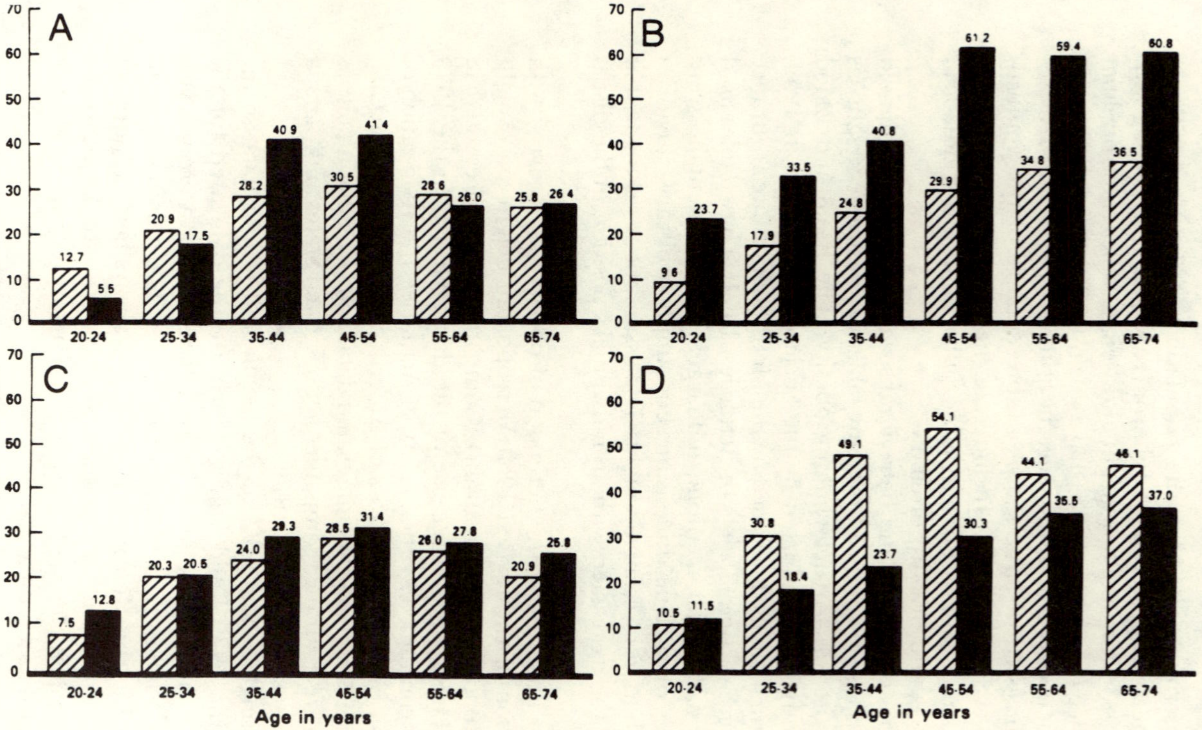

FIG. 6-1.

(A) Percentage of males overweight by race and age. Cross-hatched bars indicate whites, and solid bars indicate blacks. (B) Percentage of nonpregnant females overweight by race and age. Cross-hatched bars indicate whites, and solid bars indicate blacks. (C) Percentage of males overweight by poverty status and age. Cross-hatched bars indicate poverty, and solid bars indicate nonpoverty. (D) Percentage of nonpregnant females overweight by poverty status and age. Cross-hatched bars indicate poverty, and solid bars indicate nonpoverty. (Reproduced with permission from: Health Implications of Overweight and Obesity in the United States. T. B. Van Itallie. *Annals of Internal Medicine*. 1985; 103:983–988. Copyright 1985 by the American College of Physicians.)

Updating the Definition of Obesity

Updated descriptive data for the population of the United States (Abraham *et al.*, 1983; Abraham, Johnson, & Najjar, 1979), along with the recent 1983 Metropolitan height and weight tables (Metropolitan Life Insurance Company, 1983), have given us new information for defining what obesity is and who meet the criteria for it. The NHANES-II studies consisted of large samples representative of the noninstitutionalized U.S. population. Included in the data base were weight and height, along with triceps and subscapular skinfolds, middle-arm circumference, and breadth of elbow.

For years, physicians and behavioral scientists have used the old Metropolitan Life Insurance Company tables of "desirable weight" as the major criterion for determining obesity. The Build and Blood Pressure Study was conducted by the Society of Actuaries in 1959, and the original tables developed by the Metropolitan Life Insurance Company were revised (Society of Actuaries, 1959). These tables used three frame sizes, small, medium, and large; these, incidentally, were not measures of skeletal dimension, but simply arbitrary categories of the distribution of relative weight. The assumption was made that skeletal size was associated with an individual's position in the distribution.

A major updating of the definition of obesity has occurred with the publication of the revised 1983 Metropolitan height and weight tables (Metropolitan Life Insurance Company, 1983), presented in Table 6-1. These tables make use of the data collected in the 1979 Build Study conducted by the Society of Actuaries and Association of Life Insurance Medical Directors of America (1980; see also McCue, 1981). The 1979 Build Study integrated data from 4.2 million policies issued by 25 life insurance companies in the United States and Canada between the years 1950 and 1971.

Interestingly, about 10% of the height and weight data on the subjects in the 1979 Build Study (which are the data used for the Metropolitan tables) were provided by self-report and were not verified by direct measurement (Harrison, 1985). The amount of modesty reflected in the Metropolitan tables has always been a source of amusement to me. The 90% of subjects who were actually measured all wore clothing, including their shoes! How many patients wear their shoes when they step on a scale?

Upon publication, these new Metropolitan tables met with considerable criticism. They are not representative of the U.S. population as a whole. The tables include, in a disproportionate amount, middle- and upper-class individuals, males, whites, and individuals less than

TABLE 6-1. 1983 Metropolitan Height and Weight Tables

Men					Women				
Height		Frame			Height		Frame		
Feet	Inches	Small	Medium	Large	Feet	Inches	Small	Medium	Large
5	2	128–134	131–141	138–150	4	10	102–111	109–121	118–131
5	3	130–136	133–143	140–153	4	11	103–113	111–123	120–134
5	4	132–138	135–145	142–156	5	0	104–115	113–126	122–137
5	5	134–140	137–148	144–160	5	1	106–118	115–129	125–140
5	6	136–142	139–151	146–164	5	2	108–121	118–132	128–143
5	7	138–145	142–154	149–168	5	3	111–124	121–135	131–147
5	8	140–148	145–157	152–172	5	4	114–127	124–138	134–151
5	9	142–151	148–160	155–176	5	5	117–130	127–141	137–155
5	10	144–154	151–163	158–180	5	6	120–133	130–144	140–159
5	11	146–157	154–166	161–184	5	7	123–136	133–147	143–163
6	0	149–160	157–170	164–188	5	8	126–139	136–150	146–167
6	1	152–164	160–174	168–192	5	9	129–142	139–153	149–170
6	2	155–168	164–178	172–197	5	10	132–145	142–156	152–173
6	3	158–172	167–182	176–202	5	11	135–148	145–159	155–176
6	4	162–176	171–187	181–207	6	0	138–151	148–162	158–179

Note. Weights at ages 25–59 based on lowest mortality. Weight in pounds according to frame (in shoes with 1-inch heels and indoor clothing weighing 5 pounds for men and 3 pounds for women). From "1983 Metropolitan Height and Weight Tables" by the Metropolitan Life Insurance Company, 1983, *Statistical Bulletin, 64*, 2–9. Copyright 1983 by the Metropolitan Life Insurance Company. Reprinted by permission.

60 years old. Although the tables can be helpful within these subgroups, they are certainly less useful with the underrepresented subgroups. In fact, the tables include data only on individuals between the ages of 20 years and 59 years, seriously limiting their use with people younger than 20 or older than 59. Harrison (1985) has pointed out that the unit of analysis in the 1979 Build Study was not the person, but the insurance policy. For example, an individual with more than one insurance policy would have been counted once for each policy. Mortality ratios could have been affected in some of the subgroups by deaths of just a few individuals who might have had more than one policy (Harrison, 1985). Confounding variables such as smoking were also not considered in the 1979 Build Study.

One of the biggest problems I have always had with the Metropolitan tables has been the concept of frame size. Guidelines for assessing frame size have been sparse, and many of my patients simply assume that they are "large." For use with the new tables, a plastic gauge is available for measuring breadth of the elbow, which, according to the company, may help determine frame size. Unfortunately, the published tables are not based on, and do not use, elbow breadth as a measure, reducing its applicability. Behavioral researchers have traditionally used the midpoint of the midrange for a given person's height and sex to determine desirable weight, and then have determined obesity by multiplying by 120%. That definition is obviously arbitrary and does not take into account a number of variables, including bone size and density; this fact limits its usefulness for both clinicians and researchers.

Despite the limitations discussed above, the new Metropolitan tables will not go away, and Americans in particular love to use them in their apparently never-ending preoccupation with being thinner than the "average" person. Since these tables will always be with us, I think that it is important that all of us in the field be aware of their strengths and weaknesses. It is especially important to remember that, when we are dealing with individuals from the subgroups on which the tables were *not* normed, we ought to be particularly careful in our assessment procedures. We certainly need tools for diagnostic and treatment purposes, but not to the exclusion of good judgment and common sense.

New Data on Weight and Mortality

Recent results from the Framingham Heart Study suggest that obesity is an independent risk factor for cardiovascular disease (Hubert, Feinleib, McNamara, & Castelli, 1983) and increases mortality in males (Garrison & Castelli, 1985). On the basis of data from 30 years of biennial examinations and mortality information on males who participated in the Framingham Study, Garrison and Castelli (1985) reported that Metropolitan relative weight, measured at baseline, was strongly related to mortality in the subsequent 30 years. (The Metropolitan relative weight was computed by determining the ratio of body weight to the reference weight, which was the midpoint of the desired weight range for medium-build men from the 1959 Metropolitan Life Insurance Company tables; this ratio was expressed as a whole-number percentage.) Males whose Metropolitan relative weight was 110% or greater were considered overweight. Those whose relative weight was 100–109% were considered at desirable weight, and those whose relative weight was less than 100% were considered underweight. Results showed that men whose relative weight was between 100% and 109% had minimum mortality. Figure 6-2 illustrates the 30-year relative risk of death for men aged 30–39 at the first biennial examination, showing data for nonsmokers and smokers separately. Overweight nonsmoking men had mortality rates that were

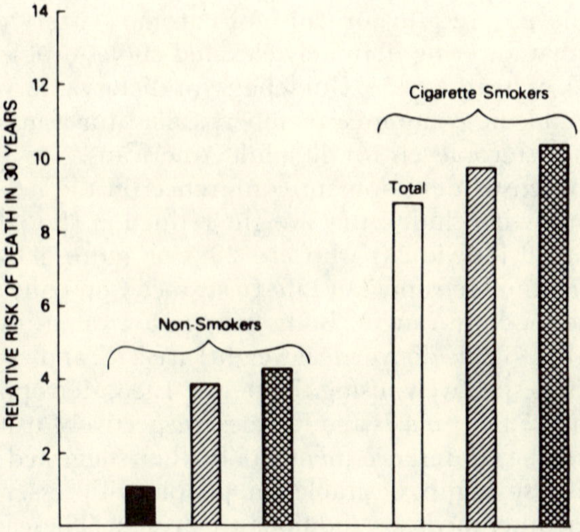

FIG. 6-2.
Thirty-year relative risk of death for men aged 30–39 years at the first biennial examination. The solid bar represents men of desirable weight (Metropolitan relative weight, 100–109%); the bar with diagonal hatching represents overweight men (relative weight, 110% or more); and the cross-hatched bar represents obese men (relative weight, 120% or more). Reproduced with permission from: R. J. Garrison and W. P. Castelli. Weight and Thirty-Year Mortality of Men in the Framingham Study. *Annals of Internal Medicine.* 1985; 103:1006–1009. Copyright 1985 by the American College of Physicians.

up to 3.9 times higher than those for nonsmoking men who were at desirable weight. The figure illustrates the increase in excess mortality with increasing degrees of overweight in both nonsmokers and smokers. This study represents further evidence that obesity does indeed affect longevity in males, and emphasizes the need from the medical viewpoint to reduce excess body weight.

Consensus Development Conferences on Cholesterol and on Health Implications of Obesity

Recently, two NIH consensus development conferences focused on health-related topics relevant to this chapter (Consensus Conference, 1985; National Institutes of Health Consensus Development Panel on the Health Implications of Obesity, 1985). The Consensus Development Conference on Cholesterol provided an integrated summary of the current state of the field, reiterated the fact that elevated blood cholesterol levels are a major cause of coronary artery disease, and concluded that lowering definitely elevated cholesterol levels will reduce the risk of heart attacks. Guidelines for dietary intervention were presented, and the committee members called for a mass screening of blood cholesterol levels for all adult Americans.

The consensus development conference on the health implications of obesity concluded that weight reduction should be recommended for all individuals who are 20% or more above desirable weights using the Metropolitan Life Insurance Company tables (midpoint of the medium range). Body mass index values (which correspond roughly to 20% above ideal weight) are 27.2 and 26.9 for males and females, respectively, using the newer 1983 Metropolitan tables, and 26.4 and 25.8 for males and females, respectively, using the older 1959 tables. The conference members further suggested that weight reduction is also highly desirable for people with lesser degrees of obesity when other medical conditions are present. These include non-insulin-dependent diabetes mellitus; a family history of diabetes mellitus; a history of gestational diabetes or a birth history of an infant large for gestational age (for women); hypertension; hypertriglyceridemia; or hypercholesterolemia. Finally, the conference members viewed with alarm the increasing frequency of obesity in young children and adolescents. They recommend that obese children be strongly encouraged to bring their weight to within normal limits.

Several recommendations for future research were suggested (National Institutes for Health Consensus Development Panel on the Health Implications of Obesity, 1985):

1. The search for biological (genetic, metabolic, or anthropometric) markers in infancy and childhood as predictors of adult obesity.
2. The study of mechanisms by which body fat distribution is associated with adverse effects of obesity; factors that regulate the regional distribution of fat; and methods to assess its distribution.
3. Studies on the regulation of energy balance, including the effects on the central and autonomic nervous system and the endocrine system; adipose tissue cellularity and metabolism; the role of various components on thermogenesis; the control of food intake (including endogenous opioids); and satiety factors (gastrointestinal hormones).
4. Investigations using cultural and physical measurements in

minority groups, low-socioeconomic-status groups, and rapidly changing societies.

5. The archiving of data from large-cohort investigations on coronary artery disease begun up to 30 years ago.
6. The development of tables of relative risk that incorporate both height–weight information and body fat distribution.
7. Clinical studies using the new advances in biology.

Unfortunately, the conference did not review a number of important areas. For example, the treatment of obesity was not covered, nor was the area of prevention of obesity or the impact of society on body weight. Clearly, these issues fundamental to behavioral science need to be addressed, and the importance of a consensus development conference in these areas cannot be overemphasized.

Behavior Therapy for Obesity

Behavior therapy continues to be one of the most widely used interventions for weight reduction. This section is, therefore, an excellent time to pause to re-examine its contributions. Readers will remember that Ferster, Nurnberger, and Levitt published their article describing a model for the control of obesity using behavioral strategies in 1962. Since that time, how much has behavior therapy really contributed to this area? Early reviews (e.g., Foreyt, Goodrick, & Gotto, 1981; Jeffery, Wing, & Stunkard, 1978; Wilson & Brownell, 1980) all found that patients undergoing behavior therapy for obesity had average weight losses of about 11 points at posttreatment. This average weight loss of 11 pounds was a remarkably robust finding for early behavioral treatment programs lasting 8–10 weeks, considering that therapists differed in training, patients differed in a number of characteristics, and treatment settings varied from university psychology departments to private clinics. However, the large variability in weight losses among patients was always a cause for concern. Some patients clearly seemed to benefit from treatment, while others apparently received no help.

Brownell and Wadden (1986) recently reviewed behavioral treatment of obesity studies covering three time periods: those conducted before and during 1974, during 1978, and during 1984. They examined characteristics of subjects, duration of treatment, follow-up, and outcome results. Table 6-2 presents their findings.

As the table indicates, average length of treatment increased, from 8.4 weeks in 1974 to 10.5 weeks in 1978 to 13.2 weeks in 1984.

TABLE 6-2. Summary of Data from Controlled Trials of Behavior Therapy for Obesity, Completed before and during 1974 and during 1978 and 1984

	1974	1978	1984
Sample size	53.1	54.0	71.3
Initial weight (pounds)	163.0	194.0	197.0
Initial % overweight	49.4	48.6	48.1
Length of treatment (weeks)	8.4	10.5	13.2
Weight loss (pounds)	8.5	9.4	15.4
Loss per week (pounds)	1.2	0.9	1.2
Attrition (%)	11.4	12.9	10.6
Length of follow-up (weeks)	15.5	30.3	58.4
Loss at follow-up (pounds)	8.9	9.1	9.8

Note. All values are means across studies. From "Behavior Therapy for Obesity: Modern Approaches and Better Results" by K. D. Brownell and T. A. Wadden, 1986, in K. D. Brownell and J. P. Foreyt (Eds.), *Handbook of Eating Disorders: Physiology, Psychology, and Treatment of Obesity, Anorexia, and Bulimia* (pp. 180–197), New York: Basic Books. Copyright 1986 by Basic Books, Inc. Reprinted by permission.

Average weight losses also increased, from 8.5 pounds in 1974 to 15.4 pounds in 1984. Weight losses per week, however, remained the same (1.2 pounds in both 1974 and 1984), suggesting that the longer formal treatment period was the cause of the better average weight losses. Attrition remained low in behavioral programs—11.4% in 1974 and 10.6% in 1984. Length of follow-up increased, from 15.5 weeks in 1974 to 58.4 weeks in 1984.

Behavioral treatment programs are different today from what they were like in the mid-1970s. Early programs emphasized self-monitoring, particularly food diaries, and stimulus control strategies. Today's programs are much more comprehensive than the earlier ones and include, in addition to self-monitoring and stimulus control, greater emphasis on cognitive–behavioral strategies, social support approaches, nutrition, and exercise.

Are today's more comprehensive programs better? Average weight losses per week have not improved, although from a nutritional standpoint they are in line with current dietary recommendations for safe, healthy losses. At first glance, however, it might appear surprising that average losses have not increased, since many clinicians who have been practicing since the mid-1970s would certainly argue that today's treatment programs are clearly superior to the earlier ones. We do not know whether the earlier programs based on self-monitoring and stimulus control would have produced the same losses as the newer ones, had they extended their treatment length to 13 weeks, but I doubt it. Clinicians realize that material presented to classes must be varied, interesting, and relevant, or participants find reasons not to attend. The newer information being included in programs today may serve to motivate participants to attend more classes, keep their interest, and therefore increase weight losses—something the earlier programs might not have been able to do, since they relied almost exclusively on two interventions (self-monitoring and stimulus control). As participants lose more weight, the newer cognitive–behavioral strategies take on more relevance, particularly for dealing with high-risk situations and for maintaining already achieved losses. Emphasizing these strategies may help participants continue to lose and to maintain their successes better (Brownell & Wadden, 1986).

As noted above, Brownell and Wadden (1986) found that length of reported follow-up increased dramatically, from 15.5 weeks in 1974 to 58.4 weeks in 1984. Interestingly, average weight loss at follow-up did not improve substantially (8.9 pounds in 1974 and 9.8 pounds in 1984). Participants were gaining back about 5.6 pounds from post-treatment to follow-up.

What can we conclude about the recent state of the science of behavior therapy for obesity? Treatment programs in 1984 averaged about 13.2 weeks in length. They resulted in weight losses of about 1.2 pounds per week. Attrition was low, averaging about 10.6%. Length of follow-up being reported was over 1 year, and the average patient gained back about 5.6 pounds, leaving him or her with a loss of 9.8 pounds a year after treatment. However, one study (Stalonas, Perri, & Kerzner, 1984) reported that at a 5-year follow-up most participants had gained back a major amount of the weight loss during treatment. The average participant had gained back 11.94 pounds and was 1.49 pounds heavier than at baseline.

There have been a number of exceptions to the summary given above. Some longer behaviorally oriented treatment programs with more aggressive approaches have produced substantially better weight losses. A 25-week program reported a loss of 24 pounds (Craighead, Stunkard, & O'Brien, 1981), and a 16-week program reported an 18-pound loss (Brownell & Stunkard, 1981). Losses of over 20 pounds were reported in studies of 15 and 16 weeks (Jeffery, Bjornson-Benson, Rosenthal, Kurth, & Dunn, 1984a; Jeffery, Bjornson-Benson, Rosenthal, Lindquist, & Johnson, 1984b; Jeffery *et al.*, 1984c). An impressive loss of 42 pounds has been reported in a 6-month program combining behavior therapy with a very-low-calorie diet (Wadden & Stunkard, 1986).

These losses are quite substantial, suggesting that behavior therapy has an extremely important role to play in a comprehensive plan of treatment. Combining behavior therapy with more aggressive strategies, especially for those with moderate or gross obesity, seems to offer considerable promise. Maintenance of losses, however, is still the exception rather than the rule.

Trends in the Behavioral Treatment of Obesity

Two challenges remain in the behavioral treatment of obesity: how to increase weight losses during treatment, and how to improve the maintenance of these losses. If, for example, a patient comes to a behavioral clinician needing to lose 60 pounds, what kind of treatment program is the most effective one to use with that particular patient? Similarly, if a patient loses 60 pounds, what behavioral program is best for helping that patient maintain those losses?

INCREASING WEIGHT LOSSES

Behavioral treatment programs as currently conducted appear to be most useful with patients needing to lose modest amounts of weight. A patient who is 20 pounds overweight stands a good chance of losing most, if not all, of the excess weight with a knowledgeable behavior therapist. Two trends have emerged to assist clinicians with patients who need to lose substantially greater amounts of weight. These trends—one promising, one disappointing—are very-low-calorie diets and pharmacotherapy.

Very-Low-Calorie Diets. For patients needing to lose 50 or more pounds, the use of very-low-calorie diets, combined with behavioral approaches for maintenance of those losses, appears promising. These diets of 300–600 calories per day, consisting of 70 to 100 grams of protein, have been shown consistently to produce rapid weight losses in relatively short periods of time. Programs today rely either on protein from lean meat, chicken, turkey, or seafood, or on a high-protein liquid using an egg-based or a milk-based formula. Studies show no significant differences in the amount of weight loss with either of the protein forms. Both produce an average weight loss of about 45 pounds in 12 weeks, three times the amount of loss in current behavioral programs. The diets seem safe when the patients are monitored regularly by physicians (Wadden, Stunkard, & Brownell, 1983).

Although the average weight losses have been extremely encouraging, a not unexpected finding has been the difficulty in maintaining those large losses. Any clinician who uses very-low-calorie diets can attest to the rapid regain of lost weight in a high percentage of treated patients, although, as with the early behavioral treatment studies, published long-term follow-up data of patients treated with these diets are not numerous.

Studies combining behavior therapy with the very-low-calorie diets show cautiously optimistic data. For example, Wadden, Stunkard, Brownell, and Day (1984) treated 17 women in a weekly program over 6 months. The women were placed on a very-low-calorie diet for 2 months, followed by exercise, cognitive–behavioral strategies, and a calorie-controlled diet for 4 months. These heavy subjects (average starting weight of 238 pounds), lost an average of 45 pounds at the end of treatment and had maintained a loss of 41 pounds at a 1-year follow-up.

In one of the few controlled clinical trials reported to date, Wadden and Stunkard (1986) randomly assigned subjects to one of three treatment conditions: (1) very-low-calorie diet alone; (2) behavior therapy alone; or (3) very-low-calorie diet plus behavior therapy (combined treatment). Subjects in the first condition received a very-low-calorie diet for 2 months and a 1,000-calorie diet for 2 months. No formal training in behavioral strategies was given. Subjects in the second condition received a comprehensive behavioral treatment program for 6 months. Subjects in the third condition received both the behavioral training and the diet strategies. Weight losses for all three groups were excellent. Patients in Group 1 (the very-low-calorie diet alone) lost 31 pounds; those in Group 2 (the behavior therapy alone) lost 31.5 pounds; and those in Group 3 (the combined treatment) lost 42.5 pounds. These results have several important implications. First, note the large average weight loss in the behavior therapy alone condition (31.5 pounds); this suggests that comprehensive behavioral programs lasting for longer periods than are now common (patients in this study met weekly for 6 months) result in significantly greater weight losses. It seems to me that it is about time that behavioral clinicians forget about their 8- to 12-week treatment programs and conduct programs *at least* 6 months long. Second, even though the literature is not clear on the importance of specific components of behavioral treatment interventions, more elements—including exercise, social support, cognitive change, and nutrition, in addition to behavior modification strategies—should be incorporated into programs, if only to maintain participants' interest and to keep them coming to treatment sessions (Brownell, 1985b).

The 1-year follow-up data in the Wadden and Stunkard (1986) study are also of great interest. Subjects in Groups 2 and 3 (those receiving the behavior therapy alone condition and the combined treatment) both regained about one-third of their losses, with those in Group 2 having an average weight loss from pretreatment of 20.9

pounds and those in Group 3 of 28.4 pounds. Subjects in Group 1 (those receiving the very-low-calorie diet alone) fared much worse, regaining two-thirds of their weight loss; at the 1-year follow-up, their average weight loss was only 10.1 pounds.

In both behavior therapy conditions (Groups 2 and 3), subjects were better able to maintain their weight losses. Subjects in the first two groups lost about the same amount of weight during treatment; however, at follow-up, the subjects receiving behavior therapy alone regained only about half as much weight as the subjects receiving the very-low-calorie diet alone (10.5 vs. 20.9 pounds); this suggests that slower weight losses may be better maintained than weight lost more rapidly. Finally, the addition of behavior therapy to very-low-calorie diets appears to help subjects lose more weight during treatment. However, I think that it is important to observe that none of the conditions showed maintenance of treatment-produced losses. Although these results are encouraging, we clearly have much to learn about the processes involved in the long-term maintenance of lost body weight. This is clearly the challenge of the 1980s for behavior therapists working with obesity.

Pharmacotherapy. Many of the patients I treat for obesity do not really want to change their diet, begin exercising, or alter their life style in any appreciable way. They just want to lose weight. These are the patients who have made the drug industry wealthy. Drug treatment for obesity has been extremely popular for at least the past 30 years. Drugs have always been seen by many as the magic bullet, allowing individuals to lose weight without having to expend much effort in the process. Reviews of the drug literature have generally teased us with their potential for increasing weight losses; however, maintenance of those losses has again been difficult. As patients are weaned from their drug therapy, weight regain appears almost inevitable. The potential for abuse of drugs and possible negative side effects also has led to the limited availability of the more powerful ones.

However, if we could find safe drugs along with effective strategies for maintaining the losses produced by drug treatment, their usefulness for behavior therapists would increase. Two studies have explored the combination of pharmacotherapy with behavior therapy; both had disappointing results. In one study (Craighead *et al.*, 1981), subjects who were treated for 25 weeks with either pharmacotherapy (fenfluramine hydrochloride) or pharmacotherapy plus behavior therapy lost significantly more weight than subjects who were treated with behavior therapy alone. Posttreatment losses were 32 pounds, 35 pounds, and 24 pounds, respectively (note the larger losses with the drug treatments). Follow-up data, however, were quite poor for the drug treatment groups: Subjects in the pharmacotherapy group regained 18 pounds, while those in the pharmacotherapy-plus-behavior-therapy group regained even more, 24 pounds. Subjects in the behavior-therapy-alone condition regained only 4 pounds at the 1-year follow-up. Neither pharmacotherapy nor the addition of behavior therapy to pharmacotherapy appeared effective in maintenance of weight losses (Craighead *et al.*, 1981).

Because the behavior therapy treatment was given at the same time that subjects were receiving the drug, it seemed logical that subjects might not be learning the behavioral strategies, since the drug itself was probably the primary agent producing weight loss. Craighead (1984) wondered whether behavior therapy might be more effective if it were administered either just before or just after the pharmacotherapy. In her second study, she examined the sequencing of the two treatments. Unfortunately the long-term results were no better in the second study (Craighead, 1984) than in the first.

So far, then, the results of the two Craighead studies suggest that behavior therapy really does not add to the effects produced by pharmacotherapy. The idea still seems to be a good one, and I think more studies ought to be done in the area. To date, however, drug treatment does not appear particularly useful, with or without behavior therapy, since regain occurs so rapidly.

MAINTAINING WEIGHT LOSSES

Does behavior therapy result in weight losses that are maintained? If not, how can we improve our track record? The answer to the first question is that in most programs patients appear to regain about one-third of their losses at a 1-year follow-up. This regain appears to be slower than that seen in patients who undergo most other kinds of treatment for obesity. We also know that once they leave a formal behavioral treatment program, patients do not continue to lose weight. The amount lost during contact with therapists in formal intervention programs is all the patients can be expected to lose. The question, then, becomes this: How can therapists help patients maintain these losses once therapists are no longer in contact with them? Although a number of approaches have been attempted through the years to improve maintenance, the three most promising approaches to date are relapse prevention training, exercise, and social support.

Relapse Prevention Training. Following any kind of treatment for obesity, most patients eventually regain some if not all of their lost weight back. An interesting paper was recently published examining the phenomenon of relapse in obesity, alcoholism, and smoking (Brownell, Marlatt, Lichtenstein, & Wilson, 1986). In it, the authors describe the natural history of relapse, its determinants and effects, and several potential methods for prevention. The authors investigated commonalities and differences among the addictive disorders and reported that at least three basic stages of behavior change were common to all of them: motivation and commitment, initial change, and maintenance. They further explored many specific behavioral strategies relevant during each of these three basic stages.

For example, to prevent relapse, individuals trying to maintain weight losses need first to identify for themselves specific high-risk situations that lead to overeating, and then to master behavioral skills to cope with these situations. When individuals do falter, they need to learn to interpret the event as a temporary "lapse" (slip) from which they can recover, rather than as a "relapse," which generally leads to regaining all of their weight back (Marlatt & Gordon, 1985).

A number of recent studies have examined relapse prevention training in obesity treatment programs, and several have found improved long-term results when relapse prevention was added to behavioral treatment (e.g., Abrams & Follick, 1983; Perri, McAdoo, Spevak, & Newlin, 1984a; Perri, Shapiro, Ludwig, Twentyman, & McAdoo, 1984b; Sternberg, 1985). Also, one study (Collins, Rothblum, & Wilson, 1986) found no effect with the addition of relapse prevention training to a behavioral program.

In the study by Perri *et al.* (1984b), individuals who received behavior therapy, relapse prevention training, and follow-up contacts by telephone and mail had a 21.2-pound weight loss at posttreatment and a 22.8-pound loss at the 1-year follow-up. Individuals who received behavior therapy with only relapse prevention training lost 18.8 pounds during treatment, but were able to maintain only a 6.5-pound weight loss at follow-up. Those who received only behavior therapy lost 16.5 pounds during treatment and 13.8 pounds at follow-up. Individuals who received behavior therapy plus contact by phone and mail lost 19.2 pounds during treatment and 12.7 pounds at follow-up. Their results suggest that the addition of regular contacts over the telephone and mail may significantly enhance maintenance of losses following formal treatment.

Clearly, additional studies in relapse prevention training are needed. Specific strategies to prevent relapse are lacking, although the work of Marlatt and Gordon (1985) is exemplary. To date, studies of relapse prevention in the obesity field are optimistic, although much more work is required in this area before any definitive statements can be made.

Exercise. About half of all people who begin exercise programs are no longer exercising within 6 months (Falls, Baylor, & Dishman, 1980). Among the obese, the statistics are even worse, although there are a number of studies suggesting that increased exercise plays a significant role in maintenance of lost body weight (e.g., Colvin & Olson, 1983; Dahlkoetter, Callahan, & Linton, 1979; Epstein, Wing, Koeske, & Valoski, 1984, 1985; Gormally, Rardin, & Black, 1980; Harris & Hallbauer, 1973; Hoiberg, Berard, Watten, & Caine, 1984; Marston & Criss, 1984; Stalonas, Johnson, & Christ, 1978). Colvin and Olson (1983) reported that 78% of females and 85% of males who participated in an obesity treatment program reported that increased exercise was an important factor in their weight maintenance. Even small amounts of exercise seem to be important during the maintenance phase. As little as an additional 200 calories expended per day can play a major role in preventing regain of body weight. Patients appear more likely to adopt exercise patterns that are conducive to current life styles, such as increasing their walking, than to add a rigorous aerobic exercise program to their daily lives (Epstein, Wing, Koeske, Ossip, & Beck, 1982).

A major challenge facing behavior therapists today is to help individuals devise strategies to help them build exercise programs into their current life styles. By doing so, behavior therapists should begin to see improved maintenance statistics following formal treatment.

Social Support. The social support literature is based on Brownell, Heckerman, Westlake, Hayes, and Monti's (1978) initial study, which suggested that individuals who received treatment for weight reduction with a cooperative spouse showed significantly greater weight maintenance at a 6-month follow-up than did those in other conditions. Since that publication, a growing number of studies have examined the role of spousal support, with varying results. Some studies appear to show an effect; others do not (Brownell & Stunkard, 1981; O'Neil *et al.*, 1979; Weisz & Bucher, 1980). The idea makes good intuitive sense. Thomas, Goodwin, and Goodwin (1985), for example, reported that individuals with good social support systems had lower serum cholesterol and uric acid levels and higher indices of immune function than those lacking such support. Studies investigating the nature of the marital interaction would seem to be particularly useful in helping tease out the role of spousal support in weight loss and maintenance.

Peer support also appears promising as a long-term maintenance strategy (e.g., Foster, Wadden, & Brownell, 1985). It is clear, for example, that in our treatment classes many patients go to see each other and occasionally form friendships. Programs like Overeaters

Anonymous and Take Off Pounds Sensibly rely strongly on support from fellow sufferers to lose weight.

Spousal, family, and peer support all deserve further attention as maintenance strategies in the obesity field.

SUMMARY OF RECOMMENDATIONS TO DATE

Several recent findings (Brownell & Wadden, 1986) provide us with guidelines and suggestions for further research and treatment:

1. Broaden the base of behavioral treatment programs. Treatment for mild obesity (less than 40 pounds overweight) should involve a program including behavior modification, exercise, nutrition, cognitive change, and social support.
2. Increase the length of formal treatment. Behavioral programs result in losses of about 1 pound a week; therefore, longer programs generally result in better weight losses. Treatment programs of 6 months or a year may be more cost-effective for patients than several programs of shorter duration.
3. Explore more aggressive approaches to obesity with patients needing to lose more than 40 pounds. Combining behavior therapy with very-low-calorie diets appears promising, although maintenance is proving difficult.
4. Improve weight maintenance by emphasizing relapse prevention techniques.
5. Emphasize the use of exercise as a weight maintenance strategy. Find ways in which patients can add activity to their daily life style. Stress the need to exercise regularly.
6. Consider social support groups as a maintenance strategy.

TOBACCO USE

While the overall percentage of people who smoke cigarettes in the United States has continued to decline during the past 20 years, the production and use of smokeless tobacco products have risen dramatically. Snuff and chewing tobacco have re-emerged as popular products in this country for the first time since the early 1900s. About 12 million Americans used some form of smokeless tobacco in 1985, with all indications that the number will continue to increase, especially among adolescent males. Growing evidence suggests that use of these products may cause oral cancer and other health problems. Because of the increasing use of smokeless tobacco, I begin this section with a review of the products, including kinds, history of use, prevalence, factors related to adoption and maintenance, effects on health, and behavior therapy's potential role in prevention and treatment. Following the review, I also provide an update on cigarette smoking, with a current perspective on what is occurring with respect to changes in smoking patterns, given the growing assertiveness of nonsmokers in this country. Are we really approaching a smoke-free society by the year 2000? I also look at the increasing trend toward the use of multicomponent programs rather than single-strategy approaches for treatment of cigarette smoking; finally, I comment briefly on the concept of self-efficacy and its role in predicting maintenance of cessation.

Smokeless Tobacco

TYPES OF SMOKELESS TOBACCO PRODUCTS

There are two major kinds of smokeless tobacco products: chewing tobacco and snuff. Table 6-3 describes both kinds and how they are used and packaged.

The three most popular kinds of chewing tobacco are looseleaf, plug, and twist. Looseleaf chewing tobacco consists of tobacco leaves that are usually sold in 3-ounce foil-lined pouches consisting of small strips of shredded tobacco, often treated with sugar and licorice. The chewer takes a piece of it about 1 inch in diameter, and puts it in between the gum and jaw in the back of the mouth. Plug chewing tobacco is made from tobacco leaves pressed into flat bars and packaged in clear plastic. The chewer bites off a portion of the block and places it between the cheek and gum. Twist chewing tobacco consists of cured and flavored leaves that are twisted into a rope-shaped hank. It is used like plug chewing tobacco. Of the three types of chewing tobacco, looseleaf has always been by far the most popular kind and today accounts for about 70% of all chewing tobacco sales. In the United States, about 87 million pounds are sold annually.

There are two types of snuff, moist and dry. The most popular kind, moist snuff, is made from cured tobacco leaves that are flavored and processed into fine particles. Often flavored with wintergreen, raspberry, or mint, moist snuff is sold in flat, round 1.2-ounce containers. Its use, called "dipping," consists of placing a pinch between the lip and gum or under the tongue. Dry snuff consists of cured tobacco that is processed into a dry, powdered substance and often flavored. It is used like moist snuff or sniffed through the nose. The use of dry snuff in the United States is declining, with about 10 million

TABLE 6-3. Characteristics of Smokeless Tobacco Products

Product	Description	How used	Packaging[a]
Chewing Tobacco			
Looseleaf	Made from air-cured, cigar-leaf tobaccos of Pennsylvania and Wisconsin. Consists of stripped and processed tobacco leaves. The leaves are stemmed, cut, or granulated and are loosely packed to form small strips of shredded tobacco. Most brands are sweetened and flavored with licorice.	A piece of tobacco, ¾ to 1 inch in diameter, is tucked between the gum and jaw, usually to the back of the mouth.	Pouch, typically 3 ounces. A few brands market a 1.5-ounce pouch.
Plug	Made from enriched tobacco leaves (burley and bright tobacco and cigar tobacco) or fragments wrapped in fine tobacco and pressed into bricks. May be firm (less than 15% moisture) or moist (15% or greater moisture). Most plug tobacco is sweetened and flavored with licorice.	Chewed or held in the cheek or lower lip. May be held in the mouth for several hours.	A compressed brick or flat block wrapped inside natural tobacco leaves. Packaged in clear plastic. Packages range from 7 to 13 ounces. Also sold by the piece.
Twist	Hand-made of dark, air-cured leaf tobacco treated with a tarlike tobacco leaf extract and twisted into strands that are dried. Majority is sold without flavoring and sweeteners.	Similar to plug.	A pliable but dry rope. Sold by the piece, packaged in plastic bags. No standard weight. Sold in small (approximately 1–2 ounces) and larger sizes based on the number of leaves in the twist.

Snuff			
Moist	Made from air-cured and fire-cured tobacco. Consists of tobacco stems and leaves that are processed into fine particles or strips. Some products are flavored. Has a moisture content of up to 50%.	A small amount ("pinch") is placed between the lip or cheek and gum and is typically held for 30 minutes or longer per pinch.	Cans and plastic containers, typically 1.2 ounces.
Dry	Most dry snuff is made from fire-cured tobaccos of Kentucky and Tennessee. After initial curing, the tobacco is fermented further and processed into a dry powdered form. Products vary in strength and flavoring. Generally has a moisture content of less than 10%.	Same as moist snuff. May also be sniffed.	Metal cans or glass containers, varying from 1.15 to 7 ounces per container.

Note. From *The Health Consequences of Using Smokeless Tobacco: A Report of the Advisory Committee to the Surgeon General* (DHHS Publication No. NIH 86-2874, p. 6) by the Advisory Committee to the Surgeon General, 1986, Washington, DC: U.S. Government Printing Office.

[a]Product weight includes moisture.

pounds now sold annually; by contrast, sales of moist snuff are increasing—currently about 37 million pounds annually.

Figure 6-3 illustrates the trends in the amounts of smokeless tobacco products manufactured in the United States from 1961 to 1985 (Advisory Committee to the Surgeon General, 1986). Total production of snuff increased by 56%, from 31.3 to 48.7 million pounds, between 1970 and 1985. Note the difference in trends in the production of moist and dry snuff, with that of moist snuff continuing to increase as that of dry snuff decreases. Figure 6-3 does not show production amounts for moist and dry snuff separately prior to 1981, as those data are not available.

Total production of chewing tobacco increased by 36%, from 63.9 to 86.9 million pounds, between 1970 and 1985. This gain was due primarily to the production of looseleaf tobacco, which increased by 87.3%, from 39.5 to 74.0 million pounds. The manufacturing of both plug and twist tobacco continues to decline in this country. Total annual sales of all smokeless tobacco products in the United States are over 134 million pounds (D. L. Davis, 1986).

A BRIEF HISTORY OF SMOKELESS TOBACCO

Tobacco has been used by humans for thousands of years. There is evidence that tobacco was used by the natives of Peru and Mexico as early as 3500 B.C. (Voges, 1984). When Columbus arrived in the New World, he found that the Indians were sniffing finely cut tobacco and smoking it in pipes. Explorers returning from the New World to Europe introduced the product there, and its use became popular. In England, sniffing very finely cut tobacco was prevalent during the 17th and 18th centuries, and many of the English colonists brought snuff back to America when they settled. The sandy soil of Virginia was perfect for the growing of tobacco; it soon became a major export of the colonies.

Along with snuff, both looseleaf and plug tobaccos were also popular. Many of the colorful pioneers who settled the West used chewing tobacco, a much easier way to use tobacco than trying to smoke it on windy plains (Christen, Swanson, Glover, & Henderson, 1982).

With the discovery in the late 1800s that germs were the cause of several diseases and that spitting could spread these germs, the practice of tobacco spitting became socially unacceptable, and the use of chewing tobacco and snuff declined. With the mass production of cigarettes in the early 1900s, use of smokeless tobacco declined even further and became associated with rural, southern America. The use

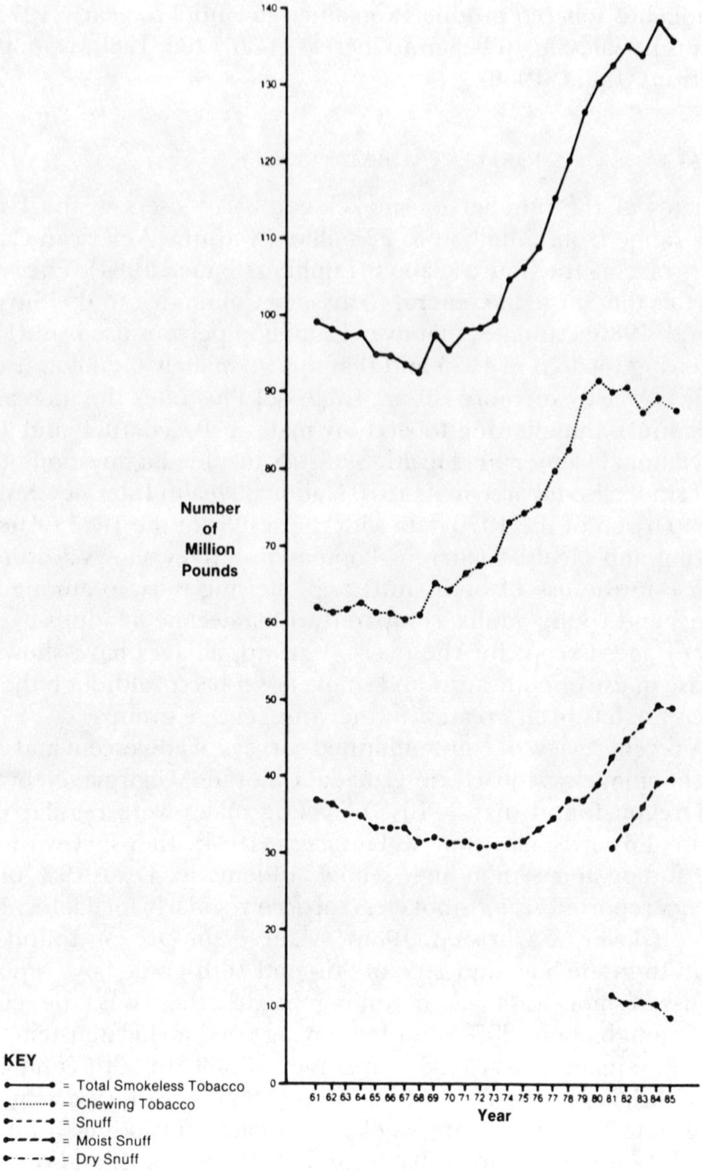

FIG. 6-3.

Manufacturing trends: Quantities of smokeless tobacco manufactured in the United States from 1961 to 1985, expressed in millions of pounds. (From *The Health Consequences of Using Smokeless Tobacco: A Report of the Advisory Committee to the Surgeon General* [DHHS Publication No. NIH 86-2874] by the Advisory Committee to the Surgeon General, 1986, Washington, DC: U.S. Government Printing Office.)

of smokeless tobacco products remained low until the early 1970s, at which time sales again began to increase (Christen, 1986; Council on Scientific Affairs, 1986).

PREVALENCE OF SMOKELESS TOBACCO USE

Estimates of the number of smokeless tobacco users in the United States range from 6 million to 22 million, with the American Cancer Society placing the figure at about 7 million (Squier, 1984). The recent report to the Surgeon General (Advisory Committee to the Surgeon General, 1986) estimates that over 12 million persons used snuff and/or chewing tobacco in 1985 and that approximately 6 million use the products weekly or more often. Table 6-4 illustrates the increase in use of snuff and chewing tobacco by males between 1970 and 1985. The National Center for Health Statistics included a question on the use of smokeless tobacco in its 1970 National Health Interview Survey. A comparison of the 1970 data with the results of the 1985 Office on Smoking and Health's Current Population Survey shows a dramatic increase in the use of both snuff and chewing tobacco among adolescents and young adults, compared with a decline in adults over 50 years of age. Except for the over-50 group, all ages have shown an increase in use of both snuff and smokeless tobacco, although the rate of increase has been greatest in the younger age groups.

A recent review of eight published surveys of adolescent and adult users of smokeless tobacco in Canada, Colorado, Georgia, Nebraska, and Oregon found that 8–10% of young males were regular users (Glover, Edwards, Christen, & Finnicum, 1984). In a survey of over 5,000 junior and senior high school students in Texas, 9% of the students reported using smokeless tobacco regularly (Schaefer, Henderson, Glover, & Christen, 1985). A survey in Oregon found that 9% of 7th-grade boys and 20% of 9th- and 10th-grade boys reported daily use of smokeless tobacco. Among the girls, there was little regular use, although about 20% reported having tried it (Lichtenstein, Severson, Friedman, & Ary, 1984). A survey of 609 8th-, 9th-, and 10th-grade students in the Pittsburgh, Pennsylvania area found that 35% of the boys reported using smokeless tobacco, including 6% using snuff, 10% using chewing tobacco, and 19% using snuff and/or chewing tobacco (Guggenheimer, Zullo, Kruper, & Verbin, 1986). None of the females reported use of smokeless tobacco. A survey of 901 high school students in Arkansas communities found that 36.7% of the males and 2.2% of the females were currently using smokeless tobacco (Marty, McDermott, & Williams, 1986). Among Texas college students, 11% reported present or past use of smokeless tobacco (Foreyt *et al.*, 1986).

TABLE 6-4. Prevalence of the Use of Snuff and Chewing Tobacco among Males by Age, 1970 National Health Interview Survey (NHIS) and 1985 Current Population Survey (CPS)

	1970 NHIS		1985 CPS	
Product	Age	Percentage of users	Age	Percentage of users
Snuff	17–19	0.3	16–19	2.9
	20–29	0.6	20–29	2.7
	30–39	0.7	30–39	1.8
	40–49	1.2	40–49	1.5
	50+	2.7	50+	1.4
	Total	1.4	Total	1.9
Chewing tobacco	17–19	1.2	16–19	3.0
	20–29	1.9	20–29	4.2
	30–39	2.8	30–39	3.7
	40–49	3.0	40–49	3.3
	50+	6.5	50+	4.2
	Total	3.8	Total	3.9

Note. "Use" not further defined with respect to frequency. From *The Health Consequences of Using Smokeless Tobacco: A Report of the Advisory Committee to the Surgeon General* (DHHS Publication No. NIH 86-2874, p. 11) by the Advisory Committee to the Surgeon General, 1986, Washington, DC: U.S. Government Printing Office.

As part of the Bogalusa (Louisiana) Heart Study, tobacco use was studied during 1976–1977 and 1981–1982 in over 2,000 children aged 8–17 years. Over the 5 years, cigarette smoking decreased; however, the use of smokeless tobacco increased, especially among 14- and 15-year-old white males. Among white males, snuff dipping tripled at all ages, with the highest use occurring in 12- and 13-year-olds (32%) in 1981. Among the white males who chewed tobacco, over 50% of them also used snuff. Of the 8- to 13-year-old white males who used snuff, over 60% of them also chewed tobacco. Of the 14- to 17-year-old snuff users, over 90% of them also chewed tobacco. Although the study reported that more boys chewed tobacco, the rate of increase was greater for snuff, with the use of snuff increasing eight-fold in the 14-year-olds over the 5-year period (Hunter *et al.*, 1986).

It appears that both snuff and chewing tobacco are being used primarily by teenage boys, with snuff the more popular of the two. Of males between 12 and 25 years of age, 16% have used some form of smokeless tobacco during the past year, and from one-third to one-half of these use the products at least once a week (Advisory Committee to the Surgeon General, 1986). The use of smokeless tobacco is an almost exclusively male behavioral pattern, although one study reported that about 20% of teenage girls try it, with about 1–2% becoming regular users (Lichtenstein *et al.*, 1984). Its use still appears higher in rural than in urban areas, although this seems to be changing. In some parts of the country, 25–35% of adolescent males report current use. It is more popular among white than among black, Asian, or Hispanic males. Its popularity appears to be increasing among young adolescents. The percentage of adolescent males who report using smokeless tobacco is now higher than the percentage using cigarettes (Lichtenstein *et al.*, 1984; Severson, 1986).

CORRELATES OF SMOKELESS TOBACCO USE

There has been little careful research reported that has studied factors related to the adoption and maintenance of smokeless tobacco use. Among the factors that have discriminated between subjects who use smokeless tobacco regularly from those who do not are the following: having tried smoking, having friends who smoke, having a sister who smokes, having smoked marijuana during the previous week, indicating an intention to smoke, and having a best friend who uses chewing tobacco (Ary, Severson, & Lichtenstein, 1985). Current smoking is related to the onset of smokeless tobacco use. Chewing has been perceived as less dangerous by users of smokeless tobacco than by smokers (Chassin, Presson, Sherman, McLaughlin, & Gioia, 1985). A survey of over 900 college students indicated that the three most important reasons for adopting smokeless tobacco use were "To see if I would enjoy it," "Most friends use it," and "To try something new" (Foreyt *et al.*, 1986).

With respect to personality factors of smokeless tobacco users, Edmundson, Glover, Alston, and Holbert (in press) reported that smokeless tobacco users at East Carolina University who were given Cattell's Sixteen Personality Factor Questionnaire were found to be more reserved and less socially outgoing than nonusers. Users tended to be more self-reliant and less sentimental, and saw themselves as realistic. They were also found to be more conforming than nonusers. Overall, the users appeared less personally optimistic and socially participating than the nonusers. The researchers found no significant difference in personality factors among the students who used varying amounts of either snuff or chewing tobacco. In a related study, Edmundson, Glover, Holbert, Alston, and Schroeder (in press) found that snuff dippers were more socially outgoing, enthusiastic, imaginative, and group-dependent than users of chewing tobacco. The tobacco chewers were more uncompromising, critical in outlook, and practical, and less easily influenced by others, than the snuff users. Both studies were based on a sample of 289 males, of whom 55 (19%) were smokeless tobacco users. Clearly, much more behavioral research is needed to factor out the reasons for both initiation and maintenance of smokeless tobacco use.

HEALTH EFFECTS OF SMOKELESS TOBACCO

A growing number of studies suggest potential health risks with habitual use of smokeless tobacco products. A study in North Carolina found that among women who used snuff but did not smoke tobacco, the risk of having oral or pharyngeal cancer was 4.2 times greater than that of women who did not use any tobacco products. Chronic users (i.e., women who had used snuff for 50 years or longer) were 48 times more likely to have cancer of the gum and buccal mucosa than were women who did not use snuff. No fewer than 87% of cancers of the gingiva and oral mucosa were attributed to the use of snuff (Winn *et al.*, 1981). Two studies of patients in India found that persons who chewed tobacco were six times more likely to develop cancer of the oral cavity or the hypopharynx and three times more likely to develop cancer of the oropharynx (Jayant, Balakrishnan, Sanghvi, & Jussawalla, 1977; Jussawalla & Deshpande, 1971). Jayant *et al.* (1977) attributed 47% of all cancer cases involving the oral cavity and 40% of the cancers of the hypopharynx to chewing tobacco.

I went to Burma and northern Thailand recently for 2 weeks. While there, I noticed that in almost every market and on many street corners men were selling betel nut (actually areca nut), wrapped in tobacco leaf and mixed with lime and a number of flavoring ingredients. This concoction was sold as a quid and then chewed. Gupta (1986) has reviewed the data on the relationship of this chewing and the amount of oral cancer throughout Southeast Asia. He concludes that the published evidence to date suggests an association between the tobacco chewing (it is the tobacco, not the nut, that is important) and oral cancer. The association is consistent across several populations, is very strong, and shows a dose–response relationship. Gupta (1986) concludes that tobacco chewing is a cause of oral cancer.

The Council on Scientific Affairs (1986) of the American Medical Association has reviewed the available literature to date on the health effects of smokeless tobacco and has found evidence demonstrating that the use of snuff or chewing tobacco is associated with adverse effects, including oral cancer. The International Agency for Research on Cancer (1985), an agency of the World Health Organization, has also concluded after a review of published evidence that oral use of snuff is carcinogenic. A consensus conference sponsored by the National Cancer Institute, the National Institute of Dental Research, and the NIH Office of Medical Applications of Research examined published reports and concluded that evidence is strong that use of snuff causes cancer of the mouth in humans. The risk is especially high for parts of the mouth where snuff is usually placed (Consensus Conference, 1986).

The Consensus Conference (1986) also stated that the data are insufficient at this time to conclude that there is a relationship of smokeless tobacco use to cancers at other sites. The panel pointed out that smokeless tobacco use increases the frequency of localized gum recession and leukoplakia at the site where the snuff is usually placed. The release of nicotine into the blood stream, like cigarette smoking, leads to long-term nicotine dependence (Consensus Conference, 1986; Henningfield, 1986).

Finally, the report from the Advisory Committee to the Surgeon General (1986; see also Cullen *et al.*, 1986) has reviewed and summarized the available data on health risks of using snuff and chewing tobacco. Their conclusions are similar to those of the Consensus Conference (1986) and other reviews to date. With respect to cancer, the committee concluded:

1. The scientific evidence is strong that the use of smokeless tobacco can cause cancer in humans. The association between smokeless tobacco use and cancer is strongest for cancers of the oral cavity.
2. Oral cancer has been shown to occur several times more frequently among snuff dippers than nontobacco users, and the excess risk of cancers of the cheek and gum may reach nearly fiftyfold among long-term snuff users.
3. Some investigations suggest that the use of chewing tobacco also may increase the risk of oral cancer.
4. Evidence for an association between smokeless tobacco use and cancers outside the oral cavity in humans is sparse. Some investigations suggest that smokeless tobacco users may face increased risks of tumors of the upper aerodigestive tract, but results are currently inconclusive.
5. Experimental investigations have revealed potent carcinogens in snuff and chewing tobacco. These include nitrosamines, polycyclic aromatic hydrocarbons, and radiation-emitting polonium. The tobacco-specific nitrosamines N-nitrosonornicotine and 4-(methylnitrosamino)-1-(3-pyridyl)-1-butanone have been detected in smokeless tobacco at levels 100 times higher than the regulated levels of other nitrosamines found in bacon, beer, and other foods. Animals exposed to these tobacco-specific nitrosamines, at levels approximately those thought to be accumulated during a human lifetime by daily smokeless tobacco users,

have developed an excess of a variety of tumors. The nitrosamines can be metabolized by target tissues to compounds that can modify cellular genetic material.

6. Bioassays exposing animals to smokeless tobacco, however, have generally shown little or no increased tumor production, although some bioassays suggest that snuff may cause oral tumors when tested in animals that are infected with herpes simplex virus. (Advisory Committee to the Surgeon General, 1986, p. xxiii)

The committee also concluded that smokeless tobacco carries other health risks:

- Smokeless tobacco use can lead into the development of oral leukoplakias (white patches or plaques of the oral mucosa), particularly at the site of tobacco placement. Based on evidence from several studies, a portion of leukoplakias can undergo transformation to dysplasia and further to cancer.
- Gingival recession is a commonly reported outcome of smokeless tobacco use.
- A number of studies have shown that nicotine exposure from smoking cigarettes can cause addiction in humans. In this regard, nicotine is similar to other addictive drugs such as morphine and cocaine. Since nicotine levels in the body resulting from smokeless tobacco use are similar in magnitude to nicotine levels from cigarette smoking, it is concluded that smokeless tobacco use can also be addictive. Besides, recent studies have shown that nicotine administered orally has the potential to produce a physiologic dependence.
- Some evidence suggests that nicotine may play a contributory or supportive role in the pathogenesis of coronary artery and peripheral vascular disease, hypertension, peptic ulcers, and fetal mortality and morbidity. (Advisory Committee to the Surgeon General, 1986, p. viii)

PREVENTION AND TREATMENT OF SMOKELESS TOBACCO USE

There is virtually no published literature to date on the prevention or treatment of smokeless tobacco use. An intervention program in India (McMichael, 1984), in which the treatment included providing information about the consequences of chewing tobacco, along with posters, films, and discussions, showed cessation of tobacco chewing in up to 5% and reduction of chewing in 16% of the subjects. Glover (1986) conducted two pilot "Quit Smokeless Tobacco" clinics, adapting material from the American Cancer Society's "Fresh Start" smoking cessation program. Although he treated 41 subjects, his success rate at 6 months was only 2.3%. Schinke, Gilchrist, Schilling, and Senechal (1986) have described a preventive intervention curriculum taught to 1,281 fifth- and sixth-graders in 12 elementary schools. Schools were randomly divided into skills, discussion, or control groups. Youths receiving the skills intervention were taught communication and problem-solving methods for handling high-risk situations in regard to tobacco use. During the 2-year study, only 3% of all smokeless tobacco users quit their habits. Gritz (1986) suggests that the behavioral technology developing for smoking cessation programs should be readily adaptable for use with smokeless tobacco. Similarly, with regard to prevention, behavioral approaches used for smoking prevention should also play a major role in the design of programs to help young people resist the pressures to begin smokeless tobacco use.

CONCLUSIONS

Behavioral methodology may play a major role in helping us understand the factors that lead to the initiation and maintenance of the smokeless tobacco habit and to the development of empirically valid strategies for the effective prevention and treatment of smokeless tobacco use, especially in the young. This is an important, clinically significant area, and behavioral scientists can make many contributions to combating this growing threat to health. I hope that by the time the next *Review of Behavior Therapy* is published, there will be a large number of studies reporting on the potential effectiveness of behavioral strategies in this area.

An Update on Cigarette Smoking: Who's Winning?

According to the Surgeon General of the United States, cigarette smoking is "the chief, single, avoidable cause of death in our society and most important public health problem of our time" (Koop, 1982, p. xi). In spite of the gains made in the areas of prevention and treatment, there is obviously much to do (McAfee, 1986):

- There are still approximately 1 million new smokers per year in the United States, most of them adolescents and young adults.
- Approximately 1,000 deaths per day in this country are attributed to the effects of tobacco.
- More than $2 billion is spent each year by the tobacco industry to advertise their products.
- The largest amount of the health care dollar in this country goes to the treatment of respiratory, malignant, and vascular diseases secondary to the use of tobacco.

- In 1986, for the first time, lung cancer became the most common malignancy in both men and women in the United States.

NEW DATA ON USE OF TOBACCO IN OTHER COUNTRIES

Greece leads the world in cigarette use per capita, followed by Japan and the United States. Also ranking high on the list are Hungary and Poland. In only four countries—Great Britain, Norway, Zambia, and Zimbabwe—are fewer cigarettes now smoked than in 1964. In the last 20 years, worldwide consumption of tobacco has increased by 75% (Goldsmith, 1986).

In 1984, U.S. manufacturers exported over 56 billion cigarettes and 246,000 tons of unmanufactured tobacco to other countries (U.S. Department of Agriculture, 1985). Approximately 31% of the total tobacco crop of the United States was exported (Tobacco Institute, 1985).

Most Third World countries have few restrictions on the advertising or sale of tobacco products (R. M. Davis, 1986). Only 5 (19%) of 26 developing countries (Cyprus, Egypt, Jordan, Mozambique, and Singapore) had major restrictions on advertising, compared to 22 (71%) of 31 developed countries in 1982 (Roemer, 1982). Unless changes are made, lung cancer from smoking will show a 50% increase worldwide by the year 2000 (Chandler, 1986).

CURRENT PRODUCTION OF TOBACCO IN THE UNITED STATES

In the United States, there has been a decline of about 1.5% in sales of tobacco between 1980 and 1985. In 1984, 124 factories in 19 states manufactured 668 billion cigarettes. Of these, 56.5 billion were exported to other countries; 9.8 billion were shipped overseas to our armed forces; and 800 million went to Puerto Rico and other U.S. possessions. In 1985, Americans spent $30.25 billion on cigarettes, compared to $3.59 billion in 1950. The sale of tobacco products brings in more than $10 billion in taxes to the federal and state governments (Mackenzie, 1986c).

Tobacco is the sixth largest crop in this country, behind corn, soybeans, hay, wheat, and cotton. Of the 23 tobacco-growing states in this country, the top five are North Carolina, Kentucky, Tennessee, Virginia, and South Carolina. The crop brought $2.8 billion in 1984.

There are about 200,000 tobacco farms, which yield about 1.74 billion pounds of tobacco from 797,400 acres. In 1985, there was a record harvest of 2,187 pounds of tobacco per acre. Gross income per acre for tobacco in 1984 was $3,940. This amount contrasts sharply with what farmers earn from other crops: $131 for wheat, $727 for peanuts, and $1,619 for fruits (Mackenzie, 1986c).

The majority of cigarettes are made in the United States by six companies: R.J. Reynolds, Phillip Morris, Inc., American Brands, Inc., Lorillard Inc., Brown and Williamson Tobacco Corp., and Ligget Group Inc. Together, they employ almost 65,000 workers (of whom 49,000 work on the production line), who earn an average of $438 for a 38.9-hour week (Mackenzie, 1986c). In 1985, 245 domestic brands of cigarettes were sold; by contrast, only 64 brands of cigarettes were sold 20 years ago. The top-selling cigarette in the United States continues to be Marlboro (21%), followed by Winston (14%) (Mackenzie, 1986c).

CURRENT PREVALENCE AND PATTERNS OF SMOKING

About 30% of Americans now smoke. Approximately 33% of men and 28% of women are smokers. Although smoking prevalence has decreased from 43% in 1964, individuals who use cigarettes now smoke more heavily: Of the smokers, 31% smoke fewer than 15 cigarettes a day, 41% smoke 15–24 cigarettes a day, and 27% smoke 25 or more a day. Occupations with the highest prevalence of smoking include painters (55%), truck drivers (53.6%), construction laborers (53%), carpenters (50.8%), automobile mechanics (50.5%), guards and watchmen (50.5%), and janitors (49.8%). Occupations showing the lowest percentages of smokers include electrical engineers (16.2%), lawyers (21.9%), secondary school teachers (24.9%), accountants (26.8%), real estate brokers (27.8%), and farmers (28.1%). In the armed forces, the rate of smoking is about 47% (Mackenzie, 1986a).

ONE MAN'S VIEW

In a recent interview, Gerald H. Long, president and chief executive officer of the R. J. Reynolds Tobacco Company, was asked the question, "Have you ever had personal doubts about being involved in the tobacco industry when you have thought of some of the health consequences of smoking?" Mr. Long's reply was as follows:

> If there was any evidence whatsoever that conclusively proved that, in some way, tobacco was harmful to people, and I believed it in my heart and my soul, then I would get out of the business and I wouldn't be involved in it. Honestly, I have not seen one piece of evidence that has been presented by anybody, anywhere that absolutely, totally said that smoking caused disease or created it. I believe this. I am sitting here

talking with you with an extremely clear conscience. (quoted in Mackenzie, 1986b, p. 15)

Multicomponent Programs for the Treatment of Smoking

Treatment programs for smoking that emphasize single strategies continue to give way to multicomponent interventions. Like programs for the reduction of obesity, smoking treatment programs are also showing an increase in the use of cognitive–behavioral strategies, training in coping skills, and increasing attention to the role of social support in maintenance of cessation.

Table 6-5 illustrates some of the options available for multicomponent programs. These programs typically involve three stages. Stage 1, preparation, involves mobilizing the client's motivation and commitment. Operant strategies, including deposit contracts, are frequently used to maintain attendance at class sessions. Self-monitoring (to increase a client's awareness of smoking patterns), self-management training (including stimulus control strategies), stress management training, and the use of alternative nonsmoking options are taught. Stage 2, the quitting stage, may utilize both aversive and nonaversive strategies. Aversive strategies may include cognitive–aversive interventions, such as covert sensitization; nonaversive strategies may include nicotine fading and writing a contract that specifies a target quitting date. Stage 3, maintenance, includes booster sessions, training in social skills (including how to avoid the abstinence violation effect), and utilization of social support.

The continuing increase in the number of multicomponent programs is based on the results of studies suggesting that no single strategy has been very effective in promoting long-term smoking cessation. Several examples of multicomponent programs have been published. Shiffman, Read, Maltese, Rapkin, and Jarvik (1985) describe a multicomponent program emphasizing relapse prevention treatment as a major part of their intervention. Other examples of multicomponent programs include those developed by Lando (Lando, 1977; Lando & McCullough, 1978), Hamilton and Bornstein (1979), Pomerleau (Pomerleau, 1980; Pomerleau & Pomerleau, 1977), and Powell and McCann (1981). Each of these programs emphasizes different components; however, each reports preliminary encouraging results.

Many of the multicomponent treatment programs have yet to be replicated. However, it is likely that with refinement they will prove to be the most effective interventions in the area. Although more

TABLE 6-5. Options for a Multicomponent Program

Preparation		
	Mobilizing client motivation and commitment	
		Deposits contingent on following through with program requirements
		Review of reasons for quitting and benefits of stopping
	Self-monitoring to increase client's awareness of smoking patterns	
	Setting target quitting date	
	Self-management training	
		Stimulus control for modifying antecedents of smoking
		Stress management training; relaxation
		Use of substitutes and alternative nonsmoking behaviors
Quitting		
	Aversive strategies	
		Electric shock
		Covert (sensitization) aversion
		Rapid smoking and satiation
		Focused smoking and smoke holding
	Nonaversive strategies	
		Nicotine fading
		Target quitting date contract
Maintenance		
	Booster sessions	
	Coping skills training	
		Transfer of self-management skills to maintenance
		Cognitive and behavioral coping (anticipating high-risk situations and planning for coping with them)
		Avoiding the abstinence violation effect
Social support		

Note. From "Review of Approaches to Smoking Treatment: Behavior Modification Strategies" by E. Lichtenstein and R. J. Mermelstein, 1984, in J. D. Matarazzo, S. M. Weiss, J. A. Herd, N. E. Miller, and S. M. Weiss (Eds.), *Behavioral Health: A Handbook of Health Enhancement and Disease Prevention* (p. 707), New York: Wiley. Copyright 1984 by John Wiley & Sons. Reprinted by permission.

research is needed to document their efficacy, preliminary results are optimistic. The addition of pharmacological approaches to behavioral strategies also shows considerable promise (Killen, Maccoby, & Taylor, 1984; Kozlowski, 1984).

Self-Efficacy and Maintenance

The concept of self-efficacy is among the most exciting developments in the field of addictive disorders. Since Bandura's (1977) original description of self-efficacy theory, a growing number of studies have shown that self-efficacy scores can be used to predict maintenance. In the smoking area, for example, Yates and Thain (1985) reported in a retrospective study of subjects who had quit smoking voluntarily that the self-efficacy total score predicted the status of all 15 subjects who had relapsed at a 4-month follow-up, while the 7 subjects it had predicted would not relapse were still abstaining. The predictive power of the measure was also maintained at an 8-month follow-up. The authors suggest that the self-efficacy measure may be a good way to identify subjects at high risk for relapse after quitting smoking. Prochaska, DiClemente, Velicer, Ginpil, and Norcross (1985) also reported that the self-efficacy measure was one of their most significant variables for predicting change in smoking status. Condiotte and Lichtenstein (1981) reported that posttreatment self-efficacy scores predicted relapse and accounted for about half the variance in length of abstinence. They found that ex-smokers were most likely to relapse in situations similar to those for which their self-efficacy was lowest. DiClemente (1981), Colletti, Supnick, and Rizzo (1981), and Supnick and Colletti (1984) also found that self-efficacy scores predicted maintenance. To date, the self-efficacy measure is proving to be particularly strong in the smoking area, and further research is encouraged.

ALCOHOLISM

This section begins, as in the past two volumes of this series, with a review of and (let us hope) a conclusion to the controversy surrounding the Sobell and Sobell (1973a, 1973b, 1976) study on controlled drinking and the subsequent accusations by Pendery, Maltzman, and West (1982) with respect to the outcome and reporting of results. With the report of a steering group of the Alcohol, Drug Abuse and Mental Health Administration (ADAMHA) now complete (Steering Group to the Administrator, 1984), the controversy appears to be over, at least for most individuals. However, the debate over controlled drinking versus abstinence goes on, and an update on that issue is also provided. The trend in the behavioral assessment and treatment of alcoholism, like that in obesity and smoking, continues to emphasize an integration of genetic, physiological, behavioral, and sociocultural variables associated with its etiology and maintenance. Behavioral models of assessment and treatment are therefore becoming increasingly complex, and this trend is also noted.

The Controlled Drinking Controversy: The Final Chapter?

Brownell devoted the entire section on alcoholism in Chapter 6 of Volume 9 of this series, and half of the alcoholism section in Volume 10, to the controversy over controlled drinking and the accusation of fraud that followed the critique of a study (Caddy, Addington, & Perkins, 1978; Sobell & Sobell, 1973a, 1973b, 1976) by Pendery *et al.* I have reviewed all of the material with respect to the accusations made by Pendery *et al.* (1982) regarding the Sobells' study, and it seems clear to me that an update on the controversy is necessary. I think that a brief review followed by a report of news since the publication of Volume 10 will enable us to lay the Sobell and Sobell part of the story to rest.

BACKGROUND AND UPDATE ON THE CONTROVERSY

The background is known to most behavior therapists interested in alcoholism. An article by Pendery *et al.* (1982) published in *Science* re-examined the results of a study of individualized behavior therapy for alcoholics conducted by Sobell and Sobell (1973a, 1973b, 1976). The re-examination covered three major areas:

1. It questioned the design of the study, particularly the nature of the sample and the comparability of groups.
2. It presented follow-up data that appeared to be different from the data reported by Sobell and Sobell (1973a, 1973b).
3. It reported new long-term follow-up data on the experimental subjects.

Specifically, Pendery *et al.* (1982) reported that only 1 of 20 subjects had successfully controlled his drinking over several years and that most of the 20 had experienced arrests, rehospitalizations, or periods of heavy drinking. Unfortunately, Pendery *et al.* (1982) did not report follow-up data on the control subjects in their *Science* article. Without comparison data on the Sobells' control subjects, valid conclusions about the experimental subjects are difficult to make. Even though Pendery *et al.* pointed out how badly the experimental subjects were faring 11 years later, it was possible that the control subjects had fared even worse. Pendery *et al.* later raised questions about the initial random assignment of subjects to groups; the amount of follow-up contact with subjects; and the integrity of the Sobells' reporting of their experimental design, procedures, and outcome data.

In answer to the Pendery *et al.* article, Sobell and Sobell (1984) published a lengthy, detailed, point-by-point response. In their response, they showed that the experimental and control subjects were justifiably classified as "gamma alcoholics," that all subjects were randomly assigned to groups, and that the two groups were comparable in terms of pretreatment characteristics. With respect to the originally reported 2-year treatment outcome data, the Sobells indicated that the Pendery *et al.* article contained no specific events that were not already documented and that had not been part of the data base for the Sobells' original publication. With respect to the new long-term outcome data, the Sobells reported that their experimental group had a lower mortality than their traditionally treated (control) group (20% vs. 30%, respectively). Sobell and Sobell (1984) concluded that the data reported by Pendery *et al.* actually strengthened, rather than weakened, the validity of their original work.

Three independent investigations examined the criticisms raised by Pendery *et al.*, and the conclusions of each of them tended to support the work of the Sobells. The first—an investigation by the Addiction Research Foundation, the Sobells' employer—was chaired by Dr. Bernard M. Dickens, professor of law, criminology, and community health at the University of Toronto; it concluded, "The Committee finds there to be no reasonable cause to doubt the scientific or personal integrity of either Dr. Mark Sobell or Dr. Linda Sobell" (Dickens, Doob, Warwick, & Winegard, 1982, p. 109). An investigator for the Subcommittee on Investigations and Oversight, Committee on Science and Technology, U.S. House of Representatives, concurred: "My review of all available [evidence] supports the findings of the Commission convened by the Addiction Research Foundation (also known as the 'Dickens Commission') and fully supports their conclusion" (Jensen, 1983 [letter]).

ADAMHA also conducted an investigation of the allegations against the Sobells. The administrator of ADAMHA established a steering group for the investigation with Robert L. Trachtenberg, deputy administrator of ADAMHA, as chairman. The steering group reported that ADAMHA, with the assistance of the NIH Division of Management and Review, investigated the matter as far as reasonably possible. The Office of the Inspector General indicated that no action by that office was warranted (Steering Group to the Administrator, 1984).

Reading the testimony and reports of the investigations, one cannot help being impressed by the Sobells' handling of the attacks on them. They had maintained extensive records, including original tapes and notebooks, over this long period of time. This is not to say that the investigations did not find some minor errors in the reporting of their data. However, none of these errors appeared to have had an effect on the outcome of the study. The outcomes of the investigations described above indicate that the results of the original study stand. I have been unable to find any solid evidence to the contrary.

What was particularly distressing about the whole controversy was the extensive involvement of the media. Clearly, the appropriate forum for issues about scientific matters and integrity of researchers is that of peer-reviewed scientific journals. If questions are raised about scientific matters, it seems to me that those bringing up the issues ought to confine their assertions to scientific outlets.

The results of the investigations put to rest the controversy surrounding the Sobells' study. However, the furor over the issue of controlled drinking versus abstinence continues unabated. None of the investigations considered the question of whether or not alcoholics can be taught to return to drinking in a moderate fashion. A brief, updated look at that question will illustrate the intensity of the debate.

AN UPDATE ON THE CONCEPT OF CONTROLLED DRINKING

In brief, the prevailing notion among most researchers and clinicians in the alcoholism field is that when a person is physically addicted to alcohol, the only goal is complete abstinence. This idea can be found, for example, in the writings of Alcoholics Anonymous (Anonymous, 1939) and Jellinek (1960). Alcoholism is a disease; its use by some people leads to physical dependence. According to Alcoholics Anonymous, the development of physical dependence on alcohol is a result of a genetic predisposition.

Sobell and Sobell (in press) recently reviewed the limitations of this viewpoint, which they term the "conventional wisdom." Problems with alcohol, they point out, do not have a single etiology. Whether or not individuals develop difficulty in handling alcohol appears to be due to a wide array of factors. For example, it is commonly believed that withdrawal symptoms will occur in physically dependent alcoholics following ingestion of a small amount of alcohol. In reality, 2–5 days of very heavy drinking, equivalent to daily consumption of more than a fifth of whiskey, are typically required to produce clinical withdrawal after drinking stops (Kissin, 1983; Sobell & Sobell, in press); research suggests that some heavy drinkers can terminate their drinking once begun and that if they do so within a reasonable period of time, they do not experience clinical withdrawal symptoms (Sobell & Sobell, in press). There are a few studies, in addition to the Sobell and Sobell investigation (1973a, 1973b), indicating that some people may return to nonproblematic drinking following treatment (for a review of these studies, see Heather & Robertson, 1983). For persons who have been physically dependent on alcohol, however, the frequency is low, and for this group completely positive outcomes are quite rare (Vaillant, 1983). Many of these studies are also reviewed in the controversial Rand Report (Armor, Polich, & Stambul, 1978).

At this time, however, despite the scattered studies supporting the use of controlled drinking with some individuals, the overwhelming evidence does not support its use with physically dependent alcoholics (Nathan, 1986). Nathan states,

> The consensus among most informed current observers is that alcoholism treatment with controlled drinking as a prime treatment goal is neither efficacious nor ethical when it is offered to chronic alcoholics. . . . The weight of the available data now suggests both that we have not developed treatment programs which can reliably teach chronic alcoholics to become controlled drinkers and that status as a controlled drinker is not in the best interest of most chronic alcoholics. (1986, p. 44)

Trends in Behavioral Assessment and Treatment of Alcoholism

All treatments for alcoholism developed to date, including that of Alcoholics Anonymous, are not very effective (Baekeland, 1977; Emrick, 1982; Miller & Hester, 1980; Vaillant, 1983). As Vaillant (1983, p. 302) states, "there is no single, best, or only treatment for alcoholism." Behaviorally oriented researchers, like their colleagues studying obesity and tobacco abuse, have increasingly recognized that a comprehensive view of the development of alcoholism is necessary if knowledge in the field is to move ahead. Its etiology is best understood within the context of a longitudinal–developmental framework, including genetic, physiological, behavioral, and sociocultural variables (Zucker & Gomberg, 1986). Surely behavior therapy's greatest strength continues to be its reliance on methodology and empiricism. A brief look at some of the contributions that behavior therapy has made to the field of alcohol research should illustrate how far we have come.

BEHAVIORAL ASSESSMENT OF ALCOHOLISM

Many behavior therapists view alcohol abuse as primarily a socially acquired behavioral pattern maintained by antecedent cues and consequent reinforcers. Five areas are typically assessed (Tharp & Wetzel, 1969) in the alcohol abuser:

1. *The target behavior itself—its frequency, intensity, and pattern.* The amount of alcohol consumed and the behavioral patterns associated with its use are measured.

2. *Antecedent events—the "setting events" for the abuser's maladaptive behavior.* A number of factors may lead an individual to abuse alcohol. Many of the common ones include problems on the job or in the marriage; problems within personal relationships; and feelings of depression, anxiety, stress, or anger.
3. *Maintaining stimuli—environmental factors that reinforce the target behaviors.* These environmental factors include the spouse or friends who provide sympathy to the abuser.
4. *Reinforcement hierarchy—the range of factors in the environment to reinforce both target and nontarget behaviors.* In spite of many potential reinforcers in the environment, many alcohol abusers tend to see only alcohol as reinforcing.
5. *Potential for remediation in the environment.* Therapists tend to make use of a wide variety of potential reinforcers for having abusers reduce or eliminate their intake of alcohol.

Behavioral assessment of alcohol abuse relies on all sources of data. Studies in the area frequently make use of self-reports, observational reports by "significant others," and direct observations by the experimenter. Behavioral patterns associated with abuse of drinking, including number of arrests or hospitalizations for alcohol-related problems, are also assessed. In addition to the assessment of alcohol-related problems, the individual's functioning in other areas of life is also measured, since drinking results in emotional, occupational, social, and marital difficulties.

Wanberg and Horn (1983) have published the results of 15 years of research based on large samples showing the complexity of the diagnosis "alcoholism." Their research indicates 15 psychometrically independent first-order factors, the interrelationships among which indicate five broad second-order dimensions. These factors provide reliable operational definitions that correspond to different concepts. They have different relationships to variables of etiology, variables of the total personality, variables of outcome following different kinds of treatment, and variables of life span development. Wanberg and Horn's work indicates that assessment of alcoholism necessitates multiple measures and that multivariate theory and measurement serve as a guide for research in this field.

Emrick and Hansen (1983) stress the need to collect reliable and valid data on alcohol abusers. They point out that treatment outcome is influenced by many external validity factors, including patient characteristics, sample selection and attrition, patients' experiences outside of treatment, time of evaluation in relation to treatment, type and definition of criterion variables, measurement of criterion variables, and the analysis and interpretation of data. Internal validity factors affecting outcome include investigator bias, demand characteristics, and efforts to compare patient self-report data with other sources of information. Any assessment of treatment effectiveness will require the use of multiple outcome criterion measures, not just drinking behavior. Several excellent reviews of the behavioral assessment literature have been published (e.g., Caddy, 1978; Caddy & Block, 1983; Nathan & Niaura, 1985), and the reader is referred to them for detailed information on the area.

BEHAVIORAL TREATMENT OF ALCOHOLISM

Behavioral treatment of alcoholism has, of course, improved greatly since the early aversion conditioning studies of Voegtlin (Lemere & Voegtlin, 1950; Voegtlin, 1940; Voegtlin & Broz, 1949). Behavioral treatment has become a recognized part of the establishment. Contributions to the area have helped investigators define the parameters of abusive drinking more precisely and have helped with the definition of objective change criteria following intervention. Multifaceted behavioral treatment packages have proliferated, and efforts at assessing their contribution to the field are increasing.

Reviews of the literature of behavioral outcome studies are encouraging. For example, Litman and Topham (1983) evaluated outcomes of treatment trials after 1975 that used behavioral strategies as their main treatment modalities. Specifically evaluated were the results of trials using aversion therapy, contingency contracting, broad-spectrum behavioral treatments, behavioral self-control, and cognitive therapy. Litman and Topham concluded that, where appropriately applied, behavioral treatment programs were at least as effective as more conventional treatments, and in some cases their success was "strikingly high." Advantages of behavioral intervention included the facts that patients stayed in treatment longer and that the use of paraprofessional and community resources made the techniques more economical in terms of professional time.

A number of questions, however, remain to be answered. Litman and Topham have pointed out that much of the work in this area is still being done by "small, enthusiastic, innovative teams" and that the nonspecifics of intervention, including the experimental effect, are difficult to evaluate. The specific effective components of broad-spectrum approaches need to be identified. Cognitive mediating variables, including deficits in cognitive flexibility and perseveration, require further study.

With the increasing emphasis on the teaching of coping skills, there has been little systematic exploration on how to teach these strategies. Sanchez-Craig (1976; Sanchez-Craig & Walker, 1982), for example, reported that many patients could not recall coping skills strategies 1 month following treatment. Chaney, O'Leary, and Marlatt (1978) and Intagliata (1978, 1979) reported that the benefits of coping skills training fell off after about 3 months. Although skills training did result in reduced levels of drinking in the Chaney *et al.* study, experimental subjects did not differ from controls in days abstinent at the 1-year follow-up. Coping behaviors may need to be taught in hierarchial fashion, from avoidance of high-risk situations to more complex cognitive control over a period of time, to help with retention of skills (Litman, 1980).

Among behavior therapy's strongest contributions to this area are the increasing sophistication and precision of its methodology. These contributions will aid in the determination of optimal combinations of interventions sequenced for maximum effectiveness, matching of individuals to treatments and treatment goals, and the increasing exploration of cognitive–behavioral interventions and their application to the treatment of alcohol abuse (Litman & Topham, 1983).

FUTURE DIRECTIONS

Reviews of the behavioral treatment literature suggest future directions similar to those in the obesity and smoking areas. Nathan and Niaura (1985) suggest five potential areas for future research:

1. Exploration of cognitive mediating processes important to the maintenance of chronic alcoholism, along with procedures for modification by behavioral means.
2. Increasing attention to efforts to "unpackage" the separate components of broad-spectrum behavioral treatment programs.
3. Systematic development of new components of broad-spectrum behavioral treatment programs, in order to expand the range of associated behavioral problems that can be confronted by these treatment packages.
4. More emphasis on primary and secondary prevention of alcohol problems and less emphasis on tertiary prevention.
5. The breaking down of conceptual and political issues that have separated behavioral clinicians from other alcoholism workers.

A FINAL COMMENT

A review of the literature in all of these areas makes it clear that there are increasing commonalities in our growing understanding of the nature and treatment of the addictive disorders. When one is reading publications in these areas, one's mind can easily begin to drift until it is not clear whether the particular article being read is about obesity, tobacco use, or alcoholism. The following is probably an obvious point, but I would like to make it anyway: It is increasingly important that researchers and clinicians in one area of addiction read the works of investigators in other areas. There are far more similarities in the development and maintenance of these behavioral patterns than differences, and we have much to learn from each other. As we continue to do that, future advances in prevention and treatment should occur with increasing frequency.

CHAPTER

7

BEHAVIOR THERAPY WITH CHILDREN AND ADOLESCENTS

CYRIL M. FRANKS

INTRODUCTION

Reviewing the literature in preparation for this chapter gave me the feeling that I had seen most of it before. A glance at previous volumes in this series soon convinced me that this was no *déjà vu* phenomenon: I had indeed read much of it before. There were the same recommendations for broadening the field; there were the same criticisms of methodology; there was the same tempered endorsement of the cognitive direction that child behavior therapy was taking.

Each year, knowledgeable commentators praise or lament "clearly evident" trends and call for the expansion of our framework. Griest and Wells (1983), for example, rightly stress the importance of sometimes neglected family variables, and Harris and Ferrari (1983) highlight the need to include developmental psychology. How much are these calls taken to heart, and are any trends apparent?

To shed light on this question, Forehand, Middlebrook, Steffe, and Rogers (1984) examined alternative volumes of four behavioral journals. Some 410 relevant articles were identified, but, in contrast to the more intuitively determined trends conjured up each year, no trend was discernible. What their survey did reveal was a focus upon specific maladaptive behaviors and a tendency to rely upon consequences for inducing change.

Of the new books, Graziano and Mooney's (1984) is among the more thoughtful. Noting the grim realities of many state institutions for children, Graziano and Mooney pose several disquieting questions: Why are accountability systems still lacking? Why cannot children be protected from abusive parents by appropriate community mechanisms? Graziano and Mooney place the responsibility for social change on behavior therapists as well as concerned citizens and administrators.

The contributors to Ollendick and Hersen's (1984) assessment compendium predictably stress the need for multimethod assessment and more attention to developmental processes (see also Campbell, 1985; Maddux, Roberts, Sledden, & Wright, 1986). But despite the intuitive appeal of this notion, the evidence with respect to the superiority of multiple assessment methods remains limited, and viable behavioral alternatives to traditional psychometrics are still in the formative stage (see also Hersen, 1986; Nelson, 1983).

Morris and Kratochwill's (1983) thorough review of fears and phobias in children is impressive but marred by a literature-based equivocation, which makes for admirable scholarship but limited clinical utility. Another mild disappointment is Meyers and Craighead's (1984) text on child cognitive-behavior therapy. The editorial promise to integrate theory and practical application is not fulfilled.

While perhaps not yet a trend, cognitive-behavior therapy with children does seem to be becoming more thoughtful and less militant. For example, a recent special issue of the *Journal of Abnormal Child Psychology* (Harris, Wong, & Keogh, 1985) brings together a series of critical yet constructive commentaries on the contemporary status of cognitive-behavior modification with children (e.g., Craighead, Meyers, & Wilcoxon-Craighead, 1985; Harris, 1985; Kendall, 1985b). Whether cognition and behaviorism can be successfully synthesized, as the section editors believe, remains to be seen. The premise that cognitive strategies are superior to traditional behavioral approaches awaits demonstration (Meador & Ollendick, 1984).

For Ellis and his associates, rational–emotive therapy (RET) is, without question, cognitive–behavioral. Indeed, one would conclude from their writings that RET is *the* cognitive–behavioral approach (e.g., Ellis & Bernard, 1983). On the other hand, when Bernard is writing without Ellis (e.g., Bernard & Joyce, 1984), RET becomes little more than a major trend within the mainstream of child behavior therapy. Pains are taken to evaluate critically what little research there is in this area.

Pediatric behavioral medicine is a growing branch of behavioral medicine and, from my perspective, shares its deficits. Too many behavior therapists enthusiastically identify with behavioral medicine, with no apparent recognition that in so doing they are departing from behavior therapy as it is customarily conceptualized (Franks, 1986). Behavioral interventions tend to be viewed by the medical fraternity as psychological analogues of physical treatment, and any child-related phenomenon that can be substantiated by data is readily subsumed under the rubric of behavioral pediatrics (e.g., Camp, 1980). If "behavioral health care"—a more appropriate term than "behavioral medicine," although it is far too late to do much about this now—is to become a respected component of mainstream behavior therapy, the emphasis needs to shift to a more behavioral perspective (Eyberg, 1985; Hobbs, Beck, & Wansley, 1984a). It is with this caveat that I turn now to a review of recent developments within specific areas of child behavior therapy.

HOME AND FAMILY IN BEHAVIOR THERAPY

Once again, pickings in the areas of home and family involvement are slim, and little of significance seems to have appeared since Volume 10. Among the more interesting publications is an invited book review by Wells (1984), really an essay about Patterson and his work. As Wells notes, *Coercive Family Process* (Patterson, 1982) is in large part the story of Patterson's professional career. As a young trainee, Patterson was busily learning the child treatment techniques in existence at that time (circa mid-1950s). These consisted primarily of intensive psychotherapy and nondirective play therapy. His initial satisfaction with occasional successes and parental global reports of "some improvement" soon subsided when he noticed a widespread failure to obtain permanent, objectively documented changes in the majority of aggressive childhood disorders. In seeking an explanation, Patterson looked first to existing theories of child aggression, but found few answers there. It was these beginnings that led him to devote his entire career to the description, understanding, and treatment of aggressive behavior, culminating in his now well-known program at the Oregon Social Learning Center and the book under review by Wells. Along the way, he developed objective methods for describing and measuring child aggression in the home, school, and community. Innovative treatment strategies using internally validated experimental designs were implemented and evaluated. Coercion theory describes and explains the variables that increase aggression within all children, and *Coercive Family Process* is the single best source of contemporary knowledge about aggression in families from a behavioral perspective.

What is of particular significance is the research stimulus that Patterson's program provides. The emphasis on precision that is the hallmark of this group greatly facilitates the posing and answering of questions that are fundamental to a behavioral approach. For example, Horne and Van Dyke (1983) asked: For whom is the Patterson social learning treatment model most appropriate? Under what conditions? What familial factors are predictive of successful treatment outcomes? Designed to pinpoint treatment outcome variables and to compare persons who continued in treatment with those who dropped out, their study was carried out with some 119 families referred to the Oregon Social Learning Center for treatment of an aggressive child. Among the more significant findings (unfortunately limited by lack of an adequate control group) were a reduction of aggressive behavior, generalization of treatment effects to siblings and mothers, and maintenance through a 12-month follow-up.

Children do not have to be problem children to be stressful; they just have to be children. In most cases, parents are able to cope with these day-to-day stresses. It is when the child is perceived as atypical or difficult that the mismatch between child and parent behavior becomes important and the increase in parent-related stress becomes a problem of significance. Mash (1984) presents compelling evidence of a strong association between childhood behavior problems and disturbances in family functioning. These include marital conflict; disruptive behavioral interactions; impaired verbal and nonverbal communication; parental mood disturbance; lowered self-esteem; disrupted sibling relationships; and difficult interactions with relatives, friends, social service agencies, and others. Whether these disturbances reflect nonspecific reactions to the stresses associated with having a problem child or specific effects related to the unique characteristics of a particular childhood disorder awaits further research.

What is becoming apparent is that when one is establishing goals and designing interventions, it is not sufficient to focus on the behavior of the referred or target child. The reactions from the environment, particularly other family members, are what help determine whether or not particular behaviors will be repeated. Baskett's (1984) systematic home observations of nonclinical families with an identified target child between the ages of 4 and 8 led her to the conclusion that fairly high levels of mutual noninvolvement can be the norm. As she points out, this is something for family therapists to consider in establishing goals for intervention. Setting up expectations that parents be actively engaged with their children all or most of the time may be unnecessary, highly unrealistic, and difficult to maintain after therapy ends. How this applies to disturbed families must await further research.

Griest and Wells (1983) hypothesize that, in addition to direct parent behavior, other parental characteristics—cognitive, marital, psychological, and social adjustment—are related either to actual child behavior or to parental perceptions of child behavior. A number of studies summarized briefly by Middlebrook and Forehand (1985) support not only the hypothesis of a relationship between parent function and parent perceptions of child deviance (a matter of particular importance in terms of which children are actually referred to a clinic), but also the probability that factors other than child deviance per se account for both parental perceptions and clinic referrals.

Using contrived vignettes rather than real-life observations, Middlebrook and Forehand found, as predicted, that neutral child behaviors were rated as more deviant in situations that were intrinsically highly stressful than in those that were less stressful. In addition, mothers of clinic-referred children rated neutral behaviors as more deviant than did mothers of non-clinic-referred children. If stress is closely associated with parent ratings of child deviance, there may be a need for stress management components in the treatment of mothers who experience high levels of stress. Parent training alone may not be adequate for such mothers.

In related studies, Forehand and his associates have delved further into the parameters of child disruptive behavior. In both clinic-referred and non-clinic-referred mothers, it was found that a combination of a high level of child disruptive behavior with a high level of marital dissatisfaction resulted in greater perceptions of child maladjustment than either a high level of child disruptive behavior combined with a low level of marital dissatisfaction or a low level of disruptive behavior combined with a high level of marital dissatisfaction (Forehand, Brody, & Smith, 1986a).

In a subsequent study, Forehand, Lautenschlager, Faust, and Graziano (1986) confirmed Patterson's (1982) hypothesis that maternal depressive mood can have a direct effect on maternal perceptions, together with an indirect effect on the child through parenting behavior. (For a contrasting finding, see Rogers & Forehand, 1983.) Pending further research, even at this stage it would seem appropriate to include measures of maternal depression in the assessment process.

Forehand and his associates make no mention of the hapless father. In these times of dual-career families, androgyny, and the breakdown of traditional parent roles, it would be of interest to explore Patterson's and Forehand's formulations as they apply to these less traditional settings. As yet, there are few studies to report. In a preliminary survey, Carlson (1984) found what we would all suspect intuitively: Paternal participation in child care and household tasks is closely related to the stereotypes young boys hold about their fathers' roles. The more housework the father performs, for example, the fewer stereotypes children have about these roles. It is of interest that fewer stereotypes about the maternal role were reported by girls than boys. What is not surprising is that boys whose parents shared responsibility for child care held fewer stereotypes about the maternal role than did boys from traditional families.

Regardless of the problem, the family is going to play a major role. For example, the success of behavioral weight loss therapy programs for young people depends heavily upon the family environment (Kirschenbaum, Harris, & Tomarken, 1984). In past years, I have discussed settings outside the home in which the family interact as a group, especially those where disruptive interactions are likely to occur. For example, in 1977 Greene, Clark, and Risley developed a program for enhancing family interactions while shopping. Now this group has extended its strategies to the family-style restaurant (Green, Hardison, & Green, 1984). Their "Table-Talk" placemats generated more social and educational dialogue than either traditional placemats or no placemat—a conclusion that might seem trivial unless one has to contend with a disruptive child in a restaurant. Social validation ratings of the experimental placemats by mental health counselors and parents were strongly favorable. As the authors note, "In a small way, such research captures the spirit of one social engineer's vision of a community in which even the nuances of dining halls and corridors are selective for the subtle pleasure they offer its inhabitants." The quotation refers, of course, to Skinner's *Walden Two* (1984, p. 507).

The home and the school can be at odds with each other or allies. Home-based reinforcement programs designed to modify classroom behaviors are by now well established. Typically, the teacher sends a note to parents reporting the child's performance at school and, depending upon the contents of the note, parents subsequently institute home contingencies. This simple procedure requires considerably less teacher effort than even the least complicated classroom intervention and therefore, if effective, is likely to be attractive to the school. While such programs can be and have been applied to disruptive behaviors, the home-based programs for academic behaviors are the ones that offer the most advantages. First, they tend to be easier for teachers to implement because it is easier to record academic behavior. Second, the parents themselves may be able to intervene directly by providing some form of home tuition. Third, the reduction of disruptive behavior does not inevitably result in a corresponding increase in adademic achievement.

Despite these advantages, the effectiveness of a home-based program that focuses primarily or exclusively on academic performance remains largely unexplored. Witt, Hannafin, and Martens (1983) found that home contingencies placed only on academic performance resulted in marked increases in academic performance and large decreases in disruptive behavior. Throughout both baseline and treatment conditions, there was a significant negative correlation between academic performance and disruptive behavior.

Although it is promising, this study possesses certain methodological limitations, some of which are noted by the authors themselves. The three target students were of average or above-average academic ability, and classroom disruptions were relatively minimal. In addition, interactions between the target children and others who might be contributing relevant effects were not taken into consideration. Furthermore, there was no control group and no follow-up. One advantage of this strategy is the ease with which it can be implemented.

Finally, brief attention is drawn to a problem that has long plagued family social workers. The term "nonorganic failure to thrive" is applied to infants and children whose growth and development are significantly below age-related norms and in whom no physical cause for this can be detected. Following a detailed examination of the complex psychological and social dimensions of this phenomenon, Iwaniec, Herbert, and McNeish (1985a, 1985b) describe a readily applicable behavioral program for social workers directed specifically toward the amelioration of this problem. Their method, more a general strategy than a formal procedure so far, illustrates the manner in which behaviorally oriented family social work can be blended into the mainstream of community support systems.

COMPLIANCE AND NONCOMPLIANCE IN CHILDREN AND THEIR PARENTS

As far as I am concerned, the year's most exciting development in this area is the emergence of the *Journal of Compliance in Health Care*. It is my informed guess that children and their families will be featured prominently in each issue and that the orientation will be broadly behavioral.

A frequent complaint of parents seeking help with their problem children is that these children fail to comply properly with parental requests (Forehand & McMahon, 1981). Focusing on consequence-controlled behavior, the usual strategy is to couple reinforcement for compliance with time out for noncompliance. But antecedent parental commands are also of significance (Hudson & Blane, 1985). For example, Forehand, Wells, and Sturgis (1978) found that the incidence of vague and interrupted commands given by mothers in the clinic situation predicted children's noncompliance in the home. When Roberts, McMahon, Forehand, and Humphreys (1978) trained mothers to use specific unitary commands, child compliance increased from 35% to approximately 64%. In virtually all these studies, the focus has been upon the verbal content of a command rather than the associated nonverbal behaviors. This is particularly curious, given that compliance training manuals stress the shaping of nonverbal commands by use of such activities as appropriate eye contact and a firm but supportive voice tone; however, it is still not known precisely which nonverbal behaviors are associated with increased child compliance and under what circumstances.

To shed light on this problem, Hudson and Blane (1985) observed clinic and nonclinic mother–child pairs in a videotape procedure, similar to that outlined by Forehand and McMahon (1981), in which the first half of the available time was designated the "child's game" and the second half the "mother's game." Mothers were instructed to interact with their children as much as possible during the child's game but not to direct them in any way. During the mother's game, they were required to direct their children to engage in three specific play activities for short periods of time. The following nonverbal elements were all found to be reliably related to child compliance: distance from child; body orientation of mother; eye contact between mother and child; tone of voice; and mother's orientation toward objects involved in the instruction. It would seem reasonable to conclude that those involved in the training of parents of noncompliant children should make a special effort to shape noverbal as well as verbal components of parental instruction giving.

On the assumption that contingent praise is reinforcing, parents of noncompliant children are trained to praise the children for compliance with instructions. Unfortunately, this notion lacks either theoretical or empirical support, and Roberts (1985) offers two alternative explanations why praising compliance and ignoring noncompliance is generally not effective. First, noncompliant children may not value parental praise. Second, there may be some other more powerful process at work that serves to reinforce noncompliance. For example, Wells and Forehand (1981) have hypothesized that persistent noncompliance coerces parents into withdrawing instructions. As a consequence, the child successfully avoids the task at hand. If this is so, then ignoring noncompliance permits the negative reinforcing mechanism (in this instance, task avoidance) to come into play, thereby strengthening the pattern of noncompliance. Even if noncompliant children were to value parental praise, such reinforcers for compliance would have to compete with this hypothesized negative reinforcement for ignoring noncompliance.

To deal with the problem of ineffective social reinforcers, Patterson (1982) recommends token-mediated activities and material reinforcers. By contrast, Forehand and McMahon (1981) advocate the use of time out in conjunction with contingent social reinforcers to suppress noncompliance. But Day and Roberts's (1983) analysis of the Forehand and McMahon procedures suggests that it is the time-out component rather than the contingent-praise component that is probably responsible for the acquisition of compliance in initially noncompliant children. Once again, if treatment components other than contingent praise contribute to additional child change, why then do clinicians continue to train parents to praise child compliance?

By way of resolution of this paradox, Roberts (1985) offers two hypotheses. First, conduct-disordered children may be less responsive to adult social reinforcers than are normal children. Second, a variety of components of parent training programs have been proposed as enhancers of child responsiveness to adult approval during therapy. These include temporal contiguity of social and material reinforcers, concurrent punishment schedules, and exposure to a high frequency and expanded range of social reinforcers during free play. If it could be demonstrated that noncompliant children are relatively unresponsive to adult praise at pretreatment but responsive at posttreatment, then training parents to praise compliance could be an effective strategy.

The emphasis in child compliance training programs is beginning to shift from the behavior of the child alone to include the parents. It is possible to differentiate children referred to clinics for noncompliant behaviors from non-clinic-referred children by observing how the parents behave toward their children (Breiner and Young, 1985). Parental perceptions of their children's behavior have also been shown to be of importance. Furthermore, as noted, mothers of clinic-referred children tend to be significantly more depressed than mothers of nonclinic-referred children. The presence of depression in either the father or the mother can also be used to help predict certain attitudes toward the child (e.g., Griest, Wells, & Forehand, 1979).

Much less is known about the characteristics of parents of noncompliant children who are developmentally delayed. According to Breiner and Forehand (1982), unlike mothers of nondelayed—noncompliant children, mothers of children who are developmentally delayed and noncompliant do not report feelings of depression. What they do report is that they socialize infrequently and that they feel isolated, tired, and distressed. An additional factor that may be closely related to the reported feelings of isolation is that these mothers typically spend the majority of their time with their children rather than in other types of daily activities. If it could be documented that such parents are experiencing a type of depression that is related to less frequent and less rewarding social interactions, this could have implications for the direction of future parent training programs. When Breiner and Young (1985) compared the social activities of mothers of noncompliant, nondelaying children wih those of mothers of noncompliant, developmentally delayed children, this is more or less what they found.

With children suffering from serious medical disorders, noncompliance can be literally life-threatening. As Varni and Wallander (1984) remind us, it is important to differentiate between short-term adherence ("adherence" and "compliance" are interchangeable terms) in acute pediatric illnesses and long-term adherence in chronic illnesses involving handicapping conditions. The relatively immediate improvement in acute illnesses serves as a powerful reinforcer for the maintenance of short-term adherence. By contrast, the management of pediatric chronic disorders usually requires long-term adherence to health care regimens that may not evidence immediately beneficial results. Under these circumstances, immediate reinforcement for engaging in routine health care regimens may not exist for either the child or the family. Simply prescribing a medical or exercise program is rarely a sufficient condition for assurance that it will be correctly implemented. Adherence to therapeutic regimens in pediatric chronic disorders encompasses a broad spectrum of health-related behaviors. These include correct intake of prescribed medications, conscientious clinical appointment attendance, appropriate eating and exercise patterns, and correct performance of home-based therapeutic procedures (Varni, 1983).

Improvements in adherence to therapeutic regimens could result in more cost-effective health care services. Ambulatory pediatric clinics, for example, are notorious for their high percentage of missed appointments. Keeping a pediatric appointment involves a complex training that begins with remembering the appointment and follows with many other responses, some of which are inherently punishing—as those who have had to wait in line with a sick child to park a car know well.

Appointment compliance research has focused primarily on the mail or telephone reminder. But the evidence is equivocal, and it may be that many additional variables need to be explored (Friman, Finney, Rapoff, & Christophersen, 1985). What is the social significance of broken appointments, and how acceptable are the interventions currently employed? How reliably are the dependent variables assessed? To what extent are simple appointment reminders cost-effective, and how appropriate are they for use in the typical pediatric clinic? In a related study, Finney, Friman, Rapoff, and Christophersen (1985) conclude that pediatric clinics could improve compliance by reminding parents when their children are scheduled for medical services and by making it easier for parents to obtain these services. But, as they cautiously point out, whether such compliance is in fact a significant prerequisite for health improvement remains to be established.

The bulk of the adherence research in pediatric chronic disorders has been conducted in three areas: hemophilia, juvenile diabetes, and spina bifida. A significant advance in the management of hemophilia occurred in the early 1960s with the discovery of the essential clotting factors and their separation from the plasma of normal blood. The intravenous infusion of this missing clotting factor allows a functional blood clot to form, and factor replacement therapy becomes literally a life-or-death matter. Serge-Deavenport and Varni (1982, 1983) used a combination of behavioral techniques and instructional strategies to increase parental adherence to factor replacement therapy. A comparison group of parents in a home care program for an average of 5 years was also studied. The performance of the treatment group increased from 15% during baseline to 92% by the end of the treatment condition, with 97% adherence maintained over long-term follow-up. By contrast, the comparison group showed only 75% adherence. (See also Gilbert & Varni, 1984; Grennan, Powell, & Varni, 1984.)

The successful management of insulin-dependent juvenile diabetes mellitus likewise requires strict adherence by patient and parents to a complex, long-term regimen involving medical procedures, diet, exercise, and hygienic precautions. Because the required knowledge base is complex, it is essential to implement and assess a patient education phase beforehand. Self-monitoring of blood glucose levels, for example, is most likely to be effective if the need for this determination is fully appreciated by both children and parents. This led Carney, Schechter, and Davis (1983) to develop a multiple-baseline intervention procedure consisting of contingent parental praise and the awarding of points for the self-monitoring of blood glucose levels at designated times each day.

Spina bifida is a common, congenital central nervous system deficit that can have serious consequences. With the development of improved medical and surgical techniques, the survival rate has increased dramatically, and the present thrust is toward rehabilitation. Marked developmental delays in everyday self-help skills generally result in much longer periods of time needed to achieve functional independence, and it is in this area that behavioral parent training has been particularly successful. For the child with spina bifida, obesity often causes additional problems, and compliance with weight rehabilitation programs assumes importance. Killam, Apodaca, Manella, and Varni (1983) designed a weight control group program for five children with spina bifida and their parents. At initiation, the children averaged 52% overweight. During treatment, the children and their parents received instructions pertaining to diet, exercise, and associated behavioral techniques. To assess therapeutic adherence, the number of self-monitoring forms completed and returned was compared with the number assigned. In addition, the number of treatment and follow-up sessions attended by each family was recorded, and a social validation questionnaire was given as part of the follow-up. Four of the five children evidenced a 13% weight loss at a 6-month follow-up.

BEHAVIORAL PARENT TRAINING

Many parents find parent education more appealing than behavioral parental training, perhaps because the implicit treatment emphasis of the latter is less acceptable than an educational focus. Parent education is part of the emerging new discipline of psychoeducation, with its stress upon education rather than therapy (Levant, 1986). In this chapter, however, the primary concern is with behavioral parent training rather than parent education. Despite considerable diversity in conceptualization, implementation, and evaluation, all behavioral parent training programs share common experimentally established principles and a commitment to empirical research.

Among the many new publications of relevance, that of Dangel and Polster (1984) is probably the most significant. With the notable omission of a contribution from Patterson and his associates at the Oregon Research Institute, this is the only volume to bring together under one set of covers all the major clinicians and researchers working in this area. As Graziano (1986) points out in his perceptive review, the title—*Parent Training*—is somewhat misleading, in that the content is primarily behavioral parent training. But the editors may be excused for this little oversight in view of the fact that most parent training research is more or less behavioral.

Behaviorally trained parents become active change agents rather than passive recipients of professional services (Graziano, 1983). The home, rather than the artificial environment of the professional's office, becomes the major setting for intervention. Personal life controls reside in the individual and in the family rather than in some external authority figure (Blechman, 1985).

O'Dell (1985) draws attention to the contemporary emphasis upon the study of failure as well as success. Parental depression, client resistance, lack of support systems, and defective client–treatment matching can all contribute to program failure. O'Dell offers helpful suggestions to those engaged in behavioral parent training. Thus, while direct shaping of behavior may be the preferred and perhaps the most effective method, it is also the most costly. Well-prepared videotaped modeling may be equally valid and more cost-effective. And for maximum setting generalization, it may be advisable to train in an environment similar to that in which the program is going to be implemented. The data also support the importance for parent involvement in training of social recognition and increased contact time. Finally, while parental reactions to training cannot as yet be predicted, O'Dell cautions the trainer to be alert to warning signs. Such characteristics as parental pre-existing causal assumptions about child behavior, parental reading skills, attention spans, and levels of anxiety in training may all be of relevance.

When Budd and O'Brien (1982) reviewed the behavioral literature published between the years 1970 and 1981, they found evidence of paternal involvement in only 13% of the families concerned, despite the fact that most researchers paid lip service to the necessity of including the father in the parent training program. While it is well known that many fathers resist involvement in parental training, the benefits to be derived from inclusion of the father are less well documented. When fathers are studied, it is invariably middle-class, highly educated male parents who are involved. In most instances, long-term follow-up data are lacking, and there is no attempt to see how well the fathers' enthusiasm holds up in the months that lie ahead (Budd & O'Brien, 1982; Horton, 1984).

The circumstances surrounding the failure of certain families to benefit from parent training are still incompletely understood. Families with significant marital disharmony, maternal depression, low income, limited parent education levels, or a lack of an adequate support network all seem to be particularly at risk both for dropping out of treatment and for failing to maintain treatment gains (Sanders, 1984). A somewhat related problem stems from the tendency of parent training researchers to confound the analysis of procedures for bringing about the generalization of parent behaviors with procedures that produce generalized changes in child behavior per se. Generalization of parenting skills to additional training settings may or may not bring about modification in the child's behavior, and different strategies may be required for each (Sanders, 1984; Sanders & James, 1983).

Many issues await investigation. For example, does generalization across settings reliably predict generalization over time? Under what circumstances is the generalization of treatment effects primary, and when should the training goal more appropriately be one of discrimination rather than generalization? For example, even when correctly applied, nondiscriminative use of particular punishment procedures may be counter-therapeutic and thereby may serve to reduce the effectiveness of parental reinforcers used to foster prosocial behavior (Sanders, 1984; Sanders & James, 1983).

Rios and Gutierrez's (1986) review of parent training with nontraditional families fits in well with Sanders's concern with potential ecological obstacles to generalization and maintenance. Most research concentrates upon middle-class families. The limited literature pertaining to other types of families suggests that behavioral parental training is of limited effectiveness with families of lower socioeconomic status and lower levels of education. In such families, generalization and maintenance tend to be sparse, and the risk for dropout during training is high. Families with marital conflicts also fare poorly. Perhaps understandably, clinicians tend to cope with such considerations by screening out their more "difficult" families beforehand. It may be necessary to intervene at the client's level—for example, by establishing "class-oriented treatment strategies" to maximize external validity and hence the success of the parent training program.

The ecobehavioral perspective of recent years is a direct reflection of such considerations. For example, mothers identified as "insular" due to their limited degree of positive extrafamilial interactions were found by Wahler (1980) to be quite different from noninsular mothers with respect to their parent training attitudes and coping mechanisms (see discussions in previous volumes of this series). Insularity may be one of the more significant predictors of parent treatment outcome (Dumas & Wahler, 1983). Insular mothers seem to be more likely to respond to their children's problems with aversive behavior, and, in turn, their children respond with aversiveness (Dumas & Wahler, 1985; Webster-Stratton, 1985).

As far as nontraditional families are concerned, it is good intentions rather than good studies that rule the day. Little is known about behavioral interventions with such families. For example, how is existing methodology to be used with a non-English-speaking, poorly educated, single parent who resides in a high-crime, skid-row urban area? Understandably, many lower-socioeconomic-status and/or minority families are concerned primarily with seeking relief from their immediate presenting problems. They are, therefore, unlikely to be active participants in lengthy training programs geared toward more distant objectives (Rios & Gutierrez, 1986).

The complexities are enormous, and both the treatment package and the manner of delivery may depend upon the demands of the total situation. While dozens of studies involving specific parameters have appeared, no integrative model has as yet emerged. The findings are often inconclusive and even contradictory. For example, most investigators find reinforcement of incompatible behavior to be the most acceptable and effective procedure, with time out falling at the opposite end of the spectrum. However, as Hobbs, Walle, and Caldwell (1984b) note, most investigations of treatment acceptability also rely entirely on written description rather than clinical observation.

Dropout might be one index of acceptability, but as yet little is known about dropout rates in behavioral parent training programs. When Forehand, Middlebrook, Rogers, and Steffe (1983) surveyed eight leading journals over the period 1972 through 1982, they found that only 22 of the 45 relevant studies reported any dropout data. Furthermore, to the extent that only studies with low dropout rates report this type of data, a positive bias may be operative. Dropout can be considered both an index of consumer satisfaction and a measure of outcome.

A related issue to which Forehand *et al.* (1983) draw attention is the identification of the primary client. In parent training, the child is the client, even though most of the therapy is with the parents. It may be that parents choose to terminate therapy for reasons unrelated to behavior change in the child. Therefore, parental characteristics may be better predictors of dropout rates than characteristics of the child. Preliminary data suggest that parents who are depressed or of low socioeconomic and educational status are more likely to drop out. Powell (1984) further concludes that the presence of limited social networks also contributes to early termination.

A much-neglected area of investigation in the parent training literature is that of cost-efficiency. Without sophisticated information about the equivalence or lack of equivalence of clients, methods, and outcome data, most cost-efficiency comparisons become relatively meaningless. At first inspection, self-help manuals might seem to be more cost-effective than other forms of parent training (e.g., Giebenhain & O'Dell, 1984). But self-help manuals are not going to be effective if they cannot be readily assimilated by the consumer. When Holcomb and Stith (1985) examined some 16 publications, they found that 10 of them required at least high-school-level reading ability. Yet such manuals are often suggested for use by families from culturally restricted environments with a reading level of eighth grade or less. Under these circumstances, cost-effectiveness estimations are relatively meaningless. But, of course, the search for more cost-effective methods in behavioral parent training programs is not confined to reading manuals. Sometimes some simple device that a parent may use, such as Hamilton and MacQuiddy's (1984) Signal Seat, can result in dramatic increase in cost-effectiveness. (The Signal Seat is an ordinary chair adapted to emit an auditory signal whenever the child gets up without permission. The inconveniences of time out are reduced to a minimum, and parental consistency is thereby encouraged.)

BEHAVIORAL TRAINING PROGRAMS FOR PARENTS OF CHILDREN WITH SPECIAL NEEDS

While most behavioral parent training programs continue to be directed towards parents of relatively normal children, researchers are turning increasingly to parents of children with special needs (see Cunningham, 1985, for a recent review). For example, Barth, Schinke, and Maxwell (1985) have reported a school-based program designed to increase the coping ability of adolescent mothers by the enhancement of interpersonal and cognitive skills. Seventy-nine pregnant or parenting teenage adolescents, approximately 50% black, were given $5.00 each for completing the various pretests, posttests, and follow-up tests. The experimental group met semiweekly for 10 hours with a team of trained social work students, and the control group attended other classes for an equal time period. The program consisted of various skills training strategies, the development of coping and cognitive skills, and a variety of assessment measures. The study suggests quite convincingly that such a program can teach new skills for avoiding conflict, and thereby provide the groundwork for a much-needed social support network among young mothers who would otherwise be at great risk.

The second example pertains to a training program for parents of overweight children (Israel, Stolmaker, & Andrian, 1985). Families were assigned either to a weight-reduction-only condition, predicated upon a multicomponent behavioral weight reduction program, or a parent training condition in which participants received the same treatment preceded by a short course in general child management skills. A third group served as a waiting-list control. Children of families in both 8-week experimental groups lost weight, whereas children in the control families gained weight. At a 1-year follow-up, maintenance and improved weight status were superior for children in the parent training group.

The third example comes from a quite different area, the development of a behavioral group training program for parents of children born with spina bifida. Due largely to advances in the development of medical and surgical techniques, the survival rate for such children has increased dramatically within the past two or three decades, as noted earlier. Unfortunately, these children are particularly likely to experience significant developmental delays in social, emotional, vocational, and daily living skills. To facilitate functional independence, behavioral techniques would seem to be ideal, and it is to the training of parents in such endeavors that considerable attention is now being given (e.g., Feldman, Manella, Apodaca, & Varni, 1982).

There are many behavioral training programs for mentally retarded children and their parents. Unfortunately, while most studies report favorable outcomes, serious methodological limitations demand that the findings be interpreted with caution. Hornby and Singh (1983, 1984) review these studies in detail and offer suggestions for improvement. There is a need for larger samples, better subject selection, and greater attention to generalization training. The systematic implementation of behavior change procedures in the home merits greater emphasis. Direct behavioral observation of parent–child interactions should be utilized in addition to the ubiquitous parental rating scales. Finally, if the full benefits of parent training are to be realized, it is essential to promote both the generalization and the maintenance of learned skills (e.g., Cowart, Iwata, & Pointer, 1984).

To conclude this section on a somewhat more optimistic note, attention is drawn to an innovative study of potential significance by Baker and McCurry (1984) of a school-based training program geared toward parents predicted to succeed minimally, at best. In an earlier study, Clark and Baker (1983) had identified the following predictors of poor posttraining teaching proficiency in parents of mentally retarded children: low family income, less than high school education, no prior experience with behavior modification, and high expectation of problems with their children. For the 20 mothers who fell into this category, Baker and McCurry (1984) developed an alternative program involving live modeling, observation of teaching, individually supervised teaching, and videotaped feedback. Didactic input was minimized, and the emphasis was placed upon more action-oriented strategies. The 85% of the mothers who completed the training made significant gains with respect to knowledge of behavioral principles, teaching skills, and reported child self-help skills. At a 6-month follow-up, mothers evaluated the program highly.

Unfortunately, as Baker and McCurry have acknowledged, outcome conclusions are limited by the absence of adequate control groups. Furthermore, despite impressive gains, the program failed to raise the scores of most participating families to the mean level of middle-income families—a finding not altogether surprising. At the 6-month follow-up, both the extent and quality of parental home teaching had fallen back to pretraining levels. Perhaps the main lesson to be learned is that further attention needs to be given to the development of effective parent training programs for the less privileged members of society.

CHILD ABUSE AND NEGLECT

There is little that is new to report in the area of child abuse and neglect. The three main approaches are still those of psychoanalysis, sociology, and social learning theory. Project 12-Ways is still one of the more comprehensive behaviorally oriented attempts to cope with this problem. As Wolfe and Manion (1984) imply, it is in the area of support services that most advances have occurred within the past decade. Ten years ago, parents had to be identified as demonstrably abusive before any help was offered. The "help" consisted primarily of limited child protection services, with perhaps a home visit or two and a few sessions wih the psychotherapist. Today, more and more communities are offering systematic support across a broad front involving a variety of primarily behaviorally oriented procedures.

Of the recent behavioral reviews, that of Gambrill (1983) is the most thorough. Her opening section offers a brief discussion of definitional problems, the incidence of child maltreatment, frameworks for viewing child abuse, and a limited survey of findings to date. Surprisingly little effort has been devoted to program evaluation, and the bulk of her chapter is concerned with the appraisal of current social learning programs. Like other leading child abuse investigators, Gambrill is convinced that many factors must be taken into account: the characteristics of parents, children, and significant others in the family; the general home environment; community factors; and the interactions of these networks.

Parent training in more effective child management skills would seem to lie at the heart of any broad-based program for prevention and intervention, and it is therefore understandable that Gambrill devotes considerable space to this topic. What is lacking as yet, with one or two notable exceptions such as the programs of Wolfe and Lutzker, would seem to be adequate outcome evaluation. As Gambrill observes, the "shotgun" approach, in which a packet of procedures is used with little regard for the relevance of individual variables, is antithetical to behavior therapy. Also underemphasized, according to Gambrill (and I concur), is the relevance of social networks and of ethnic and class differences. For example, Caucasian mothers are likely to be quite different from black mothers in the manner in which they interact with their children. Such mothers are also likely to have different attitudes with respect to the social service support systems that are available. If well-motivated, "compatible" parents have difficulties in accepting social service facilities, it seems even more likely that socially alienated parents are going to erect barriers to effective intervention.

Wolfe (1985) has reviewed the literature pertaining to child-abusive parents in an attempt to pinpoint relevant differences between this population and nonabusive parents. Whereas few studies have reported significant differences along traditional psychological dimensions, abusers are more likely to report stress-related symptoms, such as depression and health problems linked to the parenting role. In terms of family interactions, abusers display patterns of behavior with both children and spouses/partners that tend to be more aversive and less social than those of nonabusers. It is a critical evaluation of such data that has strengthened Wolfe's conceptualization of child abuse as an interactive process involving parental and situational demands. For the future, he suggests that greater attention be paid to cognitive abilities, family roles, standards, expectations, and child-related experiences among diverse parent populations.

A 1981 survey by Plotkin, Azar, Twentyman, and Perri of some 270 articles on child abuse found that only 25% were based on data collected by the authors. Plotkin *et al.*'s conclusion that much of the child abuse literature is based on impression and speculation rather than empirical evidence is probably less valid now, but only marginally so. One problem to which Smith (1984) draws attention is that of definition. The three main approaches to definition —in terms of outcome (e.g., injuries), in terms of intentionality, and in terms of community censure—are rarely delineated clearly in the behavioral literature, and this makes comparative studies less meaningful. Smith suggests a simple schema for all investigators to apply. The first step is a careful delineation of criteria, together with clear demographic descriptions of the families concerned. Next comes a detailed functional analysis of each situation and the formulation of an individually tailored and carefully recorded treatment program. Smith also draws attention to matters of legal sanction. How far are legal sanctions necessary or desirable to get families to behave in "socially acceptable" ways in a society with diverse ethnic, religious, and cultural mores? In attempts to answer this question, treatment goals should be conceptualized in terms of quality of life for the child more than changes within the parents. Long-term outcome measures must also be in terms of the child's quality of life as well as benefits to the parents.

Ten families participated in a controlled trial of a behavioral approach to child abuse based on Smith's recommendations. While the final outcome was inconclusive, the available data point to the feasibility of a program designed along the lines indicated above (Smith & Rachman, 1984). Noting the problems involved in the conduct of such studies (in particular, sample heterogeneity, a high rate of noncooperation, and sample attrition), Smith, Rachman, and Yule (1984) have drawn up guidelines for more innovative research. These include controlled treatment trials, clear definition of treatment goals and outcome measures, emphasis upon individualized program tailoring predicated upon adequate assessment, and long-term follow-up. One problem that may never be totally resolved pertains to the adequacy of the no-treatment control group. A complete no-treatment control group presents serious ethical difficulties, and a postponed-treatment control group can never form a good basis for comparisons.

Child abuse interventions seem to be moving toward a multidimensional social learning model. Child abuse per se is but one component of the deprived world in which these children are forced to live (e.g., Friedrich & Einbender, 1983; Lorber, Felton, & Reid, 1984; Reid & Kavanagh, 1985). The psychodynamic model of child abuse views the problem as stemming primarily from personality conflicts within the parents; it is the child-abusing parent who is seen as "sick" and in need of psychotherapeutic intervention. The sociological model sees child abuse as stemming from problems within the family's environment, such as unemployment, marital discord, and poor housing. The social learning model views the problem largely in terms of learned coercion among the family members. Each family member learns to rely on aversive control techniques that all too readily escalate into abuse incidents. For Lutzker and his associates, all three models have something to offer, and it is this premise that laid the foundations for their ecobehavioral approach. By "ecobehavioral," they mean that child abuse and neglect are multifaceted problems in need of multifaceted treatments. Parental inadequacies, child behavior problems, sociological factors, and learning variables are all seen as potential contributors to the problem. It was this view that gave birth to Project

12-Ways, perhaps the most ambitious and successful approach to date (Lutzker, 1984; Lutzker, Wesch, & Rice, 1984).

The program of outcome evaluation that these authors describe involves assessment at four levels: data collected for clinical purposes, data from single-case experiments, single-subject designs applied to small groups, and program evaluation. Despite largely unavoidable methodological limitations, which they are at pains to report, their comparative evaluation of 50 families served by Project 12-Ways and 47 comparison families receiving routine state services is encouraging (Lutzker & Rice, 1984).

What is of particular interest about Project 12-Ways is the manner in which it pays attention to facets of child abuse other than the traditional "psychological" parameters. Parents may be charged with child abuse or neglect on the basis of a variety of diverse circumstances. Child neglect, for example, can occur when the home is so poorly kept that it presents an environment in which young children have ready access to lethal hazards (e.g., poisons, exposed wall outlets, and firearms). Numerous attempts have been made to institute programs of safety education, and a variety of school health and public service facilities have been instituted. Unfortunately, most of these programs are cumbersome and of limited utility (Dershewitz & Christophersen, 1984).

Tertinger, Greene, and Lutzker (1984) conclude from their review of these attempts to improve home safety conditions that more intensive methods are needed. Modeling, behavioral rehearsal, and feedback may be required. Tertinger *et al.*'s Home Accident Prevention Inventory is a comprehensive assessment protocol for recording the nature, quantity, and accessibility of items that have been incriminated as the leading causes of death in young children: poisoning by solids and liquids; suffocation by mechanical objects; fire and electrocution; ingestion of objects; and firearms. Following the collection of baseline data, Project 12-Ways parents were presented with the treatment package of instructions, shown ways of making such hazards inaccessible to children, and offered feedback about observed occasions of possible hazards. A multiple-baseline design showed decreases in both accidents and accessible hazards, with improvements maintained over an extended period of unannounced follow-ups. Most important, social validation data indicated satisfaction with the program and a desire to continue. (See Barone, Greene, & Lutzker, in press, for a discussion of problems still to be resolved.)

It is possible to explore the contributory role of parents in child abuse without espousing a psychodynamic model. For example, Perry, Wells, and Doran (1983) compared parent characteristics in families in which physical child abuse occurred with those of nonabusing families matched on socioeconomic status and other demographic variables. Mothers from abusing families evidenced lower self-esteem, less family cohesion, and more limited expression. They expected slower development in their children and consistently reported higher incidents of anxiety and family conflict. Fathers from abusing families likewise reported less family cohesion and a decreased emphasis upon moral and religious variables. They also expected slow development in their children and reported more family conflict. Such studies point to the need both to evaluate fathers and mothers separately and to study the interactions between abuse perpetrators and their spouses.

A myriad of parent characteristics merit attention as probable contributors to the etiology and maintenance of child abuse. What, for example, is the relationship between intelligence of parents and maltreatment of their children? When Schilling, Schinke, Blythe, and Barth (1982) reviewed the relevant literature, they concluded that there is an increased risk of maltreatment for children reared by mentally retarded parents. If cognitive and social factors are important in child rearing, mentally retarded parents are likely to experience more difficulty in the provision of adequate care. It therefore seems reasonable to assume that children of such parents are at a greater risk of maltreatment than those of nonretarded parents.

Knowing something about the characteristics of abusive as contrasted with nonabusive parents is only one side of the coin. It is of at least equal importance to make a detailed study of the abused children themselves. The abused child is often described as being difficult to manage and delayed in psychosocial development in comparison with normal children. But although considerable attention has been given to the developmental consequences of abuse, there is apparently little agreement with respect to the extent and nature of the behavior problems that occur. Wolfe and Mosk (1983) compared school-age abused children, nonabused children from a child welfare agency, and nonabused children living in the community. Parental reports of strength and weaknesses were examined by means of the Achenbach and Edelbrock (1983) Child Behavior Checklist. Consistent with previous studies, abused children were found to display a significantly greater number of behavior problems and fewer social competencies than normals. In addition, the behavior patterns of these abused children closely resembled the range of problems evidenced by children from distressed families in which abuse was not present. The conclusion drawn by Wolfe and Mosk is that future studies should be expanded to include children raised in highly distressed family environments in which aversive elements other than physical aggression are operative. Disturbances in social and behavioral development may be more a function of family events and interaction patterns than of isolated abusive episodes.

In sum, the recent literature points to an increasing recognition that child abuse is not to be considered as a homogeneous category (Ross, 1984). The complexities involved suggest the need for an ecobehavioral framework in which a perspective based on social learning theory is not pursued at the expense of either parent and child characteristics or sociological variables. The other encouraging development is the increasing recognition of this problem by all members of society rather than mental health professionals alone. The development of a supportive social network is particularly encouraging.

AUTISM AND BEHAVIOR THERAPY

While no spectacular new development in the area of autism, behavioral or otherwise, is in sight, three trends are apparent: a family and systems approach to behavioral intervention with the autistic child; incidental teaching as contrasted with traditional educational procedures; and, wherever feasible, integration into the mainstream educational system.

These three trends are closely related to changing professional perspectives. Until the early 1970s, autism was viewed as a psychogenic emotional disorder in which cognitive and social impairments were secondary or derivative. During the 1970s, increasing evidence suggested that autism was more to be associated with biological deficits than with inner-directed psychogenic variables. It is significant that the *Diagnostic and Statistical Manual of Mental Disorders*, third edition (DSM-III) categorizes Infantile Autism as a pervasive developmental disorder (American Psychiatric Association, 1980), and that the *Journal of Autism and Child Schizophrenia* is now the *Journal of Autism and Developmental Disorders*. It is now recognized that autism can occur at all levels of intelligence with or without demonstrable organic pathology. This does not imply that most autistic children do not exhibit one or more "soft" neurological signs, or that deficits of various degrees of severity are not going to show up on formal intelligence testing; in both cases, they do. For an excellent review of these matters and their implications for behavior therapy, the reader is referred to a chapter by Romanczyk, Kistner, and Ponzetti-Dyer (1983).

Until recently, the commendable emphasis upon training programs for parents of autistic children has been at the expense of the family. Harris's (1984) behavioral systems approach takes into consideration the family and the extended family. She sees five major problem areas that are likely to confront virtually every family of an autistic child over the course of time: diagnostic; management in early and middle childhood; reactions of siblings; management in adulthood; and, finally, the attitudes and responses of the extended family and community. In discussing these problems, Harris cautions her readers not to assume that the presence of the autistic child is invariably the crucial factor in the maladaptive pattern of any particular family. There are certain families whose structure is so maladaptive as to be dysfunctional under even mild stress. In such a family, the autistic child may be presented as the identified patient, but the assessment and intervention of the therapist must go beyond the understandably limited vision of the parents to an appreciation of the full context in which they are living. To illustrate these points, Harris and Powers (1984) adopt a case history format. Unfortunately, as Harris would probably affirm, the best of case histories is no substitute for data, controlled investigation, and outcome evaluation.

Incidental teaching procedures have been documented for almost two decades, but it was not until recently that widespread research on and clinical interest in such procedures emerged. "Incidental teaching" is the process that occurs when the natural environment is deliberately arranged to induce children to respond positively to specific materials and other desired activities, and a teacher is available to provide appropriate attention, praise, and instruction whenever the child concerned initiates an interaction related to the topic of immediate interest (Hart & Risley, 1982). Incidental teaching enhances generalization of descriptive language by disadvantaged preschoolers and autistic children alike (e.g., Carr & Kologinsky, 1983; McGee, Krantz, Mason, & McClannahan, 1983). Generalization occurs not only to different settings, but also to different activities occurring at different times of the day. Linguistic facility can be accelerated by incidental instruction provided in the course of shaping other school and home living skills.

McGee, Krantz, and McClannahan (1985) spell out some of the major distinctions between traditional and incidental teaching that are of relevance to the autistic child. In traditional teaching, it is the teacher who paces and controls opportunities to respond at specified intertrial intervals; in incidental teaching, the episodes are child-initiated, usually in relationship to preferred items of the child's choice. Traditional teaching usually occurs in sit-down sessions arranged to minimize distraction; by contrast, incidental teaching takes place within the context of other activities, usually those occurring naturally within the child's total environment. In traditional teaching, the learning stimuli are usually teacher-selected, and consequent stimuli in the child's environment tend to be unrelated to the learning stimuli; in incidental teaching, the learning stimuli are child-selected, and contingent access to these items is used as a reinforcement. Traditional language training makes use of standard prompts until the child has achieved a predetermined criterion level; in incidental teaching, the prompts are varied according to the child's initiating responses.

In its own fashion, this is possibly the nearest thing to a minor breakthrough in the training of autistic children that has occurred to date, and it is surprising that so little comparative research has been conducted. McGee *et al.*'s (1985) study of incidental teaching versus traditional training in language-delayed autistic children is an important exception to this generalization. Three language-delayed children were taught expressive use of prepositions to describe the locations of edibles and preferred toys. Traditional and incidental teaching procedures were employed within a classroom setting, and generalization was assessed during free play. The obtained superiority of incidental teaching in terms of promoting greater generalization and more response in its use of prepositions has important implications both for language programming and for teacher training. Despite numerous unresolved problems, incidental teaching may now be ready for inclusion as a standard component of language development programs for autistic and other developmentally delayed children.

The notion that autistic children can become part of the mainstream educational milieu is relatively new, and there are still those who voice vociferous objections. Autistic students, it is argued, need specialized learning environments, specially trained staffs, and separate programs—a situation still common in North America. The rationale for this point of view is documented in detail by Donnellan and Neel (1986) and, at least from their perspective, effectively demolished. If everyday social skills are to be taught, a normal environment would seem on the face of it to offer the most opportunity for social interactions. Most investigations to date have focused on preschool children, and few procedures have been developed for the teaching of social skills to older students. In one study, Gaylord-Ross, Haring, Breen, and Pitts-Conway (1984) examined social skills development in a high school setting. In contrast to customary procedures in which efforts are directed towards the training of a nonhandicapped peer to be the primary agent of social behavior change, their strategy depended upon the direct training of autistic students to *initiate* and elaborate interactions with their nonhandicapped peers. In further contrast to most previous studies, which have focused upon a specific setting with only limited success in promoting generalization to other situations and individuals, Gaylord-Ross *et al.* focused upon generalization strategies across both settings and persons.

There are many obvious advantages to mainstream peer training. Adult professional reinforcement is not always readily available. Furthermore, such social interactions usually bear little resemblance to the normal patterns of children's experiences with their peers. The possibilities for meaningful research are great. Shafer, Egel, and Neef (1984), for example, were interested in the following: (1) whether or not a direct prompting procedure, in which peer trainers would practice directly with the target children, would increase generalized social interaction between autistic and nonautistic children; (2) the largely unexplored impact of such a procedure on the peer trainers; (3) the extent to which peer-mediated interventions would result in sustained rather than brief interactions; (4) the extent of cross-setting generalization (Strain, 1983, had already compared generalized social responding by autistic children in settings containing either socially responsive or socially nonresponsive peers); and (5) whether changes in social behavior would be evident to others in the autistic students' environment. Teachers were asked to rate the effectiveness of the treatment on the social behavior of both autistic students and peer trainers. Direct prompting procedures were found to be effective in the promotion of positive social interactions between the peer trainers and the autistic students. These increases were maintained across time and independently judged by the teachers concerned as being socially valid. Interactions in different settings were initially above baseline levels, but thereafter decreased rapidly. It was only after specific programming that interactions increased and maintained themselves above baseline levels. It may be, as Shafer *et al.* suggest, that the problem is one of maintenance rather than transfer. Research is necessary to identify those variables that are likely to facilitate generalization and durable social interaction skills.

Despite the sustained interest in social and interpersonal skill deficits in handicapped children, the research literature is sparse (Schopler & Mesibov, 1983). To show what can be accomplished, Mesibov (1984) has described a still-ongoing social skills training program for verbal but autistic adolescents and adults. Clients were residing either in their parents' homes or in group homes for retarded citizens. Some were not involved in any daily activity at all, while others were in public school or sheltered work programs. The program was designed to achieve four long-term goals: (1) provision of positive peer-related experiences in a supportive atmosphere; (2) development of long-term peer relationships; (3) improvement in the specific interpersonal skills of the participants; and (4) enhancement of self-esteem. It is important to note that most participants were functioning at higher levels than the average autistic person and that many had been mainstreamed during much of their school careers. Although mainstreaming probably had some advantages, one difficulty was that other children tended to pick on them continually, and peer relationships were never very satisfactory. Such concerns determined the first two of Mesibov's long-term goals. Short-term training focused upon meeting other people, staying with a topic of conversation, asking appropriate questions, paying attention, and expressing personal feelings and emotions. The teaching techniques included modeling, coaching, and role playing.

By and large, the preliminary findings—the project as noted, is still under way—are encouraging. As autistic young people grow older (Mesibov's subjects ranged in age from 14 to 35 years), their interest in others increases significantly. It would seem that one major problem confronting autistic individuals is not so much a lack of social interests as a lack of social skills. The implication is that helping autistic individuals develop these skills may also enable them to lead fuller and richer lives. Another implication pertains to the demonstrable effectiveness of role playing. Hitherto, some question had arisen whether autistic people were capable of such complex activity. But as Mesibov notes, although role playing is abstract to the extent that it is a make-believe situation, viewed in another way it is an extremely concrete way of teaching behavior. A somewhat related question pertains to changes in self-perception. Do modeling, coaching, and role playing help autistic people improve their self-perceptions as well as their social skills and interpersonal behaviors?

As Strain and his associates have noted on several occasions (e.g., Strain, Hoyson, & Jamieson, 1985), the use of peer-mediated intervention is particularly attractive from an efficiency standpoint. Despite this benefit, attempts to incorporate a peer-based model into a total program are rare. In Strain's Learning Experiences:—An Alternative Program for Preschoolers and Parents (LEAP), normally developing children aged 3–5 are systematically taught to aid in the instruction of their autistic classmates. When compared to a group of nominated "stars" in developmentally segregated classes, Strain *et al.*'s (1985) normally developing LEAP children engaged in less disruptive behavior and equal amounts of on-task behavior, appropriate use of language, and positive peer interactions. Treatment gains for the autistic participants, as measured by positive peer interactions, were at least equivalent to the levels exhibited by their nonhandicapped classmates. These findings do much to counter the often-voiced criticism of mainstreaming that normally developing children will somehow "pick up" the less desirable characteristics of their disabled classmates.

One of the more difficult problems encountered in working with autistic children is that of lack of motivation. Typically, these children do not respond to smiles, praise, or the closeness of others, and this makes it difficult for the natural environment to shape and reinforce new behaviors. Efforts to establish generalized social reinforcers have met with little success. The benefits of edible reinforcers are limited and children quickly become satiated, with the result that responding becomes inconsistent and new learning difficult to program. Recent research reviewed by Rincover and Newsom (1985) suggests a number of alternatives to food. Forms of sensory stimulation (e.g., music and other sounds) have been suggested as a more powerful and durable class of reinforcers. Rincover and Newsom (1985) deployed a within-subject design to compare single and multiple sensory and edible reinforcers. The multiple sensory reinforcers maintained responding over more trials than did the multiple edible reinforcers. However, single sensory reinforcers and single edible reinforcers were about equally effective. Both multiple and single sensory reinforcers produced higher percentages of direct responses than did edible reinforcers.

If substantiated and refined, these findings could have implications for treatment and further research. Do children continue to work longer and learn more when multiple sensory events are used for extended periods of time? Would they continue to enjoy these sensory sessions in spite of their length? Do sensory reinforcers actually promote greater and more sustained interactions between children and their environments, as Rincover and Newsom suggest? Sensory reinforcers offer several advantages, not least of which is the fact that there are certain ethical constraints on the use or withholding of food reinforcers. And most autistic children eventually show preference for one sensory event or another, even when they are not particularly motivated by food.

Dunlap and Johnson (1985) investigated a different problem. Progress in the establishment of productive responding by autistic children in structured educational settings continues to be hampered by a lack of knowledge about generalization. The problem becomes even more apparent when these children are left to engage in unsupervised activity. The removal of close supervision quickly leads to a re-emergence of stereotypic and other off-task behaviors and a decline in appropriate, productive responding. This leads to management problems in classrooms, homes, and other community settings in which continuous supervision is neither feasible nor desirable.

Autistic children, it is argued, may be especially likely to display off-task responding when the teacher's or therapist's departure indicates that no contingency is to be applied for an extended period of time. In order for stimulus control to occur, it is necessary to employ some form of structural training. It is such considerations that have led researchers to explore ways in which indistinguishable, unpredictable contingencies can facilitate generalization. In the Dunlap and Johnson (1985) study, the therapist's presence on a random, intermittent, and unpredictable basis was found to be more effective than a similar supervisory condition in which the therapist was present for a regular period of time and absent for the remainder of the session. Unpredictable supervision produced much higher levels of on-task responding during the therapist's absence for all three of the children who were the subjects of their study.

Although entitled *Behavioral Assessment of Severe Developmental Disabilities*, Powers and Handleman's (1984) text is really about children with autism. Collaboration of this sort between psychologists and educators could provide a more effective assessment model than the traditional psychometrics of most school psychologists and psychoeducators. In any event, behavioral assessment would be facilitated by the development of an objective method for the description of these children. Since 1976, Freeman and his associates have been conducting a large-scale research project designed to develop a behavioral observation system to accomplish just this. In 1983, Freeman and Schroth reported a preliminary scale. The revision that emerged a year later (Freeman, Ritvo, & Schroth, 1984) contains 24 items subgrouped according to the system being measured. Different behaviors differentiate each autistic subgroup from its control, with much overlap between low-functioning autistic and mentally retarded children and between high-functioning autistic and normal children. "Relation to Examiner" behaviors best differentiate the low-functioning autistic group, whereas "Solitary Stereotypic and Language" behaviors best describe the high-functioning autistic group. According to Freeman *et al.* (1984), these data confirm the generally accepted notion that autism is a syndrome rather than a single entity. This notion seems intuitively plausible, but, once again, face validity is no substitute for data.

Finally, attention is drawn to a behavioral assessment process stemming from a totally different perspective. Ecological psychologists have long stressed the importance of the environment in determining the behavior of individuals (see previous volumes in this series). Specific behaviors are wedded to particular settings, argue the ecologists, and interactions between person and environment have to be examined if behavior is to be studied properly. The stimulus control literature points clearly to the significant effects that the environment can have on the behavior of autistic children. But, as Charlop, Schreibman, Mason, and Vesey (1983) note, behavior acquired in specific environments (such as clinics or classrooms) often fails to transfer to other environments. If classroom configurations could be manipulated so as to facilitate appropriate generalization, it could benefit all concerned. The teacher could arrange for the classroom environment to maximize the occurrence of a particular pattern of behavior, or to decrease inappropriate behavior so that it would not generalize to other environments.

Teachers, parents, and therapists are often asked to indicate which environments they feel are most likely to be associated with the occurrence of appropriate or inappropriate behaviors for particular children. However, as Charlop *et al.* (1983) point out, behavior only needs to occur once in a particular setting for that setting to be associated with the behavior. For example, an autistic child who throws toys in a temper tantrum only once in the free-play area may be rated high on disruption and perhaps forbidden by the teacher to play in that area. A trained observer, observing 15-minute daily sessions, would most likely miss such an isolated occurrence. A methodology is needed for systematic and repeated observation of autistic children in a variety of settings, and it was this task that Charlop *et al.* set themselves.

The naturalistic observation technique now known as "behavioral mapping" was designed for the observation of behaviors as they occur or fail to occur in various settings. The term "behavioral map" originated from the use of a prototype architectural floor plan used in the development of the technique. Charlop *et al.* (1983) adapted these procedures to the systematic observation of autistic children in different classroom settings. A methodology for the observation and assessment of which environments were associated with what behaviors was developed. When eight behaviors were observed in five classroom settings, particular settings were associated with high rates of some behaviors and low rates of others. Thus, rather than viewing behavior as an exclusive product of the children themselves, an ecological perspective studies behavior as an interaction between individuals and settings. While this study provides bold suggestions for classroom designs that invite further research, certain cautions are in order. For example, as Charlop *et al.* note, specific findings as reported may have been a function of the prior history and training of the children concerned. Behavioral mapping with other autistic children may yield quite different results.

HYPERACTIVITY: BEHAVIORAL APPROACHES

Prior to 1980, the terms "hyperactivity," "hyperkinesis," and "minimal brain damage" were used interchangeably. Confusion was compounded by the use of the word "hyperactivity" to indicate sometimes a specific problem behavior (e.g., overactivity), sometimes a complex set of behavior patterns that tend to covary, and sometimes a clinical syndrome (Whalen, 1982). Despite the lead offered by DSM-III (American Psychiatric Association, 1980), with its introduction of the diagnosis Attention Deficit Disorder with Hyperactivity (ADD/H), the terms given above are still used interchangeably. In addition, as Wallander and Hubert (1985) observe, there has been a shift in emphasis from motor activity as a key problem in hyperactivity to cognitive disorder. This shift, together with the problems noted above, makes comparative evaluation difficult.

Overviews and reviews continue to dominate the literature rather than empirical research—a signal that all is not yet well. The journal *Clinical Psychology Review* has devoted an entire issue (Volume 5, 1985) to the assessment and intervention of hyperactivity. In his introduction to the issue, Loney (1985) suggests that the literature is now characterized by empirical investigation that "has increased the ratio of light to heat in writing on the subject" (p. 403); however, the five review articles in this special issue, excellent in themselves, come up with equivocal conclusions (other than a unanimous endorsement of the need for further research) and not too much light.

Two of these articles are mentioned here. In the social realm, Whalen and Henker's (1985) perceptive review exposes critical gaps in empirical knowledge about interpersonal functioning in hyperactive children. These gaps are duc in large part to methodological research limitations and the use of heterogeneous measuring instruments. In the same issue, Gadow (1985) critically evaluates 16 comparative studies of the effects of medication and behavioral interventions on academic performance. While it is recognized that stimulant drugs can enhance academic performance in some children and can even facilitate the efficacy of a behavioral intervention, this effect is "not pervasive enough to expect such benefits in the general population of HA (hyperactive), LD (learning disabled), or HA–LD children" (p. 529). As far as Gadow is concerned, there is little doubt that an effective behavioral intervention can be a more powerful treatment for academic underachievers. Although the cautious use of stimulant drugs could be considered when academic underachievement is identified as a serious *clinical* problem, in general the addition of medication solely for the purpose of enhancing the behavioral intervention would seem to be superfluous and possibly undesirable.

Whalen and Henker (1984), in an earlier publication, have arrived at similar conclusions. Certain stimulants can have positive short-term effects on performance, but they do not ameliorate academic deficits. Furthermore, even when these stimulants do increase socialization, they fail to be helpful with respect to aggressive and antisocial activities. In addition, there are numerous side effects, and long-term outcomes tend to be disappointing. Hyperactive children do not fare as well during adolescence and young adulthood as had originally been hoped and even believed. For the effects of behavioral programs to maintain themselves, some form of internalized control may be necessary (e.g., Kauffman & Hallahan, 1979). This is unlikely to occur spontaneously.

Wallander and Hubert (1985) suggest a competency-based approach aimed at improving social behaviors in addition to a cognitive thrust. The tendency for ADD/H children to behave inappropriately in social situations may be due to deficient social skills. It may be, as these authors speculate, that this defect can be lastingly reduced through adequate social skills training. As yet, relevant data are few and long-term outcome evaluation is nonexistent.

Hersher (1985) briefly reviews all controlled studies of the effectiveness of behavioral modification for the treatment of "hyperkinesis"—to use his term—published over the last 20 years. Each paper is categorized according to the magnitude of impulsiveness and activity before treatment, the timing of the positive reinforcement, whether the results were reported as global judgments or assessments of discrete behaviors, and whether the results were positive or negative. Highly impulsive children were less likely to respond well to behavior modification than those who were only moderately impulsive. According to Hersher, the data suggest that very active children improve when rewards for decrease in activity are given immediately. When rewards are slightly delayed, behavior remains unaffected.

Statistically significant treatment effects may be necessary to demonstrate positive outcome, but these in themselves are rarely sufficient. One way of determining the clinical meaningfulness of treatment is to assess whether treated and normal, untreated children behave similarly. Abikoff and Gittelman (1984) evaluated the effectiveness of an intensive school and home contingency reinforcement program supplemented by cognitive modeling procedures in reducing the problem behaviors of hyperactive children to levels characteristic of their normal classmates. Twenty-eight children with ADD/H were paired with same-sex classmates reported by the teacher as presenting average classroom behavior, and children were observed in the classroom by individuals who were blind to diagnoses. Following treatment, there was no significant change in the percentage of hyperactive children classified as normal. The primary features of ADD/H—attention, activity, and impulsivity—were not normalized. Only aggression was consistently and fully normalized. The hyperactive children remained deviant in many aspects of classroom conduct.

The possibility that normalization might have occurred had the 8-week program been extended is rejected by Abikoff and Gittelman in view of the absence of improvement from the midpoint to the end of treatment. According to Ross and Ross (1982), a frequent outcome of classroom behavioral interventions is an initial dramatic improvement followed by a marked worsening of behavior, often to pretreatment levels. Abikoff and Gittelman's findings tend to follow this pattern. Improvement and deterioration may both be functions of the treatment.

The diet controversy offers another example of mounting failure. It will be recalled that in 1975 Feingold suggested a possible link between the ingestion of certain substances found in food and hyperactive behavior. Detailed critical reviews can be found in Conners (1980) and Ross and Ross (1982). Most studies that support the Feingold diet are unquestionably weaker in methodology than those that yield contrary findings. In searching for alternative explanations, Conners argues that the diet succeeds because of a placebo effect. Rippere (1983), however, considers that it may be premature to reject the Feingold hypothesis on the basis of the research, since there are methodological weaknesses on both sides. Studies that indicate sucrose consumption as a factor in children's hyperactivity are also assailed by Barling and Bullen (1984) on methodological grounds. In their own well-designed study, no significant relationship emerged between sucrose consumption and either hyperactivity or aggression.

Finally, attention is drawn to the great cognitive controversy raging in this as in all other areas of behavior therapy. There are good intuitive reasons to endorse cognitive-behavior therapy for the treatment of hyperactivity. On the one hand, opponents of pharmacotherapy have been pressed to develop therapeutic alternatives; on the other hand, proponents of pharmacotherapy have become increasingly disenchanted with the limited effects of their medications (Ross & Ross, 1982). Cognitive-behavior therapy seems to offer many appealing advantages: The strategies are easy to learn and apply, few demands are made on the teacher's time, and all offer promise of ready transfer across behavior and context (Whalen, Henker, & Hinshaw, 1985). But intuitive endorsement is not sufficient, and more research is required.

For most investigators, cognitive-behavior therapy and self-control become synonymous. For example, Barkley, Copeland, and Sivage (1980) demonstrated significant improvements in both attention and behavior when children recorded their own on-task activities. Each child was signaled to engage in self-recall at random intervals by a sound delivered through a tape recorder. Treatment effects were observed in an experimental classroom in which each child was required to work individually at his or her desk. However, no improvement with respect to regular classroom behavior was obtained during the treatment phase of the study; the situation-specific nature of the attentional deficits apparently requires procedures that can be used in the regular classroom environment with actual classroom tasks. Accordingly, Christie, Hiss, and Lozanoff (1984) examined the possibility of having teachers intermittently signal children to record their behavior at the teachers' convenience. The hope was that, in this way, the generalization problem that has hampered many studies attempting to use self-control training procedures in the laboratory would be circumvented. Using an appropriate AB design for two subjects and ABAB strategy for one subject, these authors succeeded in demonstrating, at least to their satisfaction, that self-recording procedures could be effectively used to modify inattentive behavior in the regular classroom. Precisely how this self-monitoring procedure modified behavior remains an unresolved issue. Christie *et al.* speculate, without benefit of data, that the mechanism for behavior change may have been differential reinforcement to desirable behavior.

Hinshaw, Henker, and Whalen (1984a) investigated the effects of two interventions on the social behavior of 24 hyperactive boys within a naturalistic playground environment. Methylphenidate was compared with a placebo, and cognitive–behavioral self-evaluation procedures were contrasted with intrinsic reinforcement alone. The primary outcome measures consisted of direct observations of positive and negative social interactions. Both methylphenidate and reinforced self-evaluation were superior to the contrast treatments. When the effects of the four treatment combinations were rank-ordered, medication plus cognitive–behavioral self-evaluation proved to be the most effective and placebo plus reinforcement alone the least. In a related study, Hinshaw, Henker, and Whalen (1984b) demonstrated that cognitive–behavioral treatments enhanced both general self-control and specific coping strategies in hyperactive boys. Combinations of methylphenidate and cognitive–behavioral interventions were *not* advantageous.

Apparently, what you believe governs what you find; the studies described above, in conjunction with that of Abikoff and Gittelman (1985), bear this out. According to these latter authors, conclusions about the usefulness of cognitive training are hampered by serious methodological limitations in the studies concerned. These include brief treatment periods, lack of control groups, limited training in the social skills, and failure to assess maintenance effects. To address these issues, Abikoff and Gittelman designed a 16-week program for hyperactive youngsters. Children were randomly assigned to groups receiving cognitive training, an attention control, or medication alone. The psychiatrists involved knew only that the children were receiving some form of training. At the end of 16 weeks, the children receiving medication alone and those receiving so-called cognitive training (actually, the attention control) were all switched to placebo without the knowledge of either teachers or parents. Of those receiving cognitive training, half were randomly assigned to remain on the medication regimen and half were switched to a placebo (also single-blind) to assess whether treatment effects due to cognitive training plus medication were differentially maintained under conditions of drug maintenance and drug withdrawal. Both teachers and parents were contacted weekly as part of an extensive follow-up.

The combination of cognitive training and stimulant medication failed to enhance academic performance. Medication was not more easily discontinued among those children who received cognitive training than among those who did not. Stimulant dosages could not even be advantageously lowered as a result of exposure to cognitive training. Such findings speak strongly against the notion that the use of nonacademic material to inculcate a general reflective response style is going to facilitate academic functioning in children with ADD/H. As has often been noted, to improve academic achievement direct training in specific academic skills is required. Cognitive therapy alone will not suffice.

To be fair, despite their positive findings, Whalen *et al.* (1985) are prudently cautious with respect to the advantages of cognitive-behavior therapy. In their own words, as far as short-term behavioral improvements are concerned, "the findings are neither as predictable nor as widespread as once expected" (p. 393). They are much more encouraging about the long-term maintenance of behavioral gains, but again, to quote their own words, "no evidence is available attesting to facilitation of long-term maintenance" (p. 393). Despite positive isolated findings, Whalen *et al.* are forced to conclude that "there is no conclusive evidence that CBT (cognitive-behavior therapy) is superior to other, less costly interventions, whether the yardstick consists of units of durability, generalization, or refractory behavior domains" (p. 396).

In Abikoff's (1985) critical review of cognitive training interventions for hyperactive children, he too concludes that self-regulation skills do not necessarily facilitate generalization and maintenance. As he puts it, "the early expectations of the potential clinical utility of cognitive training in ADD/H children have been tempered by almost a decade of research" (p. 507). However, to conclude on a more hopeful note, what George Bernard Shaw said about Christianity—it has failed because it has not been tried—may be true of studies of cognitive-behavior therapy for the treatment of hyperactivity. In defense of this position, attention is drawn to Abikoff's detailed suggestions for the conduct of future research. These include the need to develop adequate and systematic overlap in training and outcome task demands; greater attention to the assessment of maintenance effects; the use of "booster" sessions during follow-up; and a more extensive focus on individual differences, in which training programs are systematically geared to the needs of individual subjects on the basis of functional behavioral analysis. It might be noted, with Abikoff, that such methodological and treatment concerns are not unique to studies of hyperactive youngsters. They are relevant to cognitive training with children in general.

BEHAVIOR MODIFICATION AND THE SCHOOL SYSTEM

Less than two decades ago, behavioral school psychologists emphasized either the techniques of individual clinical behavior therapy or a few circumscribed group procedures such as classroom token economies. Contemporary behavioral school psychology is more sophisticated, with a diversity of ingenious individual and group approaches in evidence, even though the trend is toward group contingencies. Earlier reviewers, summarized by Pigott and Heggie (1985), concluded from the seemingly conflicting comparative data that there is no consistent differential effect between these two types of contingencies. Pigott and Heggie argue otherwise. Unlike most reviewers, Pigott and Heggie differentiate among the comparative studies of individual versus group contingencies according to the target behaviors, thereby finding differences that have previously been overlooked. In these studies, group contingencies were generally found to be superior to individual ones when academic performance was the target. When social responding was the treated behavior, there was no consistent difference in effectiveness between the two contingencies. Verbal threats and other forms of coercive control were reported when group contingencies were utilized to correct socially undesirable behavior. In direct contrast, there was no report of increased negative peer comments when a group strategy was used to treat academic performance. Pigott and Heggie conclude that group contingencies targeting academic behavior are not only more effective than individually administered contingency programs for increasing academic performance, they also utilize teacher time more cost-effectively and appear to have the added benefit of increasing prosocial behavior.

Lundell's (1982) group procedures for dealing with school discipline problems is based upon seven hierarchical levels organized around three stages of control. The first three levels are procedures for use within the classroom; the second three are for use within the school building; and the last is a home–school cooperative effort. Movement from one level to another as necessary to increase appropriate behavior is recommended. What we are not told, however, is how to combine the various procedures or to determine the necessary order in which they are to be used.

Whatever the procedure, and however the behavioral consultant views his or her role within the school system, what teachers and parents think is of primary significance. Witt and Elliott (1982) have identified three types of resistance by classroom teachers to techniques that have been proven effective in well-controlled studies. First, some interventions require extra personnel (e.g., trained observers) who are not readily available to regular teachers. Second, many interventions require resources (e.g., material reinforcers or complex clock and light systems) that are not otherwise available to the teachers. Finally, and most important from the teachers' perspective, some interventions require too much teacher time.

To identify some of the salient factors related to teacher judgements of acceptability, Witt, Elliott, and Martens (1984) asked 180 preservice and student teachers to read selected case studies involving classroom interventions. They were then invited to judge the acceptability of the intervention according to five factors: whether the intervention was generally acceptable; whether it posed undue risk to the child; whether it required excessive teacher time; whether it had negative effects on nontarget children; and whether it required too high levels of teacher skill for ready implementation. Although one should bear in mind that the conclusions generated only apply to the particular techniques presented, and that the study utilized a paper-and-pencil analogue format applied to student teachers rather than those already in the field, Witt *et al*'s. findings point clearly to the complex nature of the notion of acceptability. Teacher time, severity of the behavior problem, and type of intervention—not to mention the possibility of variables not included in their analysis—all seemed to be relevant.

Teachers were the exclusive subjects of the Witt *et al.* (1984) study. When parents and teachers differ in their patterns of acceptability, problems can arise. It was this possibility that motivated Norton, Austen, Allen, and Hilton (1983) to compare parents' and teachers' views about the acceptability of various home and classroom procedures for the reduction of inappropriate behavior. The investigators had 48 teachers and 48 parents evaluate the effectiveness and the acceptability of five procedures for reducing disruptive behavior in 5-year-old and in 10-year-old children. The teachers, by and large, evaluated all procedures as more effective and more acceptable than did the parents. The procedures rated as most effective and most acceptable by parents and teachers alike were reinforcement, isolation, and contractual agreement. Both groups rated all procedures as more effective and acceptable for 5-year-olds than for 10-year-olds.

Teachers are far from being a homogeneous population, and it is reasonable to assume that different types of teachers in different settings are likely to evidence a broad range of attitudes. The tolerance that teachers have for specific behaviors is going to affect both expectations and teacher–student interactions—a problem that attracted the attention of Safran, Safran, and Barcikowski (1985) in their comparative studies of regular and special educators. One should bear in mind that reported tolerance of various school situations on paper-and-pencil scales may not be the same as that observed in real life; however, Safran *et al.* were unable to determine any significant difference between these two groups of teachers with respect to any of the 11 behavioral clusters measured by their Teacher Tolerance Scale. Special educators and regular teachers may be more alike in their tolerance levels than has been assumed.

Acceptance and tolerance in both teachers and pupils have been shown to be influenced by such individual qualities as attractiveness, gender, socioeconomic status, and ethnic identification (e.g., Stevens, 1980). The acceptability of various procedures may also be related in part to the teacher's tolerance for these approaches, and this, in turn, may be related to the teacher's overall level of anxiety. Kahn (1981), for example, describes a model of occupational stress in which the organizational environment combines with the personal characteristics and interpersonal needs of the individual to bring about a variety of potentially adverse emotional, physiological, and behavioral coping responses. In evaluating this stress–anxiety literature, it should be noted that the too-facile identification of stress with anxiety may be unwarranted. While the terms "anxiety" and "stress" are often used interchangeably in the literature, anxiety is just one possible reaction to work-produced stress (Turk, Meeks, & Turk, 1982).

Most behavioral self-management approaches to stress and anxiety reduction for teachers focus on coping techniques for altering maladaptive psychological and physiological responses to potential stressors. Sharp and Forman (1985) compared two approaches to anxiety management: stress inoculation training and behavior management skills training. Teachers were randomly assigned either to one of these two groups or to a no-treatment control group. Consistent with Forman's (1982) previous report, stress inoculation training was found to be highly effective; however, certain significant differences were also noted. Forman (1982) found decreases in self-reported anxiety and motoric indicators of anxiety, but no change in verbal classroom behavior. Perhaps because of videotape modeling added to the instruction procedures, Sharp and Forman's (1985) study generated more positive findings. In addition, it was noted that behavioral skills training decreased self-reports of anxiety. It would seem that more effective change can be brought about when the training utilizes a variety of instructional procedures (see also Allen & Forman, 1984). But little is known about the use of these two procedures in combination, or the relative contributions of each.

Behavior modifiers continue to extol the virtues of self-management, perhaps because they still smart under the accusation of seeking to impose control from without. Whatever the reasons, self-management programs for young people attract much attention. As far as academic performance is concerned, these procedures seem to be as effective as adult-imposed contingencies. But naturalistic evaluations, especially with other than well-functioning children, are limited. The majority of studies have been conducted with elementary school children in laboratory settings with experimenters as program mediators (Kelley & Stokes, 1984). Regardless of context, it is important to prepare the students for effective self-management beforehand. Kelley and Stokes (1982) advocate contingency contracting to negotiate work standards and determine consequences. Contracting requires students to be motivated and trained for goal setting and actively involved in establishing reward contingencies, while adults still maintain a significant amount of control over performance. A single-subject reversal design by Kelley and Stokes (1984) demonstrates that student–teacher contracting could substantially increase productivity. In a subsequent study, students were trained to set their own goals and initiate their own controls. The findings were equally positive.

Brigham, Hopper, Hill, deArmas, and Newsom (1985) sought to develop a behaviorally oriented self-management program for middle-school students with adjustment problems. The program was conducted for 3 consecutive school years with 103 students. Multiple-baseline analyses indicated that the majority of students reduced their levels of disruptive behavior. Even more encouraging was the fact that follow-up data for periods as long as 2 years showed continued improvement. Even the failures generated important information. For example, students with increased detention time over the years were generally more disturbed. Noting that their program was operated on a strictly instructional fashion, with no contingencies outside the self-management class, Brigham *et al.* conclude that a totally instructional program is not probably sufficient for students characterized as predelinquent. What to do about this awaits further research.

Individual variability in responsiveness to self-reinforcement is a complex issue, and it is surprising that such obvious parameters as age, sex, and personality have been inadequately explored (Harris & Ferrari, 1983). Tiedemann and McMahon (1985) developed an analogue study to examine possible developmental differences in responsiveness to self-rewards and external rewards in boys and girls in third and sixth grades. Sixty children completed a brief arithmetic test under one of three conditions: self-reinforcement (scoring their own work and awarding themselves tokens), external reinforcement (the experimenter scored the work and awarded tokens), and control (the experimenter scored the work, but no token was awarded).

Grade was not differentially predictive of either immediate or generalized response to the reinforcement conditions. Boys showed superior performance to the controls in the self-reinforcement condition, and girls tended to be superior to the controls in both reinforcement conditions. Thus, while grade was not an important predictor of outcome, there were marked sex differences in response to degree of adult control of the token reinforcement system. When one is designing and testing self-reinforcement interventions, sex differences may be more important than age in the prediction of outcome.

Many self-management procedures are implicitly mentalistic. In sharp contrast, Maher's (1985) professional self-management program is rigorously behavioral. Professional self-management can be conceptualized along a variety of dimensions pertaining to work control. Whether the setting is the school or any other organization, similar problems arise with respect to the parameters of self-management and the manner in which individuals manipulate the environment to maximum benefit. Maher offers a program of self-control based upon systematic organization of the external and internal environments in strict accordance with the principles of applied behavior analysis. Unfortunately, much of the more clinically oriented self-management literature does not comply with this injunction.

While school phobia, or "school refusal" as it is now more usually called, has been the subject of considerable investigation, most studies consist of single-case interventions. Blagg and Yule's (1984) notable exception compared 30 school refusers receiving outpatient behavioral treatment with 16 hospitalized school refusers and 20 who received psychotherapy and home tuition. Their behavioral treatment was predicated upon Yule, Hershov, and Treseder's (1980) additive stress model. When faced with mounting worries at home and school, certain children become very anxious, and school refusal eventuates. Once a child is away from school, secondary factors arise that tend to maintain the problem. The behavioral treatment began with a detailed analysis of pertinent home, school, and within-child variables. Precipitating and maintaining factors were isolated and a range of appropriate behavioral principles used to deal with them. Following detailed clarification of the children's problems, the therapists engaged in realistic discussion of these and related matters with children, parents, and teachers. The teaching staff was fully prepared for the children's re-entry, and, once the decision was made to return the children to school, parents received help in dealing with their own worries. A 6-week follow-up was minimal.

Blagg and Yule's second condition, hospital inpatient treatment, involved children in a resident psychiatric unit attending a hospital and school program geared specifically toward the treatment of school refusal. Within this milieu, the emphasis was upon educational and occupational therapy, drug treatment, working with the parents, and discharge management. In the third condition, the children were allowed to remain out of school and to receive home tuition and psychotherapy. The rationale was that many of these children were too distressed to cope with an immediate return to school and that the home tuition would provide a needed breathing space for both the children and their families. Parents and children received fortnightly psychotherapy at a local child guidance clinic.

The behavioral treatment group showed superior outcome as compared with the other two groups. The home tuition group did particularly badly. On this basis, behavior therapy would seem to be the treatment of choice for school refusal. As Blagg and Yule note, behavior therapy is the least intrusive and the most cost-effective. But, as Kirschenbaum (1983) observes, no matter how successful the intervention, prevention is probably the most cost-effective strategy of all.

Evaluation is essential to behavioral intervention. Usually, this takes the form of a behavioral analysis of the relevant stimulus–response (S-R) contingencies, and this is all to the good. But in the words of Bob Dylan, "the times they are a-changin'," and the current trend in evaluation is toward systems and ecobehavioral approaches in addition to or as part of the more customary S-R procedures. For several decades, ecology has effectively linked persons and their environments. But ecobehavioral assessment has had to await an appropriate technology, and it is to this matter that Greenwood, Delquadri, Stanley, Terry, and Hall (1985) addressed themselves. Their main purpose was to develop a method for describing and assessing the quality and frequency of instructional arrangements within and across divergent classroom groups, in order to attempt an ecobehavioral explanation of differences in academic performance. Observational records spanning the entire school day were obtained for 40 fourth-grade students differing in socioeconomic status. Two otherwise equivalent samples of 20 fourth-grade students were randomly drawn from 14 classrooms in four different elementary schools. The children were 90% black and 60% male. Fourteen teachers, all females, participated in the project. Trained observers who were subjected to periodic reliability checks recorded carefully defined ecological events.

This pioneering project has major methodological limitations, such as the correlational rather than causal nature of the design. Nevertheless, it points the way for future research. As noted by Bronfenbrenner in 1979, a data base concerning the structure and distribution of ecological context variables within applied settings is notoriously lacking. To determine how these context variables relate to performance from moment to moment will necessitate the evolution of a technology of ecologically based behavioral assessment; in this respect alone, the Greenwood *et al.* study is of significance. Eventually, this methodology may help to pinpoint the more persisting problems of academic retardation in inner-city children. It may be such data that pave the way for the development of the next generation of intervention procedures within the school (Patterson, 1982).

Merrett and Wheldall (1984) have reviewed the literature pertaining to behavioral training for teachers. In 1981, Wheldall presented the Behavioural Approach to Teaching Package (BATPACK) to the Third Annual Conference of the Australian Behaviour Modification Association. This 10-year program for British teachers is one of the few methodologically sophisticated surveys in the literature, behavioral or otherwise. Unlike most projects, BATPACK specifies in advance, in precise terms, what is expected and what the course tutor will provide. Limitations are made explicit and deliberate to all concerned. The aim is not to provide training in behavior therapy; the only aim is to train teachers in the application of a selective series of key behavioral techniques, and the primary concern is with the improvement of classroom management skills rather than the remediation of individual problems (Wheldall & Merrett, 1985). But exemplary as it is, long-term effects still need to be documented (Murphy, 1985). A decade ago, Bergan and Tombari (1976) found that only 31% of seemingly successful behavioral projects were actually put into practice. It will be of interest to see how Wheldall and Merrett's strategies match up to this pessimistic conclusion.

If the behavioral training of teachers is to be implemented, the training of behavioral consultants for the schools must assume high priority. A variety of behavioral consultation models are now in effect. Competency-based training, as developed by Kratochwill and his associates, is one such approach. Details of this cost-efficient method of delivering psychological services have been outlined in a variety of publications, of which the most recent are articles by Kratochwill and Van Someren (1984, 1985). Kratochwill and Van Someren are careful to note current limitations and the methodological problems that await resolution, such as the lack of consultant standardization, the lack of specific training for consultants in how to overcome consumer resistance, and so on. In 1975, Quilitch observed that the technology of training might have already surpassed the technology of program implementation. In contemporary perspective, both the training of consultants *and* the technology of program implementation may be inadequate.

BEHAVIOR MODIFICATION AND THE EDUCATION OF THE ATYPICAL CHILD

Of three new books pertaining to the education of the atypical child, each, in its own way, makes a contribution that is worthy of note. The first, by Morris (1985), is probably of least significance for the professional. Geared toward students and practitioners planning to work with developmentally disabled children, this text presupposes no previous knowledge of behavior therapy or even of learning theory. Unlike its many competitors, it is well organized, clearly written, jargon-free, and behaviorally sound. If supplemented by formal instruction, it is likely to be the text that most instructors will use and recommend.

The second book, edited by Certo, Harring, and York (1984) for the Association for the Severely Handicapped, offers an unusually comprehensive overview of the ongoing dilemma that confronts all whose concern is the integration of mentally retarded and autistic students into the educational mainstream. Despite mandated public education for such children, segregated education is still the rule in much of the United States. It is hard to believe that Public Law 94-142, the Education For All Handicapped Children Act, has been with us since 1974. This volume goes a long way toward presenting the issues and available alternatives to professionals and public alike. Its impact might have been greater had the proposed interventions been substantiated by empirical validation. It is not as if strategies for program evaluation do not exist; they do (e.g., Maher & Bennett, 1984). To this extent, this volume is a little disappointing, despite its bold and extensive canvas.

The third volume, Evans and Meyer's (1985), *An Educative Approach to Behavior Problems*, aptly subtitled *A Practical Model for Interventions with Severely Handicapped Learners*, is unusual. Unlike most texts in behavior therapy these days, not to mention the past, this is more than a catalogue of techniques or case histories. Applied behavior analysis is used as the core of Evans and Meyer's treatment planning model. The role of the teacher is presented as that of active decision maker rather than passive administrator of a package program. Step by step, the reader is shown how to utilize the model to develop an appropriate intervention program for the severely handicapped learner (by which the authors mean primarily the autistic and/or mentally impaired child). The model is not limited to the classroom, and three major dimensions of behavioral intervention are categorized. Ecological intervention, the strategy of choice, involves modification of the environment by simple procedures such as seating rearrangement or removing tempting toys from imminent reach. Because ecological interventions are always necessary but rarely sufficient, curriculum components are added to treatment. Curriculum components teach specific skills that can eventually replace the problem behaviors. But even this combination is sometimes insufficient, and, distasteful as it may be, there may be a need to apply negative consequences. Evans and Meyers have written this text primarily for teachers of the severely handicapped; for the reasons stated, however, it serves as a model for all therapists seeking to bring a behavioral approach back to behavior therapy.

In view of a recent review by Wood and Lakin (1982) of research published prior to the 1974 implementation of Public Law 94-142, Skiba and Casey (1985) decided to confine their meta-analysis to research published since 1977. They chose *Psychological Abstracts* as their data base and confined their investigation to studies in which school-age subjects received some form of special program rather than merely behavioral programs within the regular classroom. Not altogether surprisingly, behavioral consultation proved to be the most effective treatment, with psychodynamic counseling and biofeedback training far less effective. This was apparently the only firm conclusion that could be drawn from the data. Regrettably but correctly, Skiba and Casey note serious methodological problems in much of the published research. Controls have tended to be inadequate; reporting of relevant variables such as subject and setting has been limited; and it is often difficult to determine what effects the treatment had on the behavior change under study. Finally, follow-up seems to have been given perfunctory attention or confined to 6 months or less in most of the studies under review.

Another recent article of significance is Scruggs, Mastropieri, and Richter's (1985) review of peer tutoring with behaviorally disordered students. In view of the individual needs of these students, peer tutoring could be a cost-effective strategy of benefit to tutors and the tutored alike. Scruggs *et al.* conclude that such tutoring could produce beneficial results in four major areas: social behavior, academic performance, enhanced interest in school and academic matters, and self-concept. In addition, tutoring has been pinpointed as a potentially valuable tool for facilitating mainstreaming. Unfortunately, the benefits of tutoring with respect to this type of student remain uncertain, at best.

Scruggs *et al.* culled 17 articles from the professional literature in which what was studied met their stringent definition of the term "peer tutoring." They came to the following conclusions. Peer tutoring can exert a positive effect on academic functioning of the tutored student, together with positive academic influences on the tutor. It can also enhance the social interactions of the tutor–tutored dyad, as well as the attitudes toward the content area being studied. In sharp contrast, the research data do not support prevailing anecdotal impressions of improved general functioning and enhanced social esteem. Many unknown factors await investigation. For example, does peer tutoring work better than other specially developed alternative instruction strategies? Is peer tutoring as reliable a method of improving social and behavioral functioning as other instructional alternatives? Scruggs, *et al.* end their discussion with a caveat originally propounded by Krouse, Gerber, and Kauffman (1981): "Although it has been demonstrated that academic and social gains are frequently obtained by the tutor, this in itself is not sufficient justification for the child to be a tutor. Instead it must be shown that, by being a tutor, specific needs are being met" (p. 293).

Bryant and Budd (1984) have examined research in training behaviorally handicapped preschool children to share. Numerous descriptive studies show that sharing occurs naturally in the play of normal preschool children and that it is likely to result in reciprocal positive social responses. Poor social relationships in childhood have been linked to social rejection by peers and to serious problems in later adjustment. If children with limited social repertoires, such as those suffering from some form of behavioral handicap, could be taught to share, this training might increase positive contacts with others and thereby might be instrumental in producing healthier long-term social outcomes.

In 1979, Barton and Ascione developed a comprehensive training package for teaching young children to share. This involved teacher instruction, modeling, and behavior rehearsal, gradually phased by teacher prompts and praise into free-play activities. Despite confirmation of the effectiveness of this approach, especially when the entire package is used and an adult is present in the setting in which generalization is assessed, Barton (1982), has identified some important research gaps. These include the dearth of information concerning both quantitative and qualitative aspects of sharing in individual children; the lack of sharing studies in actual classroom settings; an absence of cost–benefit analysis of treatment approaches; and inadequate attention to social validity of treatment effects. To shed light on these problems, Bryant and Budd (1984) worked with six children in a remedial classroom setting specifically designed for behaviorally handicapped youngsters. In a multiple-baseline design across three pairs of children, substantial increases in sharing were reported for five of the six children. Analyses of negative interaction were less clear but suggested that concomitant decreases did occur.

It was once believed that punishment could not work. But as Rosen, O'Leary, Joyce, Conway, and Pfiffner (1984), among other investigators, have noted, the data suggest otherwise. When special education teachers in Rosen *et al*'s. study stopped providing negative feedback to students who had been functioning successfully with a combination of positive and negative consequences, academic and social behavior deteriorated markedly. In their study, the positive reinforcements were relatively weak (they consisted of verbal praise, together with occasional special privileges such as a story or a supportive note home). Therefore, as Pfiffner, Rosen, and O'Leary (1985) have observed, it is premature to reject the notion of an entirely positively managed classroom being sufficient until more powerful incentive systems have been employed.

To address this issue, Pfiffner *et al.* (1985) compared strongly enhanced positive consequences to typical positive consequences with and without the addition of negative consequences. Their subjects were eight youngsters attending a special educational facility for children with behavior problems. Both on-task behavior and academic performance were examined. The authors found that an all-positive approach relying primarily on praise was not effective; however, when an individualized reward system was used, the children's rates of on-task behavior became high and stable. Similar effects were observed for academic productivity. It would seem that the classroom can be managed utilizing only positive consequences, provided that (and this is a very important proviso) the teacher is prepared to devote considerable attention to the task at hand, particularly in maintaining high rates of praise and carefully selecting specific rewards in terms of the children's preferences. Whether this strategy is going to be feasible in the special educational classroom for the behaviorally disordered remains to be seen.

Many studies have investigated the effects of goal-setting procedures on classroom behavior and performance. For example, Bandura and Schunk (1981) compared short-term goals to long-term goals and found that short-term goals significantly enhanced the learning of children with academic defects, whereas long-term goals had no such effect. But what has not been considered is the private as contrasted with public nature of the goal-setting processes. Several studies cited by Lyman (1984) attest to the effectiveness of public feedback over private feedback in the improvement of performance. Public posting of previous accomplishments can enhance the levels of both academic and nonacademic performance.

Lyman (1984) examined the effects of participatory goal setting on the classroom behavior of emotionally disturbed, academically deficient children, and the effects of public posting of these goals as contrasted with a more private strategy. Six children were sequentially exposed to private and public goal-setting conditions within a multiple-baseline-across-subjects design. On-task behavior increased significantly during public goal setting, whereas the improvements were considerably less evident during the private goal-setting condition. Significant increases in on-task behavior were obtained without the use of tangible reinforcers, suggesting that public posting of goals could be a powerful and economic contingency management procedure for increasing this type of behavior. As noted, the fact that this research focused exclusively on on-task behavior rather than academic achievement is a limitation. Also unknown are the factors that influence the generalizability and maintenance of these effects.

The third study of goal-setting procedures is not a study at all. It is a report of an on-campus program that Vetter-Zemitzsch *et al.* (1984) refer to as a "systematic/behavioral approach" to behavior disorders in the high school. Their program, which is still ongoing, is beginning to demonstrate success in helping disturbed students develop the necessary behavioral, social, emotional, and academic skills necessary for satisfactory readjustment to mainstream education and eventually to society at large. The authors go to great pains to describe their intervention strategies, but meaningful outcome evaluation is virtually nonexistent. For this reason, their study is of significance primarily as a pointer to further evaluation.

Failure to generalize learned behaviors remains a problem in working with retarded children, and research to date offers no effective solution. Noting the failure of behavior and cognitive therapists alike to provide an adequate conceptual framework to explain why this is so, Scruggs and Mastropieri (1984) offer an explanatory model of their own based upon individual differences in the capacity for analogical reasoning. Is generalization the goal in itself, they ask, or merely one possible means to the larger goal of maximal control over the environment? It may be that long-term maintenance designed simply to facilitate generalization is not the optimal use of the child's time. It could be, they further speculate, that many tasks, such as work skills and certain social skills, need not generalize ubiquitously for benefit to occur. Loper and Hallahan (1982) likewise criticize researchers who "assume the procedures have not passed the ultimate test of worth unless they have resulted in generalization effects" (p. 66). Recent work suggests that in many instances, exceptional children can be retaught the target behavior in a new setting by means of simple instructional hierarchies alone. The time gained may then allow them to learn other necessary skills (Mastropieri & Scruggs, 1984).

One emerging consensus is that educational programs for severely handicapped children should be directly applicable in their everyday nonclassroom environments. All too often, severely handicapped students are involved in classroom activities that do not seem to be functional outside of that particular environment. Reid *et al.* (1985) have suggested that this is due in part to reliance on traditional classroom curricula designed for less seriously disturbed students. Furthermore, there is less formal educational time available for these unfortunate young people. Bearing these limitations in mind, Reid *et al.* designed a program for the increasing classroom involvement of severely handicapped students in functional educational tasks. A subsidiary goal was the generation of information about the criteria used to determine functional versus nonfunctional educational tasks.

Behaviors considered on-task were classified as either functional or nonfunctional. The criteria for functional tasks rested upon two components: functional materials and functional activities. Functional materials were those encountered in the nonclassroom living situation or used by equivalent nonhandicapped persons in the nonclassroom setting. Functional activities had to meet the criteria for at least one of the following five skill domains: (1) likely to occur among an equivalent nonhandicapped population during leisure time; (2) part of a vocational class in which, once mastered, the skill would become one for which a student could be paid; (3) an interpersonal interaction that the student would perform, once mastered, at least weekly outside of the classroom; (4) part of an activity that, once mastered, would be likely to occur among an equivalent nonhandicapped population within a community setting; or (5) purposively performed by someone for the student outside of the classroom if the student did not perform the task for himself or herself. The program itself consisted of brief in-service training followed by supervisory prompts and feedback. In all three classrooms studied, the program was accompanied by large increases in functional tasks. In addition, generalized increases occurred during nontargeted times in the classroom, and these changes were maintained over a 45-week period. In two subsequent experiments, experienced clinicians consistently rated tasks categorized as functional as more useful for severely handicapped persons than nonfunctional tasks.

Most classroom teachers within the public school system have had little or no appropriate experience in working with the severely handicapped. It has therefore been suggested on more than one occasion that regular classroom teachers receive in-service training prior to any attempt at integration. S. Stainback and Stainback (1982) showed that the attitudes of elementary education students about the integration of severely handicapped students into regular schools can easily be influenced. Whether these results would hold true for experienced, practicing teachers is another matter (Stainback, Stainback, Strathe, & Dedrick, 1983). Also open to speculation is whether and how such attitude changes modify behavior and whether these changes are maintained over time. Stainback *et al.* bring these issues to our attention but accomplish little by way of resolution.

Mainstreaming, in itself, is likely to improve neither the social skills of these mentally handicapped youngsters nor their levels of integration with other children. Somehow, adult caregivers must learn to develop good social interactions in these children. To this end, an exploratory social competence intervention program at Vanderbilt University concentrated on four major goals: the identification of the social behaviors most likely to set the occasion for positive social encounters; an evaluation of the effectiveness of critical social initiations used by handicapped children; the development of empirically valid teaching procedures; and the incorporation of these studies into teacher training materials (Day, Fox, Shores, Lindeman, & Stowitschek, 1982).

Remediation projects for learning-disabled children proceed along two lines—teacher- and self-administered—and questions are now arising with respect to their relative efficacies. While the most common response is that there is no reliable difference, Bowers, Clement, Fantuzzo, and Sorensen (1985) predicted that self-administered reinforcers would be more effective. The subjects of their study were six 8- to 11-year-old-boys with attention deficits who were enrolled in their school's special program for such children. Both teacher- and self-administered reinforcers were found to strengthen targeted academic behaviors. Unfortunately, serious methodological deficits, too numerous to list here, limit the value of their investigation.

Assessment is important for all children, but especially so for the atypical child. Kazdin, Esveldt-Dawson, and Loar's (1983) study of the correspondence between teacher ratings and direct observation of classroom behavior in psychiatrically hospitalized children provides an excellent model of behavioral methodology in this area. Teachers, extraclass raters, and observers completed standard rating scales and/or measures of overt classroom behaviors of 22 inpatient children. Their major findings were as follows: Teacher and rater checklist evaluations and estimates of overt behavior correlated with each other and with direct observations of overt classroom behavior only moderately well at best; rater evaluations tended to correspond more closely to direct observational data than did teacher evaluations. Both teachers and raters evaluated the children as engaging in more on-task and less disruptive behavior than was evident from direct observation of ongoing behavior. The teachers tended to rate the classroom behavior as more deviant than did checklist raters but did not differ from these raters with respect to estimates of overt behavior. Teachers, raters, and observers were all able to distinguish clearly between hyperactive and nonhyperactive children. However, on the checklist ratings, the hyperactive and nonhyperactive children were delineated much more sharply by teachers than by raters. In this respect, it might be noted that the classroom behavior of hyperactive children is generally rated as more deviant than the behavior of clinically referred children with other diagnoses (Abikoff, Gittelman, & Klein, 1980).

As Kazdin *et al.* suggest, their findings have potential implications for clinical research. Teacher-completed measures could be useful in delineating diagnostic groups, especially within the area of hyperactivity. Teachers might perform the initial selection and screening of subjects. On the other hand, direct observations of overt behavior might be more useful in tracking specific behaviors over time. It will be recalled that teacher estimates of overt behavior showed little correlation with direct observation.

Behavior-disordered children are thought to differ from either learning-disabled or educable mentally retarded children in terms of social adjustment. Although these differences may not lead to radically different teaching approaches, they are of relevance to the selection of initial training goals. Age is another neglected factor that might influence the behavior of these children. Sindelar, King, Cartland, Wilson, and Meisel (1985) investigated the differences in social behavior of behavior-disordered and learning-disordered children as a function of both student placement and age. The data were derived from ratings of classroom behavior by special education teachers. As one might expect, the behavior-disordered children were more easily recognized by their teachers than were those suffering from a learning disorder. Less predictable was the conclusion that the distinction between learning- and behavior-disordered children was quantitative rather than qualitative. That is to say, some learning-disordered and some behavior-disordered students exhibited each of the behavior patterns; the distinction lay in the relative proportions.

In most classrooms, the teacher can expect to have at least one behaviorally agressive student, and it is this type of behavior that is most likely to be labeled "deviant" and to result in referral for special educational services (Murray & Whittenberger, 1983). The purpose of a recent study by Ruhl and Hughes (1985) was to assess the nature and extent of aggression in special educational settings for behaviorally disordered children, as well as the common methods of coping with these behaviors within the classroom. A wide range of aggressive behaviors was encountered. While a diversity of intervention strategies was reported, the three most common were referral to school-based counseling, alternative school placement, and in-school suspension. Of interest, but not surprising, were the frequent reports by participants of a lack of administrative involvement with agressive students. As Ruhl and Hughes suggest, it would seem that it is the classroom teacher who is going to bear the major responsibility for dealing with these aggressive students.

Nonhandicapped children and their regular class teachers differ in their perception of the social skills needs of mainstreamed learning handicapped children (Cartledge, Frew, & Zaharias, 1985). Teachers have been shown to be less accepting of emotionally disturbed students (e.g., Vacc, 1968), and student teachers tend to retain initial negative impressions of aggressive children despite well-documented behavioral improvement (Lewin, Nelson, & Tollefson, 1983). Such perceptions can affect placement decisions and contribute to fears of a behavioral contrast effect. The identification of specific factors related to negative perceptions has been the subject of recent research (e.g., Safran *et al.* 1985).

Handicapped children tend to be rejected by other children much more often than their nonhandicapped peers (e.g., W. Stainback & Stainback, 1982). But minimal attention has been directed toward the determination of which problem behaviors are most disturbing to the children concerned. The Children's Tolerance Scale was developed by Safran and Safran (1985) to measure common classroom behaviors as observed by the elementary school child. In a pilot survey, 25 third-graders were told that the researchers were interested in their feelings and opinions about handicapping behaviors other than those displayed in class. The concept of "disturbedness" was discussed, and response choices were explained and practiced. Each item on the 29-item scale was read aloud and the children asked to cross out the best choice. The participants in the actual study were 506 rural and semirural third- through sixth-graders (99% white and primarily lower- to middle-class).

Older children were generally the most tolerant. The more outer-directed behaviors (negative aggression and poor peer cooperation) were rated as the most disturbing. When the handicapping condition is sensory or physical, increasing positive peer attitudes would seem to be essential. However, in dealing with disruptions, it would seem from this study that emphasis on normalizing behavior rather than increasing peer acceptance might better facilitate integration. Furthermore, the finding of significant grade-level differences has suggested to Safran and Safran that the varying chronology of peer tolerance norms should be taken into consideration *prior* to mainstreaming a behaviorally disordered student. More rigorous modification of such a child's behavior would be required to optimize peer acceptance in the lower grades.

CONCLUSIONS

Child behavior therapy has shown no recent breakthrough, dramatic or otherwise. In a way, this is a healthy sign, since—as documented in this chapter—steady, cautiously consolidated advances on a variety of fronts are what usually characterize an emerging science. The increasing acceptance of child behavior therapy by mainstream clinical psychology and psychiatry and by the general public is another favorable sign. Behavioral principles and strategies are now acknowledged, either directly or implicitly, within virtually every facet of education, parent training, and administration.

It is also encouraging to see child behavior therapists take accountability and social validation out of the domain of opinion and wish-fulfillment into the arena of science. For example, Singh and Katz (1985) compared the acceptability of three very different child behavior therapy techniques before and after systematic instruction in the use of these respective procedures. Similar strategies have been applied to an understanding of parental participation in the decision-making process involved in the education of their children (e.g., Barnett, Zins, & Wise, 1984).

Equally encouraging are the changing perceptions with respect to the roles of the behavioral school psychologist. The behavior therapist is viewed increasingly as a consultant and the school as a system. There are, of course, still those who, from my perspective, think in antiquated terms: for example, Clarizio's (1985) call for the traditional treatment of depression in school children (even if couched in cognitive phraseology); Frith's (1985) fiat that "behavior management is an art, not a science"; Maurer's (1983) heated discussion of what she believes is an ongoing shock rod controversy, an act of violence against the next generation.[1] (Much more healthy is Salend, Esquivel, & Pine's [1984] pursuit of data rather than causes. If there has to be ventilation in such a sensitive area as the use of aversion techniques within the schools, then it is better that it be through formal debate: see Patterson & Zakel, 1985.)

None of this should be construed as an invitation to complacency. There is much that remains to be done. For example, studies of the gifted child are extremely rare. With few exceptions, "atypical" or "exceptional" is assumed to be synonymous with "pathological." Belcastro's (1985) exhaustive literature search uncovered only eight dated studies in which behavior modification was used with gifted students. Two of these were in laboratory settings, five in counseling or testing centers, and only one within the classroom itself. In 1971, Hamblin,

1. Maurer is Executive Director of End Violence Against the Next Generation. She was a member of the first American Psychological Association's Task Force on Children's Rights and chairperson of several APA committees pertaining to advocacy for children. I make these points to illustrate the nature of the diminished but still present resistance to behavior therapy within the psychological community.

Hathaway, and Wodarski evaluated the effects of reinforcement procedures with gifted fourth-grade students. Little has happened in this area since then. Behavior therapists continue to neglect this important segment of our society.

If, then, child behavior therapy is making slow but steady progress, there is no occasion to rest easy. The drift toward methodological refinements and technology at the expense of science, understanding, and what Wilson (1978) terms "the importance of being theoretical" is still predominant in the behavior therapy literature, be it with children or adults. It is for such reasons that I view Evans and Meyer's (1985) focus upon the *principles* of behavior therapy in their discussion of behavior therapy in education as one of the more positive events in the recent annals of child behavior therapy. It is on this encouraging note that I conclude this survey of recent developments in the area of behavior therapy with children and adolescents.

CHAPTER

8

CLINICAL ISSUES AND STRATEGIES IN THE PRACTICE OF BEHAVIOR THERAPY

G. TERENCE WILSON

To maintain continuity with previous volumes in this series, this chapter addresses such frequently covered topics as resistance (or client noncompliance), the therapist–patient relationship in behavior therapy, clinical inference, the impact of research on clinical practice, and the integration of psychoanalytic approaches with behavior therapy. In addition, I comment on the implications of such disparate approaches as hermeneutics on the one hand, and meta-analysis on the other, for the evaluation of treatment outcome.

RESISTANCE

Resistance or noncompliance has been a topic that has been repeatedly emphasized in previous volumes in this series. The emphasis has been based on the importance of this phenomenon in all therapies or interventions aimed at behavior change, including behavior therapy. Nevertheless, despite the conceptual and practical significance of resistance or noncompliance, the topic has received relatively little systematic attention in the behavior therapy literature (see Wilson, 1984a). An exception has been the more recent trend within behavioral medicine toward research on the nature of noncompliance, with strategies designed to facilitate health-promoting behavior or reduce health-damaging behavior. Indeed, the start of a new publication, the *Journal of Compliance in Health Care*, has recently been announced. Svarstad (1986) has presented a theoretical model and outlined specific strategies for facilitating compliance with prescribed medical regimens. Both the model and the suggested interventions overlap considerably with the analyses and strategies put forward within the behavior therapy literature on compliance, as summarized in previous volumes in this series. Thus Svarstad (1986) emphasizes the importance of insuring that the patient understands and can recall prescribed medical regimens; she draws heavily on Ley's (1977) recommendations for improving comprehension and recall (e.g., be explicit, explain the purpose, provide written reinforcement of prescriptions, chunk or categorize information, and repeat information) (see Volume 7, pp. 367–375, of this series). As for enhancing motivation, she notes the importance of reinforcement, positive expectations, and increasing the patient's participation in the process. It is a mark of the fragmentation of the field that, coming from a more sociological background, Svarstad (1986) seems unaware of the overlap between her perspective and the theory and research within a cognitive–behavioral framework. The latter, particularly with respect to the role of reinforcement, self-monitoring, and the setting of appropriate goals, provides a more complete and sophisticated account (O'Leary & Wilson, 1987).

Empirical Research

The empirical analysis of resistance or noncompliance in behavior therapy for other problems has been relatively neglected. A welcome exception has been the work of Patterson and his associates at the Oregon Social Learning Center. In the first study, Chamberlain, Patterson, Reid, Kavanagh, and Forgatch (1984) coded client resistance during therapeutic interviews at what they called a "molecular level" by using a direct observational system. The clients were families who were experiencing problems in managing their children. Resistance was defined as "those client statements that block or impede the therapist's efforts towards change" (p. 146). Clients' statements in videotapes of therapy sessions were coded either as "cooperative" or "resistant." Clients' responses "that followed the direction set by the therapist's immediately previous verbalization were coded as cooperative. Clients' responses that diverted or impeded the direction set by the therapist were coded as resistant (p. 147). The "resistant" category was actually a pooled category of five more specific categories: "interrupt/talkover," "negative attitude," "challenge/confront," "own agenda," and "not tracking" (p. 148). The categories were "rationally derived based on group discussions and the clinical experience of the authors" (p. 147).

Chamberlain *et al.* (1984) obtained acceptable reliability and assessed the validity of their measure in several ways. Construct validity was demonstrated by the finding that significantly more resistant families dropped out of treatment than those who were coded as showing less resistance. In line with this finding, families that were self-referred were less resistant than families that were referred by the court. Predictive validity is suggested by the finding that therapists' ratings of successful outcome were positively correlated with reduction in clients' resistance over treatment.

As the authors themselves have noted, resistance can be defined in many ways. The typical connotation of "resistance" in the psychotherapeutic literature is negative; it describes an obstacle to successful treatment, which must be overcome by the therapist's skill or (as is clearly the case in behavior therapy) by the use of specific strategies. Chamberlain *et al.* (1984) have taken a more neutral stance, qualifying their measure of client "resistance" in the following manner:

> It should be noted that the authors have no preconceived notion that client resistance, as measured by the CRC, is necessarily inappropriate or counterproductive behavior on the part of the client. In fact, occurrences of resistance may represent appropriate attempts to slow down or modify the course of therapy. The goal of this study was simply to obtain a measure of occurrences of client resistance that could be reliably coded. (p. 147).

Nevertheless, the choice of criteria whereby construct validity was assessed, as well as the actual findings (e.g., treatment successes were less resistant), would seem to confirm the widely held view of resistance as a negative property.

In the Chamberlain *et al.* study, the focus was on verbal statements during sessions. Most of the attention that noncompliance has received in the behavior therapy and behavioral medicine literature to date has centered on actual client behavior—namely, complying with specific homework assignments (e.g., self-monitoring of target behavior and its context, engaging in *in vivo* exposure tasks, practicing relaxation training, counting calories, etc.). Patterson (1984, cited in Patterson & Forgatch, 1985), calls for the analysis of noncompliance both during treatment sessions and in the completion of homework assignments between sessions; he calls these the micro and macro levels of noncompliance, respectively. Patterson's model also requires that these two levels of noncompliance covary. An initial study of this covariation had observers rate videotapes of treatment sessions and correlate this measure with ratings of compliance with homework assignments between sessions. The correlation was an encouraging .64. Patterson argues that, together, micro-level and macro-level measures of noncompliance will provide a useful predictor of treatment outcome.

Two subsequent studies used this measure of client noncompliance to analyze the role of therapist behavior in determining noncompliance (Patterson & Forgatch, 1985). In the Chamberlain *et al.* (1984) study, parents' noncompliance rates were highest during mid treatment. Patterson and Forgatch then studied whether this pattern reflected therapists' attempts to change clients' behavior. To complement the measure of client resistance described above, a therapist behavior code was developed, consisting of seven mutually exclusive categories: "support, teach, question, confront, reframe, talk, and facilitate" (p. 847).

In the first of the two studies, the therapist behaviors "teach" and "confront" were shown to be associated with immediate increases in noncompliance, whereas the behaviors of "support" and "facilitate" were associated with significant decreases in noncompliance. In the second study, Patterson and Forgatch used a single-case experimental design (ABAB) to establish directly that therapist behavior caused noncompliance. During the B phase, therapists in each of seven therapist–parent dyads increased their use of "teach" and "confront" strategies. During the A phase, they avoided these strategies. The results were consistent with those from the first study, indicating that the therapists' behaviors did produce predictable changes in clients' noncompliance.

Two major implications stem from these studies. First, as Patterson and Forgatch (1985) observe, even skilled behavior therapists will encounter resistance: "[I]t seems that social learning therapists require a dual set of technologies. One set describes parent training skills; the other describes means for coping effectively with client noncompliance" (p. 850). Simply providing support and facilitating conditions does not result in effective therapy, and behavior therapy is demonstrably more successful than alternative methods in producing improvement in the very cases Patterson and Forgatch describe. It follows from this that the resistance provoked by active intervention does not preclude successful therapy. We need more analysis on how therapists overcome this resistance. Second, Patterson and his colleagues have developed an innovative methodology for studying a much-discussed but empirically neglected area of behavior change. The link between these in-session analyses of verbal behavior with other behavioral indices of compliance requires further study. And the adaptation of this sort of methodology to the examination of resistance in other patient samples with different problems would seem to be a useful focus of future research.

Noncompliance with Homework Assignments

One of the hallmarks of behavior therapy as a form of directive treatment is the use of specific homework activities between sessions. Regardless of problem, clients are typically asked to engage in new or different activities (cognitive and behavioral) between therapy sessions, and there is good reason to believe that treatment success often hinges on the degree to which these assignments are faithfully completed. Not surprisingly, therefore, the focus on homework assignments has been central to analyses of resistance in behavior therapy (see Wilson, 1984a, pp. 328–337). Goisman (1985) has recently focused on the assignment of homework activities in behavioral treatment as a means of exploring what he views as the commonalities between behavior therapy and psychodynamic therapy. His main thesis that the best way to compare the two forms of therapy is to "examine interventions dictated by one system according to their implications for another" (p. 675). Goisman argues for the value of examining the "psychodynamic meaning" to the client of therapeutic assignments in behavior therapy. He then proceeds to examine noncompliance with several standard behavioral techniques, offering illustrative clinical vignettes and suggesting psychodynamic views of such noncompliance.

Goisman's paper is a nonpartisan attempt to improve the use of behavioral methods. His clinical examples are informative, and he addresses some important issues. Nevertheless, I am struck by two considerations. First, in emphasizing the "meaning" of interventions for the client, Goisman is preaching to the converted. Contemporary cognitive-behavior therapy, as I have emphasized in Volumes 9 and 10 in this series (Wilson, 1984a, 1985a), would seem to accommodate this concern. Second, while I would concur with Goisman about the clinical importance of taking the meaning of therapy and particular interventions into account, this does not commit one to a psychodynamic view of such meaning. Meaning can be viewed from multiple perspectives, including those advanced by cognitive-behavior therapists (e.g., Beck, 1986; Meichenbaum & Gilmore, 1982).

Consider, for example, Goisman's discussion of relaxation training. He points out several factors that might impede relaxation:

> [Patients with] a strong work ethic or severe obsessional traits may feel anxious, guilty, or self-conscious about practicing relaxation or relaxing in the presence of the therapist. . . . Obsessionality may also produce a desire to achieve perfect relaxation, so that the patient more observes the process than participates in it; this is called "spectatoring" by Masters and Johnson with reference to sexual functioning. . . . [In addition,] there may be eroticization of or magical dependence on the sound of the therapist's voice instructing the patient to relax, factors that may indicate the use of professionally prepared relaxation tapes with an anonymous voice instead of personalized instruction by the therapist. (p. 676).

There is little in the foregoing that most behavior therapists would not essentially concede. Nor do these clinical observations tell us what to do in combating the noncompliance. What is missing is the recognition that this matter has been taken up in the behavior therapy literature. And the way in which it has been studied exemplifies the difference between the two approaches.

Heide and Borkovec (1983) have discussed the anecdotal reports in the literature of negative effects of relaxation training. Referring to the phenomenon as "relaxation-induced anxiety" (RIA), they studied its occurrence in 14 individuals with chronic anxiety. Five of these individuals responded to a single session of relaxation training (progressive relaxation or meditation) with clinical anxiety; roughly 31% reported increased tension during progressive relaxation, and 54% reported the comparable reaction during meditation. These laboratory-based findings have led Heide and Borkovec (1984) to examine possible mechanisms that could account for RIA, and to try to define effective strategies for overcoming this problematic response. They have proposed five distinguishable but not necessarily mutually exclusive mechanisms:

> (a) Clients may become frightened of sensations, physiological–behavioral reactions and cognitive–affective events that are released automatically through relaxation. (b) Clients may fear losing control or may attempt to achieve relaxation through active, effortful strategies. (c) Clients may fear the experience of their anxiety, to which their attention is drawn during relaxation. (d) Clients may fear attending to their internal experience in general as a result of dissatisfaction with self. (e) Clients may engage in worrisome cognitive activity about matters unrelated to relaxation. (p. 2)

In their analysis of each of the five possible mechanisms of RIA, Heide and Borkovec draw on a variety of sources, ranging from well-researched formulations to psychodynamic speculation. An example of the former is Denny's (1976) view that interoceptive stimuli produced by incipient relaxation may become conditioned to fear under certain circumstances. The latter is illustrated by the view that relaxation may lead to the fear of loss of ego control (Martin, 1951). Another possibility Heide and Borkovec (1984) raise is that relaxation helps to focus attention on the self, and to the extent that there are aspects of the self one does not like, this is aversive and elicits anxiety (Sackheim & Gur, 1978). The greater an individual's cognitive discrepancy between self-image and ideal self, the greater the anxiety is predicted to be. This hypothesis of Sackheim and Gur's is similar to Martin's notion of fear of intrapsychic conflicts. The advantages of Sackheim and Gur's hypothesis are, first, that it does not assume that this fear is rooted in the unconscious, and second, that it is testable.

Further empirical analysis along the lines of the researchable possibilities summarized by Heide and Borkovec promises to lead to a better understanding of RIA and the development of effective methods for overcoming it. The limitations of the psychodynamic speculation are that it is just that—speculation—and that the usual interpretations about the fear of losing control or the fear of self-focus are at best descriptions of the phenomena that do little to change cognition or behavior. Even at this preliminary stage, clinical experience with behavior therapy enables Heide and Borkovec (1984) to offer some practical suggestions about coping with RIA.

The first suggestion they make is that the therapist switch from the relaxation method producing RIA to another method. Heide and Borkovec (1983) showed that it was rare for an individual to show RIA to more than one technique. This is an important finding. It directs attention to the development of effective methods, and away from passive preoccupation with interpretations about the nature of the patient receiving the treatment. A second suggestion calls for repeated exposure to relaxation cues. Here the RIA reaction is conceptualized as other forms of anxiety, which have been shown to be modifiable by exposure treatment. Heide and Borkovec do recommend that this exposure be graduated.

Finally, Goisman (1985), carefully avoiding the discredited notion of symptom substitution, notes that successful behavior change in therapy may not always have totally benign effects for the patient. Among the possible reactions, he mentions "overgratitude toward the therapist or, conversely, resentment at not having accomplished the task by oneself . . . . fear of the 'adult' responsibilities of being non-neurotic, mourning the loss of dependency gratification in the symptom, and so on" (p. 678). The likelihood that a particular therapeutic intervention will have both positive and negative effects has been discussed elsewhere (e.g., Kazdin & Wilson, 1978). As for Goisman's examples, it cannot be said that they are not familiar to the behavior therapist, although it must be emphasized that in most problems they are the exception rather than the rule. And as I have pointed out before (Wilson, 1982c), psychodynamic theory does not provide us with an effective means of coping with such untoward reactions. According to Goisman, "Careful diagnostic assessment of the patient in terms of the symptom's meaning before treatment may help to predict the consequences, positive or adverse, of its loss after treatment" (p. 678). The absence of any empirical evidence for this assertion is telling.

THE THERAPIST–PATIENT RELATIONSHIP

Throughout this series, I have emphasized that, negative stereotypes to the contrary notwithstanding, the therapist–patient relationship is important in behavior therapy. In Volume 10, Arnkoff's (1983) analysis of the therapeutic relationship in the more cognitive forms of behavior therapy was discussed. Two recent studies have further examined the therapist's role in the outcome of Beck's cognitive therapy.

Persons and Burns (1985) assessed both technical and interpersonal factors in the process of cognitive therapy with depressed and anxious patients. Specifically, patients' automatic thoughts and moods were assessed at the beginning and end of each session by the therapist. In addition, patients rated their interpersonal relationship with the therapist at the end of each session. Statistical analyses revealed that both changes in patients' automatic thoughts and their ratings of the therapeutic relationship were associated, independently and additively, with improvements in mood. Persons and Burns conclude that these findings support the assumption of cognitive–behavioral therapy that a good therapeutic relationship is necessary but not sufficient for improvement:

> An excessively positive or negative relationship with the therapist could result in part from distorted cognitions about the therapist. These can be explored and modified as part of the treatment process. Failure to address these reactions could significantly impair therapeutic progress. The current findings suggest that training therapists to handle interpersonal issues skillfully is as important in cognitive therapy as in any other form of psychological or medical treatment. An excessive enthusiasm for the rational and technical aspects of cognitive therapy could have detrimental effects on treatment outcome. (p. 548)

Methodological limitations of the study make interpretation difficult, however. As the authors themselves observe, the causal chain cannot be determined from these data. It may have been that cognitive changes improved mood, which then led to more positive ratings of the therapist. This would make the measure of the therapeutic relationship a consequence or correlate rather than the cause of improvement in mood. Also, it becomes essential to relate these within-session changes in mood to between-session measures and independent measures of therapeutic outcome.

Luborsky, McLellan, Woody, O'Brien, and Auerbach (1985) have reported a better-controlled study of the therapist's contribution to treatment outcome. Drug-addicted patients were randomly assigned to one of three treatment conditions: supportive-expressive psychotherapy with drug counseling; cognitive–behavioral therapy with drug counseling; and drug counseling alone. The cognitive–behavioral therapy was based on Beck's (1976) approach. Nine therapists were studied, three in each of the different treatment conditions. All therapists "were trained and regularly supervised using manuals that explicitly defined and described the specific techniques employed in the performance of each therapy. These manuals provided specific criteria that could be used by independent raters to derive reliable, valid, and discriminable evaluations of the content of the three therapies" (p. 603). All sessions were tape-recorded for later analysis. The major measure of therapeutic outcome was a clinical and research interview, the Addiction Severity Index (ASI), completed at the beginning of treatment and after 7 months. This index examines several areas of functioning: medical employment/support, drug abuse, alcohol abuse, legal, family/social, and psychiatric.

The different therapists achieved varying results, with the supportive–expressive and cognitive–behavioral therapies showing essentially comparable results (Woody *et al.*, 1983). Luborsky *et al.* (1985) suggest that this finding may explain what they allege is the absence of evidence of differences in outcome among different forms of therapy.[1] They argue that the amount of variability within each therapy,

> based on therapist performance differences, would make it difficult to show a significant between-therapies effect. This suggests that the effectiveness of a given therapy can vary considerably depending on the group of therapists providing the treatment. This in turn suggests that the therapist is not simply the transmitter of a standard therapeutic agent. Rather, the therapist is an important, independent agent of change

1. Dissent from this view, particularly within the behavior therapy literature, is of course often marked (e.g., Kazdin & Wilson, 1978; Rachman & Wilson, 1980).

> with the ability to magnify or reduce the effects of a therapy. This, of course, may be obvious to clinicians who are in the position of making referrals to colleagues; however, there has been little quantitative evidence to support this clinical impression. (p. 609).

Luborsky *et al.* (1985) have also tried to examine the determinants of this variability in outcome. An obvious explanatory contender would be patient characteristics, but after analysis of a range of different measures related to this factor, Luborsky *et al.* dismiss it. As for therapist qualities, independent ratings of the factors "interest in helping patients" and "therapist skill" were related to outcome, albeit not at a statistically significant level. A measure of the therapist–patient relationship taken early in treatment did, however, significantly predict outcome. And this leads the authors to conclude that "the therapist's ability to form an alliance is possibly the most crucial determinant of his effectiveness" (p. 610). An intriguing finding was that a measure of treatment "purity," or exclusive adherence to a single theoretical/therapeutic orientation, was associated with superior outcomes. Luborsky *et al.* observe that this "purity" measure "provides information on the relative benefits associated with therapy based on a single orientation [versus] eclectic therapy, i.e., therapy that draws on techniques from more than one approach" (p. 610). They hasten to add, however, that this finding was correlational only, and more than one interpretation of the data is possible: "The inference could be that the more pure the technique—that is, the less it is eclectic—the more beneficial is the therapy and therefore the better the outcome. Another inference could be that when a treatment is proceeding toward a more positive outcome, the therapist is freer to engage in purer techniques" (p. 610). Although this latter caution is warranted, the finding raises questions about the usually uncritically accepted value of eclectic approaches.

Within behavior therapy, Lazarus (1971, 1981), among others, has long emphasized the importance of flexibility not only in selecting different treatment techniques, but also in the type of therapeutic relationship that is fostered. Linehan (in press-c) has recently reasserted this point:

> As with other factors in the therapeutic endeavor, however, it is overly simplistic to think that one can arrive at a consensus about the importance of client-therapist relationship factors with all clients, for all problems, for all phases of the treatment. There are many types of therapeutic relationships and multiple client and therapist relationship variables which can influence outcomes across diverse client populations and problem areas.

In behavior therapy, the therapist–client relationship often serves, indirectly, as the context for therapeutic change, but it may also be used directly as a means of facilitating behavior change. This latter function, and the challenge in treating seriously disturbed patients, is exemplified in the case of borderline personality disorder.

Borderline personality disorder, much in vogue these days in the United States if not in the United Kingdom, has among its defining characteristics, according to DSM-III, severe interpersonal problems and affective instability. Patients with this disorder are conflicted, hostile, demanding, manipulative, and labile in their relationships, including the therapeutic relationship. Linehan (in press-a, in press-b), based on her extensive experience in treating this type of patient, not surprisingly notes that patients are frequently referred to her by therapists who "have either given up on their client or passed the limits of their ability to give the enormous amount of time and attention required by these clients." Predictably, most clinicians contend that the therapeutic relationship is critical to the effective treatment of these patients, and Linehan's innovative behavioral treatment is no exception to this belief.

Linehan (in press-a, in press-b) calls her approach dialectical behavior therapy;[2] it is conducted in groups with concurrent individual sessions. It is not possible to adequately summarize the details of this approach here. Suffice it to note, however, that the

> term dialectical is meant to convey the multiple tensions that co-exist and must be dealt with in doing therapy with severely suicidal and borderline patients. The overriding dialectic is that of the necessity of acceptance of the client as she is within the context of trying to teach her to change and be different than she is. . . . The essential component of the dialectic approach is the notion that all elements of reality are intimately interconnected. Constant change, and therefore growth, occurs as a result of opposition between contradictory, but interacting, forces (thesis and antithesis) and their continual reconciliation on a higher level (synthesis). From this perspective, every element in reality contains within it an opposing force, like two sides of a coin. The rigid adherence to either pole of the dialectic contributes to stagnation and inhibits change. The task of the therapist in dialectical behavior therapy is to facilitate change by highlighting both aspects of the dialectical oppositions, fostering their successive reconciliation and resolution at increasingly more functional levels for the individual client. (Linehan, in press-a).

2. Elsewhere, I have described the "retronymic fervor" that has gripped behavior therapists over the years (Wilson, 1982b). Linehan's newly minted term is the most recent—and distinctive—in this tradition.

Within the context of familiar behavior therapy strategies and the dialectical focus described above, Linehan uses specific relationship strategies, namely, relationship enhancement, relationship problem solving, and relationship generalization. Relationship enhancement requires warmth and empathy, and the nurturing of cohesiveness among therapist and group members. Self-disclosure on the part of therapists, particularly about important current events in their lives, is said to be essential. To facilitate group cohesiveness, group members congregate in a waiting room prior to therapy, during explicitly scheduled session breaks, and after the session for a "debriefing" period.

Problems between therapist and group members are discussed openly in the group, using a problem-solving approach. To quote Linehan (in press-a)

> It is essential that the therapist be prepared to change the structure, format, or other details of the group if necessary. Changes should be arrived at through a process of negotiation, with everyone encouraged to express openly their wishes and opposition to proposed solutions. It was this process that led to the development of our debriefing process and the institution of two breaks instead of one. In these situations, the leader should model the skills taught in the interpersonal effectiveness part of the group and encourage and reinforce group members efforts to apply the same skills.

Relationship generalization strategies attempt to relate difficulties that occur within group sessions to the natural environment.

These relationship strategies and group treatment ground rules closely resemble the principles and procedures of Lazarus's (1968, 1971a) broad-spectrum behavior therapy which were used, primarily, with a more heterogeneous population of patients.

The literature on behavior therapy has had little to say about the treatment of such difficult patients as those now diagnosed as borderline or parasuicidal—or about personality disorders in general (Turkat & Maisto, 1985). Until recently the literature reflected only psychodynamic and pharmacological strategies. Linehan's clinical investigations serve as an important impetus to apply behavioral analyses to these problems. Of ultimate importance is the question of efficacy. Does dialectical behavior therapy succeed? Linehan (in press-b) issued an interim report on a controlled clinical trial of parasuicides meeting the criteria of borderline personality disorder. Comparing her approach to treatment-as-usual in the community she states that: "At the four-month point (the only point with complete data), DBT is more effective than other community treatment at reducing both the incidence and number of parasuicides. Interestingly, DBT, compared to usual treatment in the community, is also very effective at maintaining individuals in treatment. To date, we have a zero drop-out rate."

CLINICAL INFERENCE

In Volume 10 of this series, I emphasized that a complete account of the therapist's contribution to treatment must take serious account of the cognitive/judgmental pitfalls to which clinicians may be unduly prone (Wilson, 1985a). The basis for my comments was an incisive analysis of the nature of clinical inference, with special reference to recent developments in cognitive psychology, by Rachman (1983). Turk and Salovey (1985a, 1985b) have similarly drawn upon recent research in information processing and social cognition, and related it to both the client's participation in treatment and the judgments and inferences of the clinician. These papers complement Rachman's earlier paper; collectively, they have significant implications for the analysis of the therapist's contribution and the training of clinicians.

It is a truism that the therapist is confronted with a complex and changing array of information during treatment sessions, and even in reviewing a clinical case as a whole. The interactions within which this information has to be received and processed are, moreover, often charged with emotion. As such, treatment sessions appear to be excellent breeding grounds for the sort of inferential errors and judgmental biases in cognitive processing that recent experimental cognitive psychology has documented (e.g., Cantor & Mischel, 1979; Nisbett & Ross, 1980). Turk and Salovey (1985b) summarize what, by now, should be familiar sources of judgmental error: confirmatory bias, illusory correlation, and the availability of representative heuristics, among others.

As Rachman (1983) has made clear, compelling evidence of problems in clinical inference has been available for years, what with Meehl's (1954) analysis of clinical versus statistical prediction and the Chapman and Chapman (1967) demonstration of illusory correlation in the interpretation of Rorschach responses. Turk and Salovey recognize that these findings have been around for some time, and continue,

> [T]he important question to consider is why these data have so often been ignored? One possible explanation is that the data are threatening to clinicians, and thus, a defensive response to ignore or criticize these findings may be quite common. . . . Rather than defensively ignoring these data, we might consider how the research literature might be used to improve upon clinical practice. (1985b, p. 28)

Turk and Salovey summarize several possible strategies for "debiasing the clinician." One approach favors catchy epigrams that capture the limitations of intuitive judgments and call attention to more formal decision-making strategies: for example, "It's an empirical question," or "That's a vivid datum (I had a client once . . .), but I think I'll consult the base rate!" Others, in one way or another, emphasize training in which clinicians would become more aware of probabilistic models and statistical considerations (e.g., base rate information) (Arkes, 1981; Kahneman, Slovic, & Tversky, 1982; Nisbett, Krantz, Jepson, & Fong, 1982). It is ironic, as I have remarked previously (Wilson, 1985a), that as identifying the limitations of clinical inference is receiving more study, and developments are being made with a view to "debiasing the clinician," some professional training programs are decreasing the training in psychology that is most likely to remedy the problem.

It is clear that therapists of all theoretical persuasions are prone to errors of clinical inference. A case can be made that psychoanalysts are especially vulnerable to such distortions (Wilson, 1985a), but behavior therapists are not immune. Psychodynamic approaches are likely to continue to shun the corrective influence of controlled psychological research, but behavior therapists, with their commitment to experimental psychology, are in a much better position to be responsive to the new research. As Turk and Salovey conclude,

> The time has come for the clinician to stop defensively avoiding these issues and the researcher to stop wagging a condescending finger at the hapless clinician. Rather, we need to develop and examine programs that may improve clinical judgement. Individuals with a cognitive–behavioral orientation are in a unique position to be at the forefront of this needed research area. (1985b, p. 31)

THE IMPACT OF RESEARCH ON CLINICAL PRACTICE

Recent Findings on Research Utilization

The much-debated relationship between research and clinical practice, and the attendant controversy over models of clinical training, were discussed in some detail in Volume 8 of this series (Wilson, 1982a). Some recent publications provide a follow-up on some of the issues taken up in the previous commentary. One source is a special issue of the *American Psychologist* on psychotherapy research. Morrow-Bradley and Elliot (1986) conducted a mail survey of the fellows and members of Division 29 (Division of Psychotherapy) of the American

Psychological Association to assess the utilization of psychotherapy research by practicing therapists. Not surprisingly, Morrow-Bradley and Elliott uncovered dismally low rates of what they call "research utilization." Most respondents replied that they gained their most useful experience from working directly with their clients. Of no surprise, either, was the finding that "the strongest, most consistent correlate of research utilization was theoretical orientation; behavioral (including cognitive) therapists reported finding therapy research more useful, whereas dynamic therapists found it less useful" (p. 191).

Most of the respondents were critical of psychotherapy research. In commenting on the implications of these findings for the continuing gap between research and practice, Morrow-Bradley and Elliot assert,

> If therapy researchers want to make their research more useful to practicing therapists, they need to place greater value on external validity or clinical verisimilitude than has been the case. One aspect of this issue involves focusing on typical populations, settings, and orientations. Another aspect involves doing justice to the complexities of the clinical situation (a) by carefully describing the treatment used, (b) by continuing research on links between in-therapy processes and posttreatment or postsession outcome, (c) by focusing on significant change events, and (d) by taking into consideration the role of the therapeutic alliance. (p. 196)

Undoubtedly, these concerns are of crucial importance to good clinical research. Nevertheless, what this easy answer does not address is the failure of research that satisfies these criteria to influence practice (Wilson, 1982c). A telling example of this more disturbing phenomenon is presented below in discussing the fate of the results of token economies.

The utilization of research by practitioners has also been the subject of an analysis by Cohen, Sargent, and Sechrest (1986). They emphasize the problems inherent in disseminating research findings to practitioners. Briefly, research publications are disliked and ineffective, and word of mouth is favored. Cohen *et al.* conclude,

> Although the traditional journal article format allows for an informed judgment of the scientific merit of research, it seemingly is not conducive to treatment adoption on the part of the clinician–reader. Previous research has shown that the diffusion of a positively evaluated innovation is best accomplished by an aggressive strategy combining interpersonal communication (e.g., workshops, consultation) and detailed training manuals. This apparently is true even for psychologists, professionals who are relatively sophisticated in their understanding of research. The

> ready dissemination of psychotherapy fads documents this point. Charismatic workshop leaders armed with readable treatment manuals have almost certainly had a significant effect on the diffusion of treatments in mental health, often independent of (or in spite of) research on treatment effectiveness. (p. 204)

Behavior therapy, as much as (perhaps more than?) any other approach, has emphasized the development of treatment manuals. The specification of treatment strategies, often in the form of manuals, is required for independent assessment of the adequacy of treatment implementation in controlled research. To judge from Cohen *et al.*'s results, it will also facilitate the dissemination of our therapeutic strategies.

Where Have All The Token Economy Programs Gone?

In Volume 8 of this series (Wilson, 1982a), I used the example of the apparent lack of impact of the landmark Paul and Lentz (1977) study to illustrate the failure of sound, clinically relevant research to close the gap between research and clinical practice. Boudewyns, Fry, and Nightingale (1986) have reported an evaluation of the influence of token economy programs similar to that so thoroughly developed and standardized by Paul and Lentz. They surveyed all 152 Veterans Administration Medical Centers that have psychology services. Based on a 100% return (a most unusual rate of success), only 20 inpatient centers reported having a "behavior modification unit/token economy" program of any kind. A follow-up survey revealed that of these centers, only 10 had programs that would qualify as similar to that developed by Paul and Lentz. Why?

Boudewyns *et al.* (1986) are unable to identify any consistent reason for the remarkable failure to apply the hard-won lessons of the Paul and Lentz (1977) study. Among the explanations they raise is staff or administrative resistance. Implementing a successful token economy program involves hard work, initiative, and significant changes from routine procedures, however ineffective or inefficient the latter are. Change, as we know, is often resisted at both the individual and the institutional level. If we are to see any improvement over this discouraging situation, we would do well to come to grips with the sorts of issues Boudewyn *et al.* (1986), among others, have raised. The familiar refrain that research is not utilized only because it is somehow clinically irrelevant can be a red herring that may distract attention from the real problem.

COMMONALITIES BETWEEN BEHAVIOR THERAPY AND PSYCHODYNAMIC THERAPIES

Critical analyses of attempts to integrate behavior therapy with psychoanalytic therapy have been featured in previous volumes in this series (e.g., Wilson, 1982a). In 1984, yet another edited volume on this topic, by Arkowitz and Messer, was published—*Psychoanalytic Therapy and Behavior Therapy: Is Integration Possible?* This text follows on the heels of books (Wachtel, 1977, 1982a), anthologies (Goldfried, 1982a; Marmor & Woods, 1980), numerous individual papers, and routine panel discussions at any number of conferences on this particular topic. It is difficult to resist the conclusion that the topic is irresistible. Certainly, it would be hard to argue that the fruits of this continuing dialogue have warranted such sustained attention.

Arkowitz and Messer (1984) bring together several seasoned campaigners in this dialogue, including Franks, Gill, Mahoney, Rhoads, and Wachtel. The usual range of opinions are represented—those who, for different reasons, do not believe integration is possible or even desirable; and those who believe that some form of integration is possible, although the actual nature of the integration varies from one commentator to another. Unfortunately, despite the scholarship that is evident in the various contributions, it cannot be said that they take us beyond previously expressed views. The arguments, pro and con, have a familiar ring, and any consensus affecting theoretical development or practical know-how remains elusive.

A question that must be asked is this: Why has there been such sustained interest in integrating behavior therapy and psychoanalytic therapy in particular? Integrationism in the psychological therapies, as Kazdin (1984) points out, may take many forms. In fact, Kazdin uses the case of self-efficacy theory as a specific form of integrationism in psychotherapy. What Kazdin views here as a blending of a behavioral and a cognitive perspective is a far cry from the arguments that rage around integrating behavior therapy and psychoanalytic therapy. Self-efficacy theory, and cognitive social learning theory more generally, is based on the method and content of experimental psychology. Behavior therapy, as I and others have discussed elsewhere (e.g., Wilson, 1982c, in press-b), has increasingly been influenced by cognitive social learning theory and experimental psychology, as opposed to being more narrowly nourished only by operant and classical conditioning. A commitment to the content and methods of experimental psychology brings with it several seminal, shared assumptions about how to conceptualize and investigate a problem. This sort of "integrationism" is natural and desirable. But as Franks (1984b), Gill (1984), and others point out, behavior therapy and psychoanalysis enjoy few if any of such shared assumptions. Of course, a distinction can be made between psychoanalysis proper and more recent, briefer psychodynamic therapies (Budman, 1981; Goldfried, 1982a). In terms of clinical strategies, there appears to be more overlap between these more directive therapies and some aspects of cognitive–behavioral methods. If the dialogue is to go anywhere, it will probably have to focus on this area of clinical activity.

Another question that must be asked is a more empirical one: Just how will integrating psychoanalytic strategies with behavior therapy improve therapeutic efficacy? Where is the evidence? And even if it is argued that the new hybrid that might be developed via integration is untested, where is the evidence suggesting that such a hybrid might be more effective? The answer to the last query depends upon one's evaluation of the current evidence for the efficacy of psychoanalysis and related psychodynamic therapies. If some of the more negative evaluations of the efficacy of the psychoanalytic approach are accepted (Rachman & Wilson, 1980; Wilson, 1985c—see below), there is little basis for assuming any incremental efficacy in treatment as a function of integration. Nevertheless, it is striking (but hardly new) to see the question of empirical evaluation of treatment effects so consistently avoided or dismissed by proponents of the psychoanalytic approach in the Arkowitz and Messer (1984) volume.

One approach to the question of outcome efficacy is to ignore the matter and resort to that weary exemplar of the representative heuristic, "I had a client who . . . " A more novel tack is taken by Salzman (1984), who offers the following critique of outcome research in behavior therapy:

> They (particularly Eysenck) amass voluminous data and use statistics about undifferentiated groups of symptoms, and they claim great success in overcoming disorders that are neither clearly identified nor defined. . . . A numbers game has become confused with scientific research. Although they gather data of doubtful entities from mixed sources, there is little searching exploration of the experimental design or definitions that have produced the data. Nor are there precise statements about the criteria used to determine the quality of improvement in these outcome studies. The categories of improvement are so arbitrary at times that it becomes questionable how much change has occurred. When the data suit their views, they seem to be accepted uncritically. Despite claims of precision, many behavior therapists persist in utilizing a single label for phenomena that may seem to be similar but, as fact, may be quite different. . . . (p. 347).

This extraordinary charge is unsupported by a single example, let alone a careful methodological critique of the literature. Nor is the reader treated to how "scientific" research might be conducted, other than the remarkable tacit assumption that it would need to be founded on a psychodynamic understanding of the causes and nature of psychiatric disorders not even embraced by the American Psychiatric Association! It is hard to envisage how this sort of contribution is likely to enlighten the debate over integration.

Another approach to the issue of evaluating the outcome of the psychological therapies is to dispute the relevance or appropriateness of an experimental or scientific method as a whole.[3] This view, too, is not unfamiliar, but has gained some recent momentum with the increasing appeal to hermeneutics. Messer (1984) identifies psychoanalysis with the hermeneutic approach, which he characterizes as follows:

> In the hermeneutic approach, one strives to construct meaning out of a diversity of phenomena to aid the emergence of hidden meanings. One seeks the coherence, consistency, and harmony of the parts underlying the seeming disparity—like fitting together pieces of a puzzle. Any one piece only makes sense in the context of the adjoining pieces, and together they offer a "narrative fit" and "narrative truth." (p. 365)

The hermeneutic construal of psychoanalysis is rejected by behavior therapists and the scientifically committed. Two recent books, one by a philosopher of science, the other by a professor of English, provide a particularly incisive critique of the attempt to salvage psychoanalysis by invoking hermeneutics. The first is Grunbaum's (1984) landmark philosophical critique of the hermeneutic approach to psychoanalysis. Grunbaum makes the case that Freud adopted scientific criteria for judging his theory and therapy:

> Flawed as Freud's own arguments . . . turn out to be . . . their caliber [is] astronomically higher, and their often brilliant content incomparably more instructive, than the gloss and the animadversions of Freud's hermeneutic critics, who so patronizingly chide him for scientism. So much for their unjustified demand that we abjure the very standards of validation by which Freud himself wanted his theory to be judged. (p. xx)

The detailed and relentless manner in which Grunbaum identifies and then discredits Freud's specific arguments for the validity of psychoanalysis is beyond the scope of the present discussion. What is

3. A recent interchange along these lines is found in Bloch and Lambert's (1985) and Ryle's (1985) responses to Shepherd's (1984) negative appraisal of the effects of psychotherapy, with rejoinders from Shepherd (1985) and Watt (1985).

critical here is the rejection of the view that scientific criteria are inappropriate for examining the effects of psychoanalytic therapy.

The second book, by Crews (1986), draws on Grunbaum's work in providing a compelling critique of psychoanalysis. Concerning the hermeneutic interpretation of psychoanalysis, Crews has the following to say:

> According to the hermeneutic school, psychoanalysis should not be held accountable to the validation of its causal assertions by received scientific standards of testing; it is just a means of arriving at particular intepretive insights which are self-certifying. That view is now fashionable among academic humanists, many of whom have little use for science to begin with. They would rather not be bothered by logical and empirical constraints when they apply their favorite cross-disciplinary doctrines to history, biography, and works of art. Grunbaum, however, demonstrates that 'besides resting on a mythic exegesis of Freud's writings, the theses of these hermeneuticians are based on profound misunderstandings of the very content and methods of the natural sciences." (p.82)

In favoring a hermeneutic construal of psychoanalysis, Messer (personal communication, 1986) himself does not reject the value of the traditional scientific criteria and methods for evaluating treatment outcome and argues that hermeneutics does not necessarily eschew such outcome evaluation. According to this view, hermeneutics is concerned with the *process* of therapy, not its outcome. There are difficulties with this position, however. I believe that many clinicians who have embraced a hermeneutic position do reject conventional scientific evaluation of treatment outcome, regardless of the philosophical niceties of this approach. And, it is understandable why these therapists would make this connection.

The argument that one can hold to a hermeneutic view of therapeutic process without abandoning scientific evaluation of outcome is flawed. Therapeutic process must be linked to treatment outcome. The old argument that the validity of psychoanalysis as a theory is unaffected by its efficacy—or lack thereof—has been discredited.[4] In

4. Perhaps nowhere is this more convincingly demonstrated than in Grunbaum's penetrating analysis of what he has called Freud's "Tally Argument." Grunbaum credits Freud with recognizing the difficulties with his theory and trying to devise a suitable defense. Freud acknowledged the criticism that the patient's free-associations during therapy are inevitably contaminated by the therapist's own views and values. However, he claimed that the patient's "conflicts will only be successfully solved and his resistances overcome if the anticipatory ideas he is given tally with what is real in him." As Crews (1986) observes, "Presumably, then, any mistaken constructions will drop away in the course of treatment, and the patient's eventual cure will validate the correctness of

the same manner, it is hard to imagine how the outcome of therapy could fail to bear critically on treatment process. How would this occur from a hermeneutic viewpoint? The validity of a theory of psychological change is inescapably related to the efficacy of the treatment methods it spawns. Perhaps it is no accident that, to my knowledge, it has not occurred. Scientific evaluation of outcome, predictably, receives short shrift in hermeneutic accounts. Emphasis on something called therapeutic process, artificially disembodied from outcome, has too often been used to avoid the investigation and implications of findings on treatment outcome.

EVALUATING TREATMENT OUTCOME: THE ROLE OF META-ANALYSIS

When it comes to clinical practice, there can be no more pressing questions than whether psychotherapy works, with whom, and with what problems. The running controversy over this fundamental question, ignited by Eysenck's (1952) classic challenge, has been enlivened but not enlightened by the advent of meta-analysis (Smith, Glass, & Miller, 1980). Meta-analyses that have been used to evaluate the effects of the psychological therapies as a whole have, in general, met with a critical reaction in the behavior therapy literature (e.g., Eysenck, 1983; Wilson & Rachman, 1983). Yet, as I have pointed out elsewhere, this critical reaction cannot be attributed to any displeasure in the pattern of outcome that the published meta-analyses have produced (Wilson, 1985c). Far from it. If one restricts oneself to the meta-analytic evaluations of the psychological therapies, cognitive–behavioral methods emerge as the most effective methods.

It is unfortunate that the original meta-analysis on psychotherapy outcome by Smith *et al.* (1980) is the one that has captured so much attention. The numerous flaws and inaccuracies of Smith *et al.*'s study have been amply documented. Nevertheless, some sort of "primacy effect" seems to have resulted in this study and its blatantly false

---

those constructions that were allegedly crucial in bringing it about" (p. 85). Here, clearly, Freud is appealing to treatment outcome to validate his notions.

Parenthetically, Crews summarizes how Freud's defense flatly fails: "Grunbaum shows that Freud's Tally Argument collapses in the face of two unanswerable considerations. First, . . . patients can get well for reasons having nothing to do with the specific content of what they 'remember' or are told. A key premise of the Tally Argument is therefore unfounded. And second, psychoanalysis never did, and still does not, effect the regular and permanent cures Freud usually claimed for it" (pp. 85–86).

conclusions being widely cited in the literature. Although Smith *et al.* stridently proclaimed that all psychotherapies are effective and that there are no significant differences among them, they seem to have contradicted themselves on this fundamental point. Despite their insistence on the unique virtues of meta-analysis, they made the following observation:

> Ex post facto statistical equating of therapies is only partly satisfactory, since many potential confounding variables remain uncontrolled. The best solution for the reduction of the influence of extraneous variables is experimental; that is, for one researcher to study the effects of two or more therapies directly, using the same kinds of client, therapy of standard duration, therapists of equivalent training, and common measurements. (p. 106)

When they followed this aspect of their own advice and selected "well-controlled" studies, they found that the behavioral therapies were significantly superior to both verbal (psychodynamic) and developmental therapies. In a further ad hoc analysis, they divided outcome measures into two classes: those that were "psychological" and those that were "less tractable." The superiority of the behavioral therapies was then limited to "psychological" measures. Among these measures were "fear–anxiety, self-esteem, global adjustment, personality traits, vocational–personal development" (p. 107). How Smith *et al.* were able to conclude, on this basis, that there are no differences between therapies is hard to fathom.

Subsequent meta-analyses have consistently concluded that behavior therapy is superior to all other forms of psychological treatments included in these statistical analyses (Andrews & Harvey, 1981; Andrews, Moran, & Hall, 1983; Shapiro & Shapiro, 1983). Nicholson and Berman (1983) even found that the results of psychological treatment were maintained at a follow-up of at least 18 months, and that relapse was not as much a concern as has been believed. Essentially, these positive but putative results were based on behavioral treatments (approximately 87% of the studies). Nicholson and Berman reported mean effect sizes (ESs) of −0.67 for nonbehavioral methods. It will be recalled that negative ESs show that an untreated control group improved more than a treated group.

The Question of Quality

The problems of including methodologically deficient studies in a meta-analysis have been addressed in previous critiques (Mintz, 1983;

Wilson & Rachman, 1983). Landman and Dawes (1982) claimed to have rebutted the quality-of-study criticism in a reanalysis of 65 randomly selected studies from Smith and Glass's (1977) data base. Among these studies, they judged 42 to be appropriately controlled. The analysis produced results similar to those of Smith *et al.* (1980), leading Landman and Dawes to conclude, erroneously, that the major conclusions of Smith *et al.* were upheld in a more rigorous evaluation. But Landman and Dawes's methodological criteria—the presence of a no-treatment control group and random assignment of subjects—do little to improve upon the procedure of Smith *et al.* As has been widely demonstrated, of course, an adequate attention placebo control condition is a must if the internal validity of a treatment outcome study is to be properly assessed. Landman and Dawes did compare specific treatment to placebo effects, but only in five studies. They found that the ES for "psychotherapy" was 0.56, compared to 0.38 for placebo. But as Erwin (1984) observes, most of these studies were done on behavior therapy, and it is unclear "that even one study was found in which a psychotherapy treatment of patients with typical clinical problems exceeded that of a placebo" (p. 430).

The problems with the methodological criteria used by Smith *et al.* (1980) and Landman and Dawes (1982) are revealed in Prioleau, Murdock, and Brody's (1983) meta-analysis of yet another subset of the data base of Smith *et al.* (1980). Prioleau *et al.* limited their analysis only to psychotherapy and selected only studies that included a placebo control treatment. Prioleau *et al.* found no evidence that any effects of psychotherapy were greater than those of placebo.

Erwin's 1984 philosophical critique of meta-analysis and the evaluation of psychotherapy highlights the logical shortcomings of the Smith *et al.* (1980) study. The latter criticized previous reviewers for "arbitrarily" excluding controlled studies of poor quality.[5] But why then not also include uncontrolled studies (i.e., case studies)? Erwin states,

> [There is] no warrant for drawing a general epistemological distinction between uncontrolled and poorly controlled studies in terms of their

5. Careful examination of the Smith *et al.* (1980) study reveals several unexplained inconsistencies and contradictions. Searles (1985) notes a case in which Smith *et al.* excluded a study from their analysis because it was "uncommonly bad" in design. Searles pointedly questions the basis for this arbitrary action and wonders "if some studies can be classified so negatively, logic dictates that some could be classified as uncommonly good. What are to be done with these? Furthermore, since 'weakness in design' has been the primary reason for removing studies in traditional reviews, the advantage that meta-analysis offers in this regard is not clear" (p. 456).

> capacity to provide firm evidence of causal connections. Both sorts of studies generally fail to rule out plausible rivals to the hypothesis that the therapy caused any beneficial therapeutic results. There is a dilemma, then, for Smith *et al.* If judgments of methodological quality should not be made because they are inevitably arbitrary, then a reviewer should cast the net very wide and include all outcome studies of psychotherapy whether controlled or uncontrolled . . . ; but if judgments of quality should be made, then some justification is needed for treating evidence from bad studies on a par with evidence from superior studies. It might be that research integration of the sort Smith *et al.* are attempting is inevitably unreliable. (p. 425)

What Does Meta-Analysis Measure?

Paul (1985) has provided a balanced and probing examination of meta-analysis. Stating that he views this technique as promising, he nonetheless points out several sources of potential error. Underscoring previous reviews, he emphasizes the importance of

> the judgments that enter meta-analysis before the final analyses. The extensive discussions in the recent literature leave no doubt that meta-analytic reviews involve a series of complex, subjective, and often arbitrary judgments prior to the time that the computer objectively aggregates or disaggregates the data—according to a program selected on the basis of human decisions. Although the sophisticated mathematical operations applied in meta-analytic reviews may appear to be more rigorous and objective than other means of integrating empirical studies, that appearance can be illusory. (p. 153)

Among the many judgments to be made prior to cranking up the computer is the choice of the dependent measure in the meta-analysis—the ES measure. Smith *et al.* (1980) counted every measure in each study as a separate ES for entry into the meta-analysis. This procedure violated statistical canons, because the meta-analysis was then based on nonindependent ES estimates, with the result that the studies were unevenly weighted according to their number of ESs. An alternative approach, which yields to purely statistical concerns about dependence in the data, has been taken by other meta-analysts (Landman & Dawes, 1982; Nicholson & Berman, 1983; Prioleau *et al.*, 1983). These investigators combined every measure in a particular study to form one, pooled ES. The conceptual and clinical consequences of this decision are considerable.

Consider a simple example of this pooling strategy. In a study of the effects of treatment of obesity, what clinical or conceptual sense does it make to lump together measures of body fat, body weight, body image, lipoproteins, systolic and diastolic blood pressure, depressed affect, and marital satisfaction into a single index (ES) of outcome? Obviously, these very different measures assess highly differentiated aspects of treatment. The different patterns of outcome (across biological and psychological domains) in the treatment of obesity are documented elsewhere (Wilson & Brownell, 1980). Reducing these different measures to a single artificial number is meaningless at best and misleading at worst.

It is now well established that treatment evaluation studies should include multiple measures of process and outcome that sample different domains of functioning (e.g., Rachman & Wilson, 1980; Strupp & Hadley, 1977). Different measures may change in response to different treatments and at different rates (Lang, 1971; Rachman, 1978). Useful theoretical and practical advances have been made by studying the nature of synchrony and desynchrony among response systems in fear and fear reduction (e.g., Rachman & Hodgson, 1974). And in a closely related vein, the analysis of response covariation promises to extend our knowledge of treatment mechanisms and effects (Kazdin, 1982). These lines of scientific and clinical inquiry are obliterated by pooling different measures within studies.

Paul (1985) provides a revealing example of how failure to consider the conceptual relevance of measures within a particular study can make nonsense of a meta-analysis. Using his study of the treatment of speech anxiety (Paul, 1966, 1967),[6] he notes that of the different scales administered at follow-up, only two were directly relevant to evaluation of outcome—focal scales of experienced and expected anxiety in the performance situation. The other measures were included

> only to aid in identifying the sample of clients and to assess other changes in client behavior predicted by the competing theoretical models underlying the insight-oriented psychotherapy ("symptom-substitution" for desensitization and attention-placebo clients) and systematic desensitization treatments ("generalization" or "no change" in nonfocal areas for all clients). Thus, to represent the conceptual integrity of the design-relevant measures, only the "focal–experienced" scale or, at most, the two focal scales should be included in a meta-analysis of treatment outcomes. (1985, p. 156)

The mistake of averaging these different measures into a single mishmashed ES is obvious. Paul shows that the mean ES of the ad-

6. Smith *et al.* (1980), in their much-cited study, included the Paul (1966) study but not the 2-year follow-up (Paul, 1967). This surprisingly erratic and inaccurate coverage of the literature characterizes their study (see Wilson & Rachman, 1983).

vantage of systematic desensitization over the attention placebo control treatment at the 6-week follow-up was 0.45 for the two focal scales. The mean of all scales, however, which would be the figure used by meta-analysts such as Landman and Dawes, was 0.04. Clearly, relying upon a pooled ES would misrepresent the study and its results, and would dramatically underestimate treatment effects. Cordray and Bootzin (1983) similarly provide examples from the Prioleau *et al.* (1983) meta-analysis in which failure to attend to the conceptual relevance of individual measures produced meaningless average figures.

Paul (1985) also demonstrates the misrepresentation of his 1966 study (and, by extension, many others) by Smith *et al.* (1980). According to the procedures of Smith *et al.*, the mean ES for the advantage of desensitization over the attention placebo control group was 0.90. This figure was based on measures of actual behavior, physiological responsiveness, and self-report of anxiety. As Table 8-1 illustrates, these different measures predictably showed differential patterns of outcome for different treatments—conceptually and clinically significant differences that are obliterated in meta-analyses such as that of Smith *et al.* (1980). However, Paul states that "for assessing the practical outcome of these treatments on the reduction of anxiety, the three assessment domains need to be aggregated into a composite measure for each individual to maintain their [*sic*] conceptual integrity" (1985, p. 155).

Composite ESs for Paul's (1966) data, calculated in this manner, are presented in Table 8-1. The mean ESs in Table 8-1 would be the

TABLE 8-1 Example of How Arbitrary Meta-Analytic Decisions (Individual or Mean Effect Size) Can Misrepresent the Conceptual Relevance (Composite Effect Size) of Findings for the Basic Data to Compare Outcomes

	Treatment effect size		Advantage of desensitization over nonspecific treatment effects
Measure	Systematic desensitization	Attention placebo	
Overt behavior effect	2.19	.88	1.31
Self-report effect size	1.24	.94	.30
Physiological effect size	1.24	.17	1.07
Mean effect size	1.56	.66	.90
Composite effect size	2.88	.83	2.05

Note. From "Can Pregnancy Be a Placebo Effect?: Terminology, Designs, and Conclusions in the Study of Psychosocial and Pharmacological Treatments of Behavioral Disorders" by G. L. Paul, 1985, in L. White, B. Tursky, and G. Schwartz (Eds.), *Placebo: Clinical Phenomena and New Insights* (p. 155), New York: Guilford Press. Copyright 1985 by The Guilford Press. Reprinted by permission.

data used in the meta-analyses of Smith *et al.* (1980) and others. Paul (1985) points out,

> Although both mean and composite effect sizes reflect a similar patterning within the study, meta-analytic procedures require effect-size indexes that are portable across studies. Therefore, failing to take into account the conceptual relevance of the measures in this instance would grossly underestimate the size of effect produced by both systematic desensitization and attention-placebo treatments—even if other studies included in the meta-analyses employed similar measures and testing conditions. (p. 156)

Finally, Paul (1985) points out that strictly statistical considerations can significantly affect (distort) the findings of a meta-analysis. As an example, he takes the different ways in which the ES—the dependent variable in the meta-analysis—is derived. To quote Paul,

> Experimenting with various ways of calculating effect sizes served to sharpen my reservations concerning ready acceptance of the conclusions from meta-analytic reviews. Applying only five different ways of calculating effect sizes—from the many employed by Smith *et al.* (1980)—to the identical data set from any single study regularly resulted in five different effect sizes, and the differences among obtained indices were substantial. For example, limiting the data set to the overt behavioral measure under stress conditions for systematic desensitization and no-treatment groups included in Table [8-1] resulted in effect size indices for systematic desensitization ranging from 1.93 to 3.06. These different effect size indices depended simply upon whether pooled variances were used to obtain the standardizing standard devision and whether the data entered were posttest data only, pre–post change data, or improvement scores. . . . In large meta-analytic reviews, the marked influence of these subjective choices and/or available primary test statistics may be buried in a morass of computations rather than being public and explicit. Such a masking of lethal errors certainly warrants extreme caution in the conduct and interpretation of large-scale meta-analyses. (p. 158)

Meta-Analysis, Conventional Reviews, and Causal Inference

Both Smith *et al.* (1980) and Shapiro and Shapiro (1983) have claimed that a meta-analysis of numerous studies is to a conventional (so-called "literary") review of the literature as a single, controlled experimental design is to an uncontrolled study. Although the validity of such a claim would not appear to be critical to the potential usefulness of meta-analysis, it is a significant claim, which, if nothing else, reiterates the alleged inherent logical superiority of meta-analysis in drawing causal inferences about treatment methods and their effects. As such, it warrants comment. The philosopher Erwin (1984) has done just that.

Erwin (1984) has rejected this view that a review of experiments can itself be viewed as an experiment:

> It is probably more illuminating to compare a review not to an experiment but a complex argument. More precisely, a review will normally contain one or more conclusions and one or more supporting arguments. To use Campbell and Stanley criteria to criticize a review effectively, it has to be shown that the failure to meet some of the criteria destroys the cogency of at least one of the reviewer's arguments. (p. 431)

Erwin then shows that Smith *et al.* (1980) (and Shapiro & Shapiro [1983], it might be added) have not made such a case and have thus failed to discredit conventional reviews in these terms.

Irrespective of the particular objection of Smith *et al.* (1980), which can be rejected, what of the more general concern that traditional reviews are inherently inadequate for integrating the results of a collection of studies? Erwin concludes that traditional (literary) reviews are not inevitably limited; there are common circumstances under which they allow causal inferences about treatment effects to be drawn. And in those circumstances where they encounter problems, and causal inferences are precluded, meta-analysis is not likely to solve the problem.

The Functions of Meta-Analysis

Proponents of meta-analysis have claimed that it is uniquely well suited to providing "guiding suggestions" for future outcome research (Shapiro & Shapiro, 1983) and even to examining the plausibility of hypotheses that have not been tested in single studies. These claims have been evaluated elsewhere. On a more negative note, we (Wilson & Rachman, 1983), have voiced concern that meta-analyses might merely paper over the inadequacies of existing studies and even, however inadvertently, discourage better-controlled investigations. Seeing the mass of studies, their various imperfections notwithstanding, might confirm believers in the efficacy of psychotherapy in their conviction that there is a reliable effect there—or, in the words of the old joke, that "there must be a pony in there somewhere" (Orlinsky & Howard, 1978).

It is not hard to find indications of this trend. Recently, Belden, Braukmann, and Wolf (1985) have criticized the American Psychological Association's (1979) document *Psychology as a Health Care Profession*. They have argued that the individual studies on which the document based its conclusion that psychotherapy is cost-effective were too methodologically flawed to permit such an unequivocal statement. Cummings (1985) has responded to this critique by asserting that the evidence generally favors this conclusion: "Despite the methodological problems, this preponderance of evidence is quite persuasive and tends to mitigate the flaws" (p. 874). Among other sources, he invokes the biased and inaccurate Smith and Glass (1977) meta-analysis to support this statement. Braukmann, Belden, and Wolf's (1985) rejoinder emphasizes, among other points, that a preponderance of flawed evidence is not necessarily persuasive—a conclusion in which both methodologists (e.g., Paul, 1985) and philosophers (e.g., Erwin, 1984) would join.

Summing Up: The Current Status of Meta-Analysis and the Evaluation of Psychological Treatments

Garfield (1983), in commenting on the emerging controversy over the value of meta-analysis for evaluating the effects of psychological treatments, has made the following observation: "The application of meta-analysis to psychotherapy outcome data appeared to usher in an era of possible objectivity and systematic analysis in this confused and controversial field (Smith & Glass, 1977). Surprisingly, the use of meta-analysis has appeared to raise the level of controversy to new heights" (p. 292). In retrospect, given the well documented limitations of meta-analysis that were ignored in their original unbridled advocacy, this outcome is hardly surprising.

In a very short period of time, meta-analyses of the psychotherapy outcome literature have generated conflicting findings that match those of the more conventional reviews. I have illustrated this state of affairs in the following comment (Wilson, 1985c):

> Smith *et al.* (1980) make the extraordinary claim that their analysis 'overwhelmingly supports the efficacy of psychotherapy'; that psychotherapy 'benefits people . . . as reliably as schooling educates them, medicine cures them, or business turns a profit' (p. 183). In contrast, Prioleau *et al.* (1983) declare that 'we are still not aware of a single convincing demonstration that the benefits of psychotherapy exceed those of placebos for real patients' (p. 284). Smith *et al.* (1980) say psychotherapy works, but its benefits 'are not permanent' (p. 183). Nicholson and Berman (1983) conclude otherwise. In short, different meta-analyses thus far have differed on (a) how to select studies for inclusion in the data

> base; (b) how to classify diverse therapies; (c) how to evaluate multiple measure with a single study; (d) how to deal with the quality of study issue; and (e) not surprisingly, what methods are effective. (p. 45)

Searles (1985) similarly notes that different meta-analyses of the same data set have yielded inconsistent findings. We are no closer to a real consensus about the efficacy of psychotherapy than we were before meta-analysis. Little change in this picture can be expected unless greater commitment is made to developing better theories, devising better methods, and carrying out better-designed outcome studies.

REFERENCES

Abeles, N. (1986). Proceedings of the American Psychological Association, Incorporated, for the year 1985: Minutes of the Annual Meeting of the Council of Representatives. *American Psychologist, 41*, 633–663.

Abikoff, H. (1985). Efficacy of cognitive training interventions in hyperactive children: A critical review. *Clinical Psychology Review, 5*, 479–512.

Abikoff, H., & Gittelman, R. (1984). Does behavior therapy normalize the classroom behavior of hyperactive children? *Archives of General Psychiatry, 41*, 449–454.

Abikoff, H., & Gittelman, R. (1985). Hyperactive children treated with stimulants: Is cognitive training a useful adjunct? *Archives of General Psychiatry, 42*, 953–961.

Abikoff, H., Gittelman, R., & Klein, D. F. (1980). Classroom observation code for hyperactive children: A replication of validity. *Journal of Consulting and Clinical Psychology, 48*, 555–565.

Abikoff, H., Gittelman-Klein, R., & Klein, D. F. (1977). Validation of a classroom observation code for hyperactive children. *Journal of Consulting and Clinical Psychology, 45*, 772–783.

Abraham, S., Carroll, M. D., Najjar, M. F., & Fulwood, R. (1983). Obese and overweight adults in the United States. *Vital and Health Statistics*, Series 11, No. 230 (DHHS Publication No. PHS 83-1680). Washington, DC: U.S. Government Printing Office.

Abraham, S., Johnson, C. L., & Najjar, M. F. (1979). Weight by height and age for adults 18–74 years: United States, 1971–1974. *Vital and Health Statistics*, Series 11, No. 208 (DHEW Publication No. PHS 79-1656). Washington, DC: U.S. Government Printing Office.

Abrams, D. B., & Follick, M. J. (1983). Behavioral weight-loss intervention at the worksite: Feasibility and maintenance. *Journal of Consulting and Clincial Psychology, 51*, 226–233.

Abramson, J. H., Gofin, R., Hopp, C., Gofin, J., Donchin, M., & Habib, J. (1981). Evaluation of a community program for the control of cardiovascular risk factors: The CHAD program in Jerusalem. *Israel Journal of Medical Sciences, 17*, 201–212.

Achenbach, T. M., & Edelbrock, C. S. (1983). *Manual for the Child Behavior Checklist and Revised Child Behavior Profile.* Burlington: University of Vermont, Department of Psychiatry.

Advisory Committee to the Surgeon General. (1986). *The health consequences of using smokeless tobacco: A report of the Advisory Committee to the Surgeon General* (DHHS

Publication No. NIH 86-2874). Washington, DC: U.S. Government Printing Office.

Alden, L. (1984). Nonassertiveness: Skill deficit or selective self-evaluation? *Behavior Therapy, 15*, 107–114.

Allen, C. T., & Forman, S. G. (1984). Efficacy of methods of training teachers in behavior modification. *School Psychology Review, 13*, 26–32.

Allen, C. T., & Madden, T. J. (1985). A closer look at classical conditioning. *Journal of Consumer Research, 12*, 301–315.

Allison, J. (1983). *Behavioral economics.* New York: Praeger.

Alloy, L. B., & Abramson, L. Y. (1979). Judgment of contingency in depressed and nondepressed students: Sadder but wiser? *Journal of Experimental Psychology: General, 108*, 441–485.

American Heart Association. (1985). *1986 heart facts.* Dallas, TX: Author.

American Heart Association. (in press). Conference on Behavioral Medicine and Cardiovascular Disease. *Circulation.*

American Psychiatric Association. (1980). *Diagnostic and statistical manual of mental disorders* (3rd ed.). Washington, DC: Author.

American Psychological Association. (1979). *Psychology as a health care profession.* Washington, DC: Author.

Amies, P. L., Gelder, M. G., & Shaw, P. M. (1983). Social phobia: A comparative clinical study. *British Journal of Psychiatry, 123*, 175–179.

Andrews, G., & Harvey, R. (1981). Does psychotherapy benefit neurotic patients? *Archives of General Psychiatry, 38*, 1203–1208.

Andrews, G., Moran, C., & Hall, W. (1983). *Agoraphobia: A meta-analysis of treatment outcome studies.* Unpublished manuscript, University of New South Wales Medical School, Australia.

Angell, M. (1985). Disease as a reflection of the psyche [Editorial]. *New England Journal of Medicine, 312*, 1570–1572.

Anonymous. (1939). *Alcoholics Anonymous.* New York: Works.

Appleby, I., Klein, D. F., Sacher, E., & Levitt, M. (1981). Biochemical indices of lactate-induced panic. In D. F. Klein & J. Rabkin (Eds.), *Anxiety: New research and changing concepts.* New York: Raven Press.

Arbuthnot, J., & Gordon, D. A. (1986). Behavioral and cognitive effects of a moral reasoning development intervention for high-risk behavior-disordered adolescents. *Journal of Consulting and Clinical Psychology, 54*, 208–216.

Arkes, H. R. (1981). Impediments to accurate clincial judgment and possible ways to minimize their impact. *Journal of Consulting and Clinical Psychology, 49*, 323–330.

Arkowitz, H., & Messer, S. B. (Eds.). (1984). *Psychoanalytic therapy and behavior therapy: Is integration possible?* New York: Plenum.

Armor, D. J., Polich, J. M., & Stambul, H. B. (1978). *Alcoholism and treatment.* New York: Wiley.

Arnkoff, D. B. (1983). Common and specific factors in cognitive therapy. In M. J. Lambert (Ed.), *Psychotherapy and patient relationships* (pp. 85–125). Homewood, IL: Dorsey Press.

Arnow, B., Taylor, C. B., Agras, W. S., & Telch, M. (1985). Enhancing agoraphobia treatment outcome by changing couple communication patterns. *Behavior Therapy, 16*, 452–467.

Arrindell, W., & Emmelkamp, P. (1985a). *Marital adjustment, intimacy and needs in female agoraphobics and their partners: A controlled study.* Unpublished manuscript, Department of Clinical Psychology, Academic Hospital, Gröningen, the Netherlands.

Arrindell, W., & Emmelkamp, P. (1985b). Psychological profile of the spouse of the female agoraphobic patient personality and symptoms. *British Journal of Psychiatry, 146*, 405–414.

Arthur, J. A., Hops, H., & Biglan, A. (1982). LIFE (Living in Familial Environments) coding system. Unpublished manuscript, Oregon Research Institute, Eugene, OR.

Ary, D. V., Severson, H. H., & Lichtenstein, E. (1985, August). *Concurrent correlates and prospective factors associated with smokeless tobacco use among adolescents.* Paper presented at the meeting of the American Psychological Association, Los Angeles.

Asarnow, J. R., & Callan, J. W. (1985). Boys with peer adjustment problems: Social cognitive processes. *Journal of Consulting and Clinical Psychology, 53*, 80–87.

Asarnow, J. R., & Carlson, G. A. (1985). Depression self-rating scale: Utility with child psychiatric inpatients. *Journal of Consulting and Clinical Psychology, 53*(4), 491–499.

Avogaro, P., Bon, G. B., Cazzolato, G., & Rorai, E. (1980). Relationship between apolipoproteins and chemical components of lipoproteins in survivors of myocardial infarction. *Atherosclerosis, 37*, 69–76.

Azar, S. T., & Twentyman, C. T. (1986). Cognitive–behavioral perspectives on the assessment and treatment of child abuse. In P. C. Kendall (Ed.), *Advances in cognitive–behavioral research and therapy* (Vol. 5, pp. 237–267). New York: Academic Press.

Baekeland, F. (1977). Evaluation of treatment methods in chronic alcoholism. In B. Kissin & H. Begleiter (Eds.), *The biology of alcoholism: Vol. 5. Treatment and rehabilitation of the chronic alcoholic* (pp. 385–440). New York: Plenum Press.

Bailey, J. S., & Reiss, M. L. (1984). The demise of the "Model-T" and the emergence of systems management in human services. *the Behavior Therapist, 7*, 65–68.

Baker, A. L., & Wilson, P. H. (1985). Cognitive-behavior therapy for depression: The effects of booster sessions on relapse. *Behavior Therapy, 16*, 335–344.

Baker, B. L., & McCurry, M. C. (1984). School-based parent training: An alternative for parents predicted to demonstrate low teaching proficiency following group training. *Education and Training of the Mentally Retarded, 19*, 261–265.

Balachandran, M. (1985). Behavioral accounting. *Behavioral and Social Sciences Librarian, 4*, 21–27.

Baltes, M. M., Burgess, R. L., & Stewart, R. B. (1980). Independence and dependence in self-care behaviors in nursing home residents: An operant–observational study. *International Journal of Behavioral Development, 3*, 489–500.

Baltes, M. M., Honn, S., Barton, E. M., Orzech, M. J., & Lago, D. (1983). On the social ecology of dependence and independence in elderly nursing home residents: A replication and extension. *Journal of Gerontology, 38*, 556–564.

Bandura, A. (1972). *The process and practice of participant modeling treatment.* Paper presented at a conference on Behavioural Basis of Mental Health, Galway, Ireland.

Bandura, A. (1977). Self-efficacy: Toward a unifying theory of behavioral change. *Psychological Review, 84*, 191–215.

Bandura, A. (1978). Reflections on self-efficacy. *Advances in Behaviour Research and Therapy, 1*, 237–269.

Bandura, A. (1986). *Social foundations of thought and action: A social cognitive theory.* Englewood Cliffs, NJ: Prentice-Hall.

Bandura, A. (in press-a). From thought to action: Mechanisms of personal agency. *New Zealand Journal of Psychology.*

Bandura, A. (in press-b). The self and mechanisms of agency. In J. Suls (Ed.), *Social psychological perspectives on the self.* Hillsdale, NJ: Erlbaum.

Bandura, A., Reese, L., & Adams, N. (1982). Microanalysis of action and fear arousal as a function of differential levels of perceived self-efficacy. *Journal of Personality and Social Psychology, 43*, 5–21.

Bandura, A., & Schunk, D. H. (1981). Cultivating competence, self-efficacy and intrinsic interest through proximal self-motivation. *Journal of Personality and Social Psychology, 41*, 586–598.

Bandura, A., Taylor, C. B., Williams, L., Mefford, I., & Barchas, J. (1985). Catecholamine secretion as a function of perceived coping self-efficacy. *Journal of Clinical and Consulting Psychology, 53*, 406–414.

Bannister, D., & Fransella, F. (1986). *Inquiring man: The psychology of personal constructs* (3rd ed.) London: Croom Helm.

Barak-Glantz, I. L. (1983). Patterns of prisoner misconduct: Toward a behavioral test of prisonization. *Sociological Focus, 16*, 129–146.

Barefoot, J. C., Dahlstrom, W. G., & Williams, R. B., Jr. (1983). Hostility, CHD incidence, and total mortality: 25-year follow-up study of 255 physicians. *Psychosomatic Medicine, 45*, 59–63.

Barkley, R. A. (1987). A review of child behavior rating scales and checklists for research in child psychopathology. In M. Rutter, A. H. Tuma, & I. Lann (Eds.), *Assessment and diagnosis in child psychopathology*. New York: Guilford Press.

Barkley, R. A., Copeland, A. P., & Sivage, C. (1980). A self-control classroom for hyperactive children. *Journal of Autism and Developmental Disorders, 10*, 75–89.

Barkley, R. A., Karlsson, J., Pollard, S., & Murphy, J. V. (1985). Developmental changes in the mother–child interactions of hyperactive boys: Effects of two dose levels of Ritalin. *Journal of Child Psychology and Psychiatry, 26*, 705–715.

Barkley, R. A., Karlsson, J., Strzelecki, E., & Murphy, J. V. (1984). Effects of age on Ritalin dosage on the mother–child interactions of hyperactive children. *Journal of Consulting and Clinical Psychology, 52*, 750–758.

Barling, J., & Bullen, G. (1984). Dietary factors and hyperactivity: A failure to replicate. *Journal of Genetic Psychology, 146*, 117–123.

Barlow, D. H. (Ed.). (1981). *Behavioral assessment of adult disorders*. New York: Guilford Press.

Barlow, D. H., Cohen, A. S., Waddell, M., Vermilyea, B. B., Klosko, J. S., Blanchard, E. B., & DiNardo, P. R. (1984). Panic and generalized anxiety disorders: Nature and treatment. *Behavior Therapy, 15*, 431–449.

Barlow, D. H., Vermilyea, J. Blanchard, E., Vermilyea, B., Dinardo, P. A. & Cerney, J. (1985). The phenomenon of panic. *Journal of Abnormal Psychology, 94*, 320–328.

Barnett, D. W., Zins, J. E., & Wise, L. (1984). An analysis of parental participation as a means of reducing bias in the education of handicapped children. *Special Services in the Schools, 1*, 71–84.

Barone, V. J., Greene, B. F., & Lutzker, J. R. (in press). Home safety with families being treated for child abuse and neglect. *Behavior Modification*.

Barrios, F. X. (1985). A comparison of global and specific estimates of self-control. *Cognitive Therapy and Research, 9*, 455–469.

Barth, R. P., Schinke, S. P., & Maxwell, J. S. (1985). Coping skills training for school-age mothers. *Journal of Social Service Research, 8*, 75–94.

Barton, E. J. (1982). Classroom sharing: A critical analysis of assessment, facilitation, and generalization procedures. In M. Hersen, R. E. Eisler, & P. M. Miller (Eds.), *Progress in behavior modification* (Vol. 13, pp. 1–50). New York: Academic Press.

Barton, E. J., & Ascione, F. R. (1979). Sharing in preschool children: Facilitation, stimulus generalization, response generalization, and maintenance. *Journal of Applied Behavior Analysis, 12*, 417–430.

Baskett, L. M. (1984). Understanding family interactions: Most probable reactions by parents and siblings. *Child and Family Behavior Therapy, 7*, 41–50.

Bauer, W. D., & Twentyman, C. T. (1985). Abusing, neglectful, and comparison mothers' response to child-related and non-child-related stressors. *Journal of Consulting and Clinical Psychology, 53*, 335–343.

Beail, N. (1985). *Reportary grid technique and personal constructs: Application in clinical and educational settings.* London: Croom Helm.

Beck, A. T. (1967). *Depression: Clinical, experimental, and theoretical aspects.* New York: Harper & Row.

Beck, A. T. (1976). *Cognitive therapy and the emotional disorders.* New York: International Universities Press.

Beck, A. T. (1986). Cognitive therapy: A sign of retrogression or progress. *the Behavior Therapist, 9*(1), 2–3.

Beck, A. T., & Emery, G. (1985). *Anxiety disorders and phobias: A cognitive perspective.* New York: Basic Books.

Beck, A. T., Rush, A. J., Shaw, B. F., & Emery, G. (1979). *Cognitive therapy of depression.* New York: Guilford Press.

Beck, A. T., Ward, C. M., Mendelson, M., Mock, J. E., & Erbaugh, J. K. (1961). An inventory for measuring depression. *Archives of General Psychiatry, 4*, 561–571.

Beck, A. T., Weissman, A., Lester, D., & Trexler, L. (1974). The measurement of pessimism: The Hopelessness Scale. *Journal of Consulting and Clinical Psychology, 42*, 861–865.

Belcastro, F. P. (1985). Gifted students and behavior modification. *Behavior Modification, 9*, 155–164.

Belden, B., Braukmann, C., & Wolf, M. (1985). *Psychology as a health care profession:* How healthy was APA's case for the cost-effectiveness of psychological health care? *Psychological Reports, 56*, 391–401.

Bergan, J. R., & Tombari, M. (1976). Consultant skill and efficiency and the implementation and outcomes of consultation. *Journal of School Psychology, 14*, 3–14.

Berkman, L. F. (1983). The assessment of social networks and social support in the elderly. *Journal of the American Geriatrics Society, 31*, 743–749.

Berkman, L. F. (1984). Assessing the physical health effects of social networks and social support. *Annual Review of Public Health, 5*, 413–432.

Berkman, L. F. (1985). Measures of social networks and social support: Evidence and measurement. In A. M. Ostfeld & E. D. Eaker (Eds.), *Measuring psychosocial variables in epidemiologic studies of cardiovascular disease: Proceedings of a workshop* (DHHS Publication No. NIH 85-2270, pp. 51–79). Washington, DC: U.S. Government Printing Office.

Berkman, L. F., & Syme, S. L. (1979). Social networks, host resistance, and mortality: A nine-year follow-up study of Alameda County residents. *American Journal of Epidemiology, 109*, 186–204.

Bernard, M. E., & Joyce, M. R. (1984). *Rational emotive therapy with children and adolescents: Theory, treatment strategies, preventative methods.* New York: Wiley.

Bernstein, D. A., Borkovec, T. D., & Coles, M. G. H. (1986). Assessment of anxiety. In A. R. Ciminero, K. S. Calhoun, & H. E. Adams (Eds.), *Handbook of behavioral assessment* (2nd ed.). New York: Wiley.

Bernstein, G. S. (1982). Training behavior change agents: A conceptual review. *Behavior Therapy, 13*, 1–23.

Bernstein, G. S. (1984). Training of behavior change agents. In M. Hersen, R. M. Eisler, & P. M. Miller (Eds.). *Progress in behavior modification* (Vol. 17, pp. 167–199). New York: Academic Press.

Bernstein, G. S., & Ziarnik, J. P. (1984). Training behavior change agents in outcome selection. *the Behavior Therapist, 7*, 103–104.

Betz, B. J., & Thomas, C. B. (1979). Individual temperament as a predictor of health or premature disease. *Johns Hopkins Medical Journal, 144*, 81–89.

Bierley, C., McSweeney, F. K., & Vannieuwerk, R. (1985). Classical conditions of preferences for stimuli. *Journal of Consumer Research, 12*, 316–323.

Biglan, A., Hops, H., Sherman, L., Friedman, L. S., Arthur, J., & Osteen, V. (1985). Problem-solving interactions of depressed women and their husbands. *Behavior Therapy, 16*, 431–451.

Billings, D. C., & Wasik, B. H. (1985). Self-instructional training with preschoolers: An attempt to replicate. *Journal of Applied Behavior Analysis, 18*, 61–67.

Biran, M., Augusto, F., & Wilson, G. T. (1981). A comparative analysis of cognitive and behavioural methods in the treatment of scriptophobia. *Behaviour Research and Therapy, 19*, 525–532.

Birleson, P. (1981). The validity of depressive disorders and the development of a self-rating scale: A research report. *Journal of Child Psychiatry and Psychology, 22*, 73–88.

Black, J. L., Muehlenhard, C. L., & Massey, F. H. (1985). Social skills training to improve job maintenance. *Journal of Employment Counseling, 22*, 151–159.

Blackburn, H., Luepker, R., Kline, F. G., Bracht, N., Carlaw, R., Jacobs, D., Mittelmark, M., Stauffer, L., & Taylor, H. L. (1984). The Minnesota Heart Health Program: A research and demonstration project in cardiovascular disease prevention. In J. D. Matarazzo, S. M. Weiss, J. A. Herd, N. E. Miller, & S. M. Weiss (Eds.), *Behavioral health: A handbook of health enhancement and disease prevention* (pp. 1171–1178). New York: Wiley.

Blackman, D. E. (1982). Psychologists and the community: Influence and counter influence. *Bulletin of the British Psychological Society, 35*, 334–341.

Blackwell, R. T., Galassi, J. P., Galassi, M. D., & Watson, T. E. (1985). Are cognitive assessments equal? A comparison of think aloud and thought listing. *Cognitive Therapy and Research, 9*, 399–413.

Blagg, N. R., & Yule, W. (1984). The behavioural treatment of school refusal—a comparative study. *Behaviour Research and Therapy, 22*, 119–127.

Bland, K., & Hallam, R. (1981). Relationship between response to graded exposure and marital satisfaction in agoraphobics. *Behaviour Research and Therapy, 19*, 335–338.

Blanton, P. D., & Gouvier, W. D. (1986). Cognitive retraining therapies for neurologically impaired patients. *the Behavior Therapist, 3*, 47–50.

Blechman, E. A. (Ed.). (1984). *Behavior modification with women.* New York: Guilford Press.

Blechman, E. A. (1985). *Solving child behavior problems at home and at school.* Champaign, IL: Research Press.

Bloch, S., & Lambert, M. (1985). What price psychotherapy? *British Journal of Psychiatry, 146*, 96–98.

Boehringer Mannheim. (1986). *Reflotron–cholesterol screening set* (Catalog No. 881937). Indianapolis, IN: Author.

Bonham, G. S., & Brock, D. B. (1985). The relationship of diabetes with race, sex, and obesity. *American Journal of Clinical Nutrition, 41*, 776–783.

Borkovec, T. (1982). Facilitation and inhibition of functional CS exposure in the treatment of phobias. In J. Boulougouris (Ed.), *Learning theory approaches to psychiatry* (pp. 95–102). Chichester, England: Wiley.

Bornstein, P. H., & Quevillon, R. P. (1976). The effects of a self-instructional package on overactive preschool boys. *Journal of Applied Behavior Analysis, 9*, 179–188.

Boudewyns, P., Fry, T. J., & Nightingale, E. J. (1986). Token economy programs in VA Medical Centers: Where are they today? *the Behavior Therapist, 9*, 126–127.

Bower, G. H. (1981). Mood and memory. *American Psychologist, 36*, 129–148.

Bowers, D. S., Clement, P. W., Fantuzzo, J. W., & Sorensen, D. A. (1985). Effects of teacher-administered and self-administered reinforcers on learning disabled children. *Behavior Therapy, 16*, 357–369.

Braswell, L., & Kendall, P. C. (1987). Cognitive–behavioral therapies for children. In K. Dobson (Ed.), *Handbook of cognitive–behavioral therapies*. New York: Guilford Press.

Braswell, L., Kendall, P. C., Braith, J. A., Carey, M. P., & Vye, C. (1985). "Involvement" in cognitive–behavioral therapy with children: Process and its relationship to outcome. *Cognitive Therapy and Research, 9*, 611–630.

Braukmann, C., Belden, B., & Wolf, M. (1985). Considering the preponderance of evidence: A reply to Cummings. *Psychological Reports, 57*, 856–858.

Breckenridge, J. S., Zeiss, A. M., Breckenridge, J. N., Gallagher, D., & Thompson, L. W. (1985). Solicitation of elderly depressives for treatment outcome research: A comparison of referral sources. *Journal of Consulting and Clinical Psychology, 53*, 552–554.

Breiner, J., & Forehand, R. (1982). Mother–child interactions: A comparison of a clinic referred developmentally delayed group and two non-delayed groups. *Applied Research in Mental Retardation, 3*, 175–183.

Breiner, J., & Young, D. L. (1985). Social interaction: A comparison of mothers with noncompliant, non-delayed and developmentally delayed children. *Child and Family Behavior Therapy, 7*, 1–6.

Breuning, S. E., Davis, V. J., & Poling, A. D. (1982). Pharmacotherapy with the mentally retarded: Implications for clinical psychologists. *Clinical Psychology Review, 2*, 79–114.

Bridge, W., Dunn, P., & Speight, I. (1981). The provison of post-basic education in psychiatric nursing. *Nursing Times, 77*, 141–144.

Brigham, T. A., Hopper, C., Hill, B., deArmas, A., & Newsom, P. (1985). A self-management program for disruptive adolescents in the school: A clinical replication analysis. *Behavior Therapy, 16*, 99–115.

Bronfenbrenner, U. (1979). *The ecology of human development: Experiments by nature and design*. Cambridge, MA: Harvard University Press.

Brown, A. L., & Palinscar, A. S. (in press). Reciprocal teaching of comprehension strategies: A natural history of one program for enhancing learning. In J. Borkowski & J. D. Day (Eds.), *Intelligence and cognition in special children: Comparative studies of giftedness, mental retardation, and learning disabilities*. Norwood, NJ: Ablex.

Brown, D. K., Kratochwill, T. R., & Bergan, J. R. (1982). Teaching interview skills for problem identification: An analogue study. *Behavioral Assessment, 4*, 63–73.

Brown, R. T., & Alford, N. (1984). Ameliorating attention deficits and concomitant academic deficiencies in learning disabled children through cognitive training. *Journal of Learning Disabilities, 17*, 20–26.

Brown, S. A. (1985). Expectancies versus background with prediction of college drinking patterns. *Journal of Consulting and Clinical Psychology, 53*, 123–130.

Brown, S. A., Goldman, M. S., & Christiansen, B. A. (1985). Do alcohol expectancies mediate drinking patterns of adults? *Journal of Consulting and Clinical Psychology, 53*(4), 512–519.

Brownell, K. D. (1985a). Behavioral medicine. In C. M. Franks, G. T. Wilson, P. C. Kendall, & K. D. Brownell (Eds.), *Annual review of behavior therapy: Theory and practice* (Vol. 10, pp. 164–187). New York: Guilford Press.

Brownell, K. D. (1985b). *The LEARN manual for weight control*. Philadelphia, PA: Author.

Brownell, K. D., Greenwood, M. R. C., Stellar, E., & Shrager, E. E. (1986). The effects of repeated cycles of weight loss and regain in rats. *Physiology and Behavior, 38*, 459–464.

Brownell, K. D., Heckerman, C. L., Westlake, R. J., Hayes, S. C., & Monti, P. M. (1978).

The effect of couples training and partner co-operativeness in the behavioural treatment of obesity. *Behaviour Research and Therapy, 16*, 323–333.

Brownell, K. D., Marlatt, G. A., Lichtenstein, E., & Wilson, G. T. (1986). Understanding and preventing relapse. *American Psychologist, 41*, 765–782.

Brownell, K. D., & Stunkard, A. J. (1981). Couples training, pharmacotherapy, and behavior therapy in the treatment of obesity. *Archives of General Psychiatry, 38*, 1224–1229.

Brownell, K. D., & Wadden, T. A. (1986). Behavior therapy for obesity: Modern approaches and better results. In K. D. Brownell & J. P. Foreyt (Eds.), *Handbook of eating disorders: Physiology, psychology, and treatment of obesity, anorexia, and bulimia* (pp. 180–197). New York: Basic Books.

Bruch, M. A., Kaflowitz, N. G., & Kuethe, M. (1986). Beliefs and the subjective meaning of thoughts: Analysis of the role of self-statements in academic test performance. *Cognitive Therapy and Research, 10*, 51–69.

Bryant, L. E., & Budd, K. S. (1984). Teaching behaviorally handicapped preschool children to share. *Journal of Applied Behavior Analysis, 17*, 45–56.

Budd, K. S., & O'Brien, T. P. (1982). Father involvement in behavioral parent training: An area in need of research. *the Behavior Therapist, 5*, 85–90.

Budman, S. H. (Ed.). (1981). *Forms of brief therapy*. New York: Guilford Press.

Buglass, D., Clarke, J., Henderson, A., Kreitman, N., & Presley, A. (1977). A study of agoraphobic housewives. *Psychological Medicine, 7*, 73–86.

Burchard, J. D., & Harrington, W. A. (1985). Deinstitutionalization: Programmed transition from the institution to the community. *Child and Family Behavior Therapy, 7*, 13–25.

Butler, G. (1985). Exposure as a treatment for social phobia: Some instructive difficulties. *Behaviour Research and Therapy, 23*, 651–658.

Butler, G., & Mathews, A. (1983). Cognitive processes in anxiety. *Advances in Behaviour Research and Therapy, 5*, 51–62.

Butler, G., Cullington, A., Munby, M., Amies, P., & Gelder, M. (1984). Exposure and anxiety management in the treatment of social phobia. *Journal of Consulting and Clinical Psychology, 52*, 642–649.

Button, E. (1985). *Personal construct theory and mental health*. London: Croom Helm.

Caddy, G. R. (1978). Toward a multivariate analysis of alcohol abuse. In P. E. Nathan, G. A. Marlatt, & T. Loberg (Eds.), *Alcoholism: New directions in behavioral research and treatment* (pp. 71–117). New York: Plenum Press.

Caddy, G. R., Addington, H. J., & Perkins, D. (1978). Individualized behavior therapy for alcoholics: A third year independent double-blind follow-up. *Behaviour Research and Therapy, 16*, 345–362.

Caddy, G. R., & Block, T. (1983). Behavioral treatment methods for alcoholism. In M. Galanter (Ed.), *Recent developments in alcoholism* (Vol. 1, pp. 139–165). New York: Plenum Press.

Caetano, R. (1985). *Patterns and problems of drinking among U.S. Hispanics*. Unpublished manuscript, Task Force on Black and Minority Health, U.S. Department of Health and Human Services.

Callaway, C. W., & Greenwood, M. R. C. (1984). Introduction to the workshop on methods for characterizing human obesity. *International Journal of Obesity, 8*, 477–480.

Camp, B. W. (Ed.). (1980). *Advances in behavioral pediatrics* (Vol. 1). Greenwich, CT: JAI Press.

Campbell, S. B. (1985). Research issues in clinical child psychology. In A. S. Bellack & M. Hersen (Eds.), *Research methods in clinical psychology* (pp. 324–352). New York: Pergamon Press.

Cantor, N., & Mischel, W. (1979). Prototypes in person perception. In L. Berkowitz (Ed.), *Advances in experimental social psychology* (Vol. 12, pp. 3–52). New York: Academic Press.

Carey, M. P., Kelley, M. L., Buss, R. R., & Scott, W. O. N. (1986). Relationship of activity to depression in adolescents: Development of the Adolescent Activities Checklist. *Journal of Consulting and Clinical Psychology, 54*, 320–322.

Carlson, B. E. (1984). The father's contribution to child care: Effects on children's perceptions of parental roles. *American Journal of Orthopsychiatry, 54*, 123–136.

Carney, R. M., Schechter, K., & Davis, T. (1983). Improving adherence to blood glucose testing in insulin-dependent diabetic children. *Behavior Therapy, 14*, 146–154.

Carpenter, P. (1984). "Green stamp therapy" revisited: The evolution of 12 years of behavior modification and psychoeducational techniques with young delinquent boys. *Psychological Reports, 54*, 99–111.

Carpenter, P., & Carom, R. (1968). Green stamp therapy: Modification of delinquent behavior through food trading stamps. *Proceedings of the 76th Annual Convention of the American Psychological Association, 3*, 531–532.

Carr, E. G., & Kologinsky, E. (1983). Acquisition of sign language by autistic children: II. Spontaneity and generalization effects. *Journal of Applied Behavior Analysis, 16*, 297–314.

Carson, T. P. (1986). Assessment of depression. In A. R. Ciminero, K. S. Calhoun, & H. E. Adams (Eds.), *Handbook of behavioral assessment* (2nd ed.). New York: Wiley.

Cartledge, G., Frew, T., & Zaharias, J. (1985). Social skill needs of mainstream students: Peer and teacher perceptions. *Learning Disability Quarterly, 8*, 132–140.

Cassileth, B. R., Lusk, E. J., Miller, D. S., Brown, L. L., & Miller, C. (1985). Psychosocial correlates of survival in advanced malignant disease? *New England Journal of Medicine, 312*, 1551–1555.

Certo, N., Haring, N., & York, R. (Eds.). (1984). *Public school integration of severely handicapped students: Rational issues and progressive alternatives*. Baltimore: Paul H. Brookes.

Chamberlain, P., Patterson, G., Reid, J., Kavanagh, K., & Forgatch, M. (1984). Observation of client resistance. *Behavior Therapy, 15*, 144–155.

Chambless, D. L. (1985). The relationship of severity of agoraphobia to associated psychopathology. *Behaviour Research and Therapy, 23*, 305–310.

Chambless, D. L., Caputo, G., Bright, P., & Gallagher, R. (1984). Assessment of fear of fear in agoraphobics: The Body Sensations Questionnaire and the Agoraphobic Cognitions Questionnaire. *Journal of Consulting and Clinical Psychology, 52*, 1090–1097.

Chambless, D. L., Caputo, G., Jasin, S., Gracely, E., & Williams, C. (1985). The Mobility Inventory for Agoraphobia. *Behaviour Research and Therapy, 23*, 35–44.

Chambless, D. L., Foa, E. B., Groves, G. A., & Goldstein, A. J. (1982). Exposure and communications training in the treatment of agoraphobia. *Behaviour Research and Therapy, 20*, 219–231.

Chambless, D. L., & Goldstein, A. (Eds.). (1982). *Agoraphobia*. New York: Wiley.

Chandler, W. U. (1986). *Banishing tobacco* (Worldwatch Paper 68). Washington, DC: Worldwatch Institute.

Chaney, E. F., O'Leary, M. R., & Marlatt, G. A. (1978). Skill training with alcoholics. *Journal of Consulting and Clinical Psychology, 46*, 1092–1104.

Chapman, L. J., & Chapman, J. P. (1967). Genesis of popular but erroneous diagnostic observations. *Journal of Abnormal Psychology, 72*, 193–204.

Charlop, M. H., Schreibman, L., Mason, J., & Vesey, W. (1983). Behavior-setting interactions of autistic children: A behavioral mapping approach to assessing classroom behaviors. *Analysis and Intervention in Developmental Disabilities, 3*, 359–373.

Chase, P. N., & Wylie, R. G. (1985). Doctoral training in behavior analysis: Training generalized problem-solving skills. *The Behavior Analyst, 8*, 159–176.

Chassin, L., Presson, C., Sherman, S. J., McLaughlin, L., & Gioia, D. (1985). Psychosocial correlates of adolescent smokeless tobacco use. *Addictive Behaviors, 10*, 431–435.

Chesney, M. A., & Rosenman, R. H. (Eds.). (1985). *Anger and hostility in cardiovascular and behavioral disorders*. Washington, DC: Hemisphere.

Chhokar, J. S., & Wallin, J. A. (1984). Improving safety through applied behavior analysis. *Journal of Safety Research, 15*, 141–151.

Christen, A. G. (1986). History of smokeless tobacco use in the United States. In W. J. Blot, G. Boyd, & J. M. Elliott (Eds.), *Proceedings of NIH Consensus Development Conference: Health implications of smokeless tobacco use* (pp. 21–24). Bethesda, MD: National Institutes of Health.

Christen, A. G., Swanson, B. Z., Glover, E. D., & Henderson, A. H. (1982). Smokeless tobacco: The folklore and social history of snuffing, sneezing, dipping, and chewing. *Journal of the American Dental Association, 105*, 821–829.

Christensen, L., & Mendoza, J. L. (1986). A method of assessing change in a single subject: An alteration of the RC Index. *Behavior Therapy, 17*(3), 305–308.

Christiansen, B. A., & Goldman, M. S. (1983). Alcohol-related expectancies versus demographic/background variables in the prediction of adolescent drinking. *Journal of Consulting and Clinical Psychology, 51*, 249–258.

Christie, D. J., Hiss, M., & Lozanoff, B. (1984). Modification of inattentive classroom behavior: Hyperactive children's use of self-recording with teacher guidance. *Behavior Modification, 8*, 391–406.

Christoff, K. A., Scott, W. O. N., Kelley, M. L., Schlundt, D., Baer, G., & Kelly, J. A. (1985). Social skills and social problem-solving training for shy young adolescents. *Behavior Therapy, 16*, 468–477.

Christopherson, E. R., Cataldo, M. F., Russo, D. C., & Varni, T. W. (1984). Behavioral pediatrics: Establishing and maintaining a program of training, research, and clinical service. *the Behavior Therapist*, 7, 43–46.

Ciminero, A. (1986). In A. Ciminero, K. Calhoun, & H. Adams (Eds.), *Handbook of behavioral assessment* (2nd ed.). New York: Wiley.

Ciminero, A., Calhoun, K., & Adams, H. (Eds.). (1986). *Handbook of behavioral assessment* (2nd ed.). New York: Wiley.

Clarizio, H. F. (1985). Cognitive–behavioral treatment of childhood depression. *Psychology in the Schools, 22*, 308–322.

Clark, D. B., & Baker, B. L. (1983). Predicting outcome in parent training. *Journal of Consulting and Clinical Psychology, 51*, 309–311.

Clark, D. M. (1986). A cognitive approach to panic. *Behaviour Research and Therapy, 24*, 461–470.

Clark, D. M., Salkovskis, P. M., & Chalkley, A. J. (1985). Respiratory control as a treatment for panic attacks. *Journal of Behavior Therapy and Experimental Psychiatry, 16*, 23–30.

Clark, H. B., Wadden, T. A., Brownell, K. D., Gordon, S. G., & Tarte, R. D. (1983). Sources of continuing education for behavior therapists: The utility of journals, conferences, and other informational sources. *the Behavior Therapist, 6*, 23–26.

Clemmer, D. (1958). *The prison community*. New York: Holt.

Cobb, J., Mathews, A. M., Childs-Clarke, A., & Blowers, C. M. (1985). The spouse as co-therapist in the treatment of agoraphobia. *British Journal of Psychiatry, 144*, 282–287.

Cohen, L. D., & Cooley, S. G. (1983). Psychology training programs for direct service to the aging (Status report: 1980). *Professional Psychology, 14*, 720–728.

Cohen, L. H., Sargent, M. M., & Sechrest, L. (1986). Use of psychotherapy research by professional psychologists. *American Psychologist, 41*, 198–206.

Coleman, R. S., & Whitman, T. L. (1984). Developing, generalizing, and maintaining physical fitness in mentally retarded adults: Toward a self-directed program. *Analysis and Intervention in Developmental Disabilities, 4*, 109–127.

Coleman, S. B. (Ed.). (1985). *Failures in family therapy*. New York: Guilford Press.

Colletti, G., Supnick, J. A., & Rizzo, A. A. (1981, August). *An analysis of relapse determinants for treated smokers*. Paper presented at the meeting of the American Psychological Association, Los Angeles.

Collins, F. (1986). Therapist behavior in behavior therapy: Comments on Thompson and Williams (1985) and Wolpe (1985). *the Behavior Therapist, 9*, 5–6.

Collins, R. L., & McNair, L. D. (1986). Black women and behavior therapy: Exploring the biases. *the Behavior Therapist, 9*, 7–10.

Collins, R. L., Parks, G. A., & Marlatt, G. A. (1985). Social determinants of alcohol consumption: The effects of social interaction and model status on the self-administration of alcohol. *Journal of Consulting and Clinical Psychology, 53*, 189–200.

Collins, R. L., Rothblum, E., & Wilson, G. T. (1986). The comparative efficacy of cognitive and behavioral approaches to the treatment of obesity. *Cognitive Therapy and Research, 10*, 299–318.

Colvin, R. H., & Olson, S. B. (1983). A descriptive analysis of men and women who have lost significant weight and are highly successful at maintaining the loss. *Addictive Behaviors, 8*, 287–295.

Condiotte, M. M., & Lichtenstein, E. (1981). Self-efficacy and relapse in smoking cessation programs. *Journal of Consulting and Clinical Psychology, 49*, 648–658.

Conners, C. K. (1980). *Food additives and hyperactive children*. New York: Plenum Press.

Consensus Conference. (1985). Lowering blood cholesterol to prevent heart disease. *Journal of the American Medical Association, 253*, 2080–2086.

Consensus Conference. (1986). Health applications of smokeless tobacco use. *Journal of the American Medical Association, 255*, 1045–1048.

Cordray, D. S., & Bootzin, R. R. (1983). Placebo control conditions: Tests of theory or of effectiveness? *Behavioral and Brain Sciences, 6*, 180–187.

Cormier, W. H., Otani, A., & Cormier, L. S. (1986). The effects of problem-solving training on two problem-solving tasks. *Cognitive Therapy and Research, 10*, 95–108.

Cottier, C., Shapiro, K., & Julius, S. (1984). Treatment of mild hypertension with progressive muscle relaxation: Predictive value of indexes of sympathetic tone. *Archives of Internal Medicine, 144*, 1954–1958.

Council on Scientific Affairs. (1986). Health effects of smokeless tobacco. *Journal of the American Medical Association, 255*, 1038–1044.

Cowart, J. D., Iwata, B. A., & Poynter, H. (1984). Generalization and maintenance in training parents of the mentally retarded. *Applied Research in Mental Retardation, 5*, 233–244.

Cox, T., & Mackay, C. (1982). Psychosocial factors and psychophysiological mechanisms in the aetiology and development of cancer. *Social Science and Medicine, 16*, 381–396.

Cox, V. C., Paulus, P. B., & McCain, G. (1984). Prison crowding research: The relevance for prison housing standards and a general approach regarding crowding phenomena. *American Psychologist, 39*, 1148–1160.

Craig, K. D., & McMahon, R. S. (Eds.). (1983). *Advances in clinical behavior therapy*. New York: Brunner/Mazel.

Craighead, L. W. (1984). Sequencing of behavior therapy and pharmacotherapy for obesity. *Journal of Consulting and Clinical Psychology, 52*, 190–199.

Craighead, L. W., Stunkard, A. J., & O'Brien, R. M. (1981). Behavior therapy and pharmacotherapy for obesity. *Archives of General Psychiatry, 38*, 763–768.

Craighead, W. E., Meyers, A. W., & Wilcoxon-Craighead, L. (1985). A conceptual model for cognitive-behavior therapy with children. *Journal of Abnormal Child Psychology, 13*(3), 331–342.

Crews, F. (1986). *Skeptikal engagements*. New York: Oxford University Press.

Cronbach, L. J., & Glaser, G. C. (1965). *Psychological tests and personnel decisions*. Urbana, IL: University of Illinois Press.

Cronbach, L. J., & Meehl, P. E. (1955). Construct validity in psychological tests. *Psychological Bulletin, 52*, 281–302.

Cross, J. G. (1983). *A theory of adaptive economic behaviour*. Cambridge, England: Cambridge University Press.

Cullen, J. W., Blot, W., Henningfield, J., Boyd, G., Mecklenburg, R., & Massey, M. M. (1986). Health consequences of using smokeless tobacco: Summary of the Advisory Committee's Report to the Surgeon General. *Public Health Reports, 101*, 355–373.

Cummings, N. A. (1985). Comment on Belden, Braukmann, and Wolf. *Psychological Reports, 56*, 874.

Cunningham, C. (1985). Training and education approaches for parents of children with special needs. *British Journal of Medical Psychology, 58*, 285–305.

Cuvo, A. J., Gonzalez, P. A., & O'Brien, S. (1985). Social validation of heterosexual social behavior in community settings: A comparison of mentally retarded and non-mentally retarded adults. *Applied Research in Mental Retardation, 6*, 429–435.

Dahlkoetter, J., Callahan, E. J., & Linton, J. (1979). Obesity and the unbalanced energy equation: Exercise versus eating habit change. *Journal of Consulting and Clinical Psychology, 47*, 898–905.

Dangel, R. F., & Polster, R. A. (Eds.). (1984). *Parent training: Foundations of research and practice*. New York: Guilford Press.

Davis, D. L. (1986). Smokeless tobacco products and their production in the United States. In W. J. Blot, G. Boyd, & J. M. Elliott (Eds.), *Proceedings of NIH Consensus Development Conference: Health implications of smokeless tobacco use* (pp. 17–20). Bethesda, MD: National Institutes of Health.

Davis, R. M. (1986). Promotion of cigarettes in developing countries. *Journal of the American Medical Association, 255*, 993.

Day, D. E., & Roberts, M. W. (1983). An analysis of the physical punishment component of a parent training program. *Journal of Abnormal Child Psychology, 11*, 141–152.

Day, R. M., Fox, J. J., Shores, R. E., Lindeman, D. P., & Stowitschek, J. J. (1983). The Social Competence Intervention Project: Developing educational procedures for teaching social intervention skills to handicapped children. *Behavioral Disorders, 8*, 120–127.

Deardorff, W. W., & Funabiki, D. (1985). A diagnostic caution in screening for depressed college students. *Cognitive Therapy and Research, 9*, 277–284.

De Backer, G., Kornitzer, M., Thilly, C., & Depoorter, A. M. (1977). The Belgian Multifactor Preventive Trial in CVD: Design and methodology. *Hart Bulletin, 8*, 143–146.

Delamater, A. M., Conners, C. K., & Wells, K. C. (1984). A comparison of staff training procedures: Behavioral applications in the chid psychiatric inpatient setting. *Behavior Modification, 8*, 39–58.

Dellario, D. J., & Anthony, W. A. (1981). On the relative effectiveness of institutional alternative placement for the psychiatrically disabled. *Journal of Social Issues, 37*, 21–33.

Denkowski, G. C., & Denkowski, K. M. (1985). Community-based residential treatment of the mentally retarded adolescent offender: Phase 1. Reduction of aggressive behavior. *Journal of Community Psychology, 13*, 299–305.

Denny, M. R. (1976). Post-aversive relief and relaxation and their implications for behavior therapy. *Journal of Behavior Therapy and Experimental Psychiatry, 7*, 315–322.

Dershewitz, R. A., & Christopherson, E. R. (1984). Childhood household safety: An overview. *American Journal of Diseases of Children, 138*, 85–88.

DeRubeis, R. J., Hollon, S. D., Evans, M. D., & Bemis, K. M. (1982). Can psychotherapies for depression be discriminated? A systematic investigation of cognitive therapy and interpersonal therapy. *Journal of Consulting and Clinical Psychology, 50*, 744–756.

DeSilva, P., & Rachman, S. (1981). Is exposure a necessary condition for fear-reduction? *Behaviour Research and Therapy, 19*, 227–232.

DeSilva, P., & Rachman, S. (1984). Does escape behaviour strengthen agoraphobic avoidance? A preliminary study. *Behaviour Research and Therapy, 22*, 87–90.

Dickens, B. M., Doob, A. N., Warwick, O. H., & Winegard, W. C. (1982). *Report of the committee of enquiry into allegations concerning Drs. Linda and Mark Sobell.* Toronto: Addiction Research Foundation.

DiClemente, C. C. (1981). Self-efficacy and smoking cessation maintenance: A preliminary report. *Cognitive Therapy and Research, 5*, 175–187.

Dobson, K. (Ed.). (1987). *Handbook of cognitive–behavioral therapies.* New York: Guilford Press.

Dobson, K. S., & Shaw, B. F. (1986). Cognitive assessment with major depressive disorders. *Cognitive Therapy and Research, 10*, 13–29.

Dodge, K. A. (1985). Attributional bias in aggressive children. In P. C. Kendall (Ed.), *Advances in cognitive–behavioral research and therapy* (Vol. 4, pp. 73–110). New York: Academic Press.

Doll, R., & Peto, R.(1981). *The causes of cancer.* New York: Oxford University Press.

Donnellan, A. M., & Neel, R. S. (1986). New directions in educating students with autism. In R. H. Horner, L. H. Meyer, & H. D. Bud Fredericks (Eds.), *Education of learners with severe handicaps: Exemplary service strategies* (pp. 99–126). Baltimore: Paul H. Brookes.

Dumas, J., & Wahler, R. G. (1983). Predictors of treatment outcome in patient training: Mother insularity and socio-economic disadvantage. *Behavioral Assessment, 5*, 301–313.

Dumas, J., & Wahler, R. G. (1985). Indiscriminate mothering as a contextual factor in aggressive–oppositional child behavior: "Damned if you do and damned if you don't." *Journal of Abnormal Child Psychology, 13*, 1–17.

Dunlap, G., & Johnson, J. (1985). Increasing the independent responding of autistic children with unpredictable supervision. *Journal of Applied Behavior Analysis, 18*, 227–236.

Durand, V. M. (1983). Behavioral ecology of a staff incentive program: Effects on absenteeism and resident disruptive behavior. *Behavior Modification, 7*, 165–181.

Durand, V. M. (1985). Employee absenteeism: A selective review of antecedents and consequences. *Journal of Organizational Behavior Management, 7*, 135–167.

D'Zurilla, T. (1986). *Problem-solving therapy: A social competence approach to clinical intervention.* New York: Springer.

D'Zurilla, T., & Nezu, A. (1982). Social problem solving in adults. In P. C. Kendall

(Ed.), *Advances in cognitive–behavioral research and therapy* (Vol. 1, 202–274). New York: Academic Press.

Eaker, E. D. (1985). Personality characteristics: Working group summary. In A. M. Ostfeld & E. D. Eaker (Eds.), *Measuring psychosocial variables in epidemiologic studies of cardiovascular disease: Proceedings of a workshop* (DHHS Publication No. NIH 85-2270, pp. 363–365). Washington, DC: U.S. Government Printing Office.

Edelstein, B. A., & Couture, E. T. (Eds.). (1984). *Behavioral assessment and rehabilitation of the traumatically brain-damaged*. New York: Plenum Press.

Edmundson, E. W., Glover, E. D., Alston, P. P., & Holbert, D. (in press). A comparison of personality traits of smokeless tobacco users and nonusers. *International Journal of the Addictions*.

Edmundson, E. W., Glover, E. D., Holbert, D., Alston, P. P., & Schroeder, K. L. (in press). Personality profiles associated with smokeless tobacco use patterns. *Addictive Behaviors*.

Eelen, P. (1982). Conditioning and attribution. In J. Boulougouris (Ed.), *Learning theory approaches to psychiatry* (pp. 3–18). Chichester, England: Wiley.

Egelston, J. D., Sluyter, G. V., Murie, S. S., & Hobbs, T. (1984). Trends in the use of restrictive and aversive procedures in a facility for developmentally disabled persons. *Education and Training of the Mentally Retarded, 19*, 306–311.

Eifert, G. H. (1984). Cognitive behaviour therapy: A critical evaluation of its theoretical–empirical bases and therapeutic efficacy. *Australian Psychologist, 19*, 179–191.

Elder, J. P., McGraw, S. A., Abrams, D. B., Ferreira, A., Lasater, T. M., Longpre, H., Peterson, G. S., Schwertfeger, R., & Carleton, R. A. (1986). Organizational and community approaches to community-wide prevention of heart disease: The first two years of the Pawtucket Heart Health Program. *Preventive Medicine, 15*, 107–117.

Ellis, A. (1962). *Reason and emotion in psychotherapy*. New York: Lyle Stuart.

Ellis, A. (1985). *Overcoming resistance: Rational–emotive therapy with difficult clients*. New York: Springer.

Ellis, A., & Bernard, M. E. (Eds.). (1983). *Rational–emotive approaches to the problems of childhood*. New York: Plenum Press.

Ellis, A., & Grieger, R. (Eds.). (1977). *Handbook of rational–emotive therapy*. New York: Springer.

Emery, R. E., & Marholin, D. (1977). An applied behavior analysis of delinquency: The irrelevancy of relevant behavior. *American Psychologist, 6*, 860–873.

Emmelkamp, P. M. G. (1982). *Phobia and obsessive–compulsive disorders*. New York: Plenum.

Emmelkamp, P. M. G., Mersch, P., Vissia, E., & van der Helm, M. (1985). Social phobia: A comparative evaluation of cognitive and behavioural interventions. *Behaviour Research and Therapy, 23*, 365–369.

Emrick, C. D. (1982). Evaluation of alcoholism psychotherapy methods. In E. M. Pattison & E. Kaufman (Eds.), *Encyclopedic handbook of alcoholism* (pp. 1152–1169). New York: Gardner Press.

Emrick, C. D., & Hansen, J. (1983). Assertions regarding effectiveness of treatment for alcoholism: Fact or fantasy? *American Psychologist, 38*, 1078–1088.

Epstein, L. H., Wing, R. R., Koeske, R., Ossip, D., & Beck, S. (1982). A comparison of lifestyle change and programmed aerobic exercise on weight and fitness changes in obese children. *Behavior Therapy, 13*, 651–665.

Epstein, L. H., Wing, R. R., Koeske, R., & Valoski, A. (1984). Effects of diet plus exercise on weight change in parents and children. *Journal of Consulting and Clinical Psychology, 52*, 429–437.

Epstein, L. H., Wing, R. R., Koeske, R., & Valoski, A. (1985). A comparison of lifestyle exercise, aerobic exercise, and calisthenics on weight loss in obese children. *Behavior Therapy, 16*, 345–356.

Erwin, E. (1978). *Behavior therapy: Scientific, philosophical and moral foundations*. New York: Cambridge University Press.

Erwin, E. (1984). Establishing causal connections: Meta-analysis and psychotherapy. *Midwest Studies in Philosophy, 9*, 421–436.

Evans, I. M., & Meyer, L. H. (1985). *An educative approach to behavior problems: A practical model for interventions with severely handicapped learners*. Baltimore: Paul H. Brookes.

Eyberg, S. M. (1985). Behavioral assessment: Advancing methodology in pediatric psychology. *Journal of Pediatric Psychology, 10*, 123–139.

Eysenck, H. J. (1952). The effects of psychotherapy: An evaluation. *Journal of Consulting Psychology, 16*, 319–324.

Eysenck, H. J. (1983). The benefits of psychotherapy. *Behaviour Research and Therapy, 21*, 315–320.

Eysenck, H. J. (1985). H. Gwynne Jones, 1918–1985—an appreciation. *Behavioural Psychotherapy, 13*, 171–173.

Eysenck, H. J., & Rachman, S. (1965). *The causes and cures of neurosis*. London: Routledge & Kegan Pual.

Falls, H. B., Baylor, A. M., & Dishman, R. K. (1980). *Essentials of fitness*. Philadelphia: Saunders College.

Fantino, E. (1985). Behavior analysis and behavioral ecology: A synergistic coupling. *The Behavior Analyst, 8*, 151–157.

Farquhar, J. W. (1978). The community-based model of life style intervention trials. *American Journal of Epidemiology, 108*, 103–111.

Farquhar, J. W., Fortmann, S. P., Flora, J. A., Taylor, C. B., Haskell, W. L., Williams, P. T., & Maccoby, N. (1986, March). *Interim results of the Stanford Five City Project*. Paper presented at the Cardiovascular Behavioral Medicine, Epidemiology and Biostatistics Training Session, San Francisco.

Farquhar, J. W., Fortmann, S. P., Maccoby, N., Wood, P. D., Haskell, W. L., Taylor, C. B., Flora, J. A., Solomon, D. S., Rogers, T., Adler, E., Breitrose, P., & Weiner, L. (1984). The Stanford Five City Project: An overview. In J. D. Matarazzo, S. M. Weiss, J. A. Herd, N. E. Miller, & S. M. Weiss (Eds.), *Behavioral health: A handbook of health enhancement and disease prevention* (pp. 1154–1165). New York: Wiley.

Farquhar, J. W., Maccoby, N., Wood, P. D., Alexander, J. K., Breitrose, H., Brown, B. W., Jr., Haskell, W. L., McAlister, A. L., Meyer, A. J., Nash, J. D., & Stern, M. P. (1977). Community education for cardiovascular health. *Lancet, i*, 1192–1195.

Farquhar, J. W., & Wood, P. D. (1985, June). *Community organization for healthy lifestyles and disease prevention*. Paper presented at the International Conference on Preventive Cardiology, Moscow.

Farrell, P. (Ed.). (1985). *EDY—Its impact on staff training in mental handicap*. Manchester, England: Manchester University Press.

Federal Bureau of Investigation. (1984). *Uniform crime reports of the United States, 1983*. Washington, DC: U.S. Department of Justice.

Feindler, E. L., Marriott, S. A., & Iwata, M. (1984). Group anger control training for junior high school delinquents. *Cognitive Therapy and Research, 8*, 299–312.

Feingold, B. (1975). *Why your child is hyperactive*. New York: Random House.

Feldman, W. S., Manella, K. J., Apodaca, L., & Varni, J. W. (1982). Behavioral group parent training in spina bifida. *Journal of Clinical Child Psychology, 11*, 144–150.

Fellner, D. J., & Sulzer-Azaroff, B. (1984). The effects of posted feedback for increasing safe practices and conditions in an industry. *Journal of Safety Research, 15*, 7–21.

Ferster, C. B., Nurnberger, J. I., & Levitt, E. (1962). The control of eating. *Journal of Mathetics, 1*, 87–109.

Fielstein, E., Klein, M. S., Fischer, M., Hanan, C., Koburger, P., Schneider, M. J., & Leitenberg, H. (1985). Self-esteem and causal attributions for success and failure in children. *Cognitive Therapy and Research, 9*, 381–398.

Fincham, F. (1985). Attributions in close relationships. In J. Harvey & G. Weary (Eds.), *Attribution: Basic issues and applications*. New York: Academic Press.

Finney, J. W., Friman, P. C., Rapoff, M. A., & Christophersen, E. R. (1985). Improving compliance with antibiotic regimens for otitis media: Randomized clinical trial in a pediatric clinic. *American Journal of Diseases of Children, 139*, 89–95.

Fischler, G., & Kendall, P. C. (in press). Social cognitive problem-solving and childhood adjustment: Qualitative and topological analyses. *Cognitive Therapy and Research.*

Fisher, L., & Wilson, G. T. (1985). A study of the psychology of agoraphobia. *Behaviour Research and Therapy, 23*, 97–108.

Fishman, D. B. (1984). The real-world imperatives of organizational adoption. *Journal of Organizational Behavioral Management, 6* 5–15.

Foa, E. B., & Emmelkamp, P. M. G. (Eds.). (1983). *Failures in behavior therapy*. New York: Wiley.

Forehand, R. L. (1985). Training behavioral clinicians for a non-behavioral world. *the Behavior Therapist, 8*, 5–8.

Forehand, R. L., Brody, G., & Smith, K. (1986a). Contribution of child behaviour and marital dissatisfaction to maternal perceptions of child maladjustment. *Behaviour Research and Therapy, 24*, 43–48.

Forehand, R. L., Lautenschlager, G. J., Faust, J., & Graziano, W. G. (1986b). Parent perceptions and parent–child interactions in clinic-referred children: A preliminary investigation of the effects of maternal depressive moods. *Behaviour Research and Therapy, 24*, 73–75.

Forehand, R. L., & McMahon, R. J. (1981). *Helping the noncompliant child: A clinician's guide to parent training*. New York: Guilford Press.

Forehand, R. L., Middlebrook, J., Rogers, T., & Steffe, M. (1983). Dropping out of parent training. *Behaviour Research and Therapy, 21*, 663–668.

Forehand, R. L., Middlebrook, J., Steffe, M., & Rogers, T. (1984). An examination of some trends in child behaviour therapy. *Behavioural Psychotherapy, 23*, 203–211.

Forehand, R. L., Wells, K. C., & Sturgis, E. T. (1978). Predictors of child non-compliant behavior in the home. *Journal of Consulting and Clinical Psychology, 46*, 179.

Foreyt, J. P., Goodrick, G. K., & Gotto, A. M. (1981). Limitations of behavioral treatment of obesity: Review and analysis. *Journal of Behavioral Medicine, 4*, 159–174.

Foreyt, J. P., Hartung, G. H., Jackson, A. S., Squires, W. G., Murray, T. D., Avent, H., & Grimes, R. (1986, March). *Determinants of adoption of smokeless tobacco use in college students*. Paper presented at the meeting of Society of Behavioral Medicine, San Francisco.

Forman, S. G. (1982). Stress management for teachers: A cognitive–behavioral program. *Journal of School Psychology, 20*, 180–187.

Foster, G. D., Wadden, T. A., Brownell, K. D. (1985). Peer-led program for the treatment and prevention of obesity in the schools. *Journal of Consulting and Clinical Psychology, 53*, 538–540.

Foster, S., Berler, E., & Collins, F. (1982). Conference report: The West Virginia Working Conference on Behavioral Training in Clinical Psychology. *the Behavior Therapist, 5*, 184.

Foster, S., & Cone, J. (1986). Design and use of direct observation procedures. In A. Ciminero, K. Calhoun, & H. Adams (Eds.), *Handbook of behavioral assessment* (2nd ed., pp. 253–324). New York: Wiley.

Fox, B. H. (1976). Psychosocial epidemiology of cancer. In J. W. Cullen, B. H. Fox, & R. N. Isom (Eds.), *Cancer: The behavioral dimensions* (pp. 11–22). New York: Raven Press.

Fox, B. H. (1978). Premorbid psychological factors as related to cancer incidence. *Journal of Behavioral Medicine, 1*, 45–133.

Fox, B. H. (1981). Behavioral issues in cancer. In S. M. Weiss, J. A. Herd, & B. H. Fox (Eds.), *Perspectives on behavioral medicine* (pp. 101–133). New York: Academic Press.

Fox, B. H. (1983). Current theory of psychogenic effects on cancer incidence and prognosis. *Journal of Psychosocial Oncology, 1*, 17–31.

Foxen, T. H., & McBrien, J. A. (1981). *The E.D.Y. in-service course for mental handicap practitioners: Trainee workbook.* Manchester, England: Manchester University Press.

Franco, L. J., Stern, M. P., Rosenthal, M., Haffner, S. M., Hazuda, H. P., & Comeaux, P. J. (1985). Prevalence, detection, and control of hypertension in a biethnic community: The San Antonio Heart Study. *American Journal of Epidemiology, 121*, 684–696.

Franks, C. M. (1981). 2081: Will we be many or one—or none? *Behavioural Psychotherapy, 9*, 287–290.

Franks, C. M. (1984a). Behavior therapy: An overview. In G. T. Wilson, C. M. Franks, K. D. Brownell, & P. C. Kendall, *Annual review of behavior therapy: Theory and practice* (Vol. 9, pp. 1–38). New York: Guilford Press.

Franks, C. M. (1984b). On conceptual and technical integrity in psychoanalysis and behavior therapy: Two fundamentally incompatible systems. In H. Arkowitz & S. B. Messer (Eds.), *Psychoanalytic therapy and behavior therapy: Is integration possible?* (pp. 223–247). New York: Plenum.

Franks, C. M. (1985). Foreword. In N. H. Hadley, *Foundations of aversion therapy* (pp. v–x). New York: Medical & Scientific Books (Spectrum).

Franks, C. M. (1986). Foreword. In N. King & A. Remenyi, *Health care: A behavioral approach.* New York: Grune & Stratton.

Franks, C. M. (in press). Behavior therapy and the AABT: Personal recollections, conceptions, and misconceptions. *the Behavior Therapist.*

Franks, C. M., & Rosenbaum, M. (1983). Behavior therapy: Overview and personal reflections. In M. Rosenbaum, C. M. Franks, & Y. Jaffe (Eds.), *Perspectives on behavior therapy in the eighties* (pp. 3–14). New York: Springer.

Franks, V., & Rothblum, E. (Eds.). (1983). *The stereotyping of women: Its effects on mental health.* New York: Springer.

Freeman, A. (1983). Cognitive therapy: An overview. In A. Freeman (Ed.), *Cognitive therapy with couples and groups* (pp. 1–36). New York: Plenum Press.

Freeman, B. J., Ritvo, E. R., & Schroth, P. C. (1984). Behavior assessment of the syndrome of autism: Behavior observation system. *Journal of the American Academy of Child Psychiatry, 23*, 588–594.

Freeman, B. J., & Schroth, P. C. (1983). The development of the behavior observation system. *Behavioral Assessment, 6* 177–187.

Frerichs, R. R., Chapman, J. M., Nourjah, P., & Maes, M. (1984). *Cardiovascular diseases in Los Angeles County, 1978–1981.* Los Angeles: American Heart Association, Greater Los Angeles Affiliate.

Friedman, S. B., Phillips, S., & Parrish, J. M. (1983). Current status of behavioral pediatric training for general pediatric residents: A study of 11 funded programs. *Pediatrics, 71*, 904–908.

Friedrich, W. N., & Einbender, A. J. (1983). The abused child: A psychological reivew. *Journal of Clinical Child Psychology, 12*, 244–256.

Friman, P. C., Finney, J. W., Rapoff, M. A., & Christophersen, E. R. (1985). Improving pediatric appointment keeping with reminders and reduced response requirement. *Journal of Applied Behavior Analysis, 18*, 315–326.

Frith, G. H. (1985). *Behavior management in the schools: A primer for parents*. Springfield, IL: Charles C Thomas.

Gadow, K. D. (1985). Relative efficacy of pharmacological, behavioral, and combination treatments for enhancing academic performance. *Clinical Psychology Review, 5*, 513–533.

Gambrill, E. D. (1983). Behavioral intervention with child abuse and neglect. In M. Hersen, R. M. Eisler, & P. M. Miller (Eds.), *Progress in behavior modification* (Vol. 15, pp. 1–56). New York: Academic Press.

Garber, J., Kriss, M., Koch, M., & Lindholm, L. B. (1987). *Depression in adolescence: A follow-up study*. Manuscript submitted for publication.

Garfield, S. L. (1982). Eclecticism and integration in psychotherapy. *Behavior Therapy, 13*, 610–623.

Garfield, S. L. (1983). Does psychotherapy work? Yes, no, maybe. *Behavioral and Brain Sciences, 6*, 292–293.

Garrison, R. J., & Castelli, W. P. (1985). Weight and thirty-year mortality of men in the Framingham Study. *Annals of Internal Medicine, 103*, 1006–1009.

Gaylord-Ross, R. J., Haring, T. G., Breen, C., & Pitts-Conway, V. (1984). The training and generalization of social interaction skills with autistic youth. *Journal of Applied Behavior Analysis, 17*, 229–247.

Gerwitz, J. (1969). Mechanisms of social learning: Some roles of stimulation and behavior in early development. In D. A. Goslin (Ed.), *Handbook of socialization theory and research* (pp. 112–148). Chicago: Rand McNally.

Gesten, E. L., Rains, M. H., Rapkin, B. D., Weissberg, R. P., Flores de Apodaca, R., Cowen, E. L., & Bowen, R. (1982). Training children in social problem-solving competencies: A first and second look. *American Journal of Community Psychology, 10*, 95–115.

Ghosh, A., Marks, I., & Carr, A. (1984). Controlled study of self-exposure treatment for phobics: Preliminary communication. *Journal of the Royal Society of Medicine, 77*, 483–487.

Giebenhain, J. E., & O'Dell, S. L. (1984). Evolution of a parent-training manual for reducing children's fear of the dark. *Journal of Applied Behavior Analysis, 17*, 121–125.

Gifford, J. L., Rusch, F. R., Martin, J. E., & White, D. M. (1984). Autonomy and adaptibility: A proposed technology for the study of work behavior. In N. W. Ellis & N. R. Bray (Eds.), *International review of research on mental retardation* (Vol. 12, pp. 285–318). New York: Academic Press.

Gilbert, A., & Varni, J. W. (1984). *Adherence to factor replacement therapy by children with hemophilia*. Unpublished manuscript.

Gill M. (1984). Psychoanalytic, psychodynamic, cognitive behavior, and behavior therapies compared. In H. Arkowitz & S. B. Messer (Eds.), *Psychoanalytic therapy and behavior therapy: Is integration possible?* (pp. 179–187). New York: Plenum.

Gillum, R. F. (1982). Coronary heart disease in black populations: I. Mortality and morbidity. *American Heart Journal, 104*, 839–851.

Glasgow, R. E., Klesges, R. C., Mizes, J. S., & Pechacek, T. F. (1985). Quitting smoking:

Strategies used and variables associated with success in a stop-smoking contest. *Journal of Consulting and Clinical Psychology, 53*, 905–912.

Glass, D. C. (1985). Acute physiologic reactivity: Working group summary. In A. M. Ostfeld & E. D. Eaker (Eds.), *Measuring psychosocial variables in epidemiologic studies of cardiovascular disease: Proceedings of a workshop* (DHHS Publication No. NIH 85-2770, pp. 479–483). Washington, DC: U.S. Government Printing Office.

Glover, E. D. (1986). Conducting smokeless tobacco cessation clinics. *American Journal of Public Health, 76*, 207.

Glover, E. D., Edwards, S. W., Christen, A. G., & Finnicum, P. (1984). Smokeless tobacco research: An interdisciplinary approach. *Health Values: Achieving High Level Wellness, 8*(3), 21–25.

Gochman, S. I., Allgood, B. A., & Greer, C. R. (1982). A look at today's behavior therapists. *Professional Psychology, 13*, 605–611.

Gofin, J., Gofin, R., Abramson, J. H., & Ban, R. (1986). Ten-year evaluation of hypertension, overweight, cholesterol, and smoking control: The CHAD program in Jerusalem: Community syndrome of hypertension, atherosclerosis, and diabetes. *Preventive Medicine, 15*, 304–312.

Goisman, R. (1985). The psychodynamics of prescribing in behavior therapy. *American Journal of Psychiatry, 142*, 675–679.

Golden, W. L. (1983). Resistance in cognitive behaviour therapy. *British Journal of Cognitive Psychotherapy, 1*, 33–42.

Goldfried, M. R. (Ed.). (1982a). *Converging theories in the practice of psychotherapy.* New York: Springer.

Goldfried, M. R. (1982b). On the history of therapeutic interpretation. *Behavior Therapy, 13*, 572–593.

Goldfried, M. R., & Robbins, C. (1983). Self-schemas, cognitive bias, and the processing of therapeutic experiences. In P. C. Kendall (Ed.), *Advances in cognitive–behavioral research and therapy* (Vol. 2). New York: Academic Press.

Goldsmith, M. F. (1986). Dark days predicted as Third World lights up. *Journal of the American Medical Association, 255*, 1000–1003.

Gomberg, E. S., & Franks, V. (Eds.). (1979). *Gender and disordered behavior: Sex differences in psychopathology.* New York: Brunner/Mazel.

Gonzales, L. R., Lewinsohn, P. M., & Clarke, G. N. (1985). Longitudinal follow-up of unipolar depressives: An investigation of predictors of relapse. *Journal of Consulting and Clinical Psychology, 53*(4), 461–469.

Gormally, J., Rardin, D., & Black, S. (1980). Correlates of successful response to a behavioral weight control clinic. *Journal of Counseling Psychology, 27*, 179–191.

Gorman, J. M., Askanazi, J., Liebowitz, M. R., Fryer, A. J., Stein, J., Kinney, J. M., & Klein, D. F. (1984). Response to hyperventilation in a group of patients with panic disorder. *American Journal of Psychiatry, 141*, 857–861.

Gorn, G. J. (1982). The effects of music in advertising on choice behavior: A classical conditioning approach. *Journal of Marketing, 46*, 94–101.

Gotlib, I. H. (1984). Depression and general psychopathology in university students. *Journal of Abnormal Psychology, 93*, 19–30.

Gottman, J. M. (1979). *Marital interaction: Experimental investigations.* New York: Academic Press.

Gottman, J. M. (1985). Observational measures: A reply to Jacobson. *Behavioral Assessment, 7*, 317–321.

Gotto, A. M., Jones, P. H., & Scott, L. W. (1986). The diagnosis and management of hyperlipidemia. *DM: Disease-A-Month, 32*, 245–311.

Graziano, A. M. (1983). Behavioral approaches to child and family systems. *The Counseling Psychologist, 11*, 47–56.

Graziano, A. M. (1986). The behavioral parent [Review of R. F. Dangel & R. A. Polster (Eds.), *Parent training: Foundations of research and practice*]. *Contemporary Psychology, 31*, 219–220.

Graziano, A. M., & Mooney, K. C. (1984). *Children and behavior therapy*. Chicago: Aldine.

Green, R. B., Hardison, W. L., & Greene, B. F. (1984). Turning the table on advice program for parents: Using placemats to enhance family interaction at restaurants. *Journal of Applied Behavior Analysis, 17*, 497–508.

Greene, B. F., Clark, H. B., & Risley, T. R. (1977). *Shopping with children*. San Rafael, CA: Academic Therapy Publications.

Greenwood, C. R., Delquadri, J. C., Stanley, S. O., Terry, B., & Vance Hall, R. (1985). Assessment of eco-behavioral interaction in school settings. *Behavioral Assessment, 7*, 331–347.

Grennan, E., Powell, C., & Varni, J. W. (1984). *Adherence to therapeutic exercise by children with hemophilia*. Unpublished manuscript.

Griest, D. L., & Wells, K. C. (1983). Behavioral family therapy with conduct disorders in children. *Behavior Therapy, 14*, 37–53.

Griest, D. L., Wells, K. C., & Forehand, R. (1979). An examination of predictors of maternal perceptions of maladjustment in clinic-referred children. *Journal of Abnormal Psychology, 88*, 277–281.

Gritz, E. R. (1986). Prevention and treatment aspects of smokeless tobacco use. In W. J. Blot, G. Boyd, & J. M. Elliott (Eds.), *Proceedings of NIH Consensus Development Conference: Health implications of smokeless tobacco use* (pp. 102–105). Bethesda, MD: National Institutes of Health.

Grunbaum, A. (1984). *The foundations of psychoanalysis: A philosophical critique*. Berkeley: University of California Press.

Guernica, A., & Kasperuk, I. (1982). *Reaching the Hispanic market effectively*. New York: McGraw-Hill.

Guevremont, D. C., Tishelman, A. C., & Hull, D. B. (1985). Teaching generalized self-control to attention-deficit boys with mothers as adjunct therapists. *Child and Family Behavior Therapy, 7*, 23–37.

Guggenheimer, J., Zullo, T. G., Kruper, D. C., & Verbin, R. S. (1986). Changing trends of tobacco use in a teenage population in western Pennsylvania. *American Journal of Public Health, 76*, 196–197.

Gupta, P. C. (1986). Carcinogenicity of chewing of tobacco-containing quids in Southeast Asia. In W. J. Blot, G. Boyd, & J. M. Elliott (Eds.), *Proceedings of NIH Consensus Development Conference: Health implications of smokeless tobacco use* (pp. 78–82). Bethesda, MD: National Institutes of Health.

Hafner, J. (1982). The marital context of the agoraphobic syndrome. In D. L. Chambless & A. Goldstein (Eds.), *Agoraphobia* (pp. 77–118). New York: Wiley.

Haley, G. M. T., Fine, S., Marriage, K., Moretti, M. M., & Freeman, R. J. (1985). Cognitive bias and depression in psychiatrically disturbed children and adolescents. *Journal of Consulting and Clinical Psychology, 53*, 535–537.

Haley, W. E. (1983). A family–behavior approach to the treatment of the cognitively impaired elderly. *The Gerontologist, 23*, 18–20.

Hamblin, R. L., Hathaway, C., & Wodarski, J. S. (1971). Group contingencies, peer tutoring and accelerating academic achievement: Experiment 1. In E. Ramp & W. Hopkins (Eds.), *A new direction for education: Behavior analysis* (pp. 41–53). Lawrence: University of Kansas Press.

Hamilton, M. (1960). A rating scale for depression. *Journal of Neurology, Neurosurgery and Psychiatry, 23*, 56–62.

Hamilton, S. B., & Bornstein, P. H. (1979). Broad-spectrum behavioral approach to smoking cessation: Effects of social support and paraprofessional training on the maintenance of treatment effects. *Journal of Consulting and Clinical Psychology, 47*, 598–600.

Hamilton, S. B., & MacQuiddy, S. L. (1984). Self-administered behavioral parent training: Enhancement of treatment efficacy using a time-out signal seat. *Journal of Clinical Child Psychology, 13*, 61–69.

Hammen, C. L. (1980). Depression in college students: Beyond the Beck Depression Inventory. *Journal of Consulting and Clincial Psychology, 48*, 126–128.

Hammen, C. L. (1983, August). *Cognitive and social processes in bipolar affective disorders: A neglected topic.* Paper presented at the convention of the American Psychological Association, Anaheim, CA.

Hand, I., Angenendt, J., Fischer, M., & Wilke, C. (1986). Exposure in-vivo with panic management for agoraphobia: Treatment rationale and longterm outcome. In I. Hand & H. Wittchen (Eds.), *Panic and phobias* (pp. 104–126). New York: Springer-Verlag.

Hand, I., Lamontagne, Y., & Marks, I. (1974). Group exposure (flooding) in vivo for agoraphobics. *British Journal of Psychiatry, 124*, 588–602.

Hand, I., & Wittchen, H. (Eds.). (1986). *Panic and phobias.* New York: Springer-Verlag.

Hansen, D. J., St. Lawrence, J. S., & Christoff, K. A. (1985). Effects of interpersonal problem-solving training with chronic aftercare patients on problem-solving component skills and effectiveness of solutions. *Journal of Consulting and Clinical Psychology, 53*, 167–174.

Harris, K. R. (1985). Conceptual, methodological, and clinical issues in cognitive–behavioral assessment. *Journal of Abnormal Child Psychology, 13*, 373–390.

Harris, K. R., Wong, B. Y. L., & Keogh, B. K. (1985). Foreword. *Journal of Abnormal Child Psychology, 13*, 329–330.

Harris, M. B., & Hallbauer, E. S. (1973). Self-directed weight control through eating and exercise. *Behaviour Research and Therapy, 11*, 523–529.

Harris, S. L. (1984). The family of the autistic child: A behavioral–systems view. *Clinical Psychology Review, 4*, 227–239.

Harris, S. L., & Ferrari, M. (1983). Developmental factors in child behavior therapy. *Behavior Therapy, 14*, 54–72.

Harris, S. L., & Powers, M. D. (1984). Behavior therapists look at the impact of an autistic child on the family system. A case history. In E. Schopter & G. B. Mesibov (Eds.), *The effects of autism on the family* (pp. 201–224). New York: Plenum.

Harrison, G. G. (1984). Purposes and types of classifications. *International Journal of Obesity, 8*, 481–490.

Harrison, G. G. (1985). Height–weight tables. *Annals of Internal Medicine, 103*, 989–994.

Hart, B., & Risley, T. R. (1982). *How to use incidental teaching for elaborating language.* Lawrence, KS: H & H Enterprises.

Hartung, G. H., Foreyt, J. P., Mitchell, R. E., Vlasek, I., & Gotto, A. M., Jr. (1980). Relation of diet to high-density-lipoprotein cholesterol in middle-aged marathon runners, joggers, and inactive men. *New England Journal of Medicine, 302*, 357–361.

Hartung, G. H., Reeves, R. S., Foreyt, J. P., Patsch, W., & Gotto, A. M., Jr. (1986). Effect of alcohol intake and exercise on plasma high-density lipoprotein cholesterol subfractions and apolipoprotein A-1 in women. *American Journal of Cardiology, 58*, 148–151.

Hartup, W. W. (1970). Peer interaction and social organization. In P. Mussen (Ed.), *Carmichael's manual of child psychology* (3rd ed.): *Vol. 2. Socialization, personality, and social development* (pp. 361–456). New York: Wiley.

Hartup, W. W. (1983). Peer relations. In E. M. Hetherington (Ed.), *Handbook of child psychology* (4th ed.): *Vol. 4. Socialization, personality, and social development* (pp. 103–196). New York: Wiley.

Hatzenbuehler, L. C., Parpal, M., & Matthews, L. (1983). Classifying college students as depressed or nondepressed using the Beck Depression Inventory: An empirical analysis. *Journal of Consulting and Clinical Psychology, 51*, 360–366.

Hawkins, D. I., Best, R. J., & Coney, K. A. (1983). *Consumer behavior: Implications for marketing strategy*. Plano, TX: Business Publications.

Hawkins, R. P. (1985). On Woolfolk and Richardson. *American Psychologist, 40*, 1138–1139.

Hawkins, R. P. (1986). Existential problems, behavior therapy, and behavior analysis. *the Behavior Therapist, 9*, 6–18.

Haywood, H. C., Brooks, P., & Burns. S. (in press). Development and evaluation of the cognitive curriculum for young children. In M. Schwebel & C. Maher (Eds.), *Facilitating cognitive development: Principles, practices, and programs*. New York: Hawthorn Press.

Hazaleus, S. L., & Deffenbacher, J. L. (1986). Relaxation and cognitive treatments of anger. *Journal of Consulting and Clinical Psychology, 54*, 222–226.

Heather, N., & Robertson, I. (1983). *Controlled drinking* (2nd ed.). New York: Methuen.

Heide, F. J., & Borkovec, T. D. (1983). Relaxation-induced anxiety: Paradoxical anxiety enhancement due to relaxation training. *Journal of Consulting and Clinical Psychology, 51*, 171–175.

Heide, F. J., & Borkovec, T. D. (1984). Relaxation-induced anxiety: Mechanisms and theoretical implications. *Behaviour Research and Therapy, 22*, 1–12.

Helsel, W., & Matson, J. (1984). The assessment of depression in children: The internal structure of the Children's Depression Inventory (CDI). *Behaviour Research and Therapy, 22*, 289–298.

Henderson, M., & Hollin, C. R. (1983). A critical review of social skills training with young offenders. *Criminal Justice and Behavior, 10*, 316–341.

Henggeler, S. W., Hanson, C. L., Borduin, C. M., Watson, S. M., & Brunk, M. A. (1985). Mother–son relationships of juvenile felons. *Journal of Consulting and Clinical Psychology, 53*, 942–943.

Henningfield, J. E. (1986). Evidence that smokeless tobacco use may lead to dependence. In *Proceedings of NIH Consensus Development Conference: Health implications of smokeless tobacco use* (pp. 95–101). Bethesda, MD: National Institutes of Health.

Heppner, P. P., & Petersen, C. H. (1982). The development and implications of a Personal Problem-Solving Inventory. *Journal of Counseling Psychology, 29*, 66–75.

Herd, J. A. (1985). Acute physiologic reactivity: Content discussion. In A. M. Ostfeld & E. D. Eaker (Eds.), *Measuring psychosocial variables in epidemiologic studies of cardiovascular disease: Proceedings of a workshop* (DHHS Publication No. NIH 85-2270, pp. 453–457). Washington, DC: U.S. Government Printing Office.

Hersen, M. (Ed.). (1986). *Pharmacological and behavioral treatment: An integrative approach*. New York: Wiley.

Hersen, M., & Bellack, A. S. (Eds.). (1984). *Behavioral assessment: A practical handbook* (2nd ed.). New York: Plenum.

Hersen, M., Bellack, A. S., & Himmelhock, J. M. (1981). A comparison of solicited and nonsolicited female unipolar depressives for treatment outcome research. *Journal of Consulting and Clinical Psychology, 49*, 611–613.

Hersher, L. (1985). The effectiveness of behavior modification on hyperkinesis. *Child Psychiatry and Human Development, 16*, 87–96.

Himadi, W., Boice, R., & Barlow, D. (1985). Assessment of agoraphobia: Triple response measurement. *Behaviour Research and Therapy, 23*, 311–324.

Hibbert, G. A. (1984). Ideational components of anxiety. *British Journal of Psychiatry, 144*, 618–624.

Hinshaw, S. P., Henker, B., & Whalen, C. K. (1984a). Cognitive–behavioral and pharmacological interventions for hyperactive boys: Comparative and combined effects. *Journal of Consulting and Clinical Psychology, 5*, 739–749.

Hinshaw, S. P., Henker, B., & Whalen, C. K. (1984b). Self-control in hyperactive boys in anger-inducing situations: Effects of cognitive–behavioral training and of methylphenidate. *Journal of Abnormal Child Psychology, 12*, 55–57.

Hjermann, I. (1980). Coronary heart disease prevention: The Oslo Study. *Journal of the Oslo City Hospital, 30*, 21–36.

Hjermann, I., Velve Byre, K., Holme, I., & Leren, P. (1981). Effect of diet and smoking intervention on the incidence of coronary heart disease: Report from the Oslo Study Group of a randomised trial in healthy men. *Lancet, ii*, 1303–1310.

Hobbs, S. A., Beck, S. J., & Wansley, R. A. (1984a). Pediatric behavioral medicine: Directions in treatment and prevention. In M. Hersen, R. M. Eisler, & R. M. Miller (Eds.), *Progress in behavior modification* (Vol. 16, pp. 1–29). New York: Academic Press.

Hobbs, S. A., Walle, D. L., & Caldwell, S. (1984b). Maternal evaluation of social reinforcement and time-out: Effects of brief parent training. *Journal of Consulting and Clinical Psychology, 52*, 135–136.

Hoiberg, A., Berard, S., Watten, R. H., & Caine, C. (1984). Correlates of weight loss in treatment and at follow-up. *International Journal of Obesity, 8*, 457–465.

Holcomb, C. A., & Stith, M. (1985). Readability of selected parent education publications. *Family Relations, 34*, 151–159.

Hollin, C. R., & Courtney, S. A. (1983). A skills training approach to the reduction of institutional offending. *Personality and Individual Differences, 4*, 257–264.

Hollin, C. R., & Henderson, M. (1981). The effects of social skills training on incarcerated delinquent adolescents. *International Journal of Behavioural Social Work and Abstracts, 1*, 145–155.

Hollin, C. R., & Henderson, M. (1984). Social skills training with young offenders: False expectations and the "failure of treatment." *Behavioural Psychotherapy, 12*, 331–341.

Hollon, S. D., & Beck, A. T. (1978). Psychotherapy and drug therapy: Comparisons and combinations. In S. L. Garfield & A. E. Bergin (Eds.), *Handbook of psychotherapy and behavior change* (2nd ed., pp. 437–489). New York: Wiley.

Hollon, S. D., & Beck, A. T. (1986). Research on cognitive therapies. In S. L. Garfield & A. E. Bergin (Eds.), *Handbook on psychotherapy and behavior change* (3rd ed., pp. 443–482). New York: Wiley.

Hollon, S. D., & Kendall, P. C. (1980). Cognitive self-statements in depression: Development of an Automatic Thoughts Questionnaire. *Cognitive Therapy and Research, 4*, 383–395.

Holowinsky, I. Z. (1985). Assessment of cognitive skills in the USSR: Historical trends and current developments. *Journal of Speical Education, 18*, 541–545.

Hornby, G., & Singh, N. N. (1983). Group training for parents of mentally retarded children: A review and methodological analysis of behavioral studies. *Child: Care, Health and Development, 9*, 199–213.

Hornby, G., & Singh, N. N. (1984). Behavioural group training with parents of mentally retarded children. *Journal of Mental Deficiency Research, 28*, 43–52.

Horne, A. M., & Van Dyke, B. (1983). Treatment and maintenance of social learning family therapy. *Behavior Therapy, 14*, 606–613.

Horton, A. M. (1979a). Behavioral neuropsychology: A clinical case study. *Clinical Neuropsychology, 1*, 44–47.

Horton, A. M. (1979b). Behavioral neuropsychology: Rationale and research. *Clinical Neuropsychology, 1*, 20–23.

Horton, A. M. (1981). Behavioral neuropsychology in the schools. *School Psychology Review, 10*, 367–372.

Horton, L. (1984). The father's role in behavioral parent training: A review. *Journal of Clinical Child Psychology, 13*, 274–279.

Houston, B. K., Fox, J. E., & Forbes, L. (1984). Trait anxiety and children's state anxiety, cognitive behaviors, and performance under stress. *Cognitive Therapy and Research, 8*, 631–642.

Howard, B. L., & Kendall, P. C. (1987). *Child interventions: Having no peers?* Manuscript submitted for publication.

Hrop, S., & Rakos, R. F. (1985). The influence of race in the social evaluation of assertion in conflict situations. *Behavior Therapy, 16*, 478–493.

Hubert, H. B., Feinleib, M., McNamara, P. M., & Castelli, W. P. (1983). Obesity as an independent risk factor for cardiovascular disease: A 26-year follow-up of participants in the Framingham Heart Study. *Circulation, 67*, 968–977.

Hudson, A., & Blane, M. (1985). The importance of non-verbal behavior in giving instructions to children. *Child and Family Behavior Therapy*, 7, 1–10.

Huesmann, L. R. (1982). Experimental methods in research in psychopathology. In P. C. Kendall & J. N. Butcher (Eds.), *Handbook of research methods in clinical psychology* (pp. 223–248). New York: Wiley.

Humphrey, L. L., Apple, R. F., & Kirschenbaum, D. S. (1986). Differentiating bulimic–anorexic from normal families using interpersonal and behavioral observational systems. *Journal of Consulting and Clinical Psychology, 54*, 190–195.

Hunter, P., & Kelso, E. N. (1985). Feminist behavior therapy. *the Behavior Therapist, 10*, 201–204.

Hunter, S. M., Croft, J. B., Burke, G. L., Parker, F. C., Webber, L. S., & Berenson, G. S. (1986). Longitudinal patterns of cigarette smoking and smokeless tobacco use in youth: The Bogalusa Heart Study. *American Journal of Public Health, 76*, 193–195.

Hursh, S. R. (1980). Economic concepts for the analysis of behavior. *Journal of the Experimental Analysis of Behavior, 34*, 219–238.

Hursh, S. R. (1984). Behavioral economics. *Journal of the Experimental Analysis of Behavior, 42*, 435–452.

Hussian, R. A. (1982). Stimulus control in the modification of problematic behavior in elderly institutionalized patients. *International Journal of Behavioral Geriatrics, 1*, 33–42.

Hussian, R. A. (1984a). Behavioral geriatrics. In M. Hersen, R. M. Eisler, & P. M. Miller (Eds.), *Progress in behavior modification* (Vol. 16, pp. 159–183). New York: Academic Press.

Hussian, R. A. (1984b). Geriatric behavior therapy. In J. P. Abrahams & V. Crooks (Eds.), *Geriatric mental health* (pp. 109–122). New York: Grune & Stratton.

Hussian, R. A. (1985). A behavioral-programming approach to treatment of the institutionalized aged. In C. M. Gaitz, G. Niederehe, & N. L. Wilson (Eds.), *Aging 2000: Our health care destiny. Volume 2. Psychosocial and policy issues* (pp. 219–225). New York: Springer-Verlag.

Hussian, R. A., & Davis, R. L. (1985). *Responsive care: Behavioral interventions with elderly persons.* Champaign, IL: Research Press.

Incagnoli, T., & Newman, B. (1985). Cognitive and behavioral rehabilitation interventions. *International Journal of Clinical Neuropsychology, 7*, 173–182.

Ingram, R. E., Kendall, P. C., Smith, T. W., Donnell, C., & Ronan, K. (in press). Cognitive specificity in emotional distress. *Journal of Personality and Social Psychology.*

Intagliata, J. C. (1978). Increasing the interpersonal problem-solving skills of an alcoholic population. *Journal of Consulting and Clinical Psychology, 46*, 489–498.

Intagliata, J. C. (1979). Increasing the responsiveness of alcoholics to group therapy: An interpersonal problem-solving approach. *Group, 3*, 106–120.

International Agency for Research on Cancer. (1985). Tobacco habits other than smoking; Betal-quid and areca-nut chewing; and some related nitrosamines. *IARC Monographs on the Evaluation of the Carcinogenic Risk of Chemicals to Humans, 37*, 1–202.

Israel, A. C., Stolmaker, L., & Andrian, C. A. G. (1985). The effects of training parents in general child management skills on a behavioral weight loss program for children. *Behavior Therapy, 16*, 169–180.

Iwaniec, D., Herbert, M., & McNeish, A. S. (1985a). Social work with failure-to-thrive children and their families: Part I. Psychosocial failures. *British Journal of Social Work, 15*, 243–259.

Iwaniec, D., Herbert, M., & McNeish, A. S. (1985b). Social work with failure-to-thrive children and their families: Part II. Behavioural social work intervention. *British Journal of Social Work, 15*, 375–389.

Jackson, H. J., King, N. J., & Heller, V. R. (1981). Social skills assessment and training for mentally retarded persons: A review of research. *Australian Journal of Developmental Disabilities, 7*, 113–123.

Jackson, S. E. (1983). Participation in decision making as a strategy for reducing job-related strain. *Journal of Applied Psychology, 68*, 3–19.

Jacobson, N. S. (1985a). The role of observational measures in behavior therapy outcome research. *Behavioral Assessment, 7*, 297–308.

Jacobson, N. S. (1985b). Uses versus abuses of observational measures. *Behavioral Assessment, 7*, 323–330.

Jacobson, N. S. (Ed.). (1987). *Psychotherapists in clinical practice: Cognitive and behavioral perspectives.* New York: Guilford Press.

Jacobson, N. S., Follette, W. C., & Revenstorf, D. (1984). Psychotherapy outcome research: Methods for reporting variability and evaluating clinical significance. *Behavior Therapy, 15*, 336–352.

Jacobson, N. S., Follette, W. C., & Revenstorf, D. (1986). Toward a standard definition of clinically significant changes. *Behavior Therapy, 17*, 308–311.

Jacobson, N. S., & Margolin, G. (1979). *Marital therapy: Strategies based on social learning and behavior exchange principles.* New York: Brunner/Mazel.

Jacobson, N. S., McDonald, D. W., Follette, W. C., & Berley, R. A. (1985). Attributional processes in distressed and nondistressed married couples. *Cognitive Therapy and Research, 9*, 35–50.

James, J. E. (1985). Desensitization treatment of agoraphobia. *British Journal of Clinical Psychology, 24*, 133–134.

Jason, L. A., & Glenwick, D. S. (1984). Behavioral community psychology: A review of recent research and applications. In M. Hersen, R. M. Eisler, & P. M. Miller (Eds.), *Progress in behavior modification* (Vol. 18, pp. 85–121). New York: Academic Press.

Jayant, K., Balakrishnan, V., Sanghvi, L. D., & Jussawalla, D. J. (1977). Quantification of the role of smoking and chewing tobacco in oral, pharyngeal and oesophageal cancers. *British Journal of Cancer, 35*, 232–235.

Jeffery, R. W., Bjornson-Benson, W. M., Rosenthal, B. S., Kurth, C. L., & Dunn, M. M.

(1984a). Effectiveness of monetary contracts with two repayment schedules on weight reduction in men and women from self-referred and population samples. *Behavior Therapy, 15*, 273–279.

Jeffery, R. W., Bjornson-Benson, W. M., Rosenthal, B. S., Lindquist, R. A., & Johnson, S. L. (1984b). Behavioral treatment of obesity with monetary contracting: Two-year follow-up. *Addictive Behaviors, 9*, 311–313.

Jeffery, R. W., Bjornson-Benson, W. M., Rosenthal, B. S., Lindquist, R. A., Kurth, C. L., & Johnson, S. L. (1984c). Calorie requirements in weight loss: An estimate based on self-reported food intake in middle-aged men. *Addictive Behaviors, 9*, 231–233.

Jeffery, R. W., Wing, R. R., & Stunkard, A. J. (1978). Behavioral treatment of obesity: State of the art 1976. *Behavior Therapy, 9*, 189–199.

Jellinek, E. M. (1960). *The disease concept of alcoholism.* New Brunswick, NJ: Hillhouse Press.

Jenkins, C. D. (1985). Type A behavior, anger, and hostility: Working group summary. In A. M. Ostfeld & E. D. Eaker (Eds.), *Measuring psychosocial variables in epidemiologic studies of cardiovascular disease: Proceedings of a workshop* (DHHS Publication No. NIH 85-2270, pp. 199–206). Washington, DC: U.S. Government Printing Office.

Jensen, B. J., & Haynes, S. N. (1986). Self-report questionnaires and inventories. In A. R. Ciminero, K. S. Calhoun, & H. E. Adams (Eds.), *Handbook of behavioral assessment* (2nd ed., pp. 150–179). New York: Wiley.

Jensen, J. E. (1983, March 23). [Letter to Drs. Mark and Linda Sobell from Subcommittee on Investigations and Oversight, Committee on Science and Technology, House of Representatives, U.S. Congress].

John, H. W. (1978). Alcoholism and criminal homicide: An overview. *Alcohol Health and Research World, 2*, 8–13.

Johnson, E., & Tversky, A. (1983). Affect, generalization and the perception of risk. *Journal of Personality and Social Psychology, 45*, 20–31.

Johnson, S. M., & Greenberg, L. S. (1985). Differential effects of experiential and problem-solving interventions in resolving marital conflict. *Journal of Consulting and Clinical Psychology, 53*, 175–184.

Joint National Committee on Detection, Evaluation, and Treatment of High Blood Pressure. (1984). The 1984 report of the Joint National Committee on Dectction, Evaluation, and Treatment of High Blood Pressure. *Archives of Internal Medicine, 144*, 1045–1057.

Jones, A. P. (1984). Organizational reward systems: Implications for climate. *Motivation and Emotion, 8*, 259–274.

Jussawalla, D. J., & Deshpande, V. A. (1971). Evaluation of cancer risk in tobacco chewers and smokers: An epidemiologic assessment. *Cancer, 28*, 244–252.

Kahana, E. F., & Kiyak, H. A. (1984). Attitudes and behavior of staff in facilities for the aged. *Research on Aging, 6*, 395–416.

Kahn, R. J., McNair, D. M., Covi, L., Downing, R. W., Fisher, S., Lipman, R. S., Rickels, K., & Smith, V. K. (1981). Effects of psychotropic agents on high anxiety subjects. *Psychopharmacology Bulletin, 17*, 97–100.

Kahn, R. J., McNair, D. M., Lipman, R. S., Covi, L., Rickels, K., Downing, R., Fisher, S., & Frankenthaler, L. M. (1986). Imipramine and chlordiazepoxide in depressive and anxiety disorders: II. Efficacy in anxious outpatients. *Archives of General Psychiatry, 43*, 79–85.

Kahn, R. L. (1981). *Work and health.* New York: Wiley.

Kahneman, D., Slovic, P., & Tversky, A. (Eds.). (1982). *Judgement under uncertainty: Heuristics and biases.* New York: Cambridge University Press.

Kaplan, J. R., Manuck, S. B., Clarkson, T. B., Lusso, F. M., Taub, D. M., & Miller, E. W. (1983). Social stress and atherosclerosis in normocholesterolemic monkeys. *Science, 220*, 733–735.

Karen, R. L., Astin-Smith, S., & Creasy, D. (1985). Teaching telephone-answering skills to mentally retarded adults. *American Journal of Mental Deficiency, 89*, 595–609.

Karoly, P. (1982). Cognitive assessment in behavioral medicine. *Clinical Psychology Review, 2*, 421–434.

Kasl, S. V. (1985). Chronic life situations and life change events: Working group summary. In A. M. Ostfeld & E. D. Eaker (Eds.), *Measuring psychosocial variables in epidemiologic studies of cardiovascular disease: Proceedings of a workshop* (DHHS Publication No. NIH 85-2270, pp. 145–149). Washington, DC: U.S. Government Printing Office.

Kauffman, J. M., & Hallahan, D. P. (1979). Learning disability and hyperactivity (with comments on minimal brain dysfunction). In B. B. Lahey & A. E. Kazdin (Eds.), *Advances in clinical child psychology* (Vol. 2, pp. 71–105). New York: Plenum Press.

Kavanagh, D. J., & Bower, G. H. (1985). Mood and self-efficacy: Impact of joy and sadness on perceived capabilities. *Cognitive Therapy and Research, 9*, 507–526.

Kazdin, A. E. (1978). Conceptual and assessment issues raised by self-efficacy. *Advances in Behaviour Research and Therapy, 1*, 177–186.

Kazdin, A. E. (1982). Symptom substitution, generalization, and response covariation. Implications for psychotherapy outcome. *Psychological Bulletin, 91*, 349–365.

Kazdin, A. E. (1984). Integration of psychodynamic and behavioral psychotherapies: Conceptual versus empirical syntheses. In H. Arkowitz & S. B. Messer (Eds.), *Psychoanalytic therapy and behavior therapy: Is integration possible?* (pp. 139–170). New York: Plenum.

Kazdin, A. E., Esveldt-Dawson, K., & Loar, L. L. (1983). Correspondence of teacher ratings and direct observations of classroom behavior of psychiatric inpatient children. *Journal of Abnormal Child Psychology, 11*, 549–564.

Kazdin, A. E., Esveldt-Dawson, K., Sherick, R. B., & Colbus, D. (1985). Assessment of overt behavior and childhood depression among psychiatrically disturbed children. *Journal of Consulting and Clinical Psychology, 53*, 201–210.

Kazdin, A. E., Rodgers, A., & Colbus, D. (1986). The Hopelessness Scale for Children: Psychometric characteristics and concurrent validity. *Journal of Consulting and Clinical Psychology, 54*, 241–245.

Kazdin, A. E., & Wilson, G. T. (1978). *Evaluation of behavior therapy: Issues, evidence and research strategies*. Cambridge, MA: Ballinger.

Kelley, M. L., Scott, O. M., Prue, D. M., & Rychtarik, R. G. (1985). A component analysis of problem-solving skills training. *Cognitive Therapy and Research, 9*, 429–441.

Kelley, M. L., & Stokes, T. F. (1982). Contingency contracting with disadvantaged youths: Improving classroom performance. *Journal of Applied Behavior Analysis, 15*, 447–454.

Kelley, M. L., & Stokes, T. F. (1984). Student–teacher contracting with goal setting for maintenance. *Behavior Modification, 8*, 223–244.

Kelly, G. A. (1955). *The psychology of personal constructs* (2 vols.). New York: Norton.

Kendall, P. C., (1977). On the efficacious use of verbal self-instructions with children. *Cognitive Therapy and Research, 1*, 331–341.

Kendall, P. C. (1982). Integration: Behavior therapy and other schools of thought. *Behavior Therapy, 13*, 559–571.

Kendall, P. C. (1984a). Behavioral assessment and methodology. In G. T. Wilson, C. M. Franks, K. D. Brownell, & P. C. Kendall, *Annual review of behavior therapy: Theory and practice* (Vol. 9, pp. 39–94). New York: Guilford Press.

Kendall, P. C. (1984b). Cognitive processes and procedures in behavior therapy. In

G. T. Wilson, C. M. Franks, K. D. Brownell, & P. C. Kendall, *Annual review of behavior therapy: Theory and practice* (Vol. 9, pp. 132–179). New York: Guilford Press.

Kendall, P. C. (1985a). Behavioral assessment and methodology. In C. M. Franks, G. T. Wilson, P. C. Kendall, & K. D. Brownell, *Annual review of behavior therapy: Theory and practice* (Vol. 10, pp. 47–86). New York: Guilford Press.

Kendall, P. C. (1985b). Toward a cognitive–behavioral model of child psychopathology and a critique of related interventions. *Journal of Abnormal Child Psychology, 13*, 357–372.

Kendall, P. C. (1986). Comments on Rubin and Krasnor: Solutions and problems in research on problem solving. In M. Perlmutter (Ed.), *Cognitive perspectives on children's social and behavioral development: The Minnesota Symposium on Child Psychology* (Vol. 18, pp. 69–76). Hillsdale, NJ: Erlbaum.

Kendall, P. C., & Bemis, K. M. (1983). Thought and action in psychotherapy: The cognitive–behavioral approaches. In M. Hersen, A. E. Kazdin, & A. S. Bellack (Eds.), *The clinical psychology handbook* (pp. 565–582). New York: Pergamon Press.

Kendall, P. C., & Braswell, L. (1982). On cognitive–behavioral assessment: Model, measures, and madness. In C. D. Spielberger & J. N. Butcher (Eds.), *Advances in personality assessment* (Vol. 1, pp. 35–82). Hillsdale, NJ: Erlbaum.

Kendall, P. C., & Braswell, L. (1985). *Cognitive–behavioral therapy for impulsive children.* New York: Guilford Press.

Kendall, P. C., & Fischler, G. (1984). Behavioral and adjustment correlates of problem solving: Validation analyses of interpersonal cognitive problem-solving measures. *Child Development, 55*, 879–893.

Kendall, P. C., & Hays, R. (1986). *Self-talk and psychopathology: The balance of positive and negative thinking*. Manuscript submitted for publication.

Kendall, P. C., & Hollon, S. D. (Eds.). (1979). *Cognitive–behavioral interventions: Theory, research, and procedures.* New York: Academic Press.

Kendall, P. C., & Hollon, S. D. (1981). Assessing self-referent speech: Methods in the measurement of self-statements. In P. C. Kendall & S. D. Hollon (Eds.), *Assessment strategies for cognitive–behavioral interventions* (pp. 85–118). New York: Academic Press.

Kendall, P. C., & Hollon, S. D. (1983). Calibrating the quality of therapy: Collaborative archiving of tape samples from therapy outcome trials. *Cognitive Therapy and Research, 7*, 199–204.

Kendall, P. C., Hollon, S. D., Beck, A. T., Hammen, C. L., & Ingram, R. E. (1987). Issues and recommendations regarding use of the Beck Depression Inventory. *Cognitive Therapy and Research, 11*, 289–299.

Kendall, P. C., & Kriss, M. R. (1983). Cognitive–behavioral interventions. In C. E. Walker (Ed.), *Handbook of clinical psychology* (Vol. 2, 770–819). Homewood, IL: Dow Jones–Irwin.

Kendall, P. C., & Little, V. L. (1977). Correspondence of brief intelligence measures to the Wechsler Scales with delinquents. *Journal of Consulting and Clinical Psychology, 45*, 660–666.

Kendall, P. C., & Norton-Ford, J. D. (1982). Therapy outcome research methods. In P. C. Kendall & J. N. Butcher (Eds.), *Handbook of research methods in clinical psychology* (pp. 429–460). New York: Wiley.

Kendall, P. C., Padawer, W., Zupan, B., & Braswell, L. (1985). Appendix. Developing self-control in children: The manual. In P. C. Kendall & L. Braswell, *Cognitive–behavioral therapy for impulsive children* (pp. 179–209). New York: Guilford Press.

Kendall, P. C., & Reber, M. (1987). Cognitive training in treatment of hyperactive children. *Archives of General Psychiatry, 44*, 296.

Kendall, P. C., & Wilcox, L. E. (1979). Self-control in children: The development of a rating scale. *Journal of Consulting and Clinical Psychology, 47*, 1020–1030.

Kendall, P. C., & Williams, C. L. (1986). Therapy with adolescents: Treating the "marginal man." *Behavior Therapy, 17*, 522–537.

Kennedy, R. E. (1984). Cognitive behavioral interventions with delinquents. In A. W. Meyers & W. E. Craighead (Eds.), *Cognitive behavior therapy with children* (pp. 351–376). New York: Plenum Press.

Keogh, D. A., Faw, G. D., Whitman, T. L., & Reid, D. H. (1984). Enhancing leisure skills in severely retarded adolescents through a self-instructional treatment package. *Analysis and Intervention in Developmental Disabilities, 4*, 333–351.

Kiesler, C. A. (1982a). Mental hospitals and alternative care: Noninstitutionalization as potential public policy for mental patients. *American Psychologist, 37*, 349–360.

Kiesler, C. A. (1982b). Public and professional myths about mental hospitalization: An empirical reassessment of policy-related beliefs. *American Psychologist, 37*, 1323–1339.

Kiesler, C. A., & Sibulkin, A. E. (1984). Episodic rate of mental hospitalization: Stable or increasing? *American Journal of Psychiatry, 141*, 44–48.

Kiesler, D. J. (1966). Some myths of psychotherapy research and the search for a paradigm. *Psychological Bulletin, 65*, 110–136.

Kihlstrom, J., & Nasby, W. (1981). Cognitive tasks in clinical assessment: An exercise in applied psychology. In P. C. Kendall & S. Hollon (Eds.), *Assessment strategies for cognitive–behavioral interventions* (pp. 287–318). New York: Academic Press.

Killam, P. E., Apodaca, L., Manella, K. J., & Varni, J. W. (1983). Behavioral pediatric weight rehabilitation for children with myelomeningcele. *MCN: American Journal of Maternal Child Nursing, 8*, 280–296.

Killen, J. D., Maccoby, N., & Taylor, C. B. (1984). Nicotine gum and self-regulation training in smoking relapse prevention. *Behavior Therapy, 15*, 234–248.

Kirkley, B. G., Schneider, J. A., Agras, W. S., & Bachman, J. A. (1985). Comparison of two group treatments for bulimia. *Journal of Consulting and Clinical Psychology, 53*, 43–48.

Kirsch, I., Tennen, H., Wickless, C., Saccone, A. J., & Cody, S. (1983). The role of expectancy in fear reduction. *Behavior Therapy, 14*, 520–533.

Kirschenbaum, D. S. (1983). Toward more behavioral early intervention programs: A rationale. *Professional Psychology: Research and Practice, 14*, 159–169.

Kirschenbaum, D. S., Harris, E. S., & Tomarken, A. J. (1984). Effects of parental involvement in behavioral weight loss therapy for preadolescents. *Behavior Therapy, 15*, 485–500.

Kissin, B. (1983). The disease concept of alcoholism. In R. G. Smart, F. B. Glaser, Y. Israel, H. Kalant, R. E. Popham, & W. Schmidt (Eds.), *Research advances in alcohol and drug problems* (Vol. 7, pp. 93–126). New York: Plenum Press.

Kleitsch, E. C., Whitman, T. L., & Santos, J. (1983). Increasing verbal interaction among elderly socially isolated mentally retarded adults: A group language training procedure. *Journal of Applied Behavior Analysis, 16*, 217–233.

Klerman, G. L., DiMascio, A., Weissman, M., Prusoff, B., & Paykel, E. (1974). Treatment of depression by drugs and psychotherapy. *American Journal of Psychiatry, 131*, 186–191.

Klerman, G. L., & Izen, J. E. (1977). The effects of bereavement and grief on physical health and general well-being. *Advances in Psychosomatic Medicine, 9*, 63–104.

Koop, C. E. (1982). Preface. In *The health consequences of smoking: Cancer. A report of the Surgeon General.* (DHHS Publication No. PHS 82-50179, p. v). Washington, DC: U.S. Government Printing Office.

Kopelman, R. E., & Schneller, G. O. (1981). A mixed-consequence system for reducing overtime and unscheduled absences. *Journal of Organizational Behavior Management, 3*, 17–28.

Kopta, S. M., Newman, F. L., McGovern, M. P., & Sandrock, D. (1986). Psychotherapeutic orientations: A comparison of conceptualizations, interventions, and treatment plan costs. *Journal of Consulting and Clinical Psychology, 54*, 369–374.

Kornitzer, M., De Backer, G., Dramaix, M., Kittel, F., Thilly, C., Graffar, M., & Vuylsteek, K. (1983). Belgian Heart Disease Prevention Project: Incidence and mortality results. *Lancet, i*, 1066–1070.

Kornitzer, M., De Backer, G., Dramaix, M., & Thilly, C. (1980). The Belgian Heart Disease Prevention Project: Modification of the coronary risk profile in an industrial population. *Circulation, 61*, 18–25.

Kovacs, M. (1979). *Children's Depression Inventory*. Pittsburgh: University of Pittsburgh School of Medicine.

Kovacs, M. (1981). Rating scales to assess depression in school aged children. *Acta Paedopsychiatrica, 46*, 305–315.

Kozlowski, L. T. (1984). Pharmacological approaches to smoking modification. In J. D. Matarazzo, S. M. Weiss, J. A. Herd, N. E. Miller, & S. M. Weiss (Eds.), *Behavioral health: A handbook of health enhancement and disease prevention* (pp. 713–728). New York: Wiley.

Krakauer, H., Grauman, J. S., McMullan, M. R., & Creede, C. C. (1983). The recent U.S. experience in the treatment of end-stage renal disease by dialysis and transplantation. *New England Journal of Medicine, 308*, 1558–1563.

Krantz, D. S., & Manuck, S. B. (1985). Measures of acute physiologic reactivity to behavior stimuli: Assessment and critique. In A. M. Ostfeld & E. D. Eaker (Eds.), *Measuring psychosocial variables in epidemiologic studies of cardiovascular disease: Proceedings of a workshop* (DHHS Publication No. NIH 85-2270, pp. 407–451). Washington, DC: U.S. Government Printing Office.

Kratochwill, T. R., Bergan, J. R., & Mace, F. C. (1981). Practitioner competencies for implementation of behavioral psychology in the schools: Issues in supervision. *School Psychology Review, 10*, 434–444.

Kratochwill, T. R., & Van Someren, K. R. (1984). Training behavioral consultants: Issues and directions. *the Behavior Therapist, 7*, 19–22.

Kratochwill, T. R., & Van Someren, K. R. (1985). Barriers to treatment success in behavioral consultation: Current limitations and future directions. *Journal of School Psychology, 23*, 225–239.

Kraus, A. S., & Lilienfeld, A. M. (1959). Some epidemiologic aspects of the high mortality rate in the young widowed group. *Journal of Chronic Diseases, 10*, 207–217.

Krouse, J., Gerber, M. M., & Kauffman, J. M. (1981). Peer tutoring: Procedures, promises, and unresolved issues. *Exceptional Education Quarterly, 1*, 107–115.

Krugman, M., Kirsch, I., Wickless, C., Milling, L., Golicz, H., & Toth, A. (1985). Neurolinguistic programming treatment for anxiety: Magic or myth? *Journal of Consulting and Clinical Psychology, 53*(4), 526–530.

Krupnick, J., Shea, T., & Elkin, I. (1986). Generalizability of treatment studies utilizing solicited patients. *Journal of Consulting and Clinical Psychology, 54*, 68–78.

Kuller, L. (1986). Stroke report. In U.S. Department of Health and Human Services, *Report of the Secretary's Task Force on Black and Minority Health: Vol. 4. Cardiovascular and cerebrovascular disease* (Part 2, pp. 475–484). Washington, DC: U.S. Government Printing Office.

Lahey, B. B., Greene, K. D., & Forehand, R. (1980). On the independence of ratings of hyperactivity, conduct problems, and attention deficits in children: A multiple regression analysis. *Journal of Consulting and Clinical Psychology, 48*, 566–574.

Lamb, H. R. (1984). Deinstitutionalization and the homeless mentally ill. In H. R. Lamb (Ed.), *The homeless mentally ill* (pp. 55–74). Washington, DC: American Psychiatric Association.

Lamb, H. R., & Grant, R. (1982). The mentally ill in an urban county jail. *Archives of General Psychiatry, 39,* 17–22.

Landman, J. T., & Dawes, R. (1982). Psychotherapy, outcome: Smith and Glass' conclusions stand up under scrutiny. *American Psychologist, 37,* 504–516.

Lando, H. A. (1977). Successful treatment of smokers with a broad-spectrum behavioral approach. *Journal of Consulting and Clinical Psychology, 45,* 361–366.

Lando, H. A., & McCullough, J. A. (1978). Clinical application of a broad-spectrum behavioral approach to chronic smokers. *Journal of Consulting and Clinical Psychology, 46,* 1583–1585.

Lang, M., & Tisher, M. (1978). *Children's Depression Scale.* Victoria: Australian Council for Educational Research.

Lang, P. J. (1969). The mechanics of desensitization and the laboratory study of fear. In C. M. Franks (Ed.), *Behavior therapy: Appraisal and status.* New York: McGraw-Hill.

Lang, P. J. (1971). The application of psychophysiological methods in the study of psychotherapy and behavior modification. In A. E. Bergin & S. L. Garfield (Eds.), *Handbook of psychotherapy and behavior change.* New York: Wiley.

Lang, P. J. (1979). A bio-informational theory of emotional imagery. *Psychophysiology, 16,* 495–512.

Lasater, T., Abrams, D., Artz, L., Beaudin, P., Cabrera, L., Elder, J., Ferreira, A., Knisley, P., Peterson, G., Rodrigues, A., Rosenberg, P., Snow, R., & Carleton, R. (1984). Lay volunteer delivery of a community-based cardiovascular risk factor change program: The Pawtucket experiment. In J. D. Matarazzo, S. M. Weiss, J. A. Herd, N. E. Miller, & S. M. Weiss (Eds.), *Behavioral health: A handbook of health enhancement and disease prevention* (pp. 1166–1170). New York: Wiley.

Lazarus, A. A. (1968). Behavior therapy in groups. In G. M. Gazda (Ed.), *Basic approaches to group psychotherapy and group counseling.* Springfield, IL: Charles C Thomas.

Lazarus, A. A. (1971a). *Behavior therapy and beyond.* New York: McGraw-Hill.

Lazarus, A. A. (1971b). Where do behavior therapists take their troubles? *Psychological Reports, 28,* 349–350.

Lazarus, A. A. (1981). *The practice of multimodal therapy.* New York: McGraw-Hill.

Lazarus, A. A. (1983). Distorting the point: A reply to Wolpe. *American Psychologist, 38,* 1028.

Lazarus, A. A. (1985). Setting the record straight. *American Psychologist, 40,* 1418–1419.

Lefkowitz, M. M., & Tesiny, E. P. (1980). Assessment of childhood depression. *Journal of Consulting and Clinical Psychology, 48,* 43–50.

Lemere, F., & Voegtlin, W. L. (1950). An evaluation of the aversion treatment of alcoholism. *Quarterly Journal of Studies on Alcohol, 11,* 199–204.

Lenfant, C. (1985). Foreword. In A. M. Ostfeld & E. D. Eaker (Eds.), *Measuring psychosocial variables in epidemiologic studies of cardiovascular disease: Proceedings of a workshop* (DHHS Publication No. NIH 85-2270, pp. vii–viii). Washington, DC: U.S. Government Printing Office.

Leren, P., Askevold, E. M., Foss, O. P., Froili, A., Grymyr, D., Helgeland, A., Hjermann, I., Holme, I., Lund-Larsen, P. G., & Norum, K. R. (1975). The Oslo Study: Cardiovascular disease in middle-aged and young Oslo men. *Acta Medica Scandinavica, 588*(Suppl.), 1–38.

Levant, R. F. (Ed.). (1986). *Psychoeducational approaches to family therapy and counseling.* New York: Springer.

Levendosky, P. G. (1986). The clinical job interview: From the ivory tower to the real world. *the Behavior Therapist, 9*(1), 11–12.

Levey, A. B., & Martin, I. (1983). Cognitions, evaluations and conditioning: Rules of sequence and rules of consequence. *Advances in Behaviour Research and Therapy, 4*, 181–195.

Levinson, R. (1984). The system that cannot say no. *American Psychologist, 39*, 811–812.

Levy, S. M. (1983). Host differences in neoplastic risk: Behavioral and social contributors to disease. *Health Psychology, 2*, 21–44.

Lewin, P., Nelson, R. E., & Tollefson, N. (1983). Teacher attitudes toward disruptive students. *Elementary School Guidance and Counseling, 17*, 188–193.

Lewinsohn, P. M., & Teri, L. (1982). Selection of depressed and nondepressed subjects on the basis of self-report data. *Journal of Consulting and Clinical Psychology, 50*, 590–591.

Lewinsohn, P. M., Teri, L., & Hautzinger, M. (1984). Training clinical psychologists for work with older adults: A working model. *Professional Psychology: Research and Practice, 15*, 187–202.

Ley, P. (1977). Psychological studies of doctor–patient communication. In S. Rachman (Ed.), *Contributions to medical psychology* (Vol. 1, pp. 9–42). Oxford: Pergamon Press.

Ley, R. (1985). Agoraphobia, the panic attack and the hyperventilation syndrome. *Behaviour Research and Therapy, 23*, 79–82.

Liberman, R. P. (1980). [Review of Paul and Lentz's *Psychological treatment for chronic mental patients: Milieu versus social-learning programs*]. *Journal of Applied Behavior Analysis, 13*, 367–371.

Liberman, R. P., Nuechterlein, K. H., & Wallace, C. J. (1982). Social skills training and the nature of schizophrenia. In J. P. Curran & P. M. Monti (Eds.), *Social skills training: A practical handbook for assessment and treatment* (pp. 5–56). New York: Guilford Press.

Lichtenstein, E., & Mermelstein, R. J. (1984). Review of approaches to smoking treatment: Behavior modification strategies. In J. D. Matarazzo, S. M. Weiss, J. A. Herd, N. E. Miller, & S. M. Weiss (Eds.), *Behavioral health: A handbook of health enhancement and disease prevention* (pp. 695–712). New York: Wiley.

Lichtenstein, E., Severson, H. H., Friedman, L. S., & Ary, D. V. (1984). Chewing tobacco use by adolescents: Prevalence and relation to cigarette smoking. *Addictive Behaviors, 9*, 351–355.

Liebowitz, M. R., Gorman, J. M., Fyer, A. J., & Klein, D. (1985). Social phobia. *Archives of General Psychiatry, 42*, 729–736.

Lineberger, M. H., & Calhoun, K. S. (1983). Assertive behavior in black and white American undergraduates. *Journal of Psychology, 113*, 139–148.

Linehan, M. (in press-a). Dialectical behavior therapy for borderline personality disorder: Theory and method. *Bulletin of the Menninger Clinic.*

Linehan, M. (in press-b). Dialectical behavior therapy in groups: Treating borderline personality disorders and suicidal behavior. In C. M. Brody (Ed.), *Women in groups*. New York: Springer.

Linehan, M. (in press-c). Perspectives on the interpersonal relationship in behavior therapy. *International Journal of Eclectic Psychotherapy.*

Lipid Research Clinics Program. (1984a). The Lipid Research Clinics Coronary Primary Prevention Trial results: I. Reduction in incidence of coronary heart disease. *Journal of the American Medical Association, 251*, 351–364.

Lipid Research Clinics Program. (1984b). The Lipid Research Clinics Coronary Primary Prevention Trial results: II. The relationship of reduction in incidence of coronary heart disease to cholesterol lowering. *Journal of the American Medical As-*

sociation, 251, 365–374.

Litman, G. K. (1980). Relapse in alcoholism: Traditional and current approaches. In G. Edwards & M. Grant (Eds.), *Alcoholism treatment in transition* (pp. 294–303). Baltimore: University Park Press.

Litman, G. K., & Topham, A. (1983). Outcome studies on techniques in alcoholism treatment. In M. Galanter (Ed.), *Recent developments in alcoholism* (Vol. 1, pp. 167–194). New York: Plenum Press.

Lobitz, W. C., & Johnson, S. M. (1975). Parental manipulations of the behavior of normal and deviant children. *Child Development, 46*, 719–726.

Lochman, J. E. (1985). Effects of different treatment lengths in cognitive–behavioral interventions with aggressive boys. *Child Psychiatry and Human Development, 16*, 45–55.

Lochman, J. E., Burch, P. R., Curry, J. F., & Lampron, L. B. (1984). Treatment and generalization effects of cognitive–behavioral and goal-setting interventions with aggressive boys. *Journal of Consulting and Clinical Psychology, 52*, 915–916.

Lochman, J. E., & Curry, J. F. (1986). Effects of social problem-solving training and self-instruction training with aggressive boys. *Journal of Clinical Child Psychology, 15*, 159–164.

Lochman, J. E., Lampron, L. B., Burch, P. R., & Curry, J. F. (1985). Client characteristics associated with behavior change for treated and untreated aggressive boys. *Journal of Abnormal Child Psychology, 13*, 527–538.

Loeber, R., Dishion, T. J., & Patterson, G. R. (1984). Multiple gating: A multistage assessment procedure for identifying youths at risk for delinquency. *Journal of Research in Crime and Delinquency, 21*, 7–32.

London, P. (1984). Behavior therapy grows a belly [Review of Wilson and Franks's *Contemporary behavior therapy: Conceptual and empirical foundations*]. *Contemporary Psychology, 29*, 376–378.

Loney, J. (Ed.). (1985). Attention deficit disorder: Issues in assessment and intervention [Special issue]. *Clinical Psychology Review, 5*.

Long, B. (1985). Stress-management interventions: A 15-month follow-up of aerobic conditioning and stress inoculation training. *Cognitive Therapy and Research, 9*, 471–478.

Loper, A. B., & Hallahan, D. P. (1982). A consideration of the role of generalization in cognitive training. *Topics in Learning and Learning Disabilities, 2*, 62–67.

Lorber, R., Felton, D. K., & Reid, J. B. (1984). A social learning approach to the reduction of coercive processes in child abusive families: A molecular analysis. *Advances in Behaviour Research and Therapy, 6*, 29–45.

Louscher, P. K., Hosford, R. E., & Moss, C. S. (1983). Predicting dangerous behavior in a penitentiary using the Megargee typology. *Criminal Justice and Behavior, 10*, 269–284.

Luborsky, L., McLellan, T., Woody, G., O'Brien, C., & Auerbach, A. (1985). Therapist success and its determinants. *Archives of General Psychiatry, 2*, 602–611.

Lum, L. C. (1976). The syndrome of habitual chronic hyperventilation. In O. W. Hill (Ed.), *Modern trends in psychosomatic medicine* (Vol. 3). London: Butterworths.

Lundell, K. T. (1982). *Levels of discipline: A complete system for behavior management*. Springfield, IL: Charles C Thomas.

Lutzker, J. R. (1984). Project 12-Ways: Treating child abuse and neglect from an ecobehavioral perspective. In R. F. Dangel & R. A. Polster (Eds.), *Parent training: Foundations of research and practice* (pp. 260–295). New York: Guilford Press.

Lutzker, J. R., & Rice, J. M. (1984). Project 12-Ways: Measuring outcome of a large in-home service for treatment and prevention of child abuse and neglect. *Child Abuse and Neglect, 8*, 519–524.

Lutzker, J. r., Wesch, D., & Rice, J. M. (1984). A review of Project "12-Ways": An ecobehavioral approach to the treatment and prevention of child abuse and neglect. *Advances in Behaviour Research and Therapy, 6*, 63–73.

Lyman, R. D. (1984). The effect of private and public goal setting on classroom on-task behavior of emotionally disturbed children. *Behavior Therapy, 15*, 395–402.

Maccoby, N., Farquhar, J. W., Wood, P. D., & Alexander, J. (1977). Reducing the risk of cardiovascular disease: Effects of a community-based campaign on knowledge and behavior. *Journal of Community Health, 3*, 100–114.

MacDonald, M. L., Davidowitz, J. J., Gimbel, B., & Foley, L. M. (1982). Physical and social environmental reprogramming as treatment for psychogeriatric patients. *International Journal of Behavioral Geriatrics, 1*, 15–32.

Mackenzie, R. (1986a, May 19). From Sir Walter Raleigh on: The who and why of smoking. *Insight*, pp. 13–14.

Mackenzie, R. (1986b, May 19). A loyalist views tobacco's fate. *Insight*, p. 15.

Mackenzie, R. (1986c, May 19). Tobacco still smells sweet to North Carolina farmers. *Insight*, pp. 10–12.

Maddux, J. E., Roberts, M. C., Sledden, E. A., & Wright, L. (1986). Developmental issues in child health care. *American Psychologist, 41*, 25–34.

Maher, C. A. (Ed.). (1985). *Professional self-management: Techniques for special service providers*. Baltimore: Paul H. Brookes.

Maher, C. A., & Bennett, R. E. (1984). *Planning and evaluating special education services*. Englewood Cliffs, NJ: Prentice-Hall.

Mahoney, M. J. (1977). Reflections on the cognitive-learning trend in psychotherapy. *American Psychologist, 32*, 5–13.

Mahoney, M. J. (1986). *Self-deception in scientists*. Paper presented at the meeting of the American Association for Advancement of Science, Philadelphia.

Mahoney, M. J., & Arnkoff, D. (1978). Cognitive and self-control therapies. In S. L. Garfield & A. E. Bergin (Eds.), *Handbook of psychotherapy and behavior change* (2nd ed., 689–722). New York: Wiley.

Malatesta, V. J. (1985). Formulation of geriatric organic syndromes. In I. D. Turkat (Ed.), *Behavioral care formulation* (pp. 259–307). New York: Plenum Press.

Marcus, A. C., & Crane, L. A. (1985). Smoking behavior among U.S. Latinos: An emerging challenge for public health. *American Journal of Public Health, 75*, 169–172.

Margraf, J., Ehlers, A., & Roth, W. T. (1986). Panic attacks: Theoretical models and empirical evidence. In I. Hand & H. Wittchen (Eds.), *Panic and phobias* (pp. 31–43). New York: Springer-Verlag.

Marks, I. M. & Mathews, A. M. (1979). Brief standard self-rating for phobic patients. *Behaviour Research and Therapy, 17*, 263–267.

Marlatt, G. A., & Gordon, J. R. (Eds.). (1985). *Relapse prevention: Maintenance strategies in the treatment of addictive behaviors*. New York: Guilford Press.

Marmor, J., & Woods, S. (Eds.). (1980). *The interface between the psychodynamic and behavioral therapies*. New York: Plenum.

Marshall, W. L. (1985). The effects of variable exposure in flooding therapy. *Behavior Therapy, 16*, 117–135.

Marston, A. R., & Criss J. (1984). Maintenance of successful weight loss: Incidence and prediction. *International Journal of Obesity, 8*, 435–439.

Martin, A. (1951). The fear of relaxation and leisure. *American Journal of Psychoanalysis, 11*, 42–50.

Martin, I., & Levey, A. B. (1985). Conditioning, evaluations, and cognitions: An axis of integration. *Behaviour Research and Therapy, 23*, 167–175.

Martin, P. H. (1985). Trends in behaviour therapy: Progression or regression? *Behaviour Change, 2*, 119–128.

Marty, P. J., McDermott, R. J., & Williams, T. (1986). Patterns of smokeless tobacco use in a population of high school students. *American Journal of Public Health, 76,* 190–192.

Mash, E. J. (1984). Families with problem children. In A. Doyle, D. Gold, & D. S. Moskowitz (Eds.), *Children in families under stress* (pp. 65–84). San Francisco: Jossey-Bass.

Mash, E. J., & Barkley, R. A. (1986). Assessment of family interaction with the Response-Class Matrix. In R. Prinz (Ed.), *Advances in the behavioral assessment of children and families* (Vol. 2). Greenwich, CT: JAI Press.

Mash, E. J., & Terdal, L. G. (Eds.). (1981). *Behavioral assessment of childhood disorders.* New York: Guilford Press.

Mash, E. J., Terdal, L. G., & Anderson, K. (1973). The Response-Class Matrix: A procedure for recording parent–child interactions. *Journal of Consulting and Clinical Psychology, 40,* 163–164.

Mastropieri, M. A., & Scruggs, T. E. (1984). Generalization: Five effective strategies. *Academic Therapy, 19,* 427–431.

Matarazzo, J. D., Weiss, S. M., Herd, J. A., Miller, N. E., & Weiss, S. M. (Eds.). (1984). *Behavioral health: A handbook of health enhancement and disease prevention.* New York: Wiley.

Mathews, A. M., Gelder, M. G., & Johnston, D. W. (1981). *Agoraphobia: Nature and treatment.* New York: Guilford Press.

Mathews, A. M., & MacLeod, C. (1985). Selective processing of threat cure in anxiety states. *Behaviour Research and Therapy, 23,* 563–570.

Mathews, A. M., Teasdale, J., Munby, M., Johnston, D., & Shaw, P. (1977). A home-based treatment program for agoraphobia. *Behavior Therapy, 8,* 915–924.

Mathews, R. M. (1984). Teaching employment interview skills to unemployed adults. *Journal of Employment Counseling, 21,* 156–161.

Mathews, R. M., & Fawcett, S. B. (1984). Building the capacities of job candidates through behavioral instruction. *Journal of Community Psychology, 12,* 123–129.

Mathews, R. M., & Fawcett, S. B. (1985). Assisting in the job search: A behavioral assessment and training strategy [Monograph]. *Journal of Rehabilitation, 51*(2), 1–18.

Matkin, R. E. (1982). Rehabilitation services offered in the private sector: A pilot investigation. *Journal of Rehabilitation, 48,* 31–33.

Matson, J. L. (1982). Independence training versus modeling procedures for training phone conversation skills in the mentally retarded. *Behaviour Research and Therapy, 20,* 505–511.

Matthews, K. A. (1985). Assessment of Type A behavior, anger, and hostility in epidemiological studies of cardiovascular disease. In A. M. Ostfeld & E. D. Eaker (Eds.), *Measuring psychosocial variables in epidemiologic studies of cardiovascular disease: Proceedings of a workshop* (DHHS Publication No. NIH 85-2270, pp. 153–183). Washington, DC: U.S. Government Printing Office.

Matthews, K. A., Jamison, J. W., & Cottington, E. M. (1985). Appendix: Assessment of Type A, anger, and hostility: A review of scales through 1982. In A. M. Ostfeld, & E. D. Eaker, (Eds.), *Measuring psychosocial variables in epidemiologic studies of cardiovascular disease: Proceedings of a workshop* (DHHS Publication No. NIH 85-2270, pp. 207–311). Washington, DC: U.S. Government Printing Office.

Maurer, A. (1983). The shock rod controversy. *Journal of Clinical Child Psychology, 12,* 272–278.

Mavissakalian, M. (1986). The Fear Questionnaire: A validity study. *Behaviour Research and Therapy, 24,* 83–86.

Mavissakalian, M., & Perel, J. (1985). Imipramine in the treatment of agoraphobia: Dose–response relationships. *American Journal of Psychiatry, 142*, 1032–1036.

Mayer, J. (1965). Genetic factors in human obesity. *Annals of the New York Academy of Sciences, 131*, 412–421.

Mays, D. T., & Franks, C. M. (Eds.). (1985). *Negative outcome in psychotherapy and what to do about it*. New York: Springer.

McAfee, R. E. (1986). Shall we continue to climb? *Journal of the American Medical Association, 255*, 1055.

McBrien, J. A. (1981)). Introducing the EDY Project. *Special Education: Forward Trends, 8*, 29–31.

McBrien, J. A., & Edmonds, M. (1985). Evaluation of an E.D.Y. training course in behavioural techniques for staff working with severely mentally handicapped children. *Behavioural Psychotherapy, 13*, 202–217.

McCormick, M. C. (1985). The contribution of low birth weight to infant mortality and childhood morbidity. *New England Journal of Medicine, 312*, 82–90.

McCue, H., Jr. (1981). The 1979 Build and Blood Pressure Study. In H. Bostrom & N. Ljungstedt (Eds.), *Medical aspects of mortality statistics* (pp. 182–198). Stockholm: Almqvist & Wiksell.

McDowell, A., Engel, A., Massey, J. T., & Maurer, K. (1981). Plan and operation of the second National Health and Nutrition Examination Survey, 1976–80. *Vital and Health Statistics*, Series 1, No. 15 (DHHS Publication No. PHS 81-1317). Washington, DC: U.S. Government Printing Office.

McFall, R. M. (1985). Nonbehavioral training for behavioral clinicians. *the Behavior Therapist, 8*, 27–30.

McGee, G. G., Krantz, P. J., Mason, D., & McClannahan, L. E. (1983). A modified incidental-teaching procedure for autistic youth: Acquisition and generalization of receptive object labels. *Journal of Applied Behavior Analysis, 16*, 329–338.

McGee, G. G., Krantz, P. J., & McClannahan, L. E. (1985). The facilitative effects of incidental teaching on preposition use by autistic children. *Journal of Applied Behavior Analysis, 18*, 17–31.

McGee, R., Williams, S., & Silva, P. A. (1985). Factor structure and correlates of ratings of inattention, hyperactivity, and antisocial behavior in a large sample of 9-year-old children from the general population. *Journal of Consulting and Clinical Psychology, 53*(4), 480–490.

McKim, B. J., Weissberg, R. P., Cowen, E. L., Gerten, E. L., & Rupkin, B. (1982). A comparison of the problem-solving ability and adjustment of suburban and urban third-grade children. *American Journal of Community Psychology, 10*, 155–170.

McMichael, A. J. (1984). Oral cancer in the Third World: Time for preventive intervention? *International Journal of Epidemiology, 13*, 403–405.

McSweeney, F. K., & Bierley, C.(1984). Recent developments in classical conditioning. *Journal of Consumer Research, 11*, 619–631.

Meador, A. E., & Ollendick, T. H. (1984). Cognitive behavior therapy with children: An evaluation of its efficacy and clinical utility. *Child and Family Behavior Therapy, 6*, 25–44.

Meehl, P. (1954). *Clinical versus statistical prediction*. Minneapolis: University of Minnesota Press.

Megargee, E. I., & Bohn, M. J. (1979). *Classifying criminal offenders: A new system based on the MMPI*. Beverly Hills, CA: Sage.

Meichenbaum, D. (1977). *Cognitive-behavior modification: An integrative approach*. New York: Plenum.

Meichenbaum, D. (1985). *Stress inoculation training*. New York: Pergamon Press.

Meichenbaum, D., & Gilmore, J. (1982). Resistance: From a cognitive–behavioral perspective. In P. Wachtel (Ed.), *Resistance* (pp. 133–156). New York: Plenum.

Meichenbaum, D., & Turk, D. (1976). The cognitive–behavioral management of anxiety, anger, and pain. In P. O. Davidson (Ed.), *The behavioral management of anxiety, depression, and pain* (pp. 1–34). New York: Brunner/Mazel.

Merker, S. L. (1985). Living systems theory: A framework for management. *Behavioral Science, 30*, 187–194.

Merrett, F., & Wheldall, K. (1984). Training teachers to use the behavioural approach to classroom management: A review. *Educational Psychology, 4*, 213–231.

Mesibov, G. B. (1984). Social skills training with verbal autistic adolescents and adults: A program model. *Journal of Autism and Developmental Disorders, 14*, 395–404.

Messer, S. B. (1984). The integration of psychoanalytic therapy and behavior therapy: Summing up. In H. Arkowitz & S. B. Messer (Eds.), *Psychoanalytic therapy and behavior therapy: Is integration possible?* (pp. 359–370). New York: Plenum.

Messer, S. B. (1985). Choice of method is value laden too. *American Psychologist, 40*, 1414–1415.

Messerer, J., Hunt, E., Meyers, G., & Lerner, J. (1984). Feuerstein's instrumental enrichment: A new approach for activating intellectual potential in learning disabled youth. *Journal of Learning Disabilities, 17*, 322–325.

Metropolitan Life Insurance Company. (1983). 1983 Metropolitan height and weight tables. *Statistical Bulletin, 64*, 2–9.

Meyers, A. W., & Cohen, R. (1984). Cognitive–behavioral interventions in educational settings. In P. C. Kendall (Ed.), *Advances in cognitive–behavioral research and therapy* (Vol. 3, pp. 131–167). New York: Academic Press.

Meyers, A. W., & Craighead, W. E. (Eds.). (1984). *Cognitive behavior therapy with children: Applied clinical psychology*. New York: Plenum Press.

Michelson, L., & Mavissakalian, M. (1985). Psychophysiological outcome of behavioral and pharmacological treatments of agoraphobia. *Journal of Consulting and Clinical Psychology, 53*, 229–236.

Michelson, L., Mavissakalian, M., & Marchione, K. (1985). Cognitive and behavioral treatments of agoraphobia: Clinical, behavioral, and psychophysiological outcomes. *Journal of Consulting and Clinical Psychology, 53*, 913–925.

Middlebrook, J. L., & Forehand, R. (1985). Maternal perception of deviance in child behavior as a function of stress and clinic versus nonclinic status of the child: An analogue study. *Behavior Therapy, 16* 494–502.

Milich, R. & Fitzgerald, G. (1985). Validation of inattention/overactivity and aggression ratings with classroom observation. *Journal of Consulting and Clinical Psychology, 53*, 139–140.

Milich, R., Loney, J., & Roberts, M. A. (1986). Brief reports. *Journal of Consulting and Clinical Psychology, 54*, 272–274.

Miller, H. W. (1973). Plan and operation of the Health and Nutrition Examination Survey, United States—1971–73. *Vital and Health Statistics*, Series 1, No. 10a and 10b (DHEW Publication No. HSM 73-1310). Washington, DC: U.S. Government Printing Office.

Miller, J. G. (1978). *Living systems*. New York: McGraw-Hill.

Miller, R. C., & Berman, J. S. (1983). The efficacy of cognitive behavior therapies: A quantitative review of the research evidence. *Psychological Bulletin, 94*, 39–53.

Miller, S. M. (1979). Controllability and human stress: Methods, evidence and theory. *Behaviour Research and Therapy, 17*, 287–304.

Miller, W. R., & Hester, R. K. (1980). Treating the problem drinker: Modern approaches. In W. R. Miller (Ed.), *The addictive behaviors: Treatment of alcoholism, drug abuse, smoking, and obesity*. (pp. 11–141). New York: Pergamon Press.

Milne, D. (1985a). An ecological validation of nurse training in behaviour therapy. *Behavioural Psychotherapy, 13*, 14–28.

Milne, D. (1985b). An observational evaluation of the effects of nurse training in behaviour therapy on unstructured ward activities and interaction. *British Journal of Clinical Psychology, 24*, 149–158.

Milne, D. (1985c). A review of the in-service training of nurses in behaviour therapy. *Behavioural Psychotherapy, 13*, 120–131.

Milne, D., Burdett, C., & Conway, P. (1985). Review and replications of a course in behaviour therapy for psychiatric nurses. *Journal of Advanced Nursing, 10*, 137–148.

Mineka, S. (in press). Animal models of anxiety-based disorders: Their usefulness and limitations. In J. Maser & A. Tuma (Eds.), *Anxiety and anxiety disorders*. Bethesda, MD: National Institute of Mental Health.

Mineka, S., Davidson, M., Cook, M., & Keir, R. (1984). Observational conditioning of snake fear in rhesus monkeys. *Journal of Abnormal Psychology, 93*, 355–372.

Mintz, J. (1983). Integrating research evidence. *Journal of Consulting and Clinical Psychology, 51*, 71–75.

Mintz, J., Mintz, L. I., & Jarvik, L. F. (1985). Cognitive–behavioral therapy in geriatric depression: Reply to Riskind, Beck, and Steer. *Journal of Consulting and Clinical Psychology, 53*, 946–947.

Miranda, A. (1985). *Escala de classificacion de auto control*. (Available from Dr. Ana Miranda, Psicologia, Universidad de Valencia, Valencia, Spain.)

Mischel, W. (1980). George Kelly's anticipation of psychology: A personal tribute. In M. J. Mahoney (Ed.), *Psychotherapy process*. New York: Plenum.

Mittelmark, M. B., Luepker, R. V., Jacobs, D. R., Bracht, N. F., Carlaw, R. W., Crow, R. S., Finnegan, J., Grimm, R. H., Jeffery, R. W., Kline, F. G., Mullis, R. M., Murray, D. M., Pechacek, T. F., Perry, C. L., Pirie, P. L., & Blackburn, H. (1986). Community-wide prevention of cardiovascular disease: Education strategies of the Minnesota Heart Health Program. *Preventive Medicine, 15*, 1–17.

Montero, J. C. (1985). *Escalar de Evaluacion del Auto Control para Ninos*. (Available from Juan Carlos Montero Ordinola, Instituto Nacional de Salud Mental, Alameda Palao s/n–Urb. Palao, San Martin de Porrar, Lima, Peru.)

Monti, P. M. (1985). Interviewing for internships. *the Behavior Therapist, 10*, 205–206.

Moos, R. H., & Lemke, S. (1985). Specialized living environments for older people. In J. E. Birren & K. W. Schaie (Eds.), *Handbook of the psychology of aging* (2nd ed., pp. 864–889). New York: Van Nostrand Reinhold.

Morgenstern, H. (1985). Socioeconomic factors: Concepts, measurement, and health effects. In A. M. Ostfeld & E. D. Eaker (Eds.), *Measuring psychosocial variables in epidemiologic studies of cardiovascular disease: Proceedings of a workshop* (DHHS Publication No. NIH 85-2270, pp. 3–35). Washington, DC: U.S. Government Printing Office.

Morris, R. J. (1985). *Behavior modification with exceptional children: Principles and practices*. Glenview, IL: Scott, Foresman.

Morris, R. J., & Kratochwill, T. R. (1983). *Treating children's fears and phobias: A behavioral approach*. New York: Plenum Press.

Morrow-Bradley, C., & Elliot, R. (1986). Utilization of psychotherapy research by practicing psychotherapists. *American Psychologist, 41*, 188–197.

Moses, A. N., & Hollandsworth, J. G. (1985). Relative effectiveness of education alone versus stress inoculation training in the treatment of dental phobia. *Behavior Therapy, 16*, 531–537.

Moss, G. R. (1983). Behavioral technology and hospital psychiatry: Considerations from the private sector. *Analysis and Internvention in Developmental Disabilities, 3*, 205–214.

Mowrer, O. H. (1960). *Learning and behavior*. New York: Wiley.

Moyes, T., Tennent, T. G., & Bedford, A. P. (1985). Long-term follow-up study of a ward-based behaviour modification programme for adolescents with acting-out and conduct problems. *British Journal of Psychiatry, 147*, 300–305.

Multiple Risk Factor Intervention Trial Research Group. (1982). Multiple Risk Factor Intervention Trial: Risk factor changes and mortality results. *Journal of the American Medical Association, 248*, 1465–1477.

Multiple Risk Factor Intervention Trial Research Group. (1985). Baseline rest electrocardiographic abnormalities, antihypertensive treatment, and mortality in the Multiple Risk Factor Intervention Trial. *American Journal of Cardiology, 55*, 1–15.

Multiple Risk Factor Intervention Trial Research Group. (1986). Relationship between baseline risk factors and coronary heart disease and total mortality in the Multiple Risk Factor Intervention Trial. *Preventive Medicine, 15*, 254–273.

Murphy, G. C. (1985). Designing an organizational environment supportive of in-service training programs: A comment on Wheldall and Merrett. *Behaviour Change, 2*, 33–35.

Murphy, G. E., Simons, A. D., Wetzel, R. D., & Lustman, P. J. (1984). Cognitive therapy and pharmacotherapy. *Archives of General Psychiatry, 41*, 33–41.

Murray, J., & Whittenberger, D. (1983). The aggressive, severely behavior disordered child. *Journal of Learning Disabilities, 16*, 76–80.

Nader, P. R., Sallis, J. F., Rupp, J., Atkins, C., Patterson, T., Buono, M., Vega, W., Senn, K. L., Abramson, I., Roppe, B., & Kaplan, R. (1985, October). *The San Diego Family Health Project: Reaching families through the schools*. Paper presented at the meeting of the American School Health Association, Little Rock, AR.

Narayanan, V. K., & Nath, R. (1982). A field test of some attitudinal and behavioral consequences of flextime. *Journal of Applied Psychology, 67*, 214–218.

Nathan, P. E. (1986). Outcomes of treatment for alcoholism: Current data. *Annals of Behavioral Medicine, 8*, 40–46.

Nathan, P. E., & Niaura, R. S. (1985). Behavioral assessment and treatment of alcoholism. In J. H. Mendelson & N. K. Mello (Eds.), *The diagnosis and treatment of alcoholism* (2nd ed., pp. 391–455). New York: McGraw-Hill.

National Center for Health Statistics. (1984, December). *Health United States, 1984* (DHHS Publication No. PHS 85-1232). Washington, DC: U.S. Government Printing Office.

National Center for Health Statistics. (1985). *Health United States, 1985* (DHHS Publication No. PHS 86-1232). Washington, DC: U.S. Government Printing Office.

National Institute on Alcohol Abuse and Alcoholism. (1980, August). *Facts in brief: Alcohol and blacks*. Rockville, MD: National Clearinghouse for Alcohol Information.

National Institutes of Health Consensus Development Panel on the Health Implications of Obesity. (1985). Health implications of obesity: National Institutes of Health consensus development conference statement. *Annals of Internal Medicine, 103*, 1073–1077.

Neimeyer, R. A. (1985). Personal constructs in clinical practice. In P. C. Kendall (Ed.), *Advances in cognitive–behavioral research and therapy* (Vol. 4, pp. 276–340). New York: Academic Press.

Nelson, R. O. (1983). Behavioral assessment: Past, present and future. *Behavioral Assessment, 5*, 195–206.

New York City Police Department. (1982). *Homicide analysis*. New York: Crime Analysis Unit.

Nezu, A. M. (1985). Differences in psychological distress between effective and ineffective problem solvers. *Journal of Counseling Psychology, 32*, 135–138.

Nezu, A. M. (1986). Efficacy of a social problem-solving therapy approach for unipolar depression. *Journal of Consulting and Clinical Psychology, 54*, 196–202.

Nezu, A. M., & D'Zurilla, T. J. (1979). An experimental evaluation of the decision making process in social problem solving. *Cognitive Therapy and Research, 3*, 269–277.

Nezu, A. M., Kalmar, K., Ronan, G. F., & Clavijo, A. (1986). Attributional correlates of depression: An interactional model including problem solving. *Behavior Therapy, 17*, 50–56.

Nicholson, R. A., & Berman, J. S. (1983). Is follow-up necessary in evaluating psychotherapy? *Psychological Bulletin, 93*, 261–278.

Nisbett, R. E., Krantz, D. H., Jepson, C., & Fong, G. (1982). Improving inductive inference. In D. Kahneman, P. Slovic, & A. Tversky (Eds.), *Judgement under uncertainty: Heuristics and biases*. New York: Cambridge University Press.

Nisbett, R., & Ross, L. (1980). *Human inference*. Englewood Cliffs, NJ: Prentice-hall.

Norcross, J. C., & Prochaska, J. O. (1982a). A national survey of clinical psychologists: Affiliations and orientations. *The Clinical Psychologist, 38*(3), 4–6.

Norcross, J. C., & Prochaska, J. O. (1982b). A national survey of clinical psychologists: Characteristics and activities. *The Clinical Psychologist, 38*(2), 1–8.

Norcross, J. C., & Prochaska, J. O. (1984). Where do behavior (and other) therapists take their troubles?: II. *the Behavior Therapist, 7*, 26–27.

Norcross, J. C., & Wogan, M. (1983). American psychotherapists of diverse persuasions: Characteristics, theories, practices, and clients. *Professional Psychology: Research and Practice, 14*, 529–539.

Norton, G. R., Austen, S., Allen, G. E., & Hilton, J. (1983). Acceptability of time out from reinforcement procedures for disruptive child behavior: A further analysis. *Child and Family Behavior Therapy, 5*, 31–41.

Novaco, R. W. (1975). *Anger control: The development and evaluation of an experimental treatment*. Lexington, MA: D. C. Heath.

Noyes, R., Jr., Anderson, D. J., Clancey, J., Crowe, R. R., Slymen, D. J., Ghoneim, M. M., & Hinrichs, J. V. (1984). Diazepam and propranolol in panic disorder and agoraphobia. *Archives of General Psychiatry, 41*, 287–292.

O'Connor, W. A., & Lubin, B. (Eds.). (1984). *Ecological approaches to clinical and community psychology*. New York: Wiley.

O'Dell, S. L. (1985). Progress in parent training. In M. Hersen, R. M. Eisler, & P. M. Miller (Eds.), *Progress in behavior modification* (Vol. 19, pp. 57–108). New York: Academic Press.

O'Dell, S. L., O'Quinn, J. A., Alford, B. A., O'Briant, A. L., Bradlyn, A. S., & Giebenhain, J. E. (1982). Predicting the acquisition of parenting skills via four training methods. *Behavior Therapy, 13*, 194–208.

O'Hara, M. W., French, C. J., Zekoski, E. M., Neunaber, D. J., & Schroeder, G. W. (1985). Discriminating adaptive attributions: Agreement between self-report and objective ratings. *Cognitive Therapy and Research, 9*, 267–275.

O'Leary, K. D., & Borkovec, T. D. (1978). Conceptual, methodological, and ethical problems of placebo groups in psychotherapy research. *American Psychologist, 33*, 821–830.

O'Leary, K. D., & Wilson, G. T. (1987). *Behavior therapy: Application and outcome* (2nd ed.). Englewood Cliffs, NJ: Prentice-Hall.

Oliver, J. M., & Baumgart, E. P. (1985). The Dysfunctional Attitude Scale: Psychometric properties and relation to depression in an unselected adult population. *Cognitive Therapy and Research, 9*, 161–167.

Oliver, J. M., & Simmons, M. E. (1984). Depression as measured by the DSM-III and the Beck Depression Inventory in an unselected adult population. *Journal of Consulting and Clinical Psychology, 52*, 892–898.

Ollendick, T. H., & Hersen, M. (Eds.). (1984). *Child behavior assessment: Principles and procedures*. New York: Pergamon Press.

O'Neil, P. M., Currey, H. S., Hirsch, A. A., Riddle, F. E., Taylor, C. I., Malcolm, R. J., & Sexauer, J. D. (1979). Effects of sex of subject and spouse involvement on weight loss in a behavioral treatment program: A retrospective investigation. *Addictive Behaviors, 4*, 167–177.

Ordman, A. M., & Kirschenbaum, D. S. (1985). Cognitive–behavioral therapy for bulemia: An initial outcome study. *Journal of Consulting and Clinical Psychology, 53*, 305–313.

Orlinsky, D. E., & Howard, K. E. (1978). The relation of process to outcome in psychotherapy. In S. L. Garfield & A. E. Bergin (Eds.), *Handbook of psychotherapy and behavior changes* (2nd ed., pp. 283–330). New York: Wiley.

Ortmeyer, C. F. (1974). Variations in mortality, morbidity, and health care by marital status. In C. L. Erhardt & J. E. Berlin (Eds.), *Mortality and morbidity in the United States* (pp. 159–188). Cambridge, MA: Harvard University Press.

Ostfeld, A. M. (1985). Social support and social networks: Working group summary. In A. M. Ostfeld & E. D. Eaker (Eds.), *Measuring psychosocial variables in epidemiologic studies of cardiovascular disease: Proceedings of a workshop* (DHHS Publication No. NIH 85-2270, pp. 99–101). Washington, DC: U.S. Government Printing Office.

Ostfeld, A. M., & Eaker, E. D. (Eds.). (1985). *Measuring psychosocial variables in epidemiologic studies of cardiovascular disease: Proceedings of a workshop* (DHHS Publication No. NIH 85-2270). Washington, DC: U.S. Government Printing Office.

Palmore, E. (1969). Predicting longevity: A follow-up controlling for age. *Gerontologist, 9*, 247–250.

Patterson, G. R. (1982). *A social learning approach to family intervention: Vol. 3. Coercive family process*. Eugene, OR: Castalia.

Patterson, G. R., & Forgatch, M. S. (1985). Therapist behavior as a determinant for client noncompliance: A paradox for the behavior modifier. *Journal of Consulting and Clinical Psychology, 53*, 846–851.

Patterson, R. L., Dupree, L. W., Eberly, D. A., Jackson, G. M., O'Sullivan, M. J., Penner, L. A., & Kelly, C. D. (1982). *Overcoming deficits of aging: A behavioral approach*. New York: Plenum Press.

Paul, G. L. (1966). *Insight versus desensitization in psychotherapy*. Stanford, CA: Stanford University Press.

Paul, G. L. (1967a). Insight versus sensitization in psychotherapy two years after termination. *Journal of Consulting Psychology, 31*, 333–345.

Paul, G. L. (1967b). Strategy of outcome research in psychotherapy. *Journal of Consulting Psychology, 39*, 109–119.

Paul, G. L. (1985). Can pregnancy be a placebo effect? Terminology, designs, and conclusions in the study of psychosocial and pharmacological treatments of behavioral disorders. In L. White, B. Tursky, & G. Schwartz (Eds.), *Placebo: Clinical phenomenon and new insights* (pp. 137–163). New York: Guilford Press.

Paul, G. L., & Lentz, R. J. (1977). *Psychological treatment for chronic mental patients: Milieu versus social-learning programs*. Cambridge, MA: Harvard University Press.

Paulus, P. B., McCain, G., & Cox, V. C. (1985). The effects of crowding in prisons and jails. In D. P. Farrington, & J. Gunn (Eds.), *Reactions to crime: The public, the police, courts, and prisons* (pp. 113–134). New York: Wiley.

Pendery, M. L., Maltzman, I. M., & West, L. J. (1982). Controlled drinking by alcoholics? New findings and a reevaluation of a major affirmative study. *Science, 217*, 169–175.

Perri, M. G., McAdoo, W. G., Spevak, P. A., & Newlin, D. B. (1984a). Effect of a multicomponent maintenance program on long-term weight loss. *Journal of Consulting and Clinical Psychology, 52*, 480–481.

Perri, M. G., Shapiro, R. M., Ludwig, W. W., Twentyman, C. T., & McAdoo, W. G. (1984b). Maintenance strategies for the treatment of obesity: An evaluation of relapse prevention training and posttreatment contact by mail and telephone. *Journal of Consulting and Clinical Psychology, 52*, 404–413.

Perry, M. A., Wells, E. A., & Doran, L. D. (1983). Parent characteristics in abusing and non-abusing families. *Journal of Clinical Child Psychology, 12*, 329–336.

Persons, J., & Burns, D. (1985). Mechanisms of action of cognitive therapy: The relative contributions of technical and interpersonal interventions. *Cognitive Therapy and Research, 9*, 539–552.

Peterson, D. (1982). *Human error reduction and safety management.* New York: Garland & TPM Press.

Peterson, D. R. (1981). Overall synthesis of the Spring Hill Symposium on the Future of Psychology in the Schools. *School Psychology Review, 10*, 307–314.

Peterson, R., & Zakel, R. (1985). Aversives in special education programs for behaviorally disordered students: A debate. *Behavioral Disorders, 10*, 295–304.

Pfeffer, C. R. (1986). *The suicidal child.* New York: Guilford Press.

Pfiffner, L. J., Rosen, L. A., & O'Leary, S. (1985). The efficacy of an all-positive approach to classroom management. *Journal of Applied Behavioral Analysis, 18*, 257–261.

Phelps, R. E., & Slater, M. A. (1985). Sequential interactions that discriminate high- and low-problem single mother–son dyads. *Journal of Consulting and Clinical Psychology, 53*, 684–692.

Pickering, J. F. (1981). A behavioral model of the demand for consumer durables. *Journal of Economic Psychology, 1*, 59–77.

Pigott, H. E., & Heggie, D. L. (1985). Interpreting the conflicting results of individual versus group contingencies in classrooms: The targeted behavior as a mediating variable. *Child and Family Behavior Therapy, 7*, 1–15.

Pinkston, E. M., & Linsk, N. L. (1984a). Behavioral family intervention with the impaired elderly. *The Gerontologist, 24*, 575–583.

Pinkston, E. M., & Linsk, N. L. (1984b). *Care of the elderly: A family approach.* New York: Pergamon Press.

Pinsof, W., & Catherall, D. (1983). *The Couples Therapy Alliance Scale Manual.* Chicago: The Chicago Center for Family Studies, Northwestern University.

Piotrowski, C., & Keller, J. W. (1984a). Psychodiagnostic testing in APA approved clinical psychology programs. *Profesional Psychology: Research and Practice, 15*, 450–456.

Piotrowski, C., & Keller, J. W. (1984b, March). *Attitudes toward clinical assessment by members of the AABT*. Paper presented at the convention of the Southeastern Psychological Association, New Orleans.

Piotrowski, C., Sherry, D., & Keller, J. W. (1985). Psychodiagnostic test usage: A survey of the Society for Personality Assessment. *Journal of Personality Assessment, 49*, 2.

Pisterman, S. J. (1985). *Adapted version of the Self-Control Rating Scale for preschool children.* (Available from S. J. Pisterman, Children's Hospital of Eastern Ontario, 401 Smyth, Ottawa, Ontario, Canada K1H 8L1.)

Plotkin, R. C., Azar, S., Twentyman, C. T., & Perri, M. G. (1981). A critical evaluation of the research methodology employed in the investigation of causative factors of child abuse and neglect. *Child Abuse and Neglect, 5*, 449–455.

Pomerleau, O. F. (1980). Why people smoke: Current psychobiological models. In P. O. Davidson & S. M. Davidson (Eds.), *Behavioral medicine: Changing health lifestyles* (pp. 94–115). New York: Brunner/Mazel.

Pomerleau, O. F., & Brady, J. P. (1979). *Behavioral medicine: Theory and practice.* Baltimore: Williams & Wilkins.

Pomerleau, O. F., & Pomerleau, C. S. (1977). *Break the smoking habit: A behavioral program for giving up cigarettes.* Champaign, IL: Research Press.

Powell, D. R., (1984). Social network and demographic predictors of length of participation in a present education program. *Journal of Community Psychology, 12*, 13–19.

Powell, D. R., & McCann, B. S. (1981). The effects of a multiple treatment and multiple maintenance procedures on smoking cessation. *Preventive Medicine, 10*, 94–104.

Powers, M. D., & Handleman, J. S. (1984). *Behavioral assessment of severe developmental disabilities.* Rockville, MD: Aspen Systems Corporation.

Poznanski, E. O. Cook, S. C. & Carroll, B. J. (1979). A depression rating scale for children. *Pediatrics*, 64, 442–450.

Prioleau, L., Murdock, M., & Brody, N. (1983). An analysis of psychotherapy versus placebo studies. *Behavioral and Brain Sciences, 6*, 275–310.

Prochaska, J. O., DiClemente, C. C., Velicer, W. F., Ginpil, S., & Norcross, J. C. (1985). Predicting change in smoking status for self-changers. *Addictive Behaviors, 10*, 395–406.

Prochaska, J. O., & Norcross, J. C. (1983). Contemporary psychotherapists: A national survey of characteristics, practices, orientations, and attitudes. *Psychotherapy: Theory, Research and Practice, 20*, 161–173.

Puente, A. E., & Horton, A. M. (1986). Behavior therapy and clinical neuropsychology: Behavioral neuropsychology. *the Behavior Therapist, 9*, 30–31.

Puig-Antich, J. (1986). *Schedule for Affective Disorders and Schizophrenia for School Age Children (6–18 years).* Unpublished manuscript, University of Pittsburgh School of Medicine.

Puig-Antich, J., & Chambers, W. (1978). *Schedule for affective disorders and schizophrenia for school-age children.* New York: New York State Psychiatric Institute.

Pulliam, H. R. (1982). A social learning model of conflict and cooperation in human services. *Human Ecology, 10*, 353–363.

Puska, P., Nissinen, A., Tuomilehto, J., Salonen, J. T., Koskela, K., McAlister, A., Kottke, T. E., Maccoby, N., & Farquhar, J. (1985). The community-based strategy to prevent coronary heart disease: Conclusions from the ten years of the North Karelia Project. *Annual Review of Public Health, 6*, 147–193.

Pynoos, J., Hade-Kaplan, B., & Fleischer, D.(1984). Intergenerational neighborhood networks: A basis for aiding the frail elderly. *The Gerontologist, 24*, 233–237.

Quilitch, R. (1975). A comparison of three staff management techniques. *Journal of Applied Behavior Analysis, 8*, 59–66.

Rachman, S. (1978). *Fear and courage*. San Francisco: W. H. Freeman.

Rachman, S. (1981). The primacy of affect: Some theoretical implications. *Behaviour Research and Therapy, 19*, 279–290.

Rachman, S. (1983). Behavioural medicine, clinical reasoning and technical advances. *Canadian Journal of Behavioural Science, 4*, 318–333.

Rachman, S. (1984). Agoraphobia—a safety-signal perspective. *Behaviour Research and Therapy, 22*, 59–70.

Rachman, S. (1986). [Review of A. Beck and G. Emery, with R. Greenberg, *Anxiety disorders and phobias: A cognitive perspective*]. *Behaviour Research and Therapy, 24*, 95–96.

Rachman, S., & Hodgson, R. (1974). Synchrony and desynchrony in fear and avoidance: I. *Behaviour Research and Therapy, 12*, 311–318.

Rachman, S., & Levitt, K. (1985). Panics and their consequences. *Behaviour Research and Therapy, 23*, 585–600.

Rachman, S., & Wilson, G. T. (1980). *The effects of psychological therapy*. Oxford: Pergamon Press.

Rapee, R. (1985a). The alleviation of panic attacks in the case of panic disorder. *Journal of Behavior Therapy and Experimental Psychiatry, 16*, 63–65.

Rapee, R. (1985b). *Distinctions between panic attacks and generalized anxiety*. Unpublished doctoral dissertation, University of New South Wales, Australia.

Rapee, R. (1985c). Distinctions in clinical presentation between panic disorder and generalized anxiety disorder. *Australian and New Zealand Journal of Psychiatry, 19*, 227–232.

Rapee, R. (1986). Differential response to hyperventilation in panic disorder and generalized anxiety disorder. *Journal of Abnormal Psychology, 95*, 24–28.

Reda, M. A., & Mahoney, M. J. (Eds.). (1984). *Cognitive psychotherapies: Recent developments in theory, research, and practice*. Cambridge, MA: Ballinger.

Reeve, R. A., & Brown, A. L. (1985). Meta cognition reconsidered: Implications for intervention research. *Journal of Abnormal Child Psychology, 13*(3), 343–356.

Reich, J. W., & Zautra, A. J. (1984). Daily event causation: An approach to elderly life quality. *Journal of Community Psychology, 12*, 312–322.

Reid, D. H., Parsons, M. B., McCarn, J. E., Green, C. W., Phillips, J. F., & Schepis, M. M. (1985). Providing a more appropriate education for severely handicapped persons: Increasing and validating functional classroom tasks. *Journal of Applied Behavior Analysis, 18*, 289–301.

Reid, J. B. (Ed.). (1978). *A social learning approach to family intervention: Vol. 2. Observation in home settings*. Eugene, OR: Castalia.

Reid, J. B., & Kavanagh, K. (1985). A social interactional approach to child abuse: Risk, prevention, and treatment. In M. A. Chesney & R. H. Rosenman (Eds.), *Anger and hostility in cardiovascular and behavioral disorders* (pp. 241–257). Washington, DC: Hemisphere.

Reiss, S., & Bootzin, R. B. (Eds.). (1985). *Theoretical issues in behavior therapy*. New York: Academic Press.

Research Group of the Rome Project of Coronary Heart Disease Prevention. (1986). Eight-year follow-up results from the Rome Project of Coronary Heart Disease Prevention. *Preventive Medicine, 15*, 176–191.

Review Panel on Coronary-Prone Behavior and Coronary Heart Disease. (1981). Coronary-prone behavior and coronary heart disease: A critical review. *Circulation, 63*, 1199–1215.

Reynolds, W. M. (1986). A model for the screening and identification of depressed children and adolescents in school settings. *Professional School Psychology, 1*, 117–129.

Reynolds, W. M., Anderson, G., & Bartell, N. (1985). Measuring depression in children: A multimethod assessment investigation. *Journal of Abnormal Child Psychology, 13*, 513–526.

Rincover, A., & Newsom, C. D. (1985). The relative motivational properties of sensory and edible reinforcers in teaching autistic children. *Journal of Applied Behavior Analysis, 18*, 237–248.

Rios, J. D., & Gutierrez, J. M. (1986). Parent training with non-traditional families: An unresolved issue. *Child and Family Behavior Therapy, 7*, 27–39.

Rippere, V. (1983). Food additives and hyperactive children: A critique of Conners. *British Journal of Clinical Psychology, 22*, 19–32.

Riskind, J. H., Beck, A. T., & Steer, R. A. (1985). Cognitive–behavioral therapy in geriatric depression: Comment on Steuer *et al. Journal of Consulting and Clinical Psychology, 53*, 944–945.

Roberts, M. W. (1985). Praising child compliance: Reinforcement or ritual? *Journal of Abnormal Child Psychology, 13*, 611–629.

Roberts, M. W., McMahon, R., Forehand, R., & Humphreys, L. (1978). The effect of parental instruction giving on child compliance. *Behavior Therapy, 9*, 793–798.

Roemer, R. (1982). *Legislative action to combat the world smoking epidemic*. Geneva: World Health Organization.

Rogers, T. R., & Forehand, R.(1983). The role of parent depression in interactions between mothers and their clinic-referred children. *Cognitive Therapy and Research, 7*, 315–324.

Rohsenow, D. J. (1985). Bungling the academic interview. *the Behavior Therapist, 8*, 185–186.

Romanczyk, R. G., Kistner, J. A., & Ponzetti-Dyer, N. (1983). Autism. In M. Hersen, V. B. Van Hassatt, & J. L. Matson (Eds.), *Behavior therapy for the developmentally and physically disabled* (pp. 155–203). New York: Academic Press.

Rose, G., Tunstall-Pedoe, H. D., & Heller, R. F. (1983). UK Heart Disease Prevention Project: Incidence and mortality results. *Lancet, i*, 1062–1066.

Rosen, G. M. (1976). The development and use of nonprescription behavior therapies. *American Psychologist, 31*, 139–141.

Rosen, G. M. (1987). Self-help treatment books and the commercialization of psychotherapy. *American Psychologist, 42*, 46–51.

Rosen, L. A., O'Leary, S. G., & Conway, S. G. (1985). Case studies and clinical replication series. The withdrawal of stimulant medication for hyperactivity: Overcoming detrimental attributions. *Behavior Therapy, 16*, 538–544.

Rosen, L. A., O'Leary, S. G., Joyce, S. A., Conway, G., & Pfiffner, L. J. (1984). The importance of prudent negative consequences for maintaining the appropriate behavior of hyperactive students. *Journal of Applied Behavior Analysis, 12*, 581–604.

Rosenbaum, M. (1980). A schedule for assessing self-control behaviors. *Behavior Therapy, 11*, 109–121.

Ross, A. O. (1984). Critical commentary. *Advances in Behaviour Research and Therapy, 6*, 75–78.

Ross, A. O. (1985). To form a more perfect union: It is time to stop standing still. *Behavior Therapy, 16*, 195–204.

Ross, D. M., & Ross, S. A. (1982). *Hyperactivity: Current issues, research, and theory* (2nd ed.). New York: Wiley.

Ross, M., & Olson, J. M. (1981). An expectancy-attribution model of the effects of placebos. *Psychological Review, 85*, 408–437.

Ross, S., & Buckalew, L. W. (1983). The placebo as an agent in behavioral manipulation: A review of problems, issues, and affected measures. *Clinical Psychology Review, 3*, 457–471.

Rostand, S. G., Kirk, K. A., Rutsky, E. A., & Pate, B. A. (1982). Racial differences in the incidence of treatment for end-stage renal disease. *New England Journal of Medicine, 306*, 1276–1279.

Rotatory, A. F., Fox, R., & Switzky, H. (1980). A multi-component behavioral program for achieving weight loss in the adult mentally retarded person. *Mental Retardation, 18*, 31–33.

Rowland, M., & Roberts, J. (1982). *Blood pressure levels and hypertension in persons ages 6–74 years: United States, 1976–80* (DHHS Publication No. PHS 82-1250; Advance Data No. 84, Vital and Health Statistics). Washington, DC: U.S. Government Printing Offfice.

Ruberman, W., Weinblatt, E., Goldberg, J. D., & Chaudhary, B. S. (1984). Psychosocial influences on mortality after myocardial infarction. *New England Journal of Medicine, 311*, 552–559.

Ruhl, K. L., & Hughes, C. A. (1985). The nature and extent of aggression in special education settings servicing behaviorally disordered students. *Behavioral Disorders, 10*, 95–104.

Rusch, F. R., Morgan, T. K., Martin, J. E., Riva, M., & Agran, M. (1985). Competitive employment: Teaching mentally retarded employees self-instructional strategies. *Applied Research in Mental Retardation, 6*, 389–407.

Rush, A. J., Beck, A. T., Kovacs, M., & Hollon, S. D. (1977). Comparative efficacy of cognitive therapy and pharmacotherapy in the treatment of depressed outpatients. *Cognitive Therapy and Research, 1*, 17–37.

Rush, A. J., Weissenberger, J., & Eaves, G.(1986). Do thinking patterns predict depressive symptoms. *Cognitive Therapy and Research, 10*, 225–236.

Russo, D. C. (1985). Clinical training in behavioral health psychology. *the Behavior Therapist, 8*, 43–46.

Ryle, A. (1985). What price psychotherapy? *British Journal of Psychiatry, 146*, 209–210.

Sacco, W. P. (1981). Invalid use of the Beck Depression Inventory to identify depressed college-student subjects: A methodological comment. *Cognitive Therapy and Research, 5*, 143–147.

Sackheim, H., & Gur, M. (1978). Self-deception, self-confrontation, and consciousness. In G. Schwartz & D. Shapiro (Eds.), *Consciousness and self-regulation* (Vol. 2). New York: Plenum.

Safran, J. S., & Safran, S. P. (1985). A developmental view of children's behavioral tolerance. *Behavioral Disorders, 10*, 87–94.

Safran, S. P., Safran, J. S., & Barcikowski, R. S. (1985). Differences in teacher tolerance: An illusory phenomena [*sic*]? *Behavioral Disorders, 11*, 11–15.

Salend, S. J., Esquivel, L., & Pine, P. B. (1984). Regular and special education teachers' estimates of use of aversive contingencies. *Behavioral Disorders, 9*, 89–94.

Salkovskis, P. M., & Clark, D. M. (1984, September). *A cognitive–behavioral approach to the treatment of panic attacks*. Paper presented at the 14th Congress of the European Association for Behaviour Therapy, Brussels.

Salkovskis, P. M., Warwick, H., Clark, D., & Wessels, D.(1986). A demonstration of acute hyperventilation during naturally occurring panic attacks. *Behaviour Research and Therapy, 24*, 91–94.

Salzman, L. (1984). Psychoanalysis and behavior therapy. In H. Arkowitz & S. B. Messer

(Eds.), *Psychoanalytic therapy and behavior therapy: Is integration possible?* (pp. 335–349). New York: Plenum.

Sanchez-Craig, M. (1976). Cognitive and behavioral coping stragegies in reappraisal of stressful social situations. *Journal of Counseling Psychology, 23*, 7–12.

Sanchez-Craig, M., & Walker, K. (1982). Teaching coping skills to chronic alcoholics in a coeducational halfway house: 1. Assessment of programme effects. *British Journal of Addiction, 77*, 35–50.

Sanders, M. R. (1984). Clinical strategies for enhancing generalization in behavioural parent training: An overview. *Behavioural Change, 1*, 25–35.

Sanders, M. R., & James, J. E., (1983). The modification of parent behaviors: A review of generalization and maintenance. *Behavior Modification, 7*, 3–27.

Santostefano, S.(1984). Cognitive control therapy with children: Rationale and technique. *Psychotherapy, 21*, 76–91.

Santostefano, S. (1986). *Cognitive control therapy with children and adolescents*. New York: Pergamon Press.

Santostefano, S., & Rieder, C. (1984). Cognitive controls and aggression in children: The concept of cognitive–affective balance. *Journal of Consulting and Clinical Psychology, 52*, 46–56.

Sartorius, N., & Ban, T. A. (Eds.). (1986). *Assessment of depression*. New York: Springer-Verlag.

Saylor, C. F., Finch, A. J., Baskin, C., Furey, W., & Kelly, M. M. (1984). Construct validity for measures of childhood depression: Application of the multitrait–multimethod methodology. *Journal of Consulting and Clinical Psychology, 52*, 977–985.

Saylor, C. F., Finch, A. J., Spirito, A., & Bennett, B. (1984). The Children's Depression Inventory: A systematic evaluation of psychometric properties. *Journal of Consulting and Clinical Psychology, 52*, 955–967.

Schaefer, M. T., & Olson, D. H. (1981). Assessing intimacy: The PAIR inventory. *Journal of Marital and Family Therapy, 1*, 47–60.

Schaefer, S. D., Henderson, A. H., Glover, E. D., & Christen, A. G. (1985). Patterns of use and incidence of smokeless tobacco consumption in school-age children. *Archives of Otolaryngology, 111*, 639–642.

Schiffman, L. G., & Kanuk, L. L. (1983). *Consumer behavior*. Englewood Cliffs, NJ: Prentice-Hall.

Schilling, R. F., Schinke, S. P., Blythe, B. J., & Barth, R. P. (1982). Child maltreatment and mentally retarded parents: Is there a relationship? *Mental Retardation, 20*, 201–209.

Schinke, S. P., Gilchrist, L. D., Schilling, R. F., II, & Senechal, V. A. (1986). Smoking and smokeless tobacco use among adolescents: Trends and intervention results. *Public Health Reports, 101*, 373–378.

Schneider, B. H., Rubin, K. H., & Ledingham, J. E. (1985). *Children's peer relations: Issues in assessment and intervention*. New York: Springer-Verlag.

Schneller, G. O., & Kopelman, R. E. (1983). Using incentives to increase absenteeism: A plan that backfired. *Compensation Review, 15*, 40–45.

Schopler, E., & Mesibov, G. B. (Eds.). (1983). *Autism in adolescents and adults*. New York: Plenum Press.

Schradle, S. B., & Dougher, M. J. (1985). Social support as a mediator of stress: Theoretical and empirical issues. *Clinical Psychology Review, 5*, 641–661.

Schwartz, G. E. (1979). The brain as a health care system. In G. C. Stone, F. Cohen, & N. E. Adler (Eds)., *Health psychology*. San Francisco: Jossey-Bass.

Schwartz, R. M., & Garamoni, G. L. (1986). A structural model of positive and negative states of mind: Asymmetry in the internal dialogue. In P. C. Kendall (Ed.), *Advances in cognitive–behavioral research and therapy* (Vol. 5, pp. 2–63). New York: Academic Press.

Scruggs, T. E., & Mastropieri, M. A. (1984). Issues in generalization: Implications for special education. *Psychology in the Schools, 21*, 397–403.

Scruggs, T. E., Mastropieri, M. A., & Richter, L. (1985). Peer tutoring with behaviorally disordered students: Social and academic benefits. *Behavioral Disorders, 10*, 283–294.

Searles, J. S. (1985). A methodological and empirical critique of psychotherapy outcome meta-analysis. *Behaviour Research and Therapy, 23*, 453–464.

Sebba, J. (1985). Evaluating the effectiveness of teaching behavioural methods to staff training in mental handicap. *Behavioural Psychotherapy, 13*, 101–109.

Serge-Deavenport, E., & Varni, J. W. (1982). Behavioral techniques in teaching hemophilia factor replacement procedures to families. *Pediatric Nursing, 8*, 416–419.

Serge-Deavenport, E., & Varni, J. W. (1983). Behavioral assessment and managment of adherence to factor replacement therapy in hemophilia. *Journal of Pediatric Psychology, 8*, 367–377.

Severson, H. H. (1986). Psychosocial factors in the use of smokeless tobacco by adolescent males. In W. J. Blot, G. Boyd, & J. M. Elliott (Eds.), *Proceedings of NIH Consensus Development Conference: Health implications of smokeless tobacco use* (pp. 38–43). Bethesda, MD: National Institutes of Health.

Shadish, W. R. (1984). Policy research: Lessons from the implementation of deinstitutionalization. *American Psychologist, 39*, 725–738.

Shadish, W. R., Orwin, R. G., Silber, B. G., & Bootzin, R. R. (1985). The subjective well-being of mental patients in nursing homes. *Evaluation and Program Planning, 8*, 239–250.

Shadish, W. R., Silber, B. G., & Bootzin, R. R. (1984). Mental patients in nursing homes: Their characteristics and treatment. *International Journal of Partial Hospitalization, 2*, 153–163.

Shafer, M. W., Egel, A. L., & Neef, N. A. (1984). Training mildly handicapped peers to facilitate changes in the social interaction skills of autistic children. *Journal of Applied Behavior Analysis, 17*, 461–476.

Shapiro, D. A., & Shapiro, D. (1983). Comparative therapy outcome research: Methodological implications of meta-analysis. *Journal of Consulting and Clinical Psychology, 51*, 42–53.

Sharp, J. J., & Forman, S. G. (1985). A comparison of two approaches to anxiety management for teachers. *Behavior Therapy, 16*, 370–383.

Sheehan, D. V. (1982). Panic attacks and phobias. *New England Journal of Medicine, 307*, 156–158.

Sheehan, D. V., (1985, May 2). [Comments during ABC News program *20/20*].

Shekelle, R. (1985). Socioeconomic factors: Working group summary. In A. M. Ostfeld & E. D. Eaker (Eds.), *Measuring psychosocial variables in epidemiologic studies of cardiovascular disease: Proceedings of a workshop* (DHHS Publication No. NIH 85-2270, pp. 47–48). Washington, DC: U.S. Government Printing Office.

Shekelle, R. B., Gale, M., Ostfeld, A. M., & Paul, O. (1983). Hostility, risk of coronary heart disease, and mortality. *Psychosomatic Medicine, 45*, 109–114.

Shepherd, M. (1984). What price psychotherapy? *British Medical Journal, 288*, 809–810.

Shepherd, M. (1985). What price psychotherapy? *British Journal of Psychiatry, 146*, 555–557.

Sheth, J. N. (Ed.). (1985). *Research in consumer behavior* (Vol. 1). Greenwich, CT: JAI Press.

Shiffman, S., Read, L., Maltese, J., Rapkin, D., & Jarvik, M. E. (1985). Preventing relapse in ex-smokers: A self-management approach. In G. A. Marlatt & J. R. Gordon (Eds.), *Relapse prevention: Maintenance strategies in the treatment of addictive behaviors* (pp. 472–520). New York: Guilford Press.

Shorr, A. (1984). *Die verhaltenstherapie*. Basel: Beltz.

Shrout, P. E., Dohrenwend, B. P., & Levav, I. (1986). A discriminant rule for screening cases of diverse diagnostic types: Preliminary results. *Journal of Consulting and Clinical Psychology, 54*, 314–319.

Shure, M. B., & Spivack, G. (1972). Means–ends thinking, adjustment, and social class among elementary-school-aged children. *Journal of Consulting and Clinical Psychology, 38*, 348–353.

Siegel, J. M. (1985). Personality and cardiovascular disease: Prior research and future directions. In A. M. Ostfeld & E. D. Eaker (Eds.), *Measuring psychosocial variables in epidemiologic studies of cardiovascular disease: Proceedings of a workshop* (DHHS Publication No. NIH 85-2270, pp. 315–344). Washington, DC: U.S. Government Printing Office.

Simons, A. D., Lustman, P. J., Wetzel, R. D., & Murphy, G. E. (1985). Predicting response to cognitive therapy of depression: The role of learned resourcefulness. *Cognitive Therapy and Research, 9*, 79–89.

Sims, E. A. H. (1979). Definitions, criteria, and prevalence of obesity. In G. A. Bray (Ed.), *Obesity in America* (DHHS Publication No. NIH 79-359, pp. 20–36). Washington, DC: U.S. Government Printing Office.

Sindelar, P. T., King, M. C., Cartland, D., Wilson, R. J., & Meisel, C. J. (1985). Deviant behavior in learning disabled and behaviorally disordered students as a function of level and placement. *Behavioral Disorders, 10*, 105–112.

Singh, N. N., & Katz, R. C. (1985). On the modification of acceptability ratings for alternative child treatments. *Behavior Modification, 9*, 375–386.

Skiba, R., & Casey, A. (1985). Intervention for behaviorally disordered students: A quantitative review and methodological critique. *Behavioral Disorders, 10*, 239–252.

Skinner, B. F. (1948). *Walden two*. New York: Macmillan.

Smith, J. C., Mercy, J. A., & Rosenberg, M. L. (1984). *Comparison of homicides among Anglos and Hispanics in five Southwestern states*. Atlanta: Centers for Disease Control.

Smith, J. E. (1984). Non-accidental injury to children: I. A review of behavioural interventions. *Behaviour Research and Therapy, 22*, 331–341.

Smith, J. E., & Rachman, S. J. (1984). Non-accidental injury to children: II. A controlled evaluation of a behavioural management programme. *Behaviour Research and Therapy, 22*, 349–366.

Smith, J. E., Rachman, S. J., & Yule, B. (1984). Non-accidental injury to children: III. Methodological problems of evaluative treatment research. *Behaviour Research and Therapy, 22*, 367–383.

Smith, M., & Dejoie-Smith, M. (1984). Behavior therapy for non-white, non-YAVIS clients: Myth or panacea? *Psychotherapy: Theory, Research, and Practice, 21*, 524–529.

Smith, M. L., & Glass, G. V. (1977). Meta-analysis of psychotherapy outcome studies. *American Psychologist, 32*, 752–760.

Smith, M. L., Glass, G. V., & Miller, T. I. (1980). *The benefits of psychotherapy*. Baltimore: Johns Hopkins University Press.

Sobell, M. B., & Sobell, L. C. (1973a). Alcoholics treated by individualized behavior therapy: One year treatment outcome. *Behaviour Research and Therapy, 11*, 599–618.

Sobell, M. B., & Sobell, L. C. (1973b). Individualized behavior therapy for alcoholics. *Behavior Therapy, 4*, 49–72.

Sobell, M. B., & Sobell, L. C. (1976). Second year treatment outcome of alcoholics treated by individualized behavior therapy: Results. *Behaviour Research and Therapy, 14*, 195–215.

Sobell, M. B., & Sobell, L. C., (1984). The aftermath of heresy: A response to Pendery *et al.*'s (1982) critique of "Individualized behavior therapy for alcoholics." *Behaviour Research and Therapy, 22*, 413–440.

Sobell, M. B., & Sobell, L. C. (in press). Conceptual issues regarding goals in the treatment of alcohol problems. *Drugs and Society*.

Society of Actuaries. (1959). *Build and Blood Pressure Study, 1959* (Vol. 1). Chicago: Author.

Society of Actuaries and Association of Life Insurance Medical Directors of America. (1980). *Build Study 1979*. Chicago: Author.

Spanier, G. B. (1976). Measuring dyadic adjustment: New scales for assessing the quality of marriage and similar dyads. *Journal of Marriage and the Family, 38*, 15–28.

Spence, S. H. (1979). Social skills training with adolescent offenders: A review. *Behavioural Psychotherapy, 7*, 49–56.

Spence, S. H., & Lee, P. (1985). Observation and social validation of staff behaviours in a residential care setting. *Behavioural Psychotherapy, 13*, 43–58.

Spielberger, C. D., Edwards, C. D., Lushene, R. E., Montouri, J., & Platzek, D. (1973). *STAIC: Preliminary manual.* Palo Alto, CA: Consulting Psychologists Press.

Spielberger, C. D., Gorsuch, R. L., & Lushene, R. E. (1970). *Manual for the State-Trait Anxiety Inventory*. Palo Alto: Consulting Psychologists Press.

Spielberger, C. D., Jacobs, G. A., Russell, S., & Crane, R. S. (1983). Assessment of anger: the State–Trait Anger Scale. In J. N. Butcher & C. D. Spielberger (Eds.), *Advances in personality assessment* (Vol. 3, pp. 112–134). Hillsdale, NJ: Erlbaum.

Spitzer, R. L., & Williams, J. B. W. (1980). Classification of mental disorders and DSM-III. In H. I. Kaplan, A. M. Freedman, & B. J. Sadock (Eds.), *Comprehensive textbook of psychiatry*. Baltimore: Williams & Wilkins.

Spivack, G., & Shure, M. B. (1974). *Social adjustment of young children: A cognitive approach to solving real-life problems*. San Francisco: Jossey-Bass.

Squier, C. A. (1984). Smokeless tobacco and oral cancer: A cause for concern? *CA—A Cancer Journal for Clinicians, 34*, 242–247.

Stainback, S., & Stainback, W. (1982). Influencing the attitudes of regular class teachers about the education of severely handicapped students. *Education and Training of the Mentally Retarded, 17*, 88–92.

Stainback, S., Stainback, W., Strathe, M., & Dedrick, C. (1983). Preparing regular classroom teachers for the integration of severely handicapped students: An experimental study. *Education and Training of the Mentally Retarded, 18*, 204–209.

Stainback, W., & Stainback, S. (1982). Social interactions between autistic students and their peers. *Behavioral Disorders, 7*, 75–81.

Stalonas, P. M., Jr., Johnson, W. G., & Christ, M. (1978). Behavior modification for obesity: The evaluation of exercise, contingency management, and program adherence. *Journal of Consulting and Clinical Psychology, 46*, 463–469.

Stalonas, P. M. Perri, M. G., & Kerzner, A. B. (1984). Do behavioral treatments of obesity last? A five-year follow-up investigation. *Addictive Behaviors, 9*, 173–183.

Steering Group to the Administrator. (1984). *Report of the Steering Group to the Administrator, Alcohol, Drug Abuse and Mental Health Administration, regarding its attempts to investigate allegations of scientific misconduct concerning Drs. Mark and Linda Sobell.* Bestheda, MD: Alcohol, Drug Abuse and Mental Health Administration.

Stein, L. I., & Test, M. A. (1980). Alternative to mental hospital treatment. *Archives of General Psychiatry, 37,* 342–397.

Stern, M. P., Gaskill, S. P., Allen, C. R., Jr., Garza, V., Gonzales, J. L., & Waldrop, R. H. (1981). Cardiovascular risk factors in Mexican Americans in Laredo, Texas: I. Prevalence of overweight and diabetes and distributions of serum lipids. *American Journal of Epidemiology, 113,* 546–555.

Stern, M. P., Gaskill, S. P., Hazuda, H. P., Gardner, L. I., & Haffner, S. M. (1983). Does obesity explain excess prevalence of diabetes among Mexican Americans? Results of the San Antonio Heart Study. *Diabetologia, 24,* 272–277.

Stern, M. P., Rosenthal, M., Haffner, S. M., Hazuda, H. P., & Franco, L. J. (1984). Sex differences in the effects of sociocultural status on diabetes and cardiovascular risk factors in Mexican Americans: The San Antonio heart study. *American Journal of Epidemiology, 120,* 834–851.

Sternberg, B. (1985). Relapse in weight control: Definitions, processes, and prevention strategies. In G. A. Marlatt & J. R. Gordon (Eds.), *Relapse prevention: Maintenance strategies in the treatment of addictive behaviors* (pp. 521–545). New York: Guilford Press.

Steuer, J. L., Mintz, J., Hammen, C. L., Hill, M. A., Jarvik, L. F., McCarley, T., Motoike, P., & Rosen, R. (1984). Cognitive–behavioral and psycho-dynamic groups psychotherapy in treatment of geriatric depression. *Journal of Consulting and Clinical Psychology, 52,* 180–189.

Stevens, G. (1980). Bias in attributions of positive and negative behavior in children by shcool psychologists, parents, and teachers. *Perceptual and Motor Skills, 50,* 1283–1290.

Stolley, P. D., Kuller, L. H., Nefzger, M. D., Tonascia, S., Lilienfeld, A. M., Miller, G. D., & Diamond, E. L. (1977). Three-area epidemiological study of geographic differences in stroke mortality: II. Results. *Stroke, 8,* 551–557.

Strain, P. S. (1983). Generalization of autistic children's social behavior change: Effects of developmentally integrated and segregated settings. *Analysis and Intervention in Developmental Disabilities, 3,* 23–34.

Strain, P. S., Hoyson, M., & Jamieson, B. (1985). Normally developing preschoolers as intervention agents for autistic-like children: Effects on class departments and social interaction. *Journal of the Division for Early Childhood, 9,* 105–115.

Strupp, H. H., & Hadley, S. W. (1977). A tripartite model of mental health and therapeutic outcomes. *American Psychologist, 32,* 187–196.

Stunkard, A. J., Foch, T. T., & Hrubec, Z. (1986a). A twin study of human obesity. *Journal of the American Medical Association, 256,* 51–54.

Stunkard, A. J., Sorenson, T. I. A., Hanis, C., Teasdale, T. W., Chakraborty, R., Schull, W. J., & Schulsinger, F. (1986b). An adoption study of human obesity. *New England Journal of Medicine, 314,* 193–198.

Sufrin, E. M. (1984). The physical rehabilitation of the brain-damaged elderly: A behavioral approach. In B. A. Edelstein & E. T. Couture (Eds.), *Behavioural assessment and rehabilitation of the traumatically brain-damaged* (pp. 191–226). New York: Plenum Press.

Suinn, R. M. (1977). *Manual—Anxiety Management Training (AMT).* (Available from Rocky Mountain Behavioral Science Institute Inc., P.O. Box 1066, Fort Collins, CO, 80523)

Suinn, R. M., & Richardson, F. (1971). Anxiety management training: A nonspecific behavior therapy program for anxiety control. *Behavior Therapy, 2,* 498–510.

Sulzer-Azaroff, B. (1982). Behavioral approaches to health and occupational safety. In L. Frederiksen (Ed.), *Handbook of organizational behavior management* (pp. 505–538). New York: Wiley.

Sulzer-Azaroff, B., & Fellner, D. (1984). Searching for performance targets in the behavioral analysis of occupational health and safety: An assessment strategy. *Journal of Organizational Behavior Management, 6*, 53–65.

Supnick, J. A., & Colletti, G. (1984). Relapse coping and problem solving training following treatment for smoking. *Addictive Behaviors, 9*, 401–404.

Svarstad, B. L. (1986). Patient–practitioner relationships and compliance with prescribed medical regimens. In L. Aiken & D. Mechanic (Eds.), *Applications of social science to clinical medicine and health policy* (pp. 438–459). New Brunswick, NJ: Rutgers University Press.

Swanson, H. L. (1985). Effects of cognitive–behavioral training on emotionally disturbed children's academic performance. *Cognitive Therapy and Research, 9*, 201–216.

Syme, S. L. (1984). Sociocultural factors and disease etiology. In W. D. Gentry (Ed.), *Handbook of behavioral medicine* (pp. 13–37). New York: Guilford Press.

Tanaka-Matsumi, J., & Kameoka, V. A. (1986). Reliabilities and concurrent validities of popular self-report measures of depression, anxiety, and social desirability. *Journal of Consulting and Clinical Psychology, 54*, 328–333.

Taylor, C., Sheikh, J., Agras, W. S., Roth, W., Margraf, J., Ehlers, A., Maddock, R., & Yossard, D. (1986). Ambulatory heart rate changes in patients with panic attacks. *American Journal of Psychiatry, 143*, 478–482.

Telch, M. J., Agras, W. S., Taylor, C. B., Roth, W. T., & Gallen, C. C. (1985). Combined pharmacological and behavioural treatment of agoraphobia. *Behaviour Research and Therapy, 23*, 325–336.

Teplin, L. A. (1983). The criminalization of the mentally ill: Speculation in search of data. *Psychological Bulletin, 94*, 54–67.

Teplin, L. A. (1984). Criminalizing mental disorder: The comparative arrest rate of the mentally ill. *American Psychologist, 39*, 794–803.

Teri, L., & Lewinsohn, P. M. (Eds.). (1986). *Geropsychological assessment and treatment: Selected topics*. New York: Springer.

Test, M. A. (1981). Effective community treatment of the chronically mentally ill: What is necessary? *Journal of Social Issues, 37*, 71–76.

Tertinger, D. A., Greene, B. F., & Lutzker, J. R. (1984). Home safety: Development and validation of one component of an ecobehavioral treatment program for abused and neglected children. *Journal of Applied Behavior Analysis, 17*, 159–174.

Tharp, R. G., & Wetzel, R. J. (1969). *Behavior modification in the natural environment*. New York: Academic Press.

Thomas, P. D., Goodwin, J. M., & Goodwin, J. S. (1985). Effect of social support on stress-related changes in cholesterol level, uric acid level, and immune function in an elderly sample. *American Journal of Psychiatry, 142*, 735–737.

Thompson, J. K., & Williams, D. E. (1985). Behavior therpay in the 80's: Evolution, exploitation, and the existential issue. *the Behavior Therapist, 8*(3), 47–50.

Thompson, T., LaBeck, L., & Zimmerman, R. (1980). Nursing staff adjustment as a function of psychiatric treatment modality. *Journal of Behavior Therapy and Experimental Psychiatry, 22*, 209–214.

Thyer, B. A. (1983). Behavior modification in social work practice. In M. Hersen, R. M. Eisler, & P. M. Miller (Eds.), *Progress in behavior modification* (Vol. 15, pp. 173–216). New York: Academic Press.

Thyer, B. A., & Himle, J. (1985). Temporal relationship between panic attack onset and phobic avoidance in agoraphobia. *Behaviour Research and Therapy, 23*, 607–608.

Thyer, B. A., Nesse, R., Cameron, O., & Curtis, G. (1985). Agoraphobia: A test of the separation anxiety hypothesis. *Behaviour Research and Therapy, 23*, 75–78.

Tiedemann, G. L., & McMahon, R. J. (1985). Individual differences in children's response to self- and externally-administered reward. *Behavior Therapy, 16*, 516–523.

Tobacco Institute. (1985). *Tobacco industry profile, 1985.* Washington, DC: Author.

Tornatzky, L. G., & Fergus, E. O. (1982). Innovation and diffusion in mental health. In A. J. Jeger & R. S. Slotnick (Eds.), *Community mental health and behavioral ecology: A handbook of theory, research, and practice* (pp. 113–126). New York: Plenum Press.

Turk, D. C., Meeks, S., & Turk, L. M. (1982). Factors contributing to teacher stress: Implications for research, prevention, and remediation. *Behavioral Counseling Quarterly, 2*, 3–25.

Turk, D. C., & Salovey, P. (1985a). Cognitive structures, cognitive processes, and cognitive-behavior modification: I. Client issues. *Cognitive Therapy and Research, 9*, 1–18.

Turk, D. C., & Salovey, P. (1985b). Cognitive structures, cognitive processes, and cognitive-behavior modification: II. Judgments and inferences of the clinician. *Cognitive Therapy and Research, 9*, 19–34.

Turk, D. C., & Speers, M. A. (1983). Cognitive schemata and cognitive processes in cognitive–behavioral interventions: Going beyond the information given. In P. C. Kendall (Ed.), *Advances in cognitive–behavioral research and therapy* (Vol. 2, pp. 3–34). New York: Academic Press.

Turkat, I., & Maisto, S. (1985). Personality disorders: Application of the experimental method to the formulation and modification of personality disorders. In D. H. Barlow (Ed.), *Clinical handbook of psychological disorders* (pp. 502–570). New York: Guilford.

Tversky, A., & Kahneman, D. (1973). Availability: A heuristic for judging frequency and probability. *Cognitive Psychology, 5*, 207–232.

Tversky, A., & Kahneman, D. (1974). Judgement under uncertainty: Heuristics and biases. *Science, 135*, 1124–1131.

Twardosz, S. (1984). Environmental organization: The physical, social, and programmatic context of behavior. In M. Hersen, R. M. Eisler & P. M. Miller (Eds.), *Progress in behavior modification* (Vol. 18, pp. 123–161). New York: Academic Press.

U.S. Bureau of the Census. (1981). *Age, sex, race, and Spanish origin of the population* (Supplementary Report No. PC-80-61-1). Washington, DC: U.S. Department of Commerce.

U.S. Department of Agriculture. (1985, March). Tobacco: World tobacco situation. *Foreign Agricultural Circular*, p. 16.

U.S. Department of Health and Human Services (DHHS). (1985). *Report of the Secretary's Task Force on Black and Minority Health: Vol. 1. Executive summary.* Washington, DC: U.S. Government Printing Office.

U.S. Department of Justice. (1985, May). *The risk of violent crime.* Washington, DC: Author.

Vacc, N. A. (1968). A study of emotionally disturbed children in regular and special classes. *Exceptional Children, 35*, 197–204.

Vaillant, G. E. (1979). Natural history of male psychologic health: Effects of mental health on physical health. *New England Journal of Medicine, 301*, 1249–1254.

Vaillant, G. E. (1983). *The natural history of alcoholism.* Cambridge, MA: Harvard University Press.

Vallis, T. M., Shaw, B. F., & Dobson, K. S. (1986). The Cognitive Therapy Scale: Psychometric properties. *Journal of Consulting and Clinical Psychology, 54,* 381–385.

VanderBos, G. R., Stapp, J., & Kilberg, R. R. (1981). Health service providers in psychology. *American Psychologist, 36,* 1395–1418.

Van Itallie, T. B. (1985). Health implications of overweight and obesity in the United States. *Annals of Internal Medicine, 103,* 983–988.

Van Itallie, T. B. (1986). Bad news and good news about obesity. *New England Journal of Medicine, 314,* 239–240.

Varni, J. W. (1983). *Clinical behavioral pediatrics: An interdisciplinary biobehavioral approach.* New York: Pergamon Press.

Varni, J. W., & Wallander, J. L. (1984). Adherence to health-related regimens in pediatric chronic disorders. *Clinical Psychology Review, 4,* 585–596.

Vetter-Zemitzsch, A., Bernstein, R., Johnstone, J., Larson, C., Simon, D., & Smith, A. (1984). The oncampus program: A systemic/behavioral approach to behavior disorders in high school. *Focus on Exceptional Children, 16,* 1–8.

Vincent, J. P., Friedman, L. C., Nugent, J., & Messerly, L. (1979). Demand characteristics in observations of marital interactions. *Journal of Consulting and Clinical Psychology, 47,* 557–566.

Voegtlin, W. L. (1940). The treatment of alcoholism by establishing a conditioned reflex. *American Journal of Medical Science, 199,* 802–810.

Voegtlin, W. L., & Broz, W. R., (1949). The conditioned reflex treatment of chronic alcoholism: X. An analysis of 3125 admissions over a period of ten and a half years. *Annals of Internal Medicine, 30,* 580–597.

Voges, E. (1984). The pleasures of tobacco—how it all began and the whole story. *Tobacco Journal International, 1,* 80–82.

Wachtel, P. L. (1977). *Psychoanalysis and behavior therapy.* New York: Basic Books.

Wachtel, P. L. (Ed.). (1982a). *Resistance: Psychodynamic and behavioral approaches.* New York: Plenum.

Wachtel, P. L. (1982b). What can dynamic therapies contribute to behavior therapy? *Behavior Therapy, 13,* 594–609.

Waddell, M. T., Barlow, D. H., & O'Brien, G. T. (1984). A preliminary investigation of cognitive and relaxation treatment of panic disorder: Effects on intense anxiety versus 'background' anxiety. *Behaviour Research and Therapy, 22,* 393–402.

Wadden, T. A., & Stunkard, A. J. (1986). Controlled trial of very low calorie diet, behavior therapy, and their combination in the treatment of obesity. *Journal of Consulting and Clinical Psychology, 54,* 482–488.

Wadden, T. A., Stunkard, A. J., & Brownell, K. D. (1983). Very low calorie diets: Their efficacy, safety, and future. *Annals of Internal Medicine, 99,* 675–684.

Wadden, T. A., Stunkard, A. J., Brownell, K. D., & Day, S. C. (1984). Treatment of obesity by behavior therapy and very low calorie diet: A pilot investigation. *Journal of Consulting and Clinical Psychology, 52,* 692–694.

Wahler, R. G. (1980). The insular mother: Her problems in parent–child treatment. *Journal of Applied Behavior Analysis, 13,* 207–219.

Wallander, J. L., & Hubert, N. C. (1983). *Peer social dysfunction in children with developmental or chronic disorder.* Unpublished manuscript.

Wallander, J. L., & Hubert, N. C. (1985). Long-term prognosis for children with attention deficit disorder with hyperactivity (ADD/H). In B. B. Lahey & A. E. Kazdin (Eds.), *Advances in clinical child psychology* (Vol. 8, pp. 113–147). New York: Plenum Press.

Wallston, B. S., Alagna, S. W., DeVellis, B. M., & DeVellis, R. F. (1983). Social support and physical health. *Health Psychology, 2*, 367–391.

Wampold, B. E., & Jenson, W. R. (1986). Clinical significance revisited. *Behavior Therapy, 17*(3), 302–305.

Wanberg, K. W., & Horn, J. L. (1983). Assessment of alcohol use with multidimensional concepts and measures. *American Psychologist, 38*, 1055–1069.

Watson, J. E., & Singh, N. N. (1985). Social skills training for schizophrenic patients. *Behaviour Change, 2*, 94–101.

Watson, D., & Clark, L. A. (1984). Negative affectivity: The disposition to experience aversive emotional states. *Psychological Bulletin, 96*, 465–490.

Watt, D. C. (1985). What price psychotherapy? *British Journal of Psychiatry, 147*, 729.

Webster-Straton, C. (1985). Predictors of treatment outcome in parent training for conduct disordered children. *Behavior Therapy, 16*, 223–243.

Weiss, R. L., & Frohman, P. E. (1985). Behavioral observation as outcome measures: Not through a glass darkly. *Behavioral Assessment. 7*, 309–315.

Weiss, R. L., & Margolin, G. (1986). Assessment of marital conflict and accord. In A. R. Ciminero, K. S. Calhoun, & H. E. Adams (Eds.), *Handbook of behavioral assessment* (2nd ed., pp. 561–600). New York: Wiley.

Weisz, G., & Bucher, B. (1980). Involving husbands in treatment of obseity–Effects on weight loss, depression, and marital satisfaction. *Behavior Therapy, 11*, 643–650.

Wells, J. A. (1985). Chronic life situations and life change events. In A. M. Ostfeld & E. D. Eaker (Eds.), *Measuring psychosocial variables in epidemiologic studies of cardiovascular disease: Proceedings of a workshop* (DHHS Publication No. NIH 85-2270, pp. 105–128). Washington, DC: U.S. Government Printing Office.

Wells, K. C. (1984). [Review of G. R. Patterson, *A social learning approach to Family intervention: Vol. 3. Coercive family process*]. *Behavior Therapy, 15*, 121–127.

Wells, K. C., & Forehand, R. (1981). Childhood behavior problems in the home. In S. M. Turner, K. S. Calhoun, & H. E. Adams (Eds.), *Handbook of clinical behavior therapy* (pp. 527–567). New York: Wiley.

Whalen, C. K. (1982). Hyperactivity, learning problems and the attention deficit disorders. In T. H. Ollendick & M. Hersen (Eds.), *Handbook of child psychopathology* (pp. 151–199). New York: Plenum Press.

Whalen, C. K., & Henker, B. (1984). Hyperactivity and the attention deficit disorders: Expanding frontiers. *Pediatric Clinics of North America, 31*, 397–427.

Whalen, C. K., & Henker, B. (1985). The social world of hyperactive (ADD/H) children. *Clinical Psychology Review, 5*, 480–511.

Whalen, C. K., Henker, B., & Hinshaw, S. P. (1985). Cognitive–behavioral therapies for hyperactive children: Premises, problems, and prospects. *Journal of Abnormal Child Psychology, 13*, 391–410.

Wheeler, S. (1961). Socialization in correctional communities. *American Sociological Review, 26*, 697–712.

Wheldall, K. (1981). *Applied behavioural analysis in British educational contexts (with particular reference to the Birmingham group).* Paper presented at the Third Annual Conference of the Australian Behaviour Modification Association, Melbourne.

Wheldall, K., & Merrett, F. (1985). The Behavioural Approach to Teaching Package (BATPACK): Evolution and evaluation. *Behaviour Change, 2*, 21–22.

Whitman, T., Burgio, L., & Johnston, M. B. (1984). Cognitive behavioral intervention with mentally retarded children. In A. W. Meyers & W. E. Craighead (Eds.), *Cognitive behavior therapy with children* (pp. 193–227). New York: Plenum Press.

Whittaker, J. K., & Garbarino, J. (Eds.). (1983). *Social support networks: Informal helping in the human services.* Chicago: Aldine.

Wiggins, J. S. (1973). *Personality and prediction.* Reading, MA: Addison-Wesley.
Williams, L., Dooseman, G., & Kleifield, E. (1984). Comparative effectiveness of guided mastery and exposure treatments for intractable phobias. *Journal of Consulting and Clinical Psychology, 52*, 505–518.
Williams, S. L., & Telch, M. J. (1984). *Self-appraisal determinants of defensive behavior and emotional arousal.* Unpublished manuscript, Lehigh University, Bethlehem, PA.
Williams, L., Turner, S., & Peer, D. (1985). Guided mastery and performance desensitization treatments for severe acrophobia. *Journal of Consulting and Clinical Psychology, 53*, 237–247.
Williams, L., & Watson, N. (1985). Perceived danger and perceived self-efficacy as cognitive determinants of acrophobic behavior. *Behavior Therapy, 16*, 136–146.
Williams, R. B., Jr., Benson, H., & Follick, M. J. (1985). Disease as a reflection of the psyche [Letter to the editor]. *New England Journal of Medicine, 313*, 1356–1357.
Wilcox, B., & Bellamy, G. (1982). *Design of high school program for severely handicapped students.* Baltimore: Paul H. Brookes.
Wilson, G. T. (1978). The importance of being theoretical: A commentary on Bandura's "Self-efficacy: Toward a unifying theory of behavioral change." *Advances in Behaviour Research and Therapy, 1*, 217–230.
Wilson, G. T. (1982a). Clinical issues and strategies in the practice of behavior therapy. In C. M. Franks, G. T. Wilson, P. C. Kendall, & K. D. Brownell, *Annual review of behavior therapy: Theory and practice* (Vol. 8, pp. 305–345). New York: Guilford Press.
Wilson, G. T. (1982b). Fear reduction methods and the treatment of anxiety disorders. In C. M. Franks, G. T. Wilson, P. C. Kendall, & K. D. Brownell, *Annual review of behavior therapy: Theory and practice* (Vol. 8, pp. 82–119). New York: Guilford Press.
Wilson, G. T. (1982c). Psychotherapy process and procedure: The behavioral mandate. *Behavior Therapy, 13*, 291–312.
Wilson, G. T. (1984a). Clinical issues and strategies in the practice of behavior therapy. In G. T. Wilson, C. M. Franks, K. D. Brownell, & P. C. Kendall, *Annual review of behavior therapy: Theory and practice* (Vol. 9, pp. 309–343). New York: Guilford Press.
Wilson, G. T. (1984b). Fear reduction methods and the treatment of anxiety disorders. In G. T. Wilson, C. M. Franks, K. D. Brownell, & P. C. Kendall, *Annual review of behavior therapy.* (Vol. 9, pp. 95–131). New York: Guilford Press.
Wilson, G. T. (1985a). Clinical issues and strategies in the practice of behavior therapy. In C. M. Franks, G. T. Wilson, P. C. Kendall, & K. D. Brownell, *Annual review of behavior therapy; Theory and practice* (Vol. 10, pp. 291–320). New York: Guilford Press.
Wilson, G. T. (1985b). Fear reduction methods and the treatment of anxiety disorders. In C. M. Franks, G. T. Wilson, P. C. Kendall, & K. D. Brownell, *Annual review of behavior therapy: Theory and practice* (Vol. 10, pp. 87–122). New York: Guilford Press.
Wilson, G. T. (1985c). Limitations of meta-analysis in the evaluation of the effects of psychological therapy. *Clinical Psychology Review, 5*, 35–47.
Wilson, G. T. (in press-a). Psychosocial treatment of anxiety disorders. In B. Shaw, F. Cashman, Z. Segal, & M. Vallis (Eds.), *Anxiety disorders: Theory, diagnosis,and treatment.* New York: Plenum.
Wilson, G. T. (in press-b). Social psychological concepts in the theory and practice of behavior therapy. In P. Eelen (Ed.), *Social cognition and behavior therapy.* Hillsdale, NJ: Erlbaum.

Wilson, G. T., & Brownell, K. D. (1980). Behaviour therapy for obesity: An evaluation of treatment outcome. *Advances in Behaviour Research and Therapy, 3*, 49–86.

Wilson, G. T., & O'Leary, K. D. (1980). *Principles of behavior therapy*. Englewood Cliffs, NJ: Prentice-Hall.

Wilson, G. T., & Rachman, S. (1983). Meta-analysis and the evaluation of psychotherapy outcome: Limitations and liabilities. *Journal of Consulting and Clinical Psychology, 51*, 54–64.

Winer, R. S. (1985). A revised behavioral model of consumer durable demand. *Journal of Economic Psychology, 6*, 175–184.

Winkler, R. C. (1985). Twenty years of token economics in psychiatric institutions: Some basic issues. *Behaviour Change, 2*, 111–118.

Winn, D. M., Blot, W. J., Shy, C. M., Pickle, L. W., Toledo, A., & Fraumeni, J. F., Jr. (1981). Snuff dipping and oral cancer among women in the southern United States. *New England Journal of Medicine, 304*, 745–749.

Winston, A. S., & Baker, J. E. (1985). Behavior analytic studies of creativity: A critical review. *The Behavior Analyst, 8*, 191–205.

Wirt, R. D., Lachar, D. Klinedienst, J., & Seat, P. D. (1977). *Multidimensional description of child personality: A manual for the Personality Inventory for Children*. Los Angeles: Western Psychological Services.

Wise, E. H., & Barnes, D. R. (1986). The relationship among life events, dysfunctional attitudes, and depression. *Cognitive Therapy and Research, 10*, 257–266.

Wisocki, P. A. (1984). Behavioral approaches to gerontology. In M. Hersen, R. M. Eisler, & P. M. Miller (Eds.), *Progress in behavior modification* (Vol. 16, (pp. 121—154). New York: Academic Press.

Wisocki, P. A., & Mosher, P. (1982). The elderly: An understudied population in behavioral research. *International Journal of Behavioral Geriatrics, 1*, 5–14.

Witt, J. C., & Elliott, S. N. (1982). The response cost lottery: A time efficient and effective classroom intervention. *Journal of School Psychology, 20*, 155–161.

Witt, J. C., Elliott, S. N., & Martens, B. K. (1984). Acceptability of behavioral interventions used in classrooms: The influence of amount of teacher time, severity of behavior problem, and type of intervention. *Behavioral Disorders, 9*, 95–104.

Witt, J. C., Hannafin, M. J., & Martens, B. K. (1983). Home-based reinforcement: Behavioral covariation between academic performance and inappropriate behavior. *Journal of School Psychology, 21*, 337–348.

Wolfe, D. A. (1985). Child-abusive parents: An empirical review and analysis. *Psychological Bulletin, 97*, 472–482.

Wolfe, D. A., & Manion, I. G. (1984). Impediments to child abuse prevention: Issues and directions. *Advances in Behaviour Research and Therapy, 6*, 47–62.

Wolfe, D. A., & Mosk, M. D. (1983). Behavioral companions of children from abusive and distressed families. *Journal of Consulting and Clinical Psychology, 51*, 702–708.

Wolfe, V. V., Finch, A. J., Saylor, C. F., Blount, R. L., Pallmeyer, T. P., & Carek, D. J. (in press). Negative affectivity in children: A multitrait–multimethod investigation. *Journal of Consulting and Clinical Psychology.*

Wolpe, J. (1984). Behavior therapy according to Lazarus. *American Psychologist, 39*, 1326–1327.

Wolpe, J. (1985a). Existential problems and behavior therapy. *the Behavior Therapist, 8*, 126–127.

Wolpe, J. (1985b). Requiem for an institution. *the Behavior Therapist, 8*, 113.

Wood, F. H., & Lakin, K. C. (1982). Defining emotionally disturbed/behaviorally disordered populations for research purposes. In F. H. Wood & K. C. Lakin (Eds.),

Disturbing, disordered or disturbed? Perspectives on the definition of problem behavior in educational settings (pp. 29–48). Reston VA: Council of Exceptional Children.

Woody, G., Luborsky, L., McLellan, A., O'Brien, C., Beck, A. T., Blaine, J., Herman, I., & Hole, A. (1983). Psychotherapy for opiate addicts: Does it help? *Archives of General Psychiatry, 40*, 639–645.

Woolfolk, R. L., & Richardson, F. C. (1984). Behavior therapy and the ideology of modernity. *American Psychologist, 39*, 777–786.

World Health Organization European Collaborative Group. (1974). An international controlled trial in the multi-factorial prevention of coronary heart disease. *International Journal of Epidemiology, 3*, 219–224.

World Health Organization European Collaborative Group. (1980). Multifactorial trial in the prevention of coronary heart disease: 1. Recruitment and initial findings. *European Heart Journal, 1*, 73–79.

Yates, A. J., & Thain, J. (1985). Self-efficacy as a predictor of relapse following voluntary cessation of smoking. *Addictive Behaviors, 10*, 291–298.

Yates, B. T. (1985). Cost effectiveness analysis and cost–benefit analysis: An introduction. *Behavioral Assessment, 7*, 207–234.

Young, J., & Beck, A. T. (1980). *Cognitive Therapy Scale: Rating Manual.* Unpublished manuscript, Center for Cognitive Therapy, Philadelphia.

Yule, W., Hersov, L., & Treseder, J. (1980). Behavioural treatments of school refusal. In L. Hersov & I. Berg (Eds.), *Out of school: Modern perspectives in truancy and school refusal* (pp. 1–24). Chichester, England: Wiley.

Zajonc, R. (1980). Feeling and thinking. *American Psychologist, 35*, 151–175.

Zane, T., Sulzer-Azaroff, B., Handen, B. L., & Fox, C. J. (1982). Validation of a competency-based training program in developmental disabilities. *Journal of the Association for the Severely Handicapped, 7*, 21–31.

Zebal, B. H., & Friedman, S. B. (1984). A nationwide survey of behavioral pediatric residency training. *Developmental and Behavioral Pediatrics, 5*, 331–335.

Zettle, R. D., & Hayes, S. C. (1982). Rule-governed behavior: A potential theoretical framework for cognitive–behavioral therapy. In P. C. Kendall (Ed.), *Advances in cognitive–behavioral research and therapy* (Vol. 1, pp. 73–118). New York: Academic Press.

Ziarnik, J. P., & Bernstein, G. S. (1982). A critical examination of the effect of in-service training on staff performance. *Mental Retardation, 20*, 109–114.

Ziarnik, J. P., & Bernstein, G. S. (1984). Effecting change in community-based facilities: Pulling staff training in perspective. *the Behavior Therapist, 7*, 39–41.

Ziarnik, J. P., Rudred, E. H., & Bernstein, G. S. (1981). Data versus reflection: A reply to Moxley and Ebert. *Mental Retardation, 19*, 251–252.

Zieffle, T. H., & Romney, D. M. (1985). Comparison of self-instruction and relaxation training in reducing impulsive and inattentive behavior of learning disabled children on cognitive tasks. *Psychological Reports, 57*, 271–274.

Zimmerman, M. (1986). The stability of the revised Beck Depression Inventory in college students: Relationship with life events. *Cognitive Therapy and Research, 10*, 37–44.

Zitrin, C. M. (1983). Differential treatment of phobias: Use of imipramine for panic attacks. *Journal of Behavior Therapy and Experimental Psychiatry, 14*, 11–18.

Zucker, R. A., & Gomberg, E. S. L. (1986). Etiology of alcoholism reconsidered: The case for a biopsychosocial process. *American Psychologist, 41*, 783–793.

Zweig, D. R., & Brown, S. D. (1985). Psychometric evaluation of a written stimulus presentation format for the Social Interaction Self-Statement Test. *Cognitive Therapy and Research, 9*, 285–295.

AUTHOR INDEX

Subject Index